To Art, my close friend —

All good wishes,

George

3/10/07

# VIRGINIA IN THE VANGUARD

# VIRGINIA IN THE VANGUARD

## Political Leadership in the 400-Year-Old Cradle of American Democracy, 1981–2006

FRANK B. ATKINSON

Published in partnership
with the

UNIVERSITY *of* VIRGINIA
CENTER *for* POLITICS

ROWMAN & LITTLEFIELD PUBLISHERS, INC.
*Lanham • Boulder • New York • Toronto • Oxford*

Published in partnership with the University of Virginia Center for Politics

ROWMAN & LITTLEFIELD PUBLISHERS, INC.

Published in the United States of America
by Rowman & Littlefield Publishers, Inc.
A wholly owned subsidiary of The Rowman & Littlefield Publishing Group, Inc.
4501 Forbes Boulevard, Suite 200, Lanham, Maryland 20706
www.rowmanlittlefield.com

PO Box 317, Oxford
OX2 9RU, UK

British Library Cataloguing in Publication Information Available

**Library of Congress Cataloging-in-Publication Data**

Atkinson, Frank B.
   Virginia in the vanguard : political leadership in the 400-year-old cradle of
American democracy, 1981–2006 / Frank B. Atkinson.
      p   cm.
   Includes bibliographical references and index.
   ISBN-13: 978-0-7425-5210-4 (cloth : alk. paper)
   ISBN-10: 0-7425-5210-1 (cloth : alk. paper)
   1. Virginia—Politics and government—1951-   2. Political leadership—
Virginia.   I. Title.
F231.2.A89   2006
975.5'043—dc22                                                      2006007510

Printed in the United States of America

∞ ™ The paper used in this publication meets the minimum requirements of American
National Standard for Information Sciences—Permanence of Paper for Printed Library
Materials, ANSI/NISO Z39.48-1992.

*For Diane and Robert and Paul,*
*with love and gratitude*

# CONTENTS

Foreword by *Larry J. Sabato*                                                    ix

Preface: Flood Tide of Freedom                                                   xiii

Acknowledgments                                                                  xxv

**Part I. Robb, Wilder, and the Democratic Decade,
1981–1992**

1  Reversal of Fortune: The Democratic Southern Strategy                         3

2  The Watershed Robb Victory of 1981                                            17

3  Improbable Journey: Wilder's Way to the Top                                    47

4  Swinging Suburbs: Making Money and Making History                             83

**Part II. George Allen and the "Virginia Renaissance,"
1993–1999**                                                                      121

5  Reagan Populism and the Positive Politics of Reform                           123

6  From Insurgent to Insider: The 1993 Allen Landslide                           153

7  John Warner and the Politics of Independence                                  179

8  New World: America's Oldest Legislature Transformed                           217

**Part III. Mark Warner and the "Sensible Center,"
2000–2006**                                                                      259

9  Taxing Times and the Tactic of Bipartisanship                                 261

Epilogue: A Concluding Reflection on Virginia's Legacy of
    Freedom                                                          297

Bibliography                                                         311

Index                                                                323

About the Author                                                     337

# FOREWORD

I n his book *Southern Politics in State and Nation*, published in 1949, the great political scientist V.O. Key penned the most famous sentence ever written about Virginia politics: "By contrast, Mississippi is a hotbed of democracy." The sentence appears in Virginia's chapter of Key's book, entitled "Virginia: Political Museum Piece."[1] Sadly, Key was right, since the Byrd Organization (and the Martin Machine before it) had managed to restrict the electorate in Virginia to a shockingly small fraction of the adult population. In most elections held during the first four decades of the twentieth century, a miserable 8 percent of the adult population effectively elected Virginia's governors and U.S. senators.[2] In Mississippi, democracy was also critically ill but not quite as comatose, with Democratic nominees for governor needing the votes of about 14 percent of the adults there to win the election. With all due respect to our friends in the Magnolia State, when one is being compared unfavorably to the segregationist Mississippi of old, a state is in serious trouble!

The Virginia of that day is no more, and Key's description has ceased to be accurate. The Old Dominion has become the Dynamic Dominion, and a new V.O. Key is on the scene to explain how and why Virginia has changed. Frank Atkinson is a man with whom Key would have been proud to share his bookshelf.

---

1. V.O. Key, Jr. *Southern Politics in State and Nation*. New York: Alfred A. Knopf, Inc., 1949.
2. According to Key's calculations, the approximate percentages of the adult population supporting the winning organization candidate in gubernatorial primaries have been as follows: 8.6 percent in 1925; 8.1 percent in 1929; 8.5 percent in 1933; 11.2 percent in 1937; 6.7 percent in 1941; and 6.2 percent in 1945.

In the splendid companion set of *Virginia in the Vanguard* and *The Dynamic Dominion*, Atkinson traces the tumultuous events that reshaped the face of Virginia in the second half of the twentieth century, focusing especially on the dramatic politics of the years between 1945 and 2005. The books began as Atkinson's undergraduate thesis at the University of Richmond in 1978, when I was pleased to supervise as second reader with Frank's guiding mentor, then-University of Richmond professor Thomas R. Morris, now Virginia's distinguished secretary of education. While Frank was once one of my students, his understanding of politics was astounding even in the classroom, and the student has long since become the teacher.

From his teenaged years onward, Frank has been involved in Virginia politics, mainly as an activist in Republican Party affairs. He has helped to run some of the statewide campaigns he describes herein, and no one in the GOP is more respected or sought after for wise counsel. Yet there is an equally weighted dimension to Frank Atkinson that is on display in each and every page of the book. Frank has the keen eye of the scholar and the modern historian. With exquisite fairness and balance aplenty, he has captured the essence of individual campaigns and decades-long trends. Hundreds of painstaking interviews with the key players, thousands of pieces of data from public opinion polls and precinct results, and research into every nook and cranny of this 7.5-million-people-strong Commonwealth have informed his writing.

*The Dynamic Dominion* and *Virginia in the Vanguard* are monumental works, absolutely indispensable to anyone interested in Virginia history, government, and politics. The careful reader will roam the halls of our state's history, remembering the people, events, and stories that have shaped our times. For any given reader, some of these people will be heroes and others villains; some events seminal and others best left in history's dustbin; some stories telling about the past and others the future. Whatever your reactions, you will be changed by these volumes, and you will treasure them as you do the title "Virginian." Frank Atkinson's books have earned a golden place alongside the great tomes of Virginia politics and history by Virginius Dabney, Allen Moger, J. Harvie Wilkinson III, and others. It is no exaggeration to call Atkinson the premier interpreter of our modern political history; he has earned the accolade.

There's an old adage that says, "To be a Virginian either by birth, marriage, adoption, or even on one's mother's side, is an introduction to any state in the union, a passport to any foreign country, and a benediction from above." While some would suggest that the anonymous author engaged in a bit of hyperbole, those of us privileged to be Virginians find no fault with the claim. The idea of "The Virginia Way" pervades our history, culture, and politics—an indefinable set of qualities that distinguishes our Commonwealth. We can be justifiably proud of much of our past, especially in providing the leadership that created and guided the American Republic for many decades. Other parts of our history, from Jim Crow to Massive Resistance, are burdens for all with conscience.

Virginia's modern history is an amalgamation of both good and bad, the constructive and the damaging. The state's steady and mainly honest leaders have left a legacy of reliable fiscal conservatism that would serve the federal government well, should it ever deign to adopt it. Our natural harbors in Hampton Roads have led to the development of one of the world's largest naval installations. The enormous expansion of the federal government since World War II has turned Northern Virginia into one of the fastest growing regions in the United States; a dynamo that has created seismic shifts in Virginia's economics, demographics, and voting patterns. The national civil rights movement dramatically expanded the Virginia electorate, bringing an end to Harry F. Byrd Sr.'s oligarchy and generating a tempestuous realignment of the political parties.

Just as art is shaped by artists, and architecture by architects, politics is influenced most directly by individual politicians. *The Dynamic Dominion* and *Virginia in the Vanguard* feature a fascinating cast of characters who have left an indelible mark on the Commonwealth. There is the senior Harry Byrd, the apple farmer who dominated every aspect of Virginia politics for more than forty years; Bill Tuck, the colorful, tough Organization governor who threatened to conscript striking members of VEPCO into the state militia; "Howlin'" Henry Howell, the liberal populist who endeavored faithfully to "Keep the Big Boys Honest"; Linwood Holton, the first Republican governor in modern times, who sought to make Virginia "a model in race relations" for the nation; the genteel Mills Godwin, Virginia's only governor so far to be elected twice, once as a Democrat and later as a Republican; youthful and passionate J. Sargeant Reynolds, whose untimely death of a brain tumor at age 34 inexorably altered the political landscape of Virginia and possibly the entire nation; Dick Obenshain, who built a powerful Republican Party and died tragically in a plane crash just as he was on the verge of winning a U.S. Senate seat; Chuck Robb and Oliver North, who waged a Senate battle that captured the attention of the entire nation; the irascible Hunter Andrews, who managed the Senate of Virginia with a sharp wit and even sharper tongue; John Warner, the debonair senior statesman with a healthy independent streak who has frequently riled his party activists; and the remarkable Douglas Wilder, whose historic election in 1989 made him the first (and to this day the only) African American elected governor in any state. The gang's all here, and Atkinson has done a masterful job in portraying these characters and their impact on Virginia and the country.

This book also profiles and illuminates two of Virginia's most accomplished adopted sons, former Governors George Allen (R) and Mark Warner (D). Both have become rising stars on the national political scene and are widely thought to have White House ambitions. Virginia, the Mother of Presidents, may finally be expecting again—perhaps with twins!

In this and in so many other ways, Virginia has found itself back in the political vanguard. After more than a century and a half of diminishing importance on the national scene, Virginia has come alive again with possibilities. Frank Atkinson tells the gripping story well, and Virginians of all stripes can share in his pride in, and fascination with, this tale of rebirth.

Professor Larry J. Sabato
Director, Center for Politics
University of Virginia
January 2006

# PREFACE:
## FLOOD TIDE OF FREEDOM

There is a tide in the affairs of men,
Which, taken at the flood, leads on to fortune;
Omitted, all the voyage of their life
Is bound in shallows and in miseries.
On such a full sea we are now afloat;
And we must take the current when it serves,
Or lose our ventures.

*—Julius Caesar*, Act IV, Sc. III

Just a few miles downstream from the storied Globe Theatre, a few years after Shakespeare penned his great Roman tragedy, three small ships slipped from their berths and began the voyage on a full sea that would bring 104 or so hearty souls to Virginia, to a settlement that would be named "Jamestown." Varied dreams of fortune and fame sailed with the English adventurers who risked all for a chance in the New World during those early years. Among their purposes—identified by one of their number in the earliest recorded indigenous Virginia poem—was this: *"We mean to plant a Nation where none before has stood."*[1]

Against all odds, the planting at Jamestown took root—and not just a nation, but a community animated by a republican ideal, flowered. Today, nearly four centuries later, that nation is the world's oldest enduring republic and sole superpower. From Athens to Rome, from Magna Carta to the U.S. Constitution, the story of *democracy* in its various forms occupies an exceedingly small quarter in the vast expanse of human history. Many in our time would find this surprising, so accustomed have we become to seeing repre-

---

1. Richard Rich, "News from Virginia," in *Virginia Reader: A Treasury of Writings from the First Voyages to the Present*, ed. Francis Coleman Rosenberger (New York: E. P. Dutton and Company, 1948), pp. 109–114.

sentative government ascendant around the world, springing forth even in war-ravaged lands thanks to a Pax Americana that now keeps hostile forces and ideologies largely in check. Yet, democracy and the liberty it enables are improbable developments. *Without America, their remarkable advance would not have occurred; and, without Virginia, America as we know it would not exist.*

A nation of refuge for freedom-seekers since its earliest days, America in the twentieth century stood abroad as a bulwark against powerful totalitarian threats to democratic principles. As he launched the Great White Fleet from the magnificent Jamestown Exposition in 1907, even the intrepid President Teddy Roosevelt could not have imagined that what lay ahead was an *American century* in which the United States would send its sons and daughters to fight and win two world wars, and would sacrifice its blood and treasure in an epic struggle against an evil empire whose central tenets were antithetical to American ideals.[2] Though the twentieth century was mainly about the projection of American power in defense of American liberty, millions around the globe were saved from servitude in the process.

With the defeat of Soviet communism and the lightning-fast advance of technology and telecommunications at the turn of the century, the tide of freedom has flowed in much of the world. In the early 1970s, there were forty democratic nations; by the end of the last century, that number had tripled to 120. Yet, the world is a big place with many still-darkened corners; traditions and conditions in many lands do not readily lend themselves to enlightened self-rule; and the enemies of democracy have many faces and startling new methods. Globalization is a powerful new reality made possible by the extension of freedom, but its acceptance is far from universal. And the sobering truth is that totalitarianism—with religious extremism as its latest handmaiden—has already claimed more casualties on American soil in this new century than did a parade of despicable despots in the twentieth century. It is all the more significant, then, that not just the defense of American interests, but the active promotion of democratic principles worldwide, has come to the fore as the stated aim of United States policy at the start of the new century. When President George W. Bush went to London in November 2003 and declared the "global expansion of democracy" to be a pillar of American policy, he was continuing a voyage begun in 1606 when three small ships set sail for Virginia.[3] America today—aided by its

---

2. After the Jamestown Exposition closed, President Roosevelt dispatched two squadrons of battleships and cruisers on a mission to sail around the world and highlight United States naval power. It came to be known as the "Great White Fleet." See Harold Evans, *American Century* (New York: Knopf Publishing, 1998), p. 104.

3. Remarks of President George W. Bush at Whitehall Palace, London, England, White House Press Office, November 19, 2003; see also President Bush's remarks upon

Mother Country and other committed allies—*means to plant free nations where none before have stood.*

During the four centuries since the settlement of Jamestown in 1607, Virginians have been central players in the remarkable story that is the rise of the United States of America and the worldwide advance of democracy. Even before the Pilgrims set foot on the North American continent, representative government—though rudimentary and selective—had blossomed at Jamestown.[4] For seventeenth-century Britons, all America was "Virginia"—an idea as much as a place, literally a new world of discovery, adventure, and opportunity that encompassed lands as far flung as present-day New England, the Great Lakes region, and the Southeast.[5] Though her geographic bounds were successively narrowed as other colonies and then other states were forged from her lands, Virginia remained, as Jefferson expressed it, the "blessed mother of us all."[6] From the arrival, survival, and perseverance of the seventeenth-century settlement to the miraculous winning of independence and inspired framing of the nation's charter in the eighteenth century, people from Virginia played pivotal roles in the seminal developments that forged America's national institutions and character. The freedom today blithely assumed in the Western world, celebrated in emerging democracies, and coveted elsewhere gained its foothold in our age largely through the soul and sword of Washington, the fiery breath of Henry, the elegant quill of Jefferson, and the extraordinary vision of Mason, Madison, and Marshall—*Virginians all.*[7]

---

the 20th anniversary of the National Endowment for Democracy (White House Press Office, Washington, DC, November 6, 2003) and Second Inaugural Address (January 20, 2005) ("[I]t is the policy of the United States to seek and support the growth of democratic movements and institutions in every nation and culture, with the ultimate goal of ending tyranny in the world.").

   4. The inception and development of representative government in the Virginia colony, beginning at Jamestown on July 30, 1619, is detailed in Warren M. Billings, *A Little Parliament* (Richmond, VA: The Library of Virginia, 2004).

   5. William Byrd II of Westover explained the matter to his contemporaries decades before the Revolution. "The other British colonies . . . have . . . been carved out of Virginia, by grants from his majesty's royal predecessors. All that part of the northern American continent now under the dominion of the king of Great Britain, and stretching quite as far as the cape of Florida, went at first under the general name of Virginia. The only distinction, in those early days, was, that all the coast to the southward of Chesapeake Bay was called South Virginia, and all to the northward of it, North Virginia." William Byrd II, *History of the Dividing Line Betwixt Virginia and North Carolina* (circa 1733) (electronic edition available through Early America Digital Archive, Maryland Institute for Technology in the Humanities, University of Maryland, College Park, MD).

   6. Jefferson to the Virginia General Assembly, 1826.

   7. "Virginia . . . was the indispensable creator of the Republic and the Constitution that has held together the world's greatest democracy." Michael Barone and Richard E.

For much of the nineteenth century and part of the twentieth, however, Virginia's voice was heard mostly in dissent. When North and South collided in the convulsion of a horrendous civil war, Virginians cast their lot with the Confederacy and proceeded to lead her through battle. Recovered eventually from the ravages of war and reconstruction, the politically cohesive South came to dominate the Congress in the mid-twentieth century, and Virginia's Senator Harry Flood Byrd and his venerable lieutenants—at one point, with a combined congressional seniority of more than a century—chaired the key committees. From there, the Virginians and their Southern brethren endeavored with mixed success to impede developments they deemed detrimental to the public interest: creation of the federal welfare state; the rapid multiplication of federal spending and debt; and the growth of central government power at the expense of state prerogatives. They also stood out among the nation's stoutest defenders against the international Communist threat. Yet, they placed themselves on the wrong side of history—and morality—by sacrificing civil rights on the altar of states' rights and seeking at length to preserve a racially discriminatory social and political order that was irreconcilable with America's most cherished values. It was because of fearless private citizens like Oliver Hill and Spottswood Robinson and the imposition of federal law, not through the efforts of Virginia's elected leaders, that Jefferson's promise of liberty finally began to be realized by African Americans—and by other ethnic minorities, including Virginia's Indian peoples[8]—in the middle decades of the twentieth century.

For nearly one hundred years—from the Civil War through World War II—Virginia aptly could be described as a "political museum piece."[9] The cataclysmic civil conflict cast a long political shadow over the Old Dominion[10] and the other states of the Old South. The region languished as a one-party political backwater, continually out of sorts and outside the

---

Cohen, *The Almanac of American Politics 2006* (Washington, DC: National Journal Group, 2005), p. 1705.

8. The state-sponsored discrimination faced by Virginia Indians in the first half of the twentieth century is chronicled in Peter Hardin, "Reclaiming History: The Struggle of Virginia's Indians," *Richmond Times-Dispatch*, March 5–6, 2000. The Commonwealth of Virginia formally recognized eight Virginia Indian tribes in the 1980s. Although recognized by the English Crown via a 1677 treaty, the Virginia Indian tribes still await long-overdue federal tribal recognition at this writing.

9. V.O. Key Jr., *Southern Politics in State and Nation* (New York: Alfred A. Knopf, Inc., 1949), p. 19.

10. Virginia's nickname as the "Old Dominion" derives from colonial times. In the mid-seventeenth century, King Charles II of England, who was especially fond of the colony, elevated Virginia to the "dominion" status enjoyed by England, Scotland, Ireland, and France. The "old" adjective was added by Virginians to reflect their status as the first of the king's settlements in the New World.

lively mainstream of American politics. But, as chronicled in *The Dynamic Dominion* and in these pages, the winds of economic, social, and political change began to blow briskly across the Virginia landscape during World War II and its aftermath, setting in motion a series of events that would revitalize the state's economy, reinvigorate its democratic processes, and realign its politics before the century was out. From a one-party Democratic state—a conservative Camelot under the deft domination of Senator Byrd and his political organization—Virginia evolved into a two-party competitive system under no party's and no person's thumb. The advent of competition paralleled the resuscitation and resurgence of the Virginia Republican Party, a long-moribund political entity that sprang to life in the second half of the century behind the lead of dynamic figures like Ted Dalton, Richard Obenshain, and later, George Allen. The transition to a competitive state brought the Virginia political parties largely into accord philosophically with their counterparts at the national level, and paralleled completion of the long post-bellum march from Southern ostracism to Southern prominence in American politics.

If the prodigal Commonwealth of Virginia had merely rejoined the Union in the latter twentieth century, its belated return to the national fold would merit little note. But today, as the nation prepares to observe the 400th anniversary of Jamestown, the tide described by the Bard's Brutus is flowing again for Virginians. Once more in the vanguard of American politics and society, the dynamic dominion is afloat on a full sea of economic gains, technological advances, cultural diversity, groundbreaking policy innovations, barrier-shattering political accomplishments, and invigorating two-party competition. To be sure, shortcomings exist and formidable challenges remain. But if competitive politics and creative governance are the business of democracy, then the once-shuttered Old Dominion clearly is open for business again.

The signs of dynamism are everywhere. In the economic arena, Virginia easily outpaced the nation during the last three decades of the twentieth century. The United States economy grew rapidly during that time, but Virginia's economy grew nearly thirty percent faster.[11] Inflation-adjusted, per capita income in Virginia increased by nearly fifty percent from 1969 to 1999, a rate of improvement eclipsing that in all but a handful of states and placing the Commonwealth among the fourteen wealthiest states—and climbing.[12] Halfway through the first decade of the new century, Virginia

---

11. W. Mark Crain, *Volatile States* (Ann Arbor: University of Michigan Press, 2003), p. 24.

12. Crain, *Volatile States*, pp. 12–13, 18–22, 82, 85. By 2005, Virginia was ranked seventh nationally in per capita personal income. *Richmond Times-Dispatch*, December 26, 2005.

already had begun to distance itself from the nation's latest economic doldrums, posting a growth rate that exceeded every other state's except gaming-fired Nevada's.[13] The long-running economic expansion was fueled not only by the Reagan defense build-up of the 1980s and, later, by post-September 11, 2001, federal spending on homeland security, but by a burgeoning service sector and a wave of technological investment and advancement centered in Northern Virginia and extending to other fast-growing areas of the state. As the information revolution transformed the world early in the new century, much of the data—more than 50 percent of the world's Internet traffic—passed through Virginia, and computer memory chips supplanted cigarettes as the state's leading manufactured export.[14] Technological progress plainly fueled the expansion, but the state's economic gains were broad-based and diverse, and they appeared at least partly to be fruits of longstanding and deeply ingrained economic and fiscal policies. With a pro-business regulatory and legal liability environment, comparatively restrained levels of state and local taxation, a balanced budget, modest debt, and—beginning in the 1990s—a "rainy day" fund to cushion economic downturns, Virginia perennially remained among the handful of states to earn the prized triple-A bond rating and routinely received national accolades as one of the best fiscally run states and one of the best states in which to live and conduct business.[15]

---

13. *Richmond Times-Dispatch,* December 7, 2004.

14. Virginia was the locus of the Internet traffic because America Online (AOL) and more than 1,300 other Internet service providers and technology companies were based in Northern Virginia. Associated Press, December 13, 2003. Computer memory chips became the state's top manufactured export in 2005, less than a decade after such chips were first produced in Virginia. *Richmond Times-Dispatch*, March 25, 2006.

15. See, e.g., Margaret Edds and Thomas R. Morris, "Virginia: Republicans Surge in the Competitive Dominion," in *Southern Politics in the 1990s*, ed. Alexander P. Lamis (Baton Rouge: Louisiana State University Press, 1999), pp. 142–143 (summarizing *Financial World* magazine's recurring ranking of Virginia as the best fiscally run state during the 1990s); Bob Lewis, "State Earns A Grade in Management Survey," Associated Press, January 31, 2005 (reporting Virginia's top ranking nationally for government management in the "Grading the States 2005" report by the Government Performance Project, an initiative of the University of Richmond and the Pew Charitable Trusts); *Richmond Times-Dispatch*, May 14, 2004 (reporting on Virginia's fourth-place overall ranking in the National Policy Research Council's "Gold Guide" of "best state" rankings, including top-ten rankings in the business climate, economic dynamism, technology, and quality of life categories); "2004 Report," *Pollina Corporate Top-10 Pro-Business States*, February 22, 2004 (ranking Virginia first among "pro-business" states); "Live Free or Move," *Forbes*, May 24, 2004 (ranking Virginia third among business-friendly states); United States Chamber of Commerce's State Liability Systems Ranking, study no. 14966, January 11, 2002 (ranking Virginia's tort laws third from the business group's perspective).

Governance is typically easier (though not necessarily better) when there is plenty of money to spend, and state government spending in Virginia grew rapidly as the economy expanded in the closing decades of the twentieth century. Indeed, government spending growth in Virginia, as in most states, easily eclipsed even the robust rate of personal income growth throughout the period.[16] Despite spirited debates in which Republicans routinely derided Democrats for profligacy and urged tax relief while Democrats complained of populist GOP shortsightedness and pressed for increased investment in public infrastructure and programs, the statistical evidence seemed largely to belie both arguments. Virginia's ranking among the states for spending growth was influenced by the way it coped with the occasional downturns that beset the national economy, but otherwise that ranking varied little even as the state was undergoing an extended period of intense political competition and transition from the 1970s through the 1990s. For example, the state legislature's research arm reported in 2004 that Virginia's ranking among the states for per capita spending was the same in 2000 as it had been in 1981—36th.[17] That meant Virginia had the fourteenth *lowest* rate of per capita state spending and the fourteenth *highest* per capita income as of the turn of the century[18]—circumstances that probably were not wholly coincidental and that seemed to justify the state's reputation as a moderate-conservative, pro-growth state.

Where Virginia stood out in the late twentieth century, however, was not in the size or growth of its government, but in its readiness to innovate and in its ability to conceive and implement innovations. Long identified with adherence to tradition, the Old Dominion suddenly seemed to break out of its bonds, becoming a policy proving ground in the years just before and after the turn of the century. It came at a time in the nation's journey when the focus of domestic policymaking was shifting back to the state capitals. Virginia's innovators passed groundbreaking educational accountability measures that were on the leading edge of a national academic reform movement. They charted new territory with initiatives on international trade, technology, and economic development. They accomplished a wholesale restructuring of adult and juvenile correctional systems and social service delivery (i.e., "welfare") systems, supplying models that would be emulated by other states and even other countries. In developing needed public infrastructure of various kinds, they led the nation in facilitating

---

16. Crain, *Volatile States*, pp. 82–93.

17. Commission Draft, "Review of State Spending: December 2004 Update," Joint Legislative Audit and Review Commission, Commonwealth of Virginia, December 13, 2004 (hereafter, "JLARC December 2004 Spending Update"), p. 51.

18. Crain, *Volatile States*, p. 18.

innovative public-private partnerships as an alternative to traditional financing approaches. And they passed a succession of reforms that enabled Virginia's widely heralded higher education system, already one of the most decentralized and diverse, to become even more so.

Some of these innovations were initiated through consensus; others were commenced through forceful demands for change; but all ultimately came to enjoy broad, bipartisan support. (In a state with a competitive political system and a single, four-year term limit on governors' service, such innovations could be sustained from conception to implementation only through bipartisan consensus.) Of course, more beneficial reform could have been accomplished on more fronts; more in fact was accomplished than is recounted here; and many more challenges remain. Structural features that seem rooted in tradition more than practicality—for example, Virginia's independent cities and counties, the one-term limit on gubernatorial service, and a host of others—remain as obstacles to change and objects for reform. But what stands out about public policy in Virginia as its four-century mark approaches is the renewed spirit of discovery, experimentation, innovation, and improvement—the spirit of *leadership*—that animates the state's governance.

The vibrancy of Virginia's communities is also worthy of comment. When three peoples—Native Americans, Europeans, and Africans—came together at Jamestown under the most divergent of circumstances and trying of conditions, the cultural diversity that would uniquely define America was born. Today, the Virginia that helped found a nation of immigrants is itself one of the most ethnically diverse states in that nation. Populous Northern Virginia is home to more varied immigrant populations, its people practice more faiths, and its schools teach children who speak more languages, than almost any other area of the country. And Virginia's diversity is not merely ethnic or religious. There is a long distance, figuratively at least, between cosmopolitan Northern Virginia and rural Southwest and Southside Virginia, and between the Commonwealth's fast-growing, prosperous suburban areas and its landlocked, struggling central cities. Virginia spends much of its time and energy coping with these differences, and it will need to spend more. Yet, there is much unity amid all this diversity, and the state seems to retain a distinctive culture. Values of faith, family, and freedom are not a source of embarrassment for most nor the province of a single party, faction, or movement. There is a sense of community and of shared destiny even while there is a strong spirit of individualism, entrepreneurship, and personal accountability.

Whether working through public or private institutions, Virginians on the whole seem engaged more than most in striving to improve their communities, help other citizens, and preserve and advance their values. Befitting the state's legacy of leadership, many Virginians are looking not only inward but outward. The Center for Politics at the University of Virginia is creatively connecting a new generation of young people to politics and government, not just in Virginia but nationally. The Mercatus Center at George Mason University is demonstrating the power of free markets to satisfy public as well as private needs, not just in Richmond or Washington but around the nation and around the world. Countless other examples of Virginia-based initiatives—public and private, secular and sectarian—could be cited. The Commonwealth of course cannot make any claim to uniqueness in this respect, and some skeptics no doubt will challenge as parochial the suggestion that Virginians today are providing notable leadership in any area. Such criticism need not cause concern; it serves to check overstatement and self-satisfaction. But the objective evidence is irresistible that Virginia—the focal point of discovery and innovation four centuries ago and at key junctures since—is again on the move and having a wide-ranging impact.

Politically, the Commonwealth has become a frequent harbinger of national trends, increasingly examined for clues about the direction of politics and governance in other competitive states and in the nation as a whole. Since the turbulent, transforming period of the late 1960s and early 1970s, Virginia politics has tended to foreshadow national political trends. The conservative coalition assembled by Virginia Republicans in the 1970s presaged the shift of "Reagan Democrats" into the GOP column nationally in the 1980s. The centrist positioning of the successful Virginia Democrats in the 1980s anticipated the Clinton-led national Democratic resurgence in the 1990s. The populist, reform-oriented appeal of George Allen's Virginia GOP during the 1990s found parallels in state capitals across the country and in the White House as the new century opened. And Virginia's moderate Democrats, led by Mark Warner, claimed midway through the first decade of the twenty-first century to have found a "sensible center" that could hold for Democrats in national contests as well. A precise correlation or cause-and-effect relationship between Virginia's leading-edge politics and the course of national events is, of course, impossible to prove. But with its off-year elections and competitive politics proximate to the nation's capital, Virginia has become—in the words of *Newsweek*'s Howard Fineman—a "test bed for political change in the country as a whole."[19]

Whether that means a Virginian will play the central role on that stage

---

19. Howard Fineman, "The Virginians," *Newsweek*, December 26, 2005–January 2, 2006, p. 70.

anytime soon is another question altogether. Dubbed the "Mother of Presidents" because of her sons' dominance of the highest office in the nation's first decades, Virginia has rarely been with child since. An alcove in the rotunda of the State Capitol awaits the bust of the ninth president from Virginia. (The likeness of an honorary Virginian, Lafayette, has been keeping the spot warm in the meantime, and Lafayette's place has long seemed secure.) Yet, with Virginia's sudden return to nationwide political prominence in the latter twentieth century, some of its contemporary leaders have been thrust into the national limelight.

When he lost his life in a 1978 airplane crash, the 42-year-old architect of Virginia's modern Republican Party, Richard Obenshain, had already held a top leadership post in the national GOP and was headed to the United States Senate where he would have been a key lieutenant in the impending Reagan "revolution" and a legitimate potential heir to the Reagan mantle. From his first arrival on the Virginia political scene in 1977, Charles Robb seemed to be angling to return to the White House with his bride Lynda, the eldest daughter of former President Lyndon Johnson. As governor, then as senator and one of the organizers of the centrist Democratic Leadership Council, Robb's presidential designs were the subject of continual speculation nationally until his scandal-tarnished star faded irretrievably in the early 1990s. Then, in 1991, the first—and, to date, only—African-American elected governor of an American state, Democrat L. Douglas Wilder, became the first Virginia-born leader since Woodrow Wilson to actually pursue a major-party presidential nomination. Wilder's timing was all wrong, though, and he fell victim to his campaign's muddled message and anger back home over his seeming neglect of the Commonwealth's recession-driven budget woes.

One can only speculate at this juncture about the national prospects for contemporary Virginia leaders, such as Republican Senator George Allen and Democratic former Governor Mark R. Warner. In the wake of the 2004 elections, the two popular Virginians became subjects of serious presidential speculation—indeed, Washington insiders in 2005 ranked them among the top two prospects in each party[20]—and each began laying the

---

20. The nonpartisan *National Journal* surveyed several hundred "insiders" identified with each party to determine whom they considered most likely to win their party's 2008 presidential nomination. George Allen was deemed the favorite in a spring 2005 survey of the Republican insiders, and he retained the pole position when the survey was repeated in December 2005. Mark Warner ranked third in the spring survey of Democratic insiders but moved up to the second spot—behind Senator Hillary Rodham Clinton—in the December 2005 poll. See James A. Barnes and Peter Bell, "Insiders Poll," *National Journal*, April 30 2005; "2008 Republican Insiders Poll" and "2008 Democratic Insiders Poll," *National Journal*, December 17, 2005.

groundwork for an expected presidential bid in 2008. But White House talk aside, Virginians now are routinely playing leadership roles and making their mark on the nation's governance. With a career of public service spanning from World War II through the Cold War to the current war against terrorism, Senator John W. Warner exerts an important influence over American military and defense policy as chairman of the Senate Armed Services Committee. Members of the Virginia congressional delegation in the last decade chaired four other congressional committees;[21] Representative Frank Wolf of the Tenth District was one of the powerful "cardinals," or subcommittee chairs, on the House Appropriations Committee; and Richmond's youthful Congressman Eric Cantor became deputy majority whip, the fourth-ranking leadership post in the GOP-controlled House of Representatives. Virginians also were tapped for prominent national political roles: Governor James Gilmore served a year-long stint as chairman of the Republican National Committee; Eleventh District Congressman Thomas M. Davis III chaired the National Republican Congressional Committee; and Senator Allen led the National Republican Senatorial Committee. Governor Warner held the prestigious chairmanship of the National Governors Association.[22]

For national significance, though, these and other Virginia developments still pale in comparison with the election of Douglas Wilder as governor in 1989. The birthplace of American liberty, Jamestown, also saw the first institution in America of the greatest affront to liberty—human slavery. So when a majority-white Virginia electorate elevated a grandson of slaves to its highest elective office, the event drew a fitting symbolic close to a supremely tragic chapter and reaffirmed Virginians' commitment to the founding promise of individual liberty. No other state has made such a powerful statement. Yet, Wilder's triumph was but a fleeting moment in an ongoing struggle to make the promise of freedom real for all people at home and abroad. And, since freedom begets opportunity and not entitlement, it was of superseding importance that Wilder overcame adversity and claimed his distinctive electoral prize mainly through his own initiative and perseverance. Though he undoubtedly would accede to Shakespearian wisdom

---

21. Before becoming chairman of the Senate Armed Services Committee, Senator John Warner was chairman of the Senate Rules and Administration Committee. Seventh District Congressman Thomas J. Bliley Jr., served as chairman of the House of Representatives Committee on Commerce; Representative Robert W. Goodlatte chaired the Committee on Agriculture; Representative Thomas M. Davis III led the Committee on Government Reform.

22. Virginia Governor Gerald Baliles served as chairman of the National Governors Association in the late 1980s, and Senator Charles Robb led the Democratic Senatorial Campaign Committee in the early 1990s.

on the importance of taking the current on a "full sea," Wilder would regularly invoke the same drama to remind listeners that freedom makes them
responsible for their own destiny: "The fault, dear Brutus, is not in our stars,
but in ourselves."[23]

This book is about politics and thus about the day-to-day practice of
democracy. Set in the cradle of American democracy as its four-century
mark approaches, the story reminds us that human history is a continuum,
and that freedom is not just a hard-won legacy but the continuing opportunity and obligation of purpose-filled lives. The immediate object of this
book is to foster a better understanding of contemporary Virginia politics
and the Commonwealth's renewed prominence on the national political
landscape. The larger object is to enhance appreciation of Virginia's political
traditions, the values that underlie those traditions, and the contemporary
application of those values at home and abroad. The ultimate object is to
prompt a new generation to ask an age-old question: *How well are we using
the gift of liberty that Providence has entrusted to us?*

---

23. *Julius Caesar*, Act I, Sc. II; see, e.g., Wilder's remarks to the National Press Club
as reported in the *Richmond Times-Dispatch*, March 21, 1990.

# ACKNOWLEDGMENTS

W hen I first began work, back during my college years, on what after more than a decade of revisions and additions finally became *The Dynamic Dominion*,[1] I had no idea that what lay ahead was a quarter-century of observing, participating in, and occasionally writing about Virginia politics and government. I was merely trying to earn the requisite credit for graduation and, in the process, satisfy several professors—Larry Sabato, Tom Morris, and John Whelan—whose lofty expectations of their students matched the high standards they set for themselves as instructors. I also had the vague notion even then that Virginia's post–World War II partisan political realignment was an unfolding story of some potential consequence for state and even national politics, and that it might be helpful to describe it for the benefit of students, observers, and contestants in the political arena.

Since then, much has changed in Virginia, but the Commonwealth's defining characteristic in the 1970s—its dynamic political competitiveness—remains its foremost attribute. And with the aid of hindsight, some of the far-reaching consequences of that competitive system have been illuminated. The venerable Old Dominion has returned to the vanguard of American politics. Its electoral battles are now watched broadly for clues about

---

1. Frank B. Atkinson, *The Dynamic Dominion: Realignment and the Rise of Virginia's Republican Party since 1945* (Fairfax, VA: George Mason University Press, 1992). The revised second edition of *The Dynamic Dominion*, published as a companion volume to this book, contains more recently available source material and new interviews and original research concerning the period of intensive partisan realignment in Virginia from 1945 to 1980. See Frank B. Atkinson, *The Dynamic Dominion: Realignment and the Rise of Two-Party Competition in Virginia, 1945–1980* (Lanham, MD: Rowman & Littlefield Publishers, 2006). Except where specified to the contrary, all citations to *The Dynamic Dominion* in this volume are to the revised second edition.

the direction of national politics. It has produced serious presidential contenders in both major political parties. It has conceived and implemented
groundbreaking public policy reforms of national significance. It has supplied highly influential figures in the United States Congress and in non-
elective posts. And it has broken the racial barrier by electing the country's
only (so far) African-American governor. Numerous other consequential
aspects could be cited, and one has the sense that more history will be made
by Virginia and Virginians in years to come. With the eyes of many turned
toward the Commonwealth for its (and America's) 400th anniversary com-
memoration in 2007, those events are unlikely to escape notice.

I have been privileged to observe many of these remarkable events and
the course of Virginia politics and government close at hand over several
decades now, and this book even more than *The Dynamic Dominion* is a
product of my firsthand perceptions. Some undoubtedly will fault my
account on this ground, suggesting that my participation in the underlying
events and my personal political proclivities may have clouded my perspective. That suggestion is one that cannot be dismissed lightly—each of us is
an exceedingly poor judge of his own preoccupations and prejudices—and
so I will not attempt to do so here. I will say only that I am content to let
these pages stand or fall on their own merit, and to have the quality of this
work considered in the full context of the substantial body of literature that
now exists and the even more insightful works that will follow as future
historians and commentators offer the enhanced perspective that time and
distance afford.

What I do wish to do, however, is express my appreciation to the
many, many people who have contributed in ways large and small to the
opportunities I have had to experience and learn about Virginia politics and
government in a variety of roles and from a variety of perspectives over
time. It is of course impossible to name them all; that would be rather like
trying to list all of the people who have had an impact on your life's journey.
But the enormous sense of gratitude I feel needs some expression, and so I
record it here.

Because this book is in every respect a continuation and outgrowth of
*The Dynamic Dominion*, all of the specific assistance that I acknowledged
when that book was first published in 1992 applies, without diminution, to
this work as well—and my gratitude to those persons likewise is undimin-
ished. In addition, I am most appreciative of those whose support, assistance,
and encouragement has made possible this, my latest foray into political history telling. Among these stand out most prominently, first, my constantly
supportive and sacrificing family, second, my wonderful colleagues at

McGuireWoods and McGuireWoods Consulting, and, third, the outstanding team at the University of Virginia Center for Politics and those who have given generously to support the center's valuable work. My thanks go especially to Beverly Dean and the top-notch administrative team at McGuireWoods; to Joshua Scott, Ken Stroupe, and the great staff at the Center for Politics; and to the center's generous benefactors who took particular interest in this project—Rick Sharp, Bob Hatcher, Bobby Ukrop, the Claude R. Lambe Foundation, and that foundation's stewards, Charles Koch and Rich Fink.

My foremost collaborators and confidants at key stages of the work on this book have been Jonathan Carr and Preston Lloyd. Both are political activists to the core (in different parties) and outstanding lawyers in the making, but on this project they made indispensable contributions as exceptionally dedicated researchers, painstaking editors, and candid sounding boards. I am indebted and very grateful to each of them.

No one during the course of this project has been more continuously supportive and helpful than Larry Sabato. It was at his instigation that I began work on an updated second edition of *The Dynamic Dominion*, which grew and grew in scope until it necessarily culminated here in a separate, companion volume to that work. Professor Sabato's incisive analysis, prolific pen, and ready, pithy commentary on all matters political are legendary in Virginia and unsurpassed by scholars across the country. Indeed, the frequency of citation to and reliance on his numerous writings in this volume attests to the depth of his body of work and the pervasiveness of his influence as analyst and commentator. But despite all of those accomplishments and demands, he remains attentive and available first and foremost to his students and to his innovative Center for Politics, where much important work in the realm of government and politics is being carried out. For me, in this and other endeavors, he has been a constant teacher, mentor, encourager, and friend, and it is impossible to convey in this space the extent of my gratitude.

Through the years, an unusually large number of persons volunteered their time to review drafts or portions of the manuscript that became *The Dynamic Dominion* and/or this book. In the former volume I acknowledged those who so assisted in the first phase of my work, and here I wish to add an expression of appreciation to the following persons who reviewed and commented on the newer chapters: Will Allcott, Ray Allen Jr., Pete Atkinson, Betsy and Jim Beamer, Warren Billings, Mark Bowles, Bob Carlson, Judge Mark Christie, Richard Cullen, Ben Dendy, Frank Donatelli, Eric Finkbeiner, Kevin Gentry, Bob Gibson, Bob Holsworth, Steve Horton, Chris LaCivita, Justice Don Lemons, Bernie McNamee, Ross Mackenzie,

Boyd Marcus, Tom Morris, Paul Nardo, L. F. Payne, Dave Robertson, Larry Sabato, Joshua Scott, Mike Shear, Todd Stottlemyer, Ken Stroupe, Susan Swecker, Mike Thomas, Tom Walls, and John Whelan.

As with *The Dynamic Dominion*, this work has been enriched by the candid observations of political leaders and activists in both parties and respected journalists and commentators who responded affirmatively to my requests for interviews. Among the Virginia public officials who took time during busy schedules to contribute to this volume were Governors Mark Warner, Jim Gilmore, Doug Wilder, and Jerry Baliles; United States Senators John Warner, George Allen, Chuck Robb, and Paul Trible; Lieutenant Governor Don Beyer; House Speakers Bill Howell and Vance Wilkins; state Senator John Chichester; and Delegate Dick Cranwell. To them and all of the others who shared their helpful insights, I express particular appreciation.

In addition to any errors herein, which are my responsibility alone, I apologize in advance to the reader who comes to this volume without having first read *The Dynamic Dominion*. Once the decision was made to publish these chapters in a new, separate volume rather than add them to the revised second edition of that book, I did my best to go back and insert background information regarding characters, concepts, and terminology that were illuminated in that work but that might be unfamiliar to the reader who begins his or her study of Virginia politics not there, but here. I also added cross-references here to the pertinent chapters of *The Dynamic Dominion* wherever it seemed likely to be useful. Ultimately, however, the only adequate remedy for the serious reader is to go back, not to 1981 where this book starts, but to 1945 where the fascinating story of Virginia's postwar political journey begins, and trace the tale in sequence.

The discerning reader also will notice that the more recent Virginia elections described in Part III (2000–2006) are not accorded the same degree of descriptive detail and analysis as are those in the first eight chapters. That is by design. Time and distance are required for accurate analysis and commentary on political trends, causes, and consequences. I thus have judged it appropriate to report the key events and salient facts about Virginia politics since the turn of the twenty-first century and to leave most of the commentary concerning this still-unfolding period to later writers. Even so, there is much to report here regarding the first years of the young century, for they have been extraordinarily busy ones in the political life of the state and the nation.

Finally, I wish to pay tribute to five incomparable Virginians who have passed away since my last published volume on Virginia politics. Each left his indelible imprint on Virginia government, politics, and history, but my purpose in paying tribute here is more personal. Each took a particular interest in my writing and other pursuits and was generous to me beyond measure with his counsel and concern. For Hunter Andrews, Herbert Bateman, Mills Godwin, Jim Latimer, and Lawrence Lewis, I give thanks to the Lord above, for He alone possesses the wit and imagination to endow earthly vessels with such wonderfully distinctive personalities and the capacity to make such a profound difference in the lives of others.

Frank B. Atkinson
Hanover, Virginia
April 26, 2006

*Part I*

# ROBB, WILDER, AND THE DEMOCRATIC DECADE, 1981–1992

# 1

## REVERSAL OF FORTUNE:
## THE DEMOCRATIC
## SOUTHERN STRATEGY

> The great leap of faith Virginians made was not in electing a black
> . . . but in electing Robb [as governor] in 1981. For a decade Vir-
> ginians had seen a Democratic Party run by liberals. . . . [Robb]
> reopened doors that had been shut to the business and money
> crowd; he firmly established the proposition that it was possible to
> be both fiscally responsible and socially enlightened. . . . [H]e rede-
> fined what it meant to be a Virginia Democrat.[1]
>
> —Dwayne Yancey, 1988

As Ronald Reagan stood on the west portico of the United States Capitol on January 20, 1981, to take the oath of office as the 40th chief
executive, launching a presidency that would rearrange American politics,
reorient the Republican Party, and remake the national and international
landscape, the Virginia Republicans in the massive crowd were basking in
the glow of their stunning successes. By the end of the 1970s, Virginia's
rapid realignment had made the state GOP the most successful such party
organization, Republican or Democratic, in the country. The autumn 1980
elections revealed a Virginia GOP at the peak of its power, and Republican
partisans eyed the new year's statewide contests with the assurance of a tried
and tested prizefighter poised to deliver a knockout punch. Pundits joined
the partisans in portraying the 1981 contests as do-or-die for the state's
Democrats. "If success eludes the Democratic Party again in 1981," warned
commentator Larry Sabato, "Democrats may find themselves in the political
wilderness indefinitely."[2] Reflecting the cockiness of many GOP activists

---

1. Dwayne Yancey, *When Hell Froze Over* (Roanoke, VA: Taylor Publishing Company, 1988), p. 373.
2. *Richmond Times-Dispatch*, November 23, 1980.

who had begun to believe their flattering press clippings, Governor John Dalton's press secretary, Charles Davis, gloated that the only way a Republican could lose statewide in 1981 would be "if all the voting machines malfunctioned on election day."[3]

A decade later, as state Republicans gazed up blurry-eyed from the canvas after three successive knock-downs in the gubernatorial races of the 1980s, neither they nor most political observers were able to fathom how the party's fortunes had been so rapidly and completely reversed. That Virginians' serial rejection of Republicanism in state elections occurred throughout the remarkable Reagan-Bush decade in Washington only added to the incomprehension. During a time of unprecedented national prosperity and foreign policy achievement under Republican presidential leadership, including outright victory in a Cold War that had consumed American lives, resources, and attention for more than a third of the Republic's existence,[4] Virginians trimmed GOP representation in the state's congressional delegation back to 50 percent—at the close of the 1980s, each party controlled one United States Senate seat and five House of Representatives seats[5]—and gave the Old Dominion's Democrats a perfect record in the nine contests for top state government posts during the decade. The Democratic winners included two history-making candidates: Douglas Wilder, who became the first African-American elected governor of an American state,[6] and Mary Sue Terry, a two-term Virginia attorney general and the first woman elected to that post.

If the 1980s belonged to Ronald Reagan nationally, the decade has to be branded the "Robb era" in Virginia. Charles Robb had burst onto the Virginia political scene with his successful bid for lieutenant governor in 1977. Winning the governorship four years later, he forged a new majority

---

3. Garrett Epps, "As Virginia Goes . . ." *Washington Post Magazine,* January 25, 1981, p. 11.

4. While the term "Cold War" is commonly used to refer to the Soviet Union's expansionism and American-led efforts to contain it in the period after World War II, it has been argued that its origins were actually much earlier—in the administration of Virginia-born Woodrow Wilson. See Donald E. Davis and Eugene V. Trani, *The First Cold War* (Columbia: University of Missouri Press, 2002).

5. The five congressional seats controlled by Virginia Democrats at the end of the 1980s represented their best share since 1968, and equaled the number of seats Democrats claimed in 1974 on the heels of the Watergate scandal. The party's gains continued in the early 1990s, when Democrats won a majority of the state's U.S. House of Representatives contests for the first time since 1966.

6. Wilder actually was the second black person to serve as governor of an American state. P.B.S. Pinchback, whose mother was a slave and whose father was a slave owner, served as acting governor of Louisiana for approximately five weeks during Reconstruction.

coalition in the state—one that resembled the broad Democratic coalition that carried his father-in-law, Lyndon Johnson, to a presidential victory in the Commonwealth in 1964 and then elected Mills Godwin governor as a Democrat in 1965. Though Robb's fame stemmed (by marriage) from the Great Society, he little resembled a latter-day liberal. His moderate platform combined tenets of economic conservatism with racial progressivism, and this—along with his considerable wealth and deliberate, reassuring manner—supplied a formula for Democratic renewal among the prosperous, forward-looking young voters in Virginia's burgeoning suburbs. Swept into office with him in 1981 were a new Democratic lieutenant governor, former Portsmouth Mayor Richard J. ("Dick") Davis Jr., and Richmond-area Delegate Gerald L. Baliles, who narrowly was elected attorney general. In the 1985 gubernatorial race, Democratic nominee Baliles embraced the popular governor's record and themes so thoroughly that reporters dubbed him "Robb II." And four years after that, Democratic gubernatorial candidate Wilder invested hundreds of thousands of dollars in television advertising to put Robb on the airwaves singing his praises. The former governor went to the United States Senate in 1988, and from there Robb continued to recommend his centrist strategy to a national Democratic Party that was eager to reclaim the White House.

The Robb-led Virginia Democrats achieved victory after victory in the 1980s, but, even so, characterizations of Democratic strength in the state often were overstated. The party's decade of successes in statewide races was accompanied by gradual erosion of its lopsided General Assembly majority and its domination of local offices. From 1979 to 1989, GOP representation climbed from 21 to 39 members in the hundred-member House of Delegates, and from six to ten members of the forty-member Virginia Senate. Moreover, the Democratic statewide winning streak of the 1980s, like the string of statewide GOP victories in the 1970s, tended to mask the reality of spirited competition between the two Virginia parties—competition that had emerged and intensified following the turbulent, transforming 1964–1975 period. State Democrats were neither as weak in the 1970s, as was generally believed at the time, nor were Virginia Republicans as feeble in the following decade as their dismal win-loss record would suggest. If the United States Senate contest in 1978 between Republican John Warner and Democrat Andrew Miller offered some encouragement for downtrodden Democrats after a decade of setbacks,[7] the razor-thin margin separating vic-

---

7. The 1978 Senate contest, which was among the closest statewide elections in Virginia history, pitted Miller, a former two-term attorney general, against first-time candidate Warner. See *The Dynamic Dominion*, Chapters 31–33. As of this writing, the closest Virginia election was the 2005 contest for attorney general. See Chapter 9.

tory from defeat in the 1989 gubernatorial race served to reassure Republicans that either party could capture the prize in contemporary Virginia.

Unlike the dramatically shifting coalitions and fast-paced change that animated Virginia politics for much of the period after World War II and reached its peak in the early 1970s, the 1980s brought more gradual evolution and the achievement of a semblance of stability. The rapid realignment process of the preceding decade gave way to a substantially de-aligned political environment in which both parties vied for the decisive support of independent voters—a situation common in the South and much of the nation. Since the demise of the Byrd organization in the 1960s, an important thread running through Virginia politics had been voters' penchant for independence from political parties. Neither major party possessed the loyalty of anything approaching a majority among the state's electorate, and opinion surveys regularly confirmed that the largest single group remained the body of unaffiliated voters who regarded themselves as independents. Even the major political benefactors in the state were, for the most part, free from party ties. Most in the business community reserved the prerogative to back candidates who were to their liking regardless of party label, and this remained generally true even as the contributor base's center-of-gravity shifted during the 1980s from the traditional Richmond-based business and financial establishment to fast-growing Northern Virginia and (to a lesser extent) the Hampton Roads area. With voters and donors roaming at large and generally choosing the person rather than the party, it was not remarkable that Virginians simultaneously embraced Robb-style Democratic leadership at the state level and Reagan Republicanism nationally.

The centrist Democratic coalition that made a fleeting debut in Virginia in the mid-1960s and then reemerged to give Charles Robb a crucial victory in 1981 contained widely divergent and sometimes antagonistic elements. In 1965, GOP gubernatorial nominee Linwood Holton had expressed amazement at the "incredible logic under which [Democrat Mills Godwin] was able to send . . . Armistead Boothe to Arlington to proclaim him a liberal in the finest tradition of the Great Society while he was also able . . . to send Bill Tuck to Danville to attest he was a conservative in the tradition of Harry Byrd."[8] In 1981, former Attorney General J. Marshall Coleman, the Republican gubernatorial nominee, could have used different names but almost identical words to describe his Democratic foe's feat. Touting Robb's candidacy simultaneously on the hustings that year—and

---

8. Jack R. Hunter, "Linwood Holton's Long Quest for the Governorship of Virginia and Its Impact on the Growth of the Republican Party," unpublished thesis, University of Richmond, 1972, p. 32.

playing clearly indispensable roles in the Democratic victory—were former Delegate W. Roy Smith, the leader of the conservative Byrd organization remnants known euphemistically as the "Coalition,"[9] and State Senator Douglas Wilder of Richmond, then the lone black in the Assembly's upper chamber and a favorite of organized labor and liberals. The two men vouched for Robb's fidelity to various principles and policies deemed fundamental by their respective constituencies, which happened to be at opposite ends of the Virginia political spectrum. For more than a decade, the divergent views and discordant voices within the Democratic Party had thwarted the party's candidates for statewide office. But as the 1980s unfolded, those Democratic divisions were healed or put on hold, and it was the GOP conservative coalition's turn to crack and crumble.

Long members of a distinctly minority party, state Republicans yearning for victories had suppressed factional differences in the late 1960s and 1970s, and their unity of purpose had played a key role in producing a decade of electoral successes. But with that success eventually came overconfidence, organizational lethargy, personal rivalries, and a renewal of factional bickering. The sudden death of conservative leader Richard Obenshain in a 1978 airplane crash left his most prominent allies vying, often bitterly, for power and influence. That critical development coincided with the growth of the "New Right," or "Christian Right," elements within the party— religious fundamentalists, evangelicals, and others primarily motivated by morality-laden social issues such as opposition to legalized abortion. By 1981, the GOP's dominant conservative wing was hemorrhaging as differing policy agendas (i.e., emphasis of economic versus social issues), contending party-building strategies, and conflicting personal ambitions came to the fore. The new divisions did not supplant, but merely supplemented, the still-simmering dispute between the traditional Republicans to the west and the more conservative GOP partisans and Democratic converts east of the Blue Ridge.

The renewed GOP factionalism in 1981 was accompanied by the first major splintering of the Byrd organization alumni and conservative business leaders who comprised the Coalition. Since 1972, the bulk of the conservative independent notables had followed former Governor Mills Godwin's overt and Senator Harry F. Byrd Jr.'s veiled direction in supporting Repub-

---

9. The loosely organized group of former Byrd Democrats often provided crucial support to Virginia Republican candidates in the 1970s. For a description of the group's origins, methods, and impact, see *The Dynamic Dominion,* Chapter 27. The convention of using a capital "C" when referring to the group has been employed in this book as a convenient way of distinguishing that specific use of the term from the broader, generic uses of the word "coalition."

lican candidates for statewide office. Republican activists, hewing to the path charted by GOP leaders Richard Obenshain and John Dalton, generally had cooperated by nominating candidates and constructing tickets that appealed to the old-line Byrd Democrats. The result had been a winning conservative coalition that elected Republicans to statewide office and left conservative non-Republicans—such as Senator Harry F. Byrd Jr., Democratic Congressmen David Satterfield and W.C. ("Dan") Daniel, and numerous state legislators and local officials—politically unmolested. In 1977, the GOP leaders' ticket-building efforts had been thwarted by rebellious delegates at the party's state convention, but the Coalition never splintered in the general election because populist-liberal former Lieutenant Governor Henry Howell deprived moderate former Attorney General Andrew Miller of the party's gubernatorial nod.[10] Republicans were not so fortunate in 1981. With neither the GOP's Coleman nor Democrat Robb regarded as distinctly more conservative or socially acceptable than the other, the Coalition split almost evenly between them.

With Republican Party division and the Coalition breach came a third key ingredient—Democratic Party unity. Sobered by their seemingly interminable hard times, Virginia Democrats had the "minority mentality"[11] necessary to forge a united front. To many in the once-proud party, winning the governorship in 1981 represented nothing less than a prerequisite for political survival, and that imperative ensured that internal party divisions would be quelled and factional interests would be subordinated. In Lieutenant Governor Charles Robb, Democrats had a candidate equal to the challenge. A well-financed celebrity, gubernatorial in appearance and demeanor, cautious and traditional by nature, conservative in style, and moderate in opinion, the lieutenant governor had been one of only two Virginia Democrats since 1969 to amass a suburban majority in a statewide race.[12] He looked like a winner, and, if few Democrats were much excited by him, he had given even fewer of them reason to be hostile. Since his 1977 election, Robb's strategy had been to meet with and placate as many influential Democrats in as many quarters of the diverse party as possible; rather than attempting to build a strongly loyal personal following, he purposely

---

10. For a description of the two political parties' nominating processes in 1977, which in both cases yielded unexpected results, see *The Dynamic Dominion*, Chapter 29.

11. The phrase was coined by Professor Larry Sabato in his *Virginia Votes 1979–1982* (Charlottesville: Institute of Government, University of Virginia, 1983), p. 81.

12. Robb's 1977 bid for lieutenant governor and Andrew Miller's landslide reelection victory in the 1973 campaign for attorney general were the only statewide Democratic efforts to garner a majority in the suburbs between 1969 and 1981. See *The Dynamic Dominion*, Chapters 25, 30.

adopted the more modest goal of "[not having] enemies out there crusading against [him]."[13] For a Democratic Party desperate to win, little more was needed.

Robb also took steps to quell the feuding between the party's liberal faction aligned with former Lieutenant Governor Henry Howell and its more moderate elements that had supported Attorney General Andrew Miller. "The personal animosity between [the Howell and Miller camps] was so strong," recalled Robb,

> that it took me two or three years of effort to bring the party back together so they wouldn't keep fighting that battle. It was very clear that they wanted to, and I had to move a number of people out of positions and a number of other people into them and keep some people very quiet in campaigns or we would have had those fights all over again.[14]

Shortly after becoming lieutenant governor, Robb asked former United States Senator William Spong to chair an informal commission that he charged with recommending steps to revitalize the state Democratic Party, and he assigned a key adviser, Stewart Gamage, to coordinate the effort. Among the commission's suggestions was a switch from the primary to the convention as the party's mechanism for nominating statewide candidates. As Robb intended, the Spong commission also concluded that the party needed new leadership. In January 1979, liberal Norfolk Senator Joseph T. Fitzpatrick resigned the Democratic state chairmanship, and the party's governing committee tapped Portsmouth Mayor Richard Davis to succeed him. The change appeared to reflect a shift toward the center by Virginia Democrats—imagery that Robb desperately wanted.[15] The new, more unified, and more moderate Democratic Party resolved to turn the page on the fiasco that was the 1970s and directed its attention to eliminating the significant technological gap in fundraising and voter turnout programs that favored the state GOP. A string of successes followed.

Though the Democratic success story of the 1980s initially centered around Robb, the decade saw another Democratic figure move from relative obscurity to the pinnacle of power in the Old Dominion and into the forefront of the national political arena. L. Douglas Wilder was a "standard-

---

13. Charles S. Robb interview, October 5, 1984, and April 16, 2005.

14. Robb interview.

15. With the acquiescence of the ostensibly neutral lieutenant governor, H. Benson ("Ben") Dendy, III, a key Robb lieutenant, worked actively at the 1980 Democratic state convention to facilitate the ouster of liberal Howell allies as the party's representatives on the Democratic National Committee. H. Benson Dendy III interview, February 7, 2005.

brand liberal"[16] state senator from the city of Richmond—the highest elected black officeholder in the Commonwealth—when he helped mobilize African-American voters behind Robb's gubernatorial candidacy in 1981. In a formula that would be repeated throughout the decade, Wilder played a key role in keeping the Democratic black and liberal base intact while Robb and his emulators fashioned a moderate-conservative image attractive to suburban whites. Acknowledging "the conservative tone of the [Robb] campaign" and his own concerns about it, Wilder wrote to his "Democratic Black Caucus of Virginia" constituents in 1981 that he had investigated Robb's stands and could attest to the gubernatorial candidate's commitment to various measures deemed important to blacks.[17] "I trust the man. . . . He has been consistent," Wilder wrote to the influential African-American political and community leaders, many of whom were wary of the conservative-sounding Democrat. Though Robb later played down the significance of Wilder's 1981 role[18] and the two engaged in a mutually debilitating feud for more than a decade thereafter, Wilder played an indispensable part in forming and fortifying what Democrats dubbed the "Robb coalition."

In stark contrast to the political stratagem of Reverend Jesse L. Jackson, the iconic black preacher-politician who used his popularity among African Americans as leverage to force the national Democratic Party and its presidential nominees to the left in the 1980s, Wilder made it possible for Democrats of a moderate-conservative stripe to run and win in Virginia with solid African-American and liberal support. In 1985, and again in 1989, it was the presence of an increasingly conservative-sounding Wilder on the statewide Democratic ticket—aided by the popular Robb's imprimatur and black Virginians' determination to break the racial barrier by electing one of their own to high office—that kept the broad Democratic coalition intact and in power. By decade's end, the winning combination could more aptly be described as the "Robb-Wilder coalition," and the nation's first elected African-American governor was stumping throughout the country, spreading the word about the formula that had brought success to Democrats even in conservative Virginia, and even at the height of the Reagan "revolution." Just a few years earlier—in 1986—Wilder had lampooned Robb's efforts to give the national Democratic Party a more centrist image, deriding the Robb-led Democratic Leadership Council as "me-too-ists who put on

---

16. Donald P. Baker, *Wilder: Hold Fast to Dreams* (Cabin John, MD: Seven Locks Press, 1989), p. 277.
17. Baker, *Wilder*, p. 121.
18. Baker, *Wilder*, p. 120.

Reagan masks."[19] But, by 1990, a largely upstaged Robb was watching in frustration as the charismatic Wilder took his moderate message—Wilder tactician Paul Goldman dubbed it the "New Mainstream" in 1989[20]—and proceeded to capture the attention of Democratic partisans around the country. Not one, but two, Virginia Democrats with apparent presidential ambitions were touting their achievements in a state that a decade earlier had been deemed the most Republican in the country.

Despite the Democratic winning streak in state elections, Virginians' enthusiasm for Reaganism never waned in the presidential contests of the 1980s. Republicans also managed to win a hard-fought contest to succeed retiring United States Senator Harry F. Byrd Jr. in 1982 when First District Representative Paul S. Trible Jr. outpolled newly elected Lieutenant Governor Richard Davis—although Trible left the seat and Charles Robb reclaimed it for Democrats six years later. To some, this two-tiered system, characterized by an evident GOP advantage in federal contests and renewed Democratic domination in state races, appeared to be a throwback to an earlier era in Virginia politics, a remnant from the Byrd years. But it was more than that. The situation reflected somewhat the immense personal popularity of the decade's leading political figures—Reagan in Washington, Robb in Richmond—as well as the inevitable benefits of incumbency during prosperous times. Yet, it also paralleled a regional, and to a lesser extent national, political trend. Virginians, like other Southerners, voted Republican in landslide proportions in the ideology-laden presidential races during the 1980s, and GOP candidates generally benefited from the tendency of United States Senate contests and races for the House of Representatives to develop along conservative-versus-liberal lines. In the less ideological competition for the largely managerial state government posts, however, Democrats thrived not only in Virginia but throughout the South.

As noted by Professors Earl and Merle Black in their seminal 1987 study, *Politics and Society in the South,* contests for federal office in the South typically focused on national security, foreign policy, and economic and fiscal issues and thus provided GOP conservatives "with more targets and symbols to employ against their opponents than [did] the more mundane and practical agendas of state politics. . . . In state politics there [was] no reliable demand for an unadulterated conservative Republicanism."[21] To the

---

19. See *Washington Post,* March 12, 1989.

20. See Margaret Edds, *Claiming the Dream: The Victorious Campaign of Douglas Wilder of Virginia* (Chapel Hill, NC: Algonquin Books, 1990), pp. 181–183.

21. Earl Black and Merle Black, *Politics and Society in the South* (Cambridge, MA: Harvard University Press, 1987), pp. 315–316; see also Larry J. Sabato, *Virginia Votes 1983–1986* (Charlottesville: Institute of Government, University of Virginia, 1987), pp. 107–108.

extent issues entered into state and local races, voters generally assessed candidates of both parties based on their practical approaches to such vexing concerns as education, transportation, public safety, and environmental protection. Also important in some state contests around the country were emotional social issues such as race relations and abortion rights, which tended to cut across traditional conservative-liberal alignments.

In Virginia, the continuing acceleration of the state's already rapid suburban growth—and the attendant increase in the proportion of younger, upper-middle-class voters in the state's electorate—worked a subtle shift in voter attitudes and political focus during the 1980s. The typical suburban voter held conservative views on economics and foreign policy, and tended to credit the Reagan administration for the notable advances made in those areas during the decade. Ironically, however, the sustained prosperity enjoyed nationally and in Virginia after 1982 advantaged the Robb Democrats in state elections. With disposable income rising steadily in the suburbs, and with state government inundated with new revenue, the preoccupying economic concerns of the 1970s gave way to widespread satisfaction in the 1980s. As the party of incumbency at the state level, Virginia's Democrats reaped the harvest of this general contentment and, with few exceptions, carefully avoided saying or doing anything that would conjure up recollections of Democratic tax-and-spend liberalism. Rather, as personal income soared in Virginia in the 1980s, Robb and his successors claimed it as their legacy. With the strong economy, Democrats had the best of both worlds—they touted Virginia's fiscal integrity and economic dynamism before conservative audiences while dramatically increasing spending on education and other state programs to the applause of Democrat-aligned interest groups. In this way, the long-running Reagan recovery provided glue that helped hold the diverse Robb-Wilder coalition together. "Unfortunately for the Republicans," chortled Delegate C. Richard Cranwell, a Roanoke County Democrat and key legislative leader, "their President [did] too good a job."[22]

With suburban concerns about the administration of state fiscal affairs largely alleviated in the 1980s, Democrats were free to concentrate on other issues and, specifically, to emphasize topics that would aggravate the tensions within the conservative coalition that had elected Republicans statewide in the 1970s. There were, of course, numerous campaign issues deemed important by suburban and other voters. But in two contexts especially— race relations and abortion policy—the attitudes of the younger voters in the suburbs tended to diverge markedly from those held by some other pro-

---

22. Yancey, *When Hell Froze Over*, p. 367.

Reagan, pro-Republican voting blocs. The more individualistic, libertarian impulse in the suburbs ran counter to the morality-driven agenda of the GOP's Christian Right, and the progressive suburban sentiments on civil rights bore little resemblance to the rigid racial codes that echoed from the Byrd era and resonated with some of its surviving symbols in the Coalition. These issues, coupled with the youth-oriented themes of change and progress, were skillfully exploited by state Democrats to varying degrees in all three gubernatorial elections of the 1980s. Their suburban strategy was a page out of the Ronald Reagan playbook—seize the future thematically, identify with the optimism of the young and upwardly mobile, and run against the "failed policies of the past." For the Reagan Republicans at the national level, the defining issues were economic growth and national security, and the foils were Jimmy Carter and the Evil Empire.[23] For the Robb Democrats in Virginia, the favorite wedge issues became race and abortion, and the polarizing symbols were Massive Resistance and Moral Majority.[24]

The explosive economic and population growth during the 1980s in Northern Virginia, and to a lesser extent in Tidewater, produced a major shift in political influence—votes, campaign contributions, and issues—away from the traditional power centers of rural Virginia and the Richmond area. The state's population grew by more than 500,000 during the decade, and roughly half of the new voters in northern and southeastern Virginia were immigrants from other states. In addition, new campaign contributors—wealthy real estate developers, home and office builders, and high-tech business men and women—emerged to give those regions dramatically increased political clout. Though both parties by decade's end had recognized the magnitude of the change and were responding to it, Democrats managed to discern and capitalize on these trends throughout the 1980s. Northern Virginia and Hampton Roads became the mainstays of Demo-

---

23. President Jimmy Carter's problem-plagued tenure in the White House ended in a landslide defeat at the hands of GOP challenger Ronald Reagan in 1980. Early in his administration, Reagan branded the Soviet Union an "evil empire," and the term, though highly controversial at the time, became synonymous with his dogged and ultimately successful rhetorical and geopolitical campaign against Soviet communism.

24. "Massive Resistance" refers to the Byrd organization's policy of legal and political resistance to school desegregation in the mid-twentieth century. See *The Dynamic Dominion*, Chapters 8–11. The "Moral Majority" political organization, led by Reverend Jerry Falwell of Lynchburg, Virginia, burst onto the national scene in the 1980 presidential election when it rallied fundamentalist and evangelical churches and their members behind the candidacy of GOP presidential nominee Ronald Reagan in his contest against incumbent President Carter. Falwell had played an active role in Virginia elections beginning in the late 1970s. See *The Dynamic Dominion,* Chapter 33.

cratic campaign financing and electoral majorities in statewide contests from 1981 to 1989 notwithstanding the regions' growing prosperity and increasingly Republican orientation in national and local elections. As these vote-rich suburban areas swung back and forth between Reagan-Bush Republicanism in Washington and Robb-Wilder Democracy in Richmond, it was apparent that state Democrats had captured—at least for a time—the alluring themes and symbols that swayed the "new" Virginia. Especially in the Washington, D.C., suburbs, where voters rarely followed Virginia statehouse developments between elections and received most of their campaign images through the *Washington Post,* the Democratic themes were reinforced throughout the 1980s by sympathetic campaign news coverage.[25]

One unexpected event during the 1980s had profound political repercussions. Former Governor John Dalton died in July 1986 at age 55, the victim of lung cancer that, after a period of remission, recurred suddenly in late 1985. The last in a trio of GOP governors in the 1970s and easily the most broadly popular of the three in the 1980s, John Dalton was esteemed by Republicans in his day much as his father Ted, Virginia's premier "Mr. Republican," had been a quarter century earlier.[26] As governor, the younger Dalton had emphasized party-building and had made the Virginia Republican Party synonymous with business-like, fiscally responsible management. "I tried to slow down the growth of government in those four years and to leave government . . . with the people having a higher percentage of their tax dollars than they had when I took office," the former governor recalled in a conversation with reporter James Latimer shortly before his death,

> and we were able to do that. We were also able to cut down the number of people employed by government as it relates to the total population of the state. I want to be remembered for those things.[27]

At a time when economic issues dominated political discourse, Dalton helped fashion a Republican image with broad appeal to the state's conservative-minded suburban voters.

---

25. See, e.g., Larry J. Sabato, *Virginia Votes 1987–1990* (Charlottesville: Center for Public Service, University of Virginia, 1991), pp. 94–99; Richard Harwood, "Tilt! Tilt!" *Washington Post,* November 19, 1989.

26. John Dalton served as Governor of Virginia from 1978 to 1982. For a description of his 1977 gubernatorial campaign, see *The Dynamic Dominion*, Chapters 29–30. His father, Ted Dalton, served as a Republican Party leader, state senator, and GOP gubernatorial nominee in 1953 and 1957 before receiving appointment to a federal judgeship. See Chapters 7–9.

27. Conversations with James Latimer, "A Different Dominion: The Republican Renaissance," WCVE-TV, 1986.

Though Dalton as governor presided over a Virginia GOP at the height of its success, he was deeply disappointed by his failure to accomplish the election of a Republican successor in 1981. He worked feverishly that year to reassemble the winning conservative coalition, only to be thwarted by the surge in GOP factionalism and by conservative defections. In 1985, with the campaign of Republican gubernatorial nominee Wyatt Durrette also flagging in the contest's waning days, the former governor took to the hustings and tried gamely to reverse the momentum with sharp attacks on Democrat Gerald Baliles for proposing state spending increases that, Dalton charged, would lead to large tax hikes. In the wake of the 1981 and 1985 statewide Democratic sweeps, Dalton sensed that he alone could rescue his strife-torn party, and with close associates he explored plans for leaving his high-powered Richmond legal practice and returning to public life in a second bid for the governorship.[28] Had his illness not suddenly intervened, Dalton might well have led the Republican Party back to the governor's mansion in 1989, derailing Douglas Wilder's history-making candidacy and vastly changing the course of state political history in the process.[29] Instead, like Richard Obenshain's untimely death eight years earlier, and Sargeant Reynolds's seven years before that, John Dalton's sudden passing left a void that hurt his political party severely.[30] "Dalton had unique standing—as a feisty party-builder and as a statesman who played the peacemaker," wrote political reporter Margie Fisher in a late-1980s article canvassing the ailing GOP's continuing woes. "No Republican has emerged to fill the leadership void left by [his] death."[31]

Long-term trends and unexpected developments combined with the vagaries of electoral politics and the ephemeral impact of personalities in the 1980s to produce a decade of election outcomes in the Old Dominion

28. Richard Cullen interview, December 15, 2004. Upon leaving office in 1982, Dalton had joined the Richmond office of McGuire, Woods, Battle & Boothe, a large law firm with longstanding, bipartisan ties to the Virginia political establishment. The firm (later called "McGuireWoods") had been home to (and bore the name of) Democratic governor John S. Battle. It was joined by a third Virginia chief executive, Republican George Allen, after his gubernatorial tenure ended in 1998. William C. Battle, the 1969 Democratic nominee for governor (and son of the former governor), and Richard D. Obenshain, who ran on the opposing GOP slate (for attorney general) in 1969 and for the United States Senate in 1978, also had been partners in the firm.

29. Wilder later observed that Dalton would have been an "enormously formidable" candidate in 1989, noting that the former Republican chief executive had a well-regarded record as governor, few political enemies, and an exceedingly strong base of financial support. L. Douglas Wilder interview, March 22, 2005.

30. See *The Dynamic Dominion,* Chapters 21, 32. For a discussion of the interrelated activities and impacts of Republican leaders Obenshain and Dalton in the 1970s, see the author's "Dalton Taught State GOP How to Win," *Richmond News Leader,* September 19, 1986.

31. *Roanoke Times & World-News,* June 10, 1988.

lopsidedly favoring the Democrats. But the Democratic streak was both more and less than it seemed on the surface. Virginia did not change precipitously between 1980 and 1990; most of the notable demographic and economic trends had been underway for several decades. Nor was the state—contrary to the superficial suggestions of observers beyond the Commonwealth's borders—suddenly transformed during or by the groundbreaking election of Governor Douglas Wilder in 1989. The election of the first African American and first female statewide officeholders in the 1980s, like the election of the first Republican governor in 1969, were reflections of Virginia's gradual and continuing evolution from the monolithic politics of the all-white, all-male, all-Democratic Byrd organization to a more competitive and pluralistic political culture.[32]

Just as Virginia Republicans' winning appeal to like-minded Democrats and independents in the 1970s had presaged the advent of "Reagan Democrats" nationally, Virginia Democrats' success under Robb and Wilder provided important cues for Democrats hoping to reclaim the White House as the Reagan era drew to a close. In 1980, the conventional wisdom would have declared Virginia the last place one should look to discover a formula for Democratic renewal nationally, but by decade's end it was quite a different story. The unexpected success of Virginia Democrats using the Robb-Wilder formula of fiscal conservatism and social progressivism gained national attention, and its lessons were pressed vigorously on partisans around the country by the moderate Democratic Leadership Council. The Old Dominion looked, politically speaking, like other major swing states across the nation; younger suburban voters held sway and had demonstrated their readiness to vote for candidates of either party depending on personalities, issues, and image. Increasingly, Virginia seemed like a national bellwether—and, more than that, a testing ground for ideas, themes, and strategies that later appeared around the country in winning state and national campaigns.

To the disappointment of Robb's and Wilder's respective supporters (and perhaps other Virginians longing for renewed fertility from the Mother of Presidents), the notable labors and successes of the two Virginia Democratic leaders would propel neither to the White House. Their interrelated fights, foibles, and ill fortunes would thwart those ambitions. But the Democratic decade in Virginia would scarcely draw to a close before another centrist Democratic governor from the South, William ("Bill") Clinton, would run the presidential race Robb and Wilder each thought could be theirs—and win.

---

32. Linwood Holton became the first Republican governor of Virginia in the twentieth century after winning election in 1969. See *The Dynamic Dominion*, Chapters 17–19.

# 2

# THE WATERSHED ROBB
# VICTORY OF 1981

We blew [the 1981] election at the convention.[1]

—Governor John N. Dalton

T he race that would set the course of Virginia politics for a decade—the
1981 campaign for governor—effectively began on election night in
1977, when Charles Robb and Marshall Coleman celebrated their successful
bids for lieutenant governor and attorney general, respectively, and instantly
became their parties' favorites for governor the next time around. Four
years later, after Robb prevailed in what was a close race throughout,
shocked Republicans immediately placed the full burden of the loss on the
shoulders of their defeated gubernatorial standard-bearer. Indeed, Coleman,
the upstart who had stunned the establishment in 1977 by becoming the
first GOP attorney general in Virginia history, was blamed not only for losing the governorship, but also for a Democratic sweep that unexpectedly
overwhelmed former Delegate Wyatt B. Durrette Jr. of Fairfax, the favorite
in the race for attorney general. As the first unsuccessful Republican gubernatorial candidate in sixteen years, Coleman could hardly have been surprised by the negative reaction, nor could he have hoped to avoid the largest
share of responsibility for the loss. But the reasons for the surprising Democratic victories and GOP defeats in 1981 were far more complicated than
most Virginia Republicans understood or wished to acknowledge. And the
simplistic GOP appraisals of the causes of the party's 1981 setbacks, including the facile indictment of Coleman, set the stage for repetition of many of
the same mistakes throughout the 1980s.

Given the considerable advantages of incumbency in the American
political system, a politician or political party typically does not lose a once-

---

1. *Richmond Times-Dispatch*, May 27, 1984.

firm grip on power without committing a lot of very big mistakes. Just as Republicans elected their first Virginia governor in modern times—Linwood Holton—primarily because of the state Democratic Party's acute division in 1969,[2] so was the stunning reversal that carried Democrats back to the executive mansion in the early 1980s a product largely of the GOP's self-inflicted wounds. To be sure, Robb, like Holton before him, played a vital role in positioning himself and his party for the breakthrough. But at the end of the day, the election outcome in each instance rested more on the incumbent party's self-defeating missteps than on successful conquest by the political opposition. How the Virginia Republicans, then the most successful state party organization in the country, managed *not* to "Keep a Good Thing Going"[3] at the height of Ronald Reagan's political revolution is neither a simple nor a short story.

A central factor in the 1981 turnabout was the state Republican Party's failure to consolidate and institutionalize its gains of the 1970s. Even as the GOP was compiling an unsurpassed winning streak in state elections during the decade, it was failing to convert its financial supporters in the business community and the influential pillars of the state's conservative establishment into Republican Party adherents who would be committed to building a durable political organization and to fighting their struggles from within. The conservative coalition that dominated Virginia politics from 1972 until 1980 depended in each election upon the galvanizing presence of a threat from the Left. In the staunch liberalism of the national Democratic Party and the menacing populism of former Lieutenant Governor Henry Howell were ample incentives for conservative coalescence. But when Virginia Democrats offered the reasonable and attractive Robb, the glue was gone. Without a long-term, institutional commitment to the GOP as their political vehicle, many of the older conservatives who comprised the Coalition fell back upon their traditional Democratic Party predilections and their network of Democratic friends and associates in the courthouses and legislature. Others made their electoral choices from year to year based upon the personality of the candidates, their own perceived political or business interests, nonideological policy goals, and other factors specific to individual contests. Party loyalty was the farthest thing from their minds.

The realignment process of the 1970s left Virginia with a Republican Party anchored to the right of center and a Democratic Party grounded to

---

2. For a description of the divisive 1969 Democratic primary contest for governor and Linwood Holton's successful general election campaign in its wake, see *The Dynamic Dominion,* Chapters 17–18.

3. The phrase was Coleman's 1981 campaign slogan.

the left—an alignment consistent with the national political arrangement. For the Republicans, that development seemed like good news, because Virginia was and remains a conservative-leaning state. The bad news was that, because so many conservative leaders, contributors, and voters staked out an independent position and refrained from Republican affiliation and identification, Virginia Democrats retained a marked advantage in any state-wide race in which philosophical differences between the candidates were not pronounced. This would change gradually in the 1980s and 1990s as older political leaders and operatives with generational Democratic loyalties, especially in rural Virginia, passed from the scene. But in the recently de-aligned political environment of 1981, a Democratic candidate whose base among African Americans, labor, and liberals was secure, and who could retain traditionalist Democratic backing in rural Virginia, needed to garner only a respectable share—not even a majority—of the suburban vote in order to gain election. In 1981, Charles Robb was well positioned to accomplish that feat.

Republicans had several options for responding to such a situation, though none guaranteed success. They could continue to pursue the conservative coalition strategy and attempt to give each race an ideological focus by emphasizing Virginia Democrats' ties to their liberal national party and by highlighting issues that would motivate conservatives. Or, they could adopt an approach similar to Coleman's successful 1977 strategy, which enabled him to hold the Republican base and to offset Democratic inroads among rural and suburban independents by targeting specific Democratic constituency groups, such as blacks and organized labor. A third option—one that combined elements of the other two and paved a middle course between them—was to take a moderate-conservative tack overall and to direct an innovative, issue-oriented appeal to the suburbs emphasizing largely nonideological concerns such as education, transportation, and public safety.

Not surprisingly, Marshall Coleman's moderate Republican supporters hoped that he would embrace one of the latter two options in his race against Charles Robb. Commenting in 1980, former Governor Linwood Holton observed that the Robb-led Democrats "are going to have a strong ticket next year," and added, "We're going to have to appeal pretty broadly to win, and I suspect that Marshall Coleman will. There we will get a chance to see not just the Obenshain elements of the [Republican] coalition, but the Obenshain *and Holton* elements of that coalition."[4] Coleman's campaign manager and trusted adviser, Anson Franklin, concurred in the

---

4. Linwood Holton interview, May 28, 1980, and April 19, 1990.

need for a broad-based campaign, but one that would emphasize his candidate's appealing conservative stands on fiscal and criminal justice issues. "Every campaign is a battle for the middle," Franklin noted in 1980.

> I think you always need to retain the capability of appealing to a broad base of people. This is a conservative state, so you are not exactly talking about going off into left field to appeal to a majority of voters. If you look at Dick Obenshain's [1978 Senate campaign after he won the nomination], you will find that, while he had a campaign based on conservative principle, he realized that you have to appeal to a lot of people who may not be as conservative as some others.[5]

A moderate-conservative campaign stressing practical problem-solving—particularly on issues of importance in the state's fast-growing metropolitan areas—was the course with which Coleman himself was most comfortable. "There are terrific responsibilities the state has," he told political writer Garrett Epps in summarizing his goals for the governorship. "[State government is] the natural protector . . . of the people against violence. We need to educate the young people, maintain a transportation system. All these things are not war-and-peace issues, but they're extremely important—and I think they are going to be where the action is in the '80s."[6]

With the GOP having won elections in Virginia for a decade by mobilizing conservatives, however, there was broad agreement in Republican ranks that assembling a conservative coalition was again the way to win in 1981. Robb had to be painted as a liberal, or at least as an unreliable captive of the liberal interests dominant in his party; Coleman had to tout his conservative views and connections and again unite the Right. No one was more fully committed to that strategy than the man who became Coleman's mentor, Governor John Dalton. Though generally regarded as more moderate in outlook than Obenshain, Godwin, and the Coalitionists, the thoroughly Republican chief executive shared the widespread view that GOP candidates won in Virginia by being perceived as more conservative than their Democratic foes. Successfully running to the right meant making common cause with the influential conservative Democratic and independent political and business leaders who generally took their cues from ex-Democrats Godwin and Byrd. The strategy had worked before, and most in the GOP assumed it would work again.

Moreover, Dalton and the Republican leadership—including Coleman

---

5. Anson Franklin interview, June 4, 1980, and September 17, 1984.
6. Epps, "As Virginia Goes. . .," p. 13.

—recognized that the liberal and African-American votes garnered by Linwood Holton in his 1969 gubernatorial bid and by Coleman in his successful 1977 campaign were largely protest votes cast *against* the Democratic candidates in those races. In 1969, disappointed Howell backers had bolted the party to "nail the coffin shut" on the Byrd organization.[7] In 1977, liberal defections were produced mainly by recollections of Democrat Edward Lane's support, however ancient and perfunctory, for Massive Resistance.[8] No comparable circumstances beneficial to the Republicans existed in 1981. In a race against Robb, the Great Society scion and nominee of a Virginia Democratic Party united for survival, a Republican would have little prospect of siphoning enough left-leaning Democratic votes to make a difference. Though Robb actually thought himself to be most vulnerable to a Coleman strategy designed to challenge him on his left flank, the GOP consensus was that the route to an electoral majority was to Robb's right.[9]

There was only one major problem with the conservative coalition strategy in 1981: it called for convincing voters that Coleman was significantly more conservative than Robb, and a lot of Coalitionists and more than a few Republican regulars simply did not believe it was true. Coleman's legislative record had been generally conservative, but his support for civil rights, consumer measures, public employee bargaining rights, and environmental initiatives had rankled General Assembly hard-liners. Even more important, his aggressive style and biting, often taunting, partisan rhetoric had infuriated Democratic legislators, especially senior members like Senate kingpin Edward E. Willey of Richmond. A product of Waynesboro and Staunton, Coleman's roots in the traditionally moderate and anti-Byrd Republicanism of the western region also engendered suspicion. But his biggest liabilities had accrued in 1977, when he overcame the Obenshain faction's Durrette to win the GOP nomination for attorney general and then outflanked Coalition favorite Lane in the general election.

To Coleman and his top aide, the candidate's conservative credentials were authentic, and impressions to the contrary were products of misfortune and misperception. "I felt strongly that Marshall was a victim of circumstances," offered campaign manager Anson Franklin.

> He ran against the Obenshain wing, and Wyatt [Durrette] automatically was anointed as the conservative candidate irrespective of issues. [And many con-

---

7. Ralph Eisenberg, "The Emergence of Two-Party Politics," in *The Changing Politics of the South*, ed. William C. Havard (Baton Rouge: Louisiana State University Press, 1972), p. 79; see *The Dynamic Dominion*, Chapter 18.

8. See *Dynamic Dominion*, Chapter 30.

9. Robb interview.

cluded] that Marshall could not be as conservative as Durrette because he was not endorsed by the Obenshain group. Then he ran against Ed Lane; he beat Main Street's boy. . . . And so there has been a sort of word-of-mouth campaign in the business community that he is [not conservative enough]. It is not so much Marshall's positions on issues, but it is the image he's gotten by virtue of whom he has run against.[10]

Coleman's critics countered that, though the choice of opponents was not within his control, his choice of tactics certainly was. In his campaigns against both Durrette and Lane, they charged, Coleman had assailed his foes unfairly.

"One of the substantial difficulties that Coleman ran into [in 1981] was the kind of campaign that he had run against Ed Lane," recalled former Governor Godwin, a Lane backer.

Ed Lane had been a staunch [Byrd] organization man; he had supported the organization in season and out. And Coleman saw fit to attack him rather bitterly about his involvement in the [Massive Resistance] legislation during the integration crisis, which had long passed. Most of our friends felt that it was not an issue and should not be an issue. I think a lot of conservative voters who were not Republicans felt that it was an unfair tactic . . . and that Coleman did it for the purpose of attracting to his candidacy the more liberal elements of the voting patterns in Virginia.[11]

"When Marshall decided on his strategy for attorney general and sought the endorsement of the [Virginia Education Association] and the Crusade [for Voters] and said that they should support him because Ed Lane had been for Massive Resistance . . . , he was really attacking Mills Godwin and Roy Smith just as much as Ed Lane," observed Governor Dalton. "They were part of it, and I can't help but think that as the years went by people who were associated with that back in the [1950s] felt that Marshall in effect was attacking them, too."[12]

The ill feeling toward Coleman among the elder Coalition members was compounded by several developments that occurred after he took office as attorney general in 1978. With Coleman's encouragement, Governor Dalton agreed to a settlement of the state's dispute with the federal Department of Health, Education and Welfare (HEW) over the desegregation of Virginia's public institutions of higher education. Governor Godwin had

10. Franklin interview.
11. Mills E. Godwin Jr., interview, September 9, 1979, September 18, 1984, and May 8, 1990.
12. John Dalton interview, July 1, 1980, and September 10, 1984.

taken a firm stand against the Carter administration's insistence upon inclusion of numerical goals that he deemed tantamount to racial quotas, and Dalton had endorsed his predecessor's position on numerous occasions during the 1977 gubernatorial campaign. But, early in the new governor's term, Coleman and state Education Secretary Wade Gilley negotiated a compromise that averted protracted litigation and, while containing significant new ameliorative language, nevertheless included race-based numerical enrollment goals. Dalton's embrace of the settlement appeared to be a Coleman-engineered reversal of a solemn campaign pledge, and it greatly annoyed Godwin, former Delegate Roy Smith, and other prominent Coalition figures. In the view of both Coleman and Dalton, avoiding further court battles over integration was important for the images of the state and the GOP. The settlement, as one commentator noted in 1981, "moved the [Republican] party away from Old South racial intransigence into a posture that stresses economics instead of race. The effect may be the same, but the emotional content is far different—and Dalton's conservatism is more palatable to the suburbanites who increasingly form the party's base."[13] To key Coalitionists, however, the compromise with HEW was just one more indication that Marshall Coleman was not their kind of conservative.

As if he did not already have enough problems with the old Byrd establishment, Coleman as attorney general took an administrative step early in his term that also had profoundly negative, though apparently unintended, consequences within the Coalition. The first attorney general of his party in the state's history, Coleman more or less perfunctorily replaced most of the private practitioners with whom his office previously had contracted for legal services related to highway condemnation proceedings, and he awarded the lucrative work to suitable Republican attorneys around the state. The dismissed Democrats and independents included numerous members of the courthouse cliques that comprised the Coalition, and among them were backers of Dalton's gubernatorial bid and several friends, allies, and even a former law partner of Mills Godwin. Judy Peachee, a frequent GOP intermediary to Godwin and the Coalitionists in earlier campaigns, described the repercussions of the Coleman move:

> The Coalition really is two parts. There's the financial part that is epitomized by Smith Ferebee and the [Main Street] people. And then there is the grassroots part . . . , those people who are the community leaders who pass the word on the local level and actually produce the votes. In replacing those attorneys in counties and cities around Virginia, Marshall went to the infrastructure [of the Coalition]. And so when the infrastructure started feeding

---

13. Epps, "As Virginia Goes . . .," p. 9.

back to the finance people that they were not going to go along with Marshall—that they did not like him because of what he had done on the grassroots level—then the money people started splitting.[14]

Had Coleman realized the adverse reaction that his action would cause,
he likely would have refrained; with Governor Dalton's help and encouragement, he was intent upon repairing his strained relations with Coalition
leaders and their allies in the business community. But Coleman the outsider
really did not understand how the nebulous Coalition functioned, nor was
he aware of the important network of personal relationships that would be
affected by his action. He was, he thought, merely dispensing patronage in
the manner of any good partisan. And, having learned from the patronage-
related mistakes of the first Virginia GOP governor in modern times,[15] the
first Republican attorney general did not intend to disappoint his supporters
or give his party cause for complaint by failing to bestow the spoils of office
on the deserving. The primary effect of the action, however, was to rein-
force the perception of Coleman as a fiercely partisan Republican. "There
was certainly nothing wrong with him being that way if he chose to,"
remarked Godwin, "but it did not endear him to those people who were
not Republicans. It had a very negative impact" on the attitudes of conservative Democrats and independents around the state.[16] It also contributed
to an early realization by Godwin that "the Coalition as we had known it
in years previous to that was just not going to come together in a united
manner" behind Marshall Coleman in 1981. To Governor Dalton, Godwin
issued the pointed warning in late 1978 that a collapse of the GOP's winning conservative coalition loomed unless decisive action was taken.[17]

Dalton and Coleman labored mightily in 1979 and 1980 to turn the
situation around. Numerous personal visits to key business leaders on Richmond's Main Street and a series of private conclaves involving Coleman,
Dalton, and a group of thirty to forty top Coalitionists from around the state
produced limited success. Some key Republican-leaning conservatives, such
as prominent benefactor Lawrence Lewis Jr., were persuaded to back the
conciliatory young attorney general, but others remained skeptical. As the
inevitability of a Coalition split over the Coleman-Robb choice became
increasingly apparent, Godwin and others began to explore options for a

---

14. Judy F. Peachee interview, September 14, 1979, August 30, 1984, and September 20, 1984.
15. Governor Holton's failure to meet the patronage expectations of the Republican
rank and file contributed to the defeat of his choice for GOP state chairman in 1972.
See *The Dynamic Dominion*, Chapters 19, 23.
16. Godwin interview.
17. Godwin interview.

viable alternative candidate for governor—either a different Republican who could capture the party's nod or someone who could mount a successful bid as an Independent in a three-way race. In Republican Party circles, doubts among GOP conservatives regarding Coleman's political philosophy, lingering resentment over his 1977 campaign against Durrette, and concern about a splintering of the Coalition produced persistent talk of possible rival candidates for the gubernatorial nomination. Among those atop the recruiters' wish list were Seventh District Congressman J. Kenneth Robinson and his predecessor, John O. Marsh Jr., a Democrat who had served as a cabinet-level adviser to President Ford in 1974–1976. Both were earnestly and repeatedly entreated by prominent Republicans and Coalitionists, but they declined.[18]

While some conservative Republicans and GOP-leaning Coalitionists scoured the landscape in search of a candidate who could derail Coleman's prospective nomination, other independents and Democrat-leaning Coalition figures pondered possibilities for recruiting a Democrat to run for governor as an Independent. Though infinitely more appealing to this group than Henry Howell, Charles Robb was hardly a favorite of the Byrd Democrats. He had actively courted the Main Street givers and especially the conservatives in the Democratic courthouses during his tenure as lieutenant governor, but, as with Coleman's overtures, Robb's efforts had generated little genuine enthusiasm for his candidacy. Except for the long-shot prospect that Harry F. Byrd Jr. could be enticed into entering the race, the Democrat-leaning Coalitionists pinned their hopes mostly on conservative state Senator Elmon Gray of Waverly. In January 1981, veteran political reporter James Latimer disclosed the behind-the-scenes maneuvering for a Gray bid and provided this insight from an unnamed Coalition pol:

> Some people feel that Coleman and Robb are two peas in a pod, very much alike—that, as George Wallace used to say, there's not a dime's worth of difference between them. Elmon offers a distinct alternative that makes him attractive to a lot of us—more of us, in fact, than I had expected.[19]

---

18. Other Republicans whose names were touted by gubernatorial candidate-seekers at various times between 1978 and 1980 included Durrette, party chief George McMath, Sixth District Congressman Caldwell Butler, First District Congressman Paul Trible, Eighth District Congressman Stanford E. ("Stan") Parris, state Senator Herbert Bateman of Newport News, recent GOP convert Thomas T. ("Tom") Byrd (son of Senator Harry F. Byrd Jr.), Hampden-Sydney College president Josiah Bunting, and Delegate Raymond R. ("Andy") Guest of Front Royal. To the extent any of them gave the idea serious consideration, the realization that Coleman would be difficult if not impossible to defeat at a GOP convention compelled a decision not to run.

19. *Richmond Times-Dispatch*, January 4, 1981.

A few weeks after Latimer's article appeared, however, Gray announced that he would not enter the race. Unmentioned but certainly factors in his decision were the results of a private poll showing him far behind Coleman and Robb, and concerns that Henry Howell might jump into the fray and make it a foursome if Gray moved to make it a three-way race.

Except for Gray's possible independent bid, there never was much of a chance that the 1981 gubernatorial contest would feature anyone other than Coleman and Robb. In fending off rivals within the GOP, Coleman had numerous advantages, including his well-known skills as a candidate, an intensely loyal personal following among some Republicans, and his status as the presumptive nominee by virtue of his statewide post. But Coleman's biggest advantage came in the person of Governor Dalton. "John Dalton made it clear from the very first day of his administration that his candidate for the gubernatorial nomination in 1981 was Marshall Coleman," recalled Stanford Parris. "Marshall had worked very hard at going around and solidifying the support that he had, and John Dalton was his campaign manager. That was a pretty tough combination."[20] Dalton later explained:

> There were some people who did not want Marshall Coleman to be the candidate, but you look back at the history of Virginia politics and you find that most of the people who have been governor had either been lieutenant governor or attorney general. Those had been the stepping-stones, and very seldom had a party denied the nomination to someone who had been in one of those roles. I became convinced that, with Marshall Coleman having been the only Republican ever to win an attorney general's race, the party was not going to say to Marshall in 1981, "You won—you've been one of only two people in the twentieth century who got elected to one of the two [lesser statewide offices]—but we're going to deny you the nomination for governor." It just wasn't in the cards. So then the question was, how do you go about bringing [the Coalition] to the table?[21]

Dalton understood that uniting the Coalition behind Coleman would require more than courting its key leaders and emphasizing conservative policy positions of importance to them, though both of these steps were necessary. The GOP had to construct a ticket on which the former Byrd Democrats had representation. The Coalition elders were not and probably never would be fond of Marshall Coleman, but Dalton and other GOP leaders were betting that most of the independent-minded conservatives would grin and bear Coleman's candidacy for governor if they had reason

---

20. Stanford E. Parris interview, September 26, 1984.
21. John Dalton interview.

for enthusiasm about the Republican nominees for lieutenant governor and attorney general. "[The Coalition] might be willing to tolerate four years of Coleman," ventured Judy Peachee in 1980, "if they think they can get eight good years after that."[22] Wyatt Durrette, the consensus Republican candidate for attorney general, was held in high regard by Mills Godwin, Roy Smith, and other key Coalition leaders. And, until late 1980, it appeared that Thomas Byrd, the senator's son, had a good shot at winning the party's nod for lieutenant governor. A Coleman-Byrd-Durrette ticket would pull together the mountain-valley Republicans, Byrd Democrats, and GOP conservatives, thus reassembling the moderate-conservative coalition that had elected three Republican governors in a row.

The Coleman-Byrd-Durrette trio seemed like a dream ticket to many Republicans and was much discussed in 1979 and 1980. The youthful Byrd—he was thirty-two years old when Senator John Warner presented him to the GOP central committee as a Republican convert in 1979— would be a first-time candidate. But his familial and political ties made him invaluable to Coleman, and the party's coalition-minded leaders, including Dalton, Godwin, and party chairman Alfred Cramer, were ready to back him for lieutenant governor. The 1977 GOP convention had shown, however, that Republican regulars would not follow the party leadership blindly. By 1980, it was clear that substantial segments of the Virginia Republican Party again had ideas of their own. State Senator Nathan Miller of Bridgewater made known his intention to seek the second spot on the ticket, and former Delegate Guy O. Farley Jr., a Warrenton lawyer and ex-Democrat with ties to Jerry Falwell and the Moral Majority, also was making thinly veiled moves in that direction. A three-way split—one that would expose the party's treacherous factional fault lines—lay ahead.

Miller's candidacy for lieutenant governor had been expected for some time. He had waged an underdog bid for the United States Senate in 1978 that was widely interpreted as a precursor to a more serious statewide effort, probably in 1981. But the 1978 venture—and specifically Miller's refusal to withdraw from that contest during lengthy balloting—had badly damaged his relations with the party's dominant Obenshain faction. Miller therefore positioned himself in 1981 as the moderate, mountain-valley prospect for the lieutenant governor nomination. Not since Linwood Holton's handpicked contender, George Shafran, received the nod for lieutenant governor in 1971 had a candidate presented himself unabashedly as the moderate alternative and prevailed at a GOP convention. But Miller's base was in the western region; he had inadvertently forfeited much of his conservative

---

22. Peachee interview.

backing at the 1978 convention; and his only hope was to be the beneficiary of a conservative split.[23]

In contrast to Miller's long-expected bid, Farley's candidacy for lieutenant governor would have been totally unpredictable as late as 1979. A three-term Democratic member of the House of Delegates in the 1960s and an unsuccessful candidate for that party's nomination for attorney general in 1969, Farley had dropped out of sight politically for almost a decade. He attended the 1978 GOP convention as an Obenshain delegate, and in 1980 he became a prominent spokesman for the Reagan campaign in Virginia. A passionate foe of abortion and the Equal Rights Amendment (ERA), Farley's sharp-edged rhetoric stressed moral values and the conservative social agenda championed by the New Right. Though he was not a member of Moral Majority, Farley's religious ardor and political agenda resembled that organization's, and its leadership included many of his friends and associates. Those ties earned him both support and intense opposition among Republican regulars. Most important, however, Farley had the backing of Ronald Reagan's Virginia coordinator, John Alderson, who used the presidential campaign to position the former Fairfax delegate for a run for lieutenant governor.

Since the death of Richard Obenshain, Alderson had been a key player in the infighting that divided the once-dominant and cohesive Obenshain faction. Aligned with him were some of the party's most resolute conservatives, including GOP national committeeman William Stanhagen, party vice chair Hugh Mulligan, and a number of Virginia Republicans with ties to the various Northern Virginia–based, nationally oriented conservative political action committees that supplied the New Right's fundraising and organizational muscle. Alderson's principal rival for influence was Judy Peachee, the GOP national committeewoman. Peachee's clout stemmed from her prominence in the Richmond-area GOP, which regularly delivered large and often decisive margins for Republican statewide candidates, and from her ties to Governor Godwin, fundraiser Smith Ferebee, and the Coalition and its financial base along Richmond's Main Street. Peachee had demonstrated remarkable resilience, serving key roles in the Godwin, Dal-

---

23. Miller's dark-horse candidacy at the 1978 Republican state convention had drawn delegates largely at the expense of frontrunner Richard Obenshain and had nearly produced an upset victory by John Warner, Obenshain's principal rival for the Senate nomination. See *The Dynamic Dominion*, Chapter 31. Moderate Delegate George Shafran won the GOP nomination for lieutenant governor in 1971 with the strong support of then-Governor Linwood Holton. Thereafter, conservative forces aligned with Richard Obenshain rather than the more moderate Holton dominated most GOP state conventions. See *Dynamic Dominion*, Chapters 21, 23.

ton, Obenshain, and Warner statewide campaigns, and her prominence and leadership style produced equally passionate friends and foes. No one in the latter category was more adamant, nor more intent upon breaking her grip on the GOP, than Alderson.

When it came time for the Reagan campaign to organize in Virginia for the 1980 election, the former California governor's operatives turned again to the Obenshain group, which had produced a Virginia delegation majority for Reagan in 1976. They found Helen Obenshain and a handful of others supportive, but others on the 1976 team, including Peachee, were reticent about committing themselves during the early going. Alderson, however, was not at all reluctant, and so the Reagan high command tapped him early to lead the frontrunner's Virginia campaign. The assignment provided the Botetourt County GOP veteran with the vehicle he needed to build his own conservative political organization in the state—one that could challenge the party power structure centered in Richmond. Guy Farley's designs on public office dovetailed nicely with Alderson's ambitions for party power, and Alderson used his leadership role to award Farley choice speaking opportunities and an appointment to the national convention's Platform Committee. Once the 1980 election was behind, Alderson's Reagan staff and much of the statewide Reagan organization appointed by him immediately switched hats and began work on Farley's campaign for lieutenant governor.

The stage thus was set in November 1980 for a fractious nomination battle featuring the party's three contending factions and their favored candidates: Nathan Miller for the party's traditional, moderate wing; Guy Farley for the New Right and the conservative forces aligned with Alderson; and Thomas Byrd for the party's Richmond-based leadership, the Godwin-led Coalition, and the Main Street financial establishment. Shortly after the November election, however, the youthful Byrd stunned Republicans and produced elation in the Robb camp with the announcement that he would forgo the race. There was immediate speculation, never confirmed, that the sudden withdrawal was prompted by Senator Harry Byrd Jr. and motivated by continuing unease among Byrd's followers over Coleman's candidacy for governor. Some surmised that the Coalition was preparing to mount an independent gubernatorial effort in support of state Senator Gray. Regardless of the reason, the younger Byrd's bombshell left Dalton, Coleman, Peachee, and other senior party strategists in a quandary; neither Farley nor Miller enjoyed particular favor in the Coalition or in the business community where Coleman needed help.

For a while it appeared that Byrd's exit would leave Farley as the lone candidate for lieutenant governor from the party's conservative wing.

Indeed, many fence-sitting conservative GOP activists signed on in support of Farley once Byrd dropped out, assuming—erroneously—that he and Miller would be the only contenders. But Farley's New Right agenda and emphasis on recruiting religious fundamentalists and evangelicals into the GOP were sources of consternation among many Republican regulars, Coalition members, and business leaders. Conservative in their views on economic, fiscal, business, defense and foreign policy issues, many of these partisans and independents had little interest in promoting a conservative social agenda emphasizing values-based issues such as abortion restrictions. There were also tactical concerns that such an agenda would adversely affect GOP fortunes in the vote-rich suburbs, where younger voters tended to be more libertarian in their outlooks. By 1981, polls showed that Reverend Jerry Falwell and his Moral Majority organization were extremely unpopular among the suburban voters who comprised a crucial element of the Republican base. The inherent tension between the principal precepts of the Reagan "revolution"—cultural conservatism and anti-government libertarianism—was evident in the Virginia GOP, and it combined with personal rivalries to ensure division among Republican conservatives in 1981.

The most likely new entrant in the race for the lieutenant governor nomination after Byrd's withdrawal was state Senator Herbert H. Bateman, a former Democrat and Godwin ally who had switched parties in 1976 and was widely touted as a potential statewide candidate. Recognizing this, Alderson and other Farley backers made a last-ditch effort to persuade Bateman to challenge Coleman for the gubernatorial nomination. Such a decision would gain them an entry in the governor's race, eliminate the need for a Coalition favorite for lieutenant governor, and give Farley an easy one-on-one contest against Miller for the second spot on the ticket. Bateman entertained the suggestion and publicly acknowledged in December 1980 that he was being urged to run for governor, but he concluded after brief deliberation that such a late-blooming challenge to Coleman would be futile. With encouragement from Governor Dalton and others eager to enhance the Coleman ticket's appeal to the Coalition, Bateman then announced in mid-January that he would enter the contest for lieutenant governor.

What ensued was an exceedingly bitter fray dominated by Bateman and Farley, with Miller avoiding most of the acrimony while his clever operatives privately egged on the conservative antagonists. As hotly contested GOP mass meetings were held in cities and counties across the state, partisans of the rival conservative candidates and their feuding factions engaged in the political equivalent of no-holds-barred guerrilla warfare. The Bateman camp seized upon Farley's ties to the fundamentalist and evangelical Christian community and stoked party regulars' fears of a "Moral Majority takeover" of the state GOP, while the Farley forces cultivated grassroots Republican resentment toward Bateman as the hand-picked candidate of the overbearing Richmond-based party leadership—"Main Street, the Third District, the Coalition, those anointed from On High to direct the unwashed masses," as Alderson sarcastically described them.[24] While their respective supporters were busy sullying each other, Bateman and Farley managed to stress a few positive themes. Positioned somewhere between his two opponents on the GOP's narrow philosophical spectrum, the Newport News senator emphasized his mainstream conservatism and the geographical balance that would be supplied by his inclusion on the ticket. With a head start and an organizational edge, frontrunner Farley played up his leadership role in the Reagan campaign and his desire to be the point man for reform-minded conservatism at the state level.

Nathan Miller was in a strange position. Much of his support had been soft—motivated by fear of Farley, Falwell, and the New Right more than enthusiasm for his own candidacy—and Bateman's last-minute entry into the race produced immediate erosion. Not only was Governor Dalton quietly encouraging Republicans to back Bateman, but no less inveterate a Valley moderate than Sixth District Congressman Caldwell Butler also signed on with the Newport News senator. Moreover, the GOP moderates who stayed with Miller were generally understood to prefer Bateman as their second choice to the more caustically conservative Farley. Nevertheless, as the competition played itself out during the spring months, Miller, Farley, and their respective campaign staffs found themselves increasingly pushed toward an alliance. "The thing that began to develop," recalled John Alderson, "was Farley and Miller against Bateman, Farley and Miller against Main Street, Farley and Miller against the party hierarchy, Farley and Miller against massa in the manor house."[25] Long antagonistic toward Mills Godwin and the Byrd Democrats who had wielded immense clout in the GOP for nearly a decade, Republican moderates now discovered that some of the most hard-core conservatives in the party shared their resentment. The stage was set for a very peculiar state convention and what longtime reporter Melville ("Buster") Carico described as the "Saturday Night Massacre" of the party leadership.[26]

When the Republican convention delegates gathered in Virginia Beach on June 5, Marshall Coleman and Wyatt Durrette knew their respec-

---

24. John E. Alderson Jr. interview, September 24, 1984, and March 11, 2005.
25. Alderson interview.
26. *Roanoke Times,* June 8, 1981.

tive spots at the top and bottom of the party's ticket would be awarded without contest. While publicly neutral, both hoped that Herbert Bateman would be joining them when the proceedings were concluded. Guy Farley arrived at the conclave with the support of a plurality of delegates and with barely concealed fury at Bateman and the party establishment for thwarting his efforts to convert that plurality into a majority. The Bateman and Miller camps both claimed second-place status, but, as the first ballot tally would confirm, it was the Bateman operatives who had the more credible vote count.

The proceedings included a symbolic display of unity that momentarily masked the most bitterly divisive assemblage of Republicans in Virginia history. Following the unanimous selection of Coleman as the party's gubernatorial nominee, the standard-bearer was joined on stage by the trio of Republicans who had borne the banner before him—Holton, Godwin, and Dalton. The importance of the moment was inescapable; Mills Godwin's embrace of Coleman, however reluctant, was something many had doubted they ever would witness. But none present on that day could have imagined that John Dalton would not live long enough to see another Republican occupy the governor's mansion, or that Linwood Holton would decline to support any future Republican gubernatorial candidate and would work actively against a number of them. The show of unity was merely a welcome respite from the fighting and seeming confirmation that the party would soon reunite its warring factions and win again.

The balloting in the contest for lieutenant governor began—and almost ended—as the pro-Bateman party leadership had hoped. With 1,690 delegate votes needed to win the nomination, Farley led narrowly on the first ballot with 1,195; Bateman was next with 1,162; and Miller had 993. The frontrunner's momentum was sapped by Bateman's strong second-place showing, and on the next two ballots Miller's total declined as several hundred of the moderate's backers shifted into the Bateman column. The Newport News senator garnered 1,461 votes on the third ballot; Farley's total inched upward to 1,236; and Miller, his collapse accelerating, dropped to 652. The trend was clear, and, as the balloting got underway for the fourth time, it was apparent that Bateman's nomination was imminent. It was for that reason that many of Bateman's supporters, including Governor Godwin, were delighted to hear Senator Joe Canada, the convention chairman, interrupt the balloting and recognize Guy Farley for the purpose of making a concession and withdrawal statement.

Farley, bowing to the inevitable, did indeed withdraw. But instead of moving that Bateman be crowned the nominee by acclamation, as many in the hall expected, he urged his delegates to vote according to the dictates of their consciences. All knew the rancor between the Bateman and Farley camps, and it took no translation to discern what Farley meant. As stunned Bateman operatives watched helplessly, Nathan Miller's previously wavering delegates promptly reverted to his camp, and the Valley candidate's supporters went to work consoling impassioned Farley delegates and supplying them with Miller lapel stickers and posters. Whole blocs of Farley supporters soon were switching to the Bridgewater senator, their intense disappointment now turned to angry defiance of the party elders. Having breached proper procedure by interrupting the fourth ballot to permit Farley to speak, convention chairman Canada next compounded the error by instructing that the balloting be started anew. "It astounded me that Joe Canada stopped the ballot and then said that we had to start all over when most of the delegations had already voted," recalled Dalton. "He should have kept calling the roll, and if he had done that Bateman would have been the nominee."[27] However innocent, Canada's action proved decisive in the convention's outcome. The votes cast prior to Farley's exodus were voided; the fourth ballot proceeded afresh over the irate but futile objections of the now-outnumbered Bateman backers; and Miller won the nomination. The final tally at approximately 9:00 p.m. on Saturday evening gave Miller 1,744 votes to Bateman's 1,541 and Farley's 30.

Farley's controversial withdrawal came despite the adamant objections of his campaign chief, John Alderson, and it embarrassed prominent GOP conservatives like Helen Obenshain and William Stanhagen, who had lent him their endorsement but strongly preferred Bateman over Miller. Though charges of a "deal" between Farley and Miller and/or their respective campaign operatives abounded after the balloting, the sketchy allegation was never supported.[28] Nevertheless, the Warrenton Republican's motives were unmistakable. Farley withdrew "believing that such a withdrawal would in fact benefit Miller," Alderson said flatly, adding that his candidate "had an uncanny grasp of the psychology and personality of that convention."[29] A majority of Farley delegates switched to Miller on the fourth ballot because of "a stupid resentment at Bateman for being so strong," commented an angry former Congressman Joel Broyhill, himself a Farley supporter. "To burn down the whole barn because you do not get your way is no way to build a party. . . . It was one of the most distasteful things I had witnessed in

---

27. John Dalton interview.
28. Charles Lihn interview, September 28, 1984. Lihn, who with campaign chief Randolf Hinaman masterminded Bateman's nearly successful bid, expressed confidence that the shift of Farley delegates to Miller was driven by emotion.
29. Alderson interview.

the party in many years."[30] In helping Miller forge what one reporter on the scene described as a "raucous, anti-establishment coalition of party moderates, Reaganite conservatives and Christian fundamentalists,"[31] Farley had paid back Bateman, Dalton, Godwin, and the GOP leadership for what he viewed—not without some justification—as an unprecedented and often mean-spirited campaign to stop him.

When the dust settled after the tumultuous Virginia Beach battle, several developments with lasting implications for the GOP were discernible, and none of them was conducive to winning elections. Confronted by the first significant influx of conservative Christian activists into state Republican Party processes, GOP regulars had given the newcomers the kind of greeting normally reserved for someone with a contagious disease. Worse still, the pro-Bateman forces had exaggerated and exploited fears of a party-wrecking Moral Majority epidemic to rally the party faithful against Farley. To be sure, the ambitious—and, to some, ominous—pronouncements of Falwell and Moral Majority officials during the previous year had contributed to takeover concerns. But the exceedingly hostile reception accorded the many well-meaning, conservative-thinking novices who had been attracted to Republican activism by Ronald Reagan's social agenda hardly foreshadowed harmonious assimilation and GOP growth in the years to follow.

A second consequence of the acrimonious 1981 nomination battle was creation of an enduring and damaging factional breach within the state GOP. What had begun as resentment and rivalry among Obenshain's top lieutenants following his death became, after the Bateman-Farley contest, a deep and personal antagonism. The hostility would constitute an impediment to party consensus and unity for several years to come. Long-time friends and allies had been forced to choose sides in the fight over the lieutenant governor nomination, and two intractable factions had been created where there had been a single dominant conservative group only a few years before. Though each camp had a cluster of influential activists rather than a single leader, one faction generally followed John Alderson's cue, while the other tended to look to Judy Peachee for direction. The former aligned itself with the New Right and the newly energized conservative Christian activists; the latter identified and cooperated with the Coalition and the Main Street business community. The Alderson-led group touted the grassroots political organization assembled during the Reagan campaign as its vital contribution to the Republican cause at election time; Peachee and her

---

30. Joel T. Broyhill interview, April 11, 1984.
31. Dale Eisman, *Richmond Times-Dispatch*, June 7, 1981.

allies cited their business community ties and ability to fill campaign money coffers as justification for their clout in party affairs. Neither conservative faction commanded a majority of votes on the GOP central committee, and thus neither could control or direct party affairs without backing from some other quarter.

This circumstance in turn gave rise to a third major development: the emergence of the party's long-declining moderate wing as an influential and potentially decisive arbiter of disputes between the two more conservative factions. For a time it appeared that Republican moderates' disdain for the New Right agenda and their fears of a Moral Majority takeover would force the mountain-valley partisans into an alliance with the Richmond-based conservative establishment. Indeed, Congressman Caldwell Butler's embrace of Bateman and the drift of Miller delegates to the Newport News legislator at the Virginia Beach convention indicated such an alignment. But Miller's eventual nomination with the support of a large bloc of Farley's New Right followers suggested another possible combination for GOP hegemony: an anti-Richmond, anti-Byrd, anti–Main Street coalition. The ambitious Alderson had just such a pragmatic arrangement in mind when he commented in 1984 that his conservative allies in the GOP stood to gain from cooperation with "the disaffected moderates who have always had a suspicion of Richmond and those with the plantation owner's mentality that they know what is best for the party."[32]

Using the independent-minded Coalition and wealthy Richmond-based business community as whipping boys to rally resentful Republican regulars may well have been a way to power and influence for Alderson and frustrated GOP moderates, but it was not a strategy calculated to help finance Republican campaigns or to forge winning center-right coalitions in statewide elections. Of all the adverse implications of the 1981 convention fight, none was more harmful than the message that the developments in Virginia Beach sent to the conservative non-Republicans around the state who had been an indispensable component of GOP wins in the 1970s. "We blew that election at the convention," declared John Dalton flatly in a 1984 interview, contending that Bateman had been the key to Coalition support for the Coleman ticket. He explained:

> There was no question in my mind that [the former Democrats'] main inter-
> est was in Herb Bateman. But this is what the average old-line Republican
> doesn't realize, some of them still don't—that you've got to have that
> [Coalition] element. That element has made a significant move; they've left
> the Democratic Party, come into the Republican Party and brought people

---

32. Alderson interview.

with them, and they like to be represented. Their main interest in that convention was Herb Bateman, who was one of them. And we in effect said to them: "We don't need you; we'll do it alone."[33]

Another life-long Republican leader, Congressman William C. Wampler of Southwest Virginia, agreed: "That was the beginning of the demise right there—the feeling caused by the convention among those who were necessary to put together the kind of coalition that could win that election."[34] In the Robb camp, meanwhile, the relief over the convention's rebuff of Bateman and his Godwin-led supporters was palpable.[35]

Not only had the GOP nominated a ticket that included three lifelong Republicans, two of whom were from the Shenandoah Valley and the Holton wing of the Republican Party; the convention delegates also had expressly and angrily repudiated the party leadership's coalition-building strategy. In a mailing to the delegates a few weeks before the June convention, Nathan Miller had moved to capitalize on Republican regulars' ill will toward the Godwin-led Coalition and Main Street financial establishment. He wrote:

> While some former Democrats have joined our party, other wealthy ones choose to remain Democrats but act as "power brokers" and exercise anointment, or at least veto power, in selecting the Republican statewide candidates. . . . . The power brokers want to use the Republican Party for their own purposes—to endorse occasionally, refuse to endorse at other times, and use the threat of lack of endorsement as a whip to keep us all in line.
>
> That is what this race is about. If I am the nominee I intend to try to build the party, *from within,* free of deals and solely responsible to its members.[36]

Former Governor Holton echoed the theme in his nominating speech for Miller at the convention; the Bridgewater senator deserved the delegates' support, he intoned, because Miller was the only "real Republican" in the race. Alderson and other Farley backers similarly incited Republican regulars with sharp attacks on the part-time party loyalty of Godwin and the Main Street benefactors who, they charged, were forever trying to impose their will on the GOP. For a Virginia Republican Party that had reconciled itself only grudgingly in the 1970s to the practical imperative of cooperation

33. *Richmond Times-Dispatch,* May 27, 1984.
34. William C. Wampler interview, February 22, 1984.
35. Dendy interview.
36. Copy on file with the author (emphasis in original).

with the Byrd Democrats, such emotional appeals fell on fertile ground. It was unsurprising, then, that when the votes were tallied and Bateman had been rejected in an orgy of resentment, Mills Godwin strode out of the Virginia Beach Pavilion, got into his car, and went home. He could take a hint, and so could his Coalition friends.

Godwin had pledged before the convention that he would back the GOP ticket, and he proceeded to support Coleman, Miller, and Durrette despite his ambivalence about the gubernatorial nominee and his dismay over the convention developments. Indeed, when Miller was beset later in the summer by charges that he had violated legislative conflict-of-interest strictures, the former governor was among the first who publicly came to his defense. And, when Coleman was locked in an apparently close duel with Robb in October, Godwin heeded a request from President Reagan and delivered a much-publicized Richmond speech designed to rally conservatives behind the Republican nominee. But, such displays of loyalty aside, there was no concealing the lack of enthusiasm and intensity on the part of the former governor and the Coalitionists who stuck with the Republican ticket. The best argument for Coalition solidarity behind Coleman and his running mates was that, over the long term, Virginia would benefit from a continuing alignment of conservatives with the GOP. But the inescapable message from the GOP state convention was that the cocky, partisan Republicans no longer were interested in sharing power with the ex-Byrd men. That scene contrasted starkly with the Democratic state convention that anointed Robb. Having spurned their more conservative elements throughout the 1980s, Democrats now made a point of welcoming and showcasing them. In one of his last public addresses, revered former Governor Colgate Darden delivered a Robb endorsement speech to the assembled Democrats that signaled the party's return to the political center.

During the competition for the second position on the Coleman ticket, the Farley and Miller camps had scoffed at assertions by Dalton and others that the GOP needed to nominate Bateman in order to win in November. The Coalition, argued Bateman's detractors, was little more than a political dinosaur slipping into irrelevance and destined for extinction. The influence of the aging Byrdites was on the wane, they contended; the Virginia electorate had become reliably Republican in its political attachments, and the presence of Reagan in the White House would assure the realignment's continued advance. There was, of course, more than a little truth in the contention that the Byrd alumni and their followers were increasing in age and declining in influence as a new generation of voters, immigrants from other states, and residents of the Commonwealth's swelling suburbs came to comprise a larger share of the electorate. But in the context of the 1981 elections, the Coalition was as important as ever, and the GOP faithful's failure to understand that fact sealed the ignominious fate of the party's ticket.

Having privately decided to back Robb over Coleman, Coalition leader Roy Smith was spurred to even greater levels of activity by the turn of events at the GOP convention. He organized a "Virginians for Robb" organization that was far more visible and active than the corresponding Coalition effort on Coleman's behalf, and during the fall campaign he played a critical role in bolstering Robb's conservative credentials and impugning Coleman's. Though Smith denied that Bateman's presence on the Republican ticket would have changed his course in the governor's race, Dalton was convinced otherwise, and Godwin asserted that Smith likely would have assumed a much less prominent role in the Robb effort out of concern for the ancillary impact his activities might have on the campaigns of Bateman and Durrette, whom he favored.[37] "Roy was a catalyst for the rallying of the Coalition toward Robb," Godwin explained. The GOP's failure to nominate Bateman "enabled [Smith] and a whole lot of people, particularly in eastern Virginia, to become active for Robb who might not have been so active."[38]

Smith, former Fourth District Congressman Watkins Abbitt, and the conservative "Virginians for Robb" were indispensable to Robb in 1981, not only in raising campaign money in the business community but also in providing a cloak of conservative authenticity, vouching for his fiscal responsibility, and confirming the outsider's fitness for acceptance into polite Virginia society.[39] Robb's governorship would dispel any lingering suspicion that he was secretly a carpetbagging liberal, but in 1981 he labored with the considerable political handicaps of being Lyndon Johnson's son-in-law, a member of Jimmy Carter's political party, and, perhaps most damaging of all, the political successor to Henry Howell. "The very fact that Roy Smith and a number of other very credible people in the establishment community would support me," explained Robb later, "relieved me of the burden of Henry Howell."[40] An indubitably conservative former House Appropriations Committee chairman, Smith accepted and ably executed the task of convincing Virginians that Robb would not tax and spend the Commonwealth into fiscal oblivion.

---

37. W. Roy Smith interview, July 21, 1980, and October 8, 1984; John Dalton, Mills Godwin interviews.

38. Godwin interview.

39. A separate "Sportsmen for Robb" group was also highly effective in rallying support for Robb in rural areas.

40. Robb interview.

Smith and his "Virginians" group also were ideally positioned to cast doubt on the sincerity of Coleman's conservative pitch. They had supplied nearly uninterrupted and seemingly automatic support to Republican candidates in Virginia for nearly a decade, so when they refused to back Coleman many voters naturally inferred that something was wrong with the GOP nominee. "While Robb stayed comfortably above the hatchet work, and behaved becomingly gubernatorial," wrote Roanoke's Ray Garland,

> his campaign apparatus brilliantly kept Coleman off-balance and on the defensive throughout. Building on nervousness and uncertainty over Coleman within the GOP hierarchy itself, the Robbites skillfully planted seeds of doubt as to his general character and fitness for high office among those Virginians susceptible to such subtle messages. The point man in this process of demolition was none other than the redoubtable W. Roy Smith of Petersburg—the High Sachem of Southside and co-chairman of "Virginians for Robb."[41]

An unrelenting barrage of Smith-led attacks on the Republican standard-bearer throughout the fall helped to drive home the impression that Coleman was not the conservative that he and his promoters claimed.

Coleman and the GOP spent much of the fall campaign endeavoring to counter the "Virginians for Robb" assaults with conservative pronouncements and pledges of fidelity to Ronald Reagan. But the more the Republican camp protested, the more doubts seemed to grow. Worse still, the raging battle on Coleman's sagging right flank gave Robb a largely uncontested field in seeking votes on the left and in the middle. Preoccupied with reinforcing the candidate's base among conservative Republicans and independents, the Coleman campaign never succeeded in penetrating the less ideological suburban consciousness with a positive message about what a new Republican administration would do to combat crime, enhance education, and alleviate mounting transportation pressures. The Robb campaign did not make that mistake; it offered a modest but forward-looking platform stressing educational investments, sustained fiscal restraint, and a Virginia "future worthy of its past." With Roy Smith and his followers successfully foiling the conservative coalition strategy on which the GOP campaign had pinned its hopes, the outcome of the contest was scarcely in doubt. "In retrospect," commented Mills Godwin several years later, "Marshall Cole-

---

41. *Roanoke Times & World-News,* July 25, 1985. Garland, a frequent commentator on Virginia politics, was also a member of the General Assembly from the Roanoke area and the Republican nominee for the United States Senate in 1970. See *The Dynamic Dominion,* Chapter 20.

man really never did have a chance to win that election because he just could not corral enough support outside of the Republican Party to do it."[42]

The Coalition split in the Coleman-Robb race was a watershed in Virginia's political realignment. Until then, both political analysts and participants generally had viewed the Coalition as a transition mechanism—a convenient stopover on the way to eventual moderate-conservative solidarity within an expanded Virginia Republican Party. But, with the split in 1981, the realignment process was derailed for the first time since the mid-1970s. Many business leaders who during the 1970s had doubted they ever would support another Democratic statewide candidate found themselves regularly backing Robb and other Democratic moderates in the 1980s. The state's once-influential conservative symbols—pillars of the Byrd establishment like Godwin, Smith, and Harry Byrd Jr.—saw the diminution of their political clout quicken as their grassroots constituency splintered. After 1981, candidates of both parties ritually drafted and distributed lists of respected "Virginians for" their candidacy, but the impact of such public relations gestures became slight. Emulating Robb's winning formula, Democrats continued to position themselves in the moderate-conservative Virginia mainstream. And, with voters alternately endorsing Reaganism at the national level and Robbism in Richmond, the electorate's tendency to shun partisan ties and ignore partisan cues was regularly reinforced.

While the dynamics were markedly different in each of the three gubernatorial elections in the 1980s, social issues unexpectedly, yet persistently, played decisive roles in the outcomes of the contests. As he looked to the 1981 gubernatorial race, Marshall Coleman had worried little about appearing too conservative on social issues for the tastes of suburban voters. Republican strategists instead were chiefly concerned with bolstering Coleman's suspect conservative credentials among the independents who took their cues from the ex-Byrd men in the Coalition. With a record that included support for civil rights measures as a state legislator and a successful appeal for the votes of African Americans in his 1977 campaign for attorney general, Coleman could hardly be portrayed as reactionary on race. Similarly, while fundamentalist congregations thought well of his efforts as attorney general to exempt church-run child care facilities from state licensing requirements, Coleman had neither taken a position on abortion nor emphasized other issues that might link him with Moral Majority. Guy Farley's strong bid for lieutenant governor had threatened to draw a very direct connection between Jerry Falwell and the GOP ticket, but it was precisely that possibility that led many partisans to strenuously and successfully resist

---

42. Godwin interview.

Farley's nomination at the June Republican convention. Nevertheless, last-minute developments in the fall campaign prompted political analyst Larry Sabato to opine that race and Falwell were among the principal reasons that an exceedingly close Coleman-Robb contest was converted at the eleventh hour into a relatively comfortable Democratic win.[43]

Coleman's difficulties on racial matters late in the 1981 contest stemmed directly from his and his party's decision to pursue a conservative coalition strategy. Aware of Coleman's problems among the Coalitionists and fearing a split by the Byrd men in the impending governor's race, Governor Dalton in March 1981 had acceded to insistence from that quarter and vetoed legislation to create a state holiday honoring the Reverend Martin Luther King Jr. Coleman privately opposed the veto but was obliged to support the Republican governor's action publicly, and in so doing he doused whatever flickering hope he entertained of garnering meaningful African-American support in his forthcoming race against Robb. With Coalition support splintering after rejection of Bateman at the GOP convention and the vigorous anti-Coleman drumbeat of the "Virginians for Robb" in the fall, Republican strategists by late October were desperately looking for a way to summon independent conservatives into the GOP camp. That need set the stage for a crucial—and controversial—last-minute visit to Richmond by Ronald Reagan and Mills Godwin.

By the close of the decade, Democrat Douglas Wilder would be expressing opposition to, or at least distancing himself from, such favorite black and liberal political causes as statehood for the District of Columbia, racial quotas and preferences, and "post-card" (i.e., mail-in) voter registration. But, in 1981, these were the main issues he raised in a widely disseminated letter urging African-American leaders to support Charles Robb for governor over Marshall Coleman. A few days later they were also among the issues Mills Godwin zeroed in on as he entreated conservatives to back Coleman over Robb. At the president's request, Godwin appeared with Reagan and the GOP ticket at a Richmond rally on October 27, 1981, and there delivered his first major campaign speech in support of Coleman. Both Reagan—whom Coleman had embraced throughout the campaign—and Godwin were immensely unpopular figures in the politically active black community, and Wilder would later report that it was the former governor's late October remarks that finally "galvanized" previously apathetic African Americans behind Robb's candidacy.[44]

---

43. See Sabato, *Virginia Votes 1979–1982*, pp. 83–84.

44. Donald P. Baker, *Wilder: Hold Fast to Dreams* (Cabin John, MD: Seven Locks Press, 1989), p. 122. While designed to rally conservatives, the Reagan and Godwin endorsements also were used heavily in Democratic voter-turnout drives in the African-American community.

Although the Godwin speech was not necessarily the one that the Coleman campaign would have preferred, the issues raised were plainly legitimate and were among the few identifiable policy differences between the two similar-sounding gubernatorial contenders. Indeed, Robb's strategists had been so determined to minimize the perceived policy differences between their candidate and Coleman that they were chagrined to learn that Wilder had raised such a controversial topic as post-card registration in his missive to blacks.[45] Nevertheless, Godwin's message was immediately controversial because of the messenger. Journalists rushed to report that the ex-champion of Massive Resistance had given a "racially tinged" speech on Coleman's behalf.[46] To the lore of Virginia politics were added two legends that would be echoed in news articles throughout the decade. One was that Mills Godwin had purposely injected racially polarizing issues into the 1981 gubernatorial campaign (and presumably would be constantly searching for opportunities to do so again). The other was that Coleman would do anything to win, even to the point of countenancing a racial appeal in his behalf.[47]

A last-minute, unsolicited endorsement by Reverend Jerry Falwell also seemed to hurt Coleman's bid. After their high-profile efforts on Ronald Reagan's behalf during the 1980 presidential campaign, prominent conservative evangelists and fundamentalists were looking for other opportunities to flex their newly found political muscle. Shortly after the 1980 Reagan landslide, Falwell declared that the "tremendous avalanche [of conservative Christian votes for Reagan] has given us the credibility we need to launch headlong into the real matters that concern us most, and that would be the moral issues."[48] Though opinion polls showed that Falwell and Moral Majority were decidedly unpopular in Virginia—a September 1981 survey found that the minister's endorsement would have an adverse impact on six people for every one that it influenced favorably[49]—the gubernatorial race in Falwell's own home state apparently was too big a plum to pass up. If the conservative preacher failed to express himself on the Coleman-Robb contest, his silence would be taken as a tacit admission that his endorsement

---

45. Baker, *Wilder*, pp. 121–122.

46. Godwin's role in Massive Resistance is described in *The Dynamic Dominion*, Chapters 8–10. In the wake of the desegregation controversy, Godwin moderated his image and advocated significant new funding for public education, compiling a record in the mid-1960s that led observers to rank him among Virginia's most progressive governors. See *Dynamic Dominion*, Chapters 11, 14, and 15.

47. Edds, *Claiming the Dream*, p. 141.

48. *Richmond News Leader*, November 5, 1980.

49. *Roanoke Times*, November 8, 1981.

was more of a liability than an asset. Falwell thus made his preference for Coleman known the weekend before the election—just as the large bloc of undecided suburban voters was preparing to make its choice. The endorsement hardly aided the GOP cause.

On election day, Robb overcame the problem-plagued Coleman by more than 100,000 votes, returning Democrats to power at the state level after more than a decade in the political wilderness, and leading the first partisan sweep of statewide offices since then-Democrat Godwin's 1965 feat.[50] The Robb victory was broad-based; he carried every congressional district (some by narrow margins) except the strongly Republican Seventh, and he won in 62 of 95 counties and 33 of 41 cities. Although Robb lost the suburbs to Coleman, the GOP tally there—50.5 percent of the vote—was a full six percentage points below the average Republican share of the suburban vote in the preceding decade's major races. As noted in Larry Sabato's post-election analysis, the Robb victory bore a remarkable resemblance to his famous father-in-law's 1964 win in the state; indeed, the Robb and LBJ statewide percentages were identical—53.5 percent—and the regional pattern of the vote was also strikingly similar.[51] In the contest for lieutenant governor, Portsmouth Mayor Richard Davis prevailed easily over the GOP's Nathan Miller.[52] And, in the day's only surprise, former Fairfax Delegate Wyatt Durrette was caught in the undertow and lost narrowly to Richmonder Gerald Baliles in the contest for attorney general.[53] Endorsed by the *Washington Post*, Durrette won decisively in the two Northern Virginia congressional districts, but Baliles benefited from the Robb-led ticket's "coattail" effect in vote-rich Hampton Roads, and he rolled up a decisive winning margin in his home area of central Virginia, denying Durrette the usual GOP majorities there.

While Virginia Democrats cheered their resounding return to power after an excruciatingly long wait, GOP activists who had basked in the glow of the nation's longest state party winning streak experienced the unfamiliar and distressing sensation of defeat. Few in either party paid much attention to the legislative election outcomes, which favored Republicans. In a

---

50. The vote totals in the governor's race were: Robb (D)—760,357 (53.5 percent); Coleman (R)—659,398 (46.4 percent). Sabato, *Virginia Votes 1979–1982*, p. 59. For a description of the Godwin-led Democrats' success in the 1965 gubernatorial election, see *The Dynamic Dominion*, Chapter 15.

51. Sabato, *Virginia Votes 1979–1982*, pp. 63, 72–74.

52. The vote totals in the contest for lieutenant governor were: Davis (D)—750,743 (55.4 percent); Miller (R)—602,714 (44.5 percent). Sabato, *Virginia Votes 1979–1982*, p. 59.

53. The vote totals in the election for attorney general were: Baliles (D)—682,410 (51.0 percent); Durrette (R)—656,284 (49.0 percent). Sabato, *Virginia Votes 1979–1982*.

realignment-related pattern that would persist during the next two decades, the GOP managed to gain ground in the state legislature even as Democrats were rolling to a decisive win in the gubernatorial battle. The House of Delegates elections in 1981 saw Republican candidates capture an unprecedented 46.6 percent of the vote in the two-party contested races and achieve a net gain of eight legislative seats, boosting GOP representation in the House of Delegates to 33 in the 100-member body.[54] It was not yet fully apparent, but Virginia was on its way to becoming a competitive, two-party state at all levels, and Republicans were poised to vie for posts in local and legislative contests in every region of the Commonwealth.

Robb's performance in the governorship gave little evidence of his executive inexperience and relative unfamiliarity with state government. His moderate methods, renowned fiscal conservatism, general aversion to partisanship, and able staff all served him well.[55] His administration benefited from a state economy that quickly recovered from national recession and, aided by the Reagan defense build-up, pumped abundant new revenues into the state's coffers. Though Robb in the 1981 campaign had defied Coleman's challenge—and even his own advisers' urgings—by refusing to pledge that he would not raise taxes, he found that no tax increase was needed. He channeled gushing growth revenues into education, where they financed a significant rise in teacher salaries and the long-sought full funding of the state's "Standards of Quality" for elementary and secondary schools. Robb's gubernatorial cabinet epitomized his administration's educational emphasis—nearly all of his cabinet officers had advanced degrees—as well as its focus on greater diversity in state government.[56] Virginia's first "New

54. Sabato, *Virginia Votes 1979–1982*, pp. 90–91. GOP representation in the House of Delegates during the 1970s was generally static; the party had averaged 21 seats during the decade and had achieved only a one-seat net gain from 1969 to 1979.

55. Robb's legislative relations as governor got off to a relatively rocky start, especially in the state Senate, and one student of his governorship attributed the difficulties partly to the new chief executive's legislative and political inexperience. See Steven Daniel Johnson, "Charles S. Robb and the Reserved Governorship," unpublished dissertation, University of Virginia, 1990, Chapter 8. Robb's lobbying operation was revamped before the second legislative session of his governorship, however, and received generally high marks thereafter. See *Richmond Times-Dispatch*, December 6, 1982.

56. Robb's secretary of finance, Stuart Connock, recalled at a 2001 conference on the Robb governorship that he was nearly alone among his peers in the Robb cabinet in not having a doctoral degree. Connock's education may have been superior for the task at hand, however. Having previously served in key finance-related posts in the executive and legislative branches and in gubernatorial administrations of both parties, Connock had unique knowledge of state government and the budget process that served Robb especially well. Transcript of Proceedings, "Virginia Governor's Project—The Honorable Charles S. Robb, Governor of Virginia, 1982–1986," Center for Politics and

South" governor, Robb's most notable achievement perhaps was his ground-breaking appointment of John Charles Thomas, a thirty-two-year-old African-American attorney from Richmond, to the Virginia Supreme Court in 1983. Years later, Thomas recalled the larger significance of his appointment:

> When you look at 1619—the first boat of blacks in the English-speaking world coming to Jamestown—and look at how our state was involved in Revolutionary America, in Civil War America, in post–World War II America, and all of the things that we have done—good, bad, and indifferent—Virginia plays a pivotal role in the whole nation's psyche. So, when Virginia stands up and says, "We can get this done," with regard to inclusion of women and minorities, it tells the whole country that it is time to do it. When [Robb] made my appointment—and not just mine, but when he appointed other women and minorities—it made people proud. It made people realize that the government wasn't going to fall if it wasn't all white guys. It made it so the whole pool from which leaders could be drawn was larger. And it stay[ed] that way.[57]

For Virginia Democrats, Robb's fiscally conservative, socially progressive tenure provided a formula for renewal and sustained success. "In the 1970s, there were two Democratic parties," explained Robb aide and veteran Democratic strategist H. Benson Dendy III.

> There was the legislative Democratic Party that was very conservative [and] fiscally responsible. . . . And there was the Democratic Party that had been so weak in 1973 that they fielded no candidate for governor, that even Henry Howell who was the darling of the liberals didn't want the Democratic nomination because he felt like it would hurt him. You had people in [party] leadership positions, national committee people and our party chairman, who in many cases just appearing with them in their local communities would cause you to get very few votes in those communities. . . . So, whereas the legislative party was very conservative we had another party in Virginia, another Democratic party, that was pretty liberal.[58]

Robb bridged the divide between those divergent Democratic camps. He secured control of the party apparatus for Democratic moderates, reflected

---

the Weldon Cooper Center for Public Service, University of Virginia, July 18–19, 2001, panel 4, p. 2. The Robb cabinet included two women and one African American.

57. Transcript of Proceedings, "Virginia Governor's Project," panel 4, p. 8. Thomas had been a partner in Hunton and Williams, a large Richmond-based law firm where United States Supreme Court Justice Lewis F. Powell Jr. had practiced before joining the Court.

58. Transcript of Proceedings, "Virginia Governor's Project," panel 1, p. 11.

the fiscal conservatism of his legislative party in administering state government, and championed racial and gender diversity and new educational investments to the satisfaction of more liberal Democratic partisans. "We . . . Democrats owe a tremendous debt of gratitude to Chuck Robb," observed legislative veteran Hunter B. Andrews in 2001. "He put it all together. It became respectable again to call yourself a 'Democrat.'"[59] Robb's pivotal election in 1981 and his successful gubernatorial tenure set the stage for a stunning decade of Democratic successes—and for a seminal event in American history.

---

59. Transcript of Proceedings, "Virginia Governor's Project," panel 1, p. 11.

# 3

## IMPROBABLE JOURNEY:
## WILDER'S WAY TO THE TOP

The fault, dear Brutus, is not in our stars, but in ourselves.[1]

—L. Douglas Wilder

Generations of Virginia school children have learned the state's motto—
*Sic Semper Tyrannis* ("Thus Always to Tyrants")—and know it appears
on the Commonwealth's flag and seal beneath the image of a prostrate mon-
arch vanquished by a Roman goddess representing the virtues of heroism,
righteousness, freedom, and valor. Few of those young students learn the
phrase that appears on the reverse side of the great seal—*Perseverando* ("By
Persevering"). To understand the extraordinary rise of a grandson of slaves
to Virginia's highest office—a story without parallel in American politics—
one has to appreciate both sides of the Virginia state seal and the many sides
of L. Douglas Wilder.

The lengthy career that positioned Wilder to become the only African
American to date elected governor of an American state began in his native
Richmond in 1931. It took him to war in Korea where he won the Bronze
Star, sent him to the nation's capital to study law because blacks did not
attend the state-run law schools in Virginia in the 1950s, saw him become
the first African American to practice law on Richmond's historic Church
Hill, and brought him to the Virginia Senate in 1970. Wilder served four
terms there, representing his majority-black urban constituency with
aplomb and waiting for the right moment to make his move.[2] The decisive

---

1. The line, often quoted by Wilder, is from Shakespeare's *Julius Caesar*, Act I, Sc.
II. See *Richmond Times-Dispatch*, March 21, 1990 (reporting on Wilder's remarks to the
National Press Club shortly after becoming governor).

2. Wilder's opening to gain election to the Senate from Richmond came when
incumbent J. Sargeant Reynolds gave up the seat to run for lieutenant governor in 1969.
Wilder set his sights early on gaining the same statewide post that Reynolds had captured. In January 1972, the Richmond senator expressed interest in running for lieutenant governor in 1973, saying, "The time is now that blacks could offer for statewide

47

events that culminated in his landmark 1989 victory can be traced to the governorship of Charles Robb and to a bizarre series of events triggered, ironically, by the retirement of Harry F. Byrd Jr. from the United States Senate.

In the close Warner-Miller contest for the Senate in 1978, both parties' nominees had vied unreservedly for association with Byrd, Virginia's popular Independent senior senator. But after the GOP captured control of the Senate in the 1980 Reagan landslide, First District Congressman Paul Trible began traveling throughout the state, seeking and obtaining assurances from Republicans and independents that they would back him for the seat if Byrd chose to retire in 1982. In an artful use of carrot and stick, Trible publicly invited Byrd to join the GOP and to seek reelection as a Republican, but he and party chief Alfred Cramer also made it abundantly clear that they expected there to be a Republican nominee in 1982 regardless of Byrd's course.[3] Such implicit threats greatly annoyed Republican Governor John Dalton, who was widely touted as a potential candidate for the same seat but had no actual interest in the post. Privately, Coalition enthusiast Dalton brusquely admonished Trible that the GOP would not field a candidate if Byrd chose to seek reelection again as an Independent. Trible, undaunted, responded that Republican regulars might well take a different view, and proceeded with his plans. When Byrd announced in November 1981 that he would not seek another term, Trible had the GOP nomination virtually sewn up. Though some Coalitionists and Republicans groused privately that the ambitious, 35-year-old congressman had elbowed Byrd out and should not be rewarded, only Eighth District Representative Stanford Parris gave serious consideration to mounting a challenge. After quietly testing the water for several weeks, Parris found broad if somewhat tepid GOP support for Trible and decided instead to seek reelection to his Northern Virginia congressional seat. The Senate nomination was Trible's without a fight.

With Charles Robb in the governor's mansion and a national economic recession impinging severely on the popularity of President Reagan, Virginia Democrats had high hopes of capturing the Senate seat as 1982 opened. Several Robb-style moderates were interested in the party's nod, but Virginia Beach Delegate Owen B. Pickett—who had succeeded Richard Davis as Democratic Party chairman a year earlier—emerged the favorite after Governor Robb and party leaders systematically rated and tallied the

---

elective office." He suggested that Virginia needed to elect an African American to statewide office to demonstrate the absence of racial bias. Yancey, *When Hell Froze Over*, p. 45.

3. See *Roanoke Times*, March 9, 1981, and April 21, 1981.

potential contenders' strengths and weaknesses. With the others stepping aside, Pickett quickly amassed the delegate support necessary to lock up the nomination. The odd developments that ensued would profoundly affect the course of state, and perhaps national, politics for many years to come. Angered by the defeat of several of his proposals during the 1982 General Assembly session, including legislation to honor Dr. Martin Luther King Jr. with a state holiday, state Senator Wilder suddenly seized upon Pickett's conservative campaign pronouncements and benign praise of retiring Senator Byrd as justification for contemplating his own bid for the Senate. Wilder even suggested that several of Pickett's statements were "anti-black,"[4] and he moved publicly toward a break with the party and an independent candidacy for the seat. Confronted with the disastrous loss of the Democrats' virtually monolithic support among African Americans, Robb intervened and pressured Pickett to withdraw from the race upon Wilder's assurance that he would do likewise. The two would-be candidates stepped aside in early May 1982—both destined for better days—and Democratic partisans thereafter awarded their Senate nomination to a reluctant draftee, the newly minted lieutenant governor, Richard Davis.[5]

Wilder's bold gambit at once consolidated and showcased his extraordinary clout within the state Democratic Party, and it guaranteed he would face no opposition for his party's nomination for lieutenant governor in 1985 or four years after that when he sought its nod for governor. *Roanoke Times & World-News* reporter Dwayne Yancey wrote:

> Wilder was not simply black—he was brazen, and not afraid to shout "racism" whenever it suited him. This was where Wilder's showdown with Pickett became so valuable. All the "experts" had figured Wilder hurt himself by not being a team player in 1982. Instead, Wilder was now untouchable. Nobody wanted to make him mad.[6]

Though observers differed in their speculation over whether Wilder's challenge to Pickett had begun as a muscle-flexing power play, the triumphant state senator wasted no time after Pickett's retreat in citing it as a turning point in the way blacks (including Wilder) would be viewed and treated in the state Democratic Party. "I am certain that our cause will no longer be pooh-poohed and ignored the way [it was] before," he declared, adding that

---

4. *Virginian-Pilot*, April 24, 1982.
5. See generally Baker, *Wilder: Hold Fast to Dreams*, pp. 124-149; Yancey, *When Hell Froze Over*, pp. 40-47.
6. Yancey, *When Hell Froze Over*, p. 71.

the "myth [that Democrats can automatically count on black votes] has been exploded."[7]

Nearly a decade later, after a simmering rivalry between Wilder and Robb boiled into a full-blown feud, *Richmond Times-Dispatch* political reporter Jeff E. Schapiro suggested it all could have been avoided:

> In 1982, when Wilder threatened to bolt the Democratic Party and seek the U.S. Senate as an independent, Robb should have held his ground and let Wilder run. Instead, Robb dumped his hand-picked candidate in a concession to Wilder. Sure, the Republicans probably would have still won the seat. But the Democrats, in general, would've been done with Wilder, and Robb, in particular, wouldn't have the self-imposed headache that lingers to this day.[8]

Schapiro's retrospective view probably was correct, but it ignored the racially polarizing effect that a Wilder independent bid in 1982 would have had within the Democratic Party. "I will probably always have a black mark against me for not somehow making that right," Robb commented in a 1984 interview,

> and yet I always thought that the strongest single political act that I performed was to get both Pickett and Wilder out of the race. It required me to spend more of my political capital. I could have let that go, but I knew that I was the only one who could unhorse either of them. [A race including Pickett and Wilder] not only would have meant certain defeat; it would have permanently polarized not only the Democratic Party but the electorate because it was going to be on black-white issues. . . . I just could not let that happen.[9]

Had the Wilder-Pickett clash not been averted, the broad coalition that elected Robb in 1981 would have been demolished, and the ensuing Democratic division likely would have made the debilitating Howell-Miller schism of the 1970s look like a minor squabble. The Democratic split would have ensured the election of a Republican, Wilder later recalled, and it "would have been the end of me politically."[10] Instead, the alliance among

---

7. Baker, *Wilder*, p. 144.

8. *Richmond Times-Dispatch*, April 22, 1990.

9. Robb interview.

10. Interviewed two decades later, Wilder recalled the dramatic events of 1982 as a "defining" and "pivotal" moment in his political career. Had Pickett not withdrawn, Wilder would have made good on his threat, mounted an independent bid, and probably thrown the election to the GOP, making him a pariah among Democrats. The gutsy state senator understood the risk, but he also perceived the reward that would accrue if Pickett and his backers blinked. "When Owen Pickett did not run, it catapulted my status, having been the determining factor in that race. And it put me in a position where I felt I had to move up in 1985 or move out," he said. Wilder interview.

Democratic moderates, blacks, labor, and liberals held throughout the 1980s, and Wilder soon joined Robb as a prime beneficiary of it.

The Trible-Davis duel for the United States Senate was set only after another unusual twist. In a move recalling the Godwin-led entreaty to the elder Senator Byrd in 1958, key backers of Senator Harry F. Byrd Jr. in May 1982 publicly urged him to reconsider his decision to forgo a reelection bid.[11] Stunned Republicans, including many with ties to Byrd, reacted to the late-breaking development by rallying emphatically around Trible at the party's state convention.[12] Byrd remained mum for several suspenseful days before reaffirming his retirement plans, and the leaders of the drive to recruit him—Mills Godwin and Roy Smith—thereafter moved to quash any appearance of Coalition division by signing on as co-chairmen of "Virginians for Trible." The autumn contest brought a barrage of mostly negative salvos fired by the combatants and their respective supporters.[13] In its wake neither candidate was accused of waging a particularly uplifting, visionary, or technically proficient campaign. The close race ended with a narrow Trible victory, his advantage secured in the First District where he was intensely popular after representing the area in the House of Representatives for six years.[14]

In amassing 51 percent of the statewide vote against Davis, Trible had overcome the effects of a national recession, ebbing Reagan popularity, vigorous opposition from a new Democratic governor, and strong Democratic campaigns in simultaneous contests for the United States House of Representatives and Virginia House of Delegates.[15] In a clear indication of the

---

11. In 1958, Senator Harry F. Byrd Sr. reversed his previously announced retirement plans in response to strong urging from fellow partisans and to avert a clash between two Democratic allies who sought to be his successor. See *The Dynamic Dominion,* Chapter 10.

12. A strong speech at the GOP convention by former Democrat Herbert H. Bateman backed Trible's candidacy and pointedly urged Byrd not to run. Such remarks by Byrd allies were pivotal in derailing the eleventh hour boomlet for the incumbent, according to Trible. Paul S. Trible Jr., interview, March 18, 2005. Also apparently influential was the *Richmond News Leader,* which editorially assailed suggestions of a Byrd reprise and warned that Democrat Davis would be the unintended beneficiary. *Richmond News Leader,* May 29, 1982.

13. A key strategist and advisor to Davis was James Carville, a fiesty Democratic operative from Louisiana who would go on to play a key role in Bill Clinton's successful presidential bids in 1992 and 1996.

14. The vote totals were: Trible (R)—724,571 (51.2%); Davis (D)—690,839 (48.8%). Sabato, *Virginia Votes 1979–1982,* p. 106. Trible carried the First District by 28,375 votes, a net gain of approximately 40,000 votes over typical GOP performances in the district in statewide races. Sabato, *Virginia Votes 1979–1982,* p. 109.

15. Pursuant to the order of a three-judge federal panel, which heard legal challenges to the 1981 Virginia House of Delegates reapportionment plan, special elections were held in newly drawn single-member House districts on November 2, 1982. The dele-

two-tiered nature of state politics and the pro-Republican tendencies of Virginia voters on national issues, Trible garnered 55 percent of the suburban vote in the Senate contest against a popular Democrat who, just twelve months earlier in a state election, had led the Robb ticket in the suburbs by polling 52 percent of the vote there.[16] Trible and his campaign successfully portrayed Davis as a liberal and identified him with the unpopular economic and foreign policies of Jimmy Carter and the national Democratic Party. That tactic enabled the Republicans to capture the Senate seat owned by the Byrd family for nearly fifty years. It also pinned the "liberal" and "loser" monikers on Davis, thereby diminishing his gubernatorial prospects and increasing the likelihood that the GOP in the 1985 race for governor would face the more moderate, and more formidable, Gerald Baliles.

The Republican enthusiasm regarding Trible's capture of the Byrd Senate seat was tempered by the gains Democrats enjoyed in the House of Representatives contests in the state. The 1980 Reagan landslide had boosted the Republican advantage in Virginia's House delegation to nine-to-one, but with the 1982 economic recession GOP congressional gains in Virginia and around the country receded. In the lively post-redistricting contests in 1982, Democrat Frederick C. Boucher narrowly toppled veteran Republican incumbent William Wampler in the Ninth District; the GOP's Robert Daniel fell to wealthy businessman and state legislator Norman Sisisky in the heavily Democratic Fourth District; Democrat James R. Olin capitalized on the fallout from a divisive GOP nomination contest to edge out Republican Kevin G. Miller in the race to succeed retiring Sixth District GOP incumbent Caldwell Butler; and conservative Fifth District Representative W. C. ("Dan") Daniel, the sole Democratic incumbent, ran unopposed. Republicans retained seats in the six other districts. In Northern Virginia, Eighth District incumbent Stanford Parris narrowly staved off another bitter challenge from two-time foe Herbert Harris, and, in the Tidewater-based First District, state Senator Herbert Bateman bounced back from his setback at the 1981 state GOP convention to easily claim the House seat being vacated by Trible.[17]

The ensuing two years were relatively calm ones politically in the Old Dominion, the eerie kind of calm that precedes a storm.[18] The national

gates chosen in the 1982 voting, like those elected a year earlier in malapportioned districts, served judicially shortened terms of one year. The normal two-year cycle was restored in November 1983. For additional information regarding the issues in the redistricting litigation, see the author's "The Reapportionment Dilemma: Lessons from the Virginia Experience," *Virginia Law Review* 68 (March 1982): 541–570.

16. Sabato, *Virginia Votes 1979–1982*, p. 110.

17. See Sabato, *Virginia Votes 1983–1986*, pp. 122–132.

18. The 1983 General Assembly contests produced no gains for either political party.

economy rebounded, and the resilient Virginia economy, powered by an infusion of new defense spending, resumed its strong growth. In 1984, President Reagan's reelection ads proclaimed it "morning again in America," a theme that resonated perfectly with Americans' improving mood and the nation's renewed self-confidence. Against the liberal Democratic team of former Vice President Walter Mondale and Representative Geraldine Ferrarro of New York, the Reagan-Bush ticket amassed a 62 percent majority in Virginia.[19] The Robb-led Democrats waged at best a perfunctory effort on behalf of their national standard-bearer, prompting conservative leader Roy Smith to observe with satisfaction that even "Mills Godwin supported Lyndon Johnson openly in 1964—and, I think, with right much more fervor—than Robb has supported Mondale."[20] Meanwhile, first-term Senator John Warner—divorced from Elizabeth Taylor in 1982 and, by 1984, recognized as a hard-working, moderate lawmaker—coasted to reelection over a little-known Norfolk Democrat, former Delegate Edythe C. Harrison. With less than 30 percent of the vote, the liberal Harrison's showing was worse even than that recorded by Hazel Barger of Roanoke, the GOP nominee for lieutenant governor in 1961 and the only woman previously tapped by either Virginia party for a statewide race.[21]

Despite the landslide successes of Ronald Reagan and John Warner, the president's infectious optimism, and the emergence of a dramatically broadened national GOP coalition, the acrimony among Virginia Republicans stoked at the 1981 state convention persisted and was reflected in everything from nomination battles in congressional and legislative contests to fights for party leadership posts. In two of the largest Republican units in the state—Fairfax County and Chesterfield County—a near-perpetual state of factional combat existed. Delegates to the 1984 GOP state convention had little of importance to do, so they fought bitterly over party leadership positions, including the choice of a successor to the retiring national committeewoman, Helen Obenshain. And, when the Seventh District's revered GOP congressman, 14-year veteran J. Kenneth Robinson, announced his retirement in 1984, a rancorous Republican nomination fight ensued between conservative former Democratic legislator D. French Slaughter Jr. of Culpeper, the irrepressible Guy Farley, and several other candidates.

---

19. The vote totals were: Reagan (R)—1,337,078 (62.3 percent); Mondale (D)—796,250 (37.1 percent). Sabato, *Virginia Votes 1983–1986*, p. 31.

20. Smith interview.

21. The vote totals in the 1984 Senate race were: Warner (R)—1,404,194 (70.0 percent); Harrison (D)—601,142 (29.9 percent). Sabato, *Virginia Votes 1983–1986*, p. 31. In 1961, Barger garnered 34 percent of the vote in losing to Mills Godwin, the Democratic nominee for lieutenant governor.

Once safely out of the Republican meat-grinder, Slaughter coasted to an easy win in November.[22]

Holding the combative Republicans together throughout this period was the party's well-regarded state chairman, Roanoke attorney Donald W. Huffman. A conservative Republican veteran, Huffman had been active in the Virginia GOP since he left the Democratic Party to join the Goldwater movement in 1964. He had strongly backed Richard Obenshain's transforming party chairmanship in the early 1970s and then had refrained from taking sides when Obenshain's supporters split after his death. He thus enjoyed the confidence of the party's two warring conservative factions and, once elected as their consensus choice in 1983, he remained the party's captain for the rest of the decade. Though Huffman's tenure produced electoral gains only in the state legislature, his chairmanship saw significant enhancement of the party's fundraising and get-out-the-vote capabilities, partly restoring a technological edge the GOP had largely forfeited in the early 1980s. Mostly, though, Huffman's fair-minded leadership and exhortations for unity provided an anchor in the storm for his contentious fellow partisans and kept the GOP ship afloat until conditions were right for a comeback.

The Republican factionalism born at the party's 1981 conclave would reach devastating maturity in the gubernatorial election of 1985, but as that contest approached it was the Virginia Democrats who most appeared bent on self-destruction. There were three credible Democratic candidates vying for governor—Lieutenant Governor Richard Davis, Attorney General Gerald Baliles, and veteran Delegate Richard M. Bagley of Hampton.[23] The real problem, however, was Wilder. Fresh off his successful face-off with Governor Robb and Democratic Party chieftains in 1982, the resolute Richmond senator had decided to mount an all-out bid for the second spot on the Democratic ticket in 1985. Dwayne Yancey, whose *When Hell Froze Over* chronicled the 1985 race, wrote that Wilder

> saw clearly the scenario he'd have to rely on to get the nomination [for lieutenant governor in 1985]: Do it my way or do without black votes in the fall. "I was convinced," [Wilder said], "if I pushed it well enough and strong enough, whoever was seeking the nomination for governor would need my support and I hoped to neutralize them so they would not pick another candidate." It was essentially Wilder's 1982 Pickett strategy in reverse: Pre-empt the field for lieutenant governor, dare someone to challenge him, make him

---

22. After remaining independent for much of the 1970s, during which he was a key Coalition leader, Slaughter became a Republican in 1980.

23. Bagley, chairman of the powerful House Appropriations Committee, acknowledged that his campaign had not caught fire and withdrew in December 1984.

think if they opposed him they'd forever outrage black voters, then try to bargain with the gubernatorial candidates for a spot on the ticket in return for black support.[24]

After Wilder launched his bid in mid-1984, numerous scenarios and alternatives were discussed among Democratic leaders Robb, Davis, and Baliles and their allies, but as fall turned to winter no challenger to Wilder stepped forward. Concerns about his candidacy prompted hushed huddles behind closed doors at the Capitol that deeply wounded Wilder;[25] later, he would lash out at Robb for trying to keep him off the ticket—a charge Robb vigorously denied. But there was no denying that in the high councils of the Robb-led party the belief was rampant that Wilder's race, along with his liberal record and penchant for provocative statements, made him virtually unelectable and a clear and present threat to the success of the entire Democratic ticket.[26] Compounding the concern was the belief among most of the Robb men that Lieutenant Governor Davis, the frontrunner for the Democratic nod for governor, was probably too liberal and lackluster to win in November, especially if saddled with Wilder as a running mate. Efforts to find a challenger to Wilder eventually gave way to attempts to coax him out of the race by offering him the party chairmanship and pledges of future support. Wilder would hear none of it, and as word of the stop-Wilder conniving became public, the aggrieved candidate charged the motive was clear: "Let's get it out on the table now. Let's not kid ourselves. The problem is that I am black."[27]

Wilder and his political confidant, Paul Goldman, found a useful target at which to lob the racial allegation in December 1984 when University of Virginia political scientist Larry Sabato publicly doubted Wilder's electability at a Capitol news conference called to present the professor's analysis of the recently concluded presidential contest. Asked about Wilder's chances, Sabato flippantly pegged them at one in 100, then added, "I think the odds are much greater that he would sink the ticket."[28] Wilder's best issue, said

---

24. Yancey, *When Hell Froze Over*, p. 53.
25. See Juan Williams, "One-Man Show," *Washington Post Magazine*, June 9, 1991, pp. 31–32.
26. Mark J. Rozell, "Virginia: The New Politics of the Old Dominion," in *The New Politics of the Old South*, eds. Charles S. Bullock III and Mark J. Rozell (Lanham, MD: Rowman & Littlefield Publishers, 2003), pp. 140–141.
27. Yancey, *When Hell Froze Over*, pp. 77–78. For a discussion of top Democrats' angst over Wilder's candidacy, efforts to derail it, and Wilder's reaction, see generally Baker, *Wilder*, pp. 173–181; Yancey, *When Hell Froze Over*, pp. 64–85; Edds, *Claiming the Dream: The Victorious Campaign of Douglas Wilder of Virginia*, pp. 45–46.
28. Yancey, *When Hell Froze Over*, p. 80.

the plain-spoken scholar, would be "white guilt, and so let's face it, he's going to try and claim that anyone opposing him for any reason is guilty of racism."[29] Sabato predicted that tactic would not succeed; the impediment, he suggested, was Wilder's long-time liberal record and unspecified personal controversies. The response from the Wilder camp was swift and sharp: "I have never known of a more blatant, direct, and open racist preachment that the Democratic Party should kick blacks in the behind," boomed the enraged candidate.[30] As for the suggestion that he was too "liberal," the black Richmonder declared flatly: "That's a code word for racism."[31] Sabato vigorously denied the charge, but the message Wilder had delivered in the 1982 Pickett episode had been conveyed again forcefully, this time at the cavalier pundit's expense.

With Wilder's place on the ticket increasingly secure, he and his backers formed a tacit alliance with those backing Baliles for the gubernatorial nomination. It was a match that made sense for both candidates. In addition to Wilder's perception that Davis and his team had been conspiring to squeeze him out, Wilder had more to offer Baliles than to Davis, who already enjoyed strong support among black, labor, and liberal partisans. Baliles's message—that he was positioned closer to the center and thus was more electable than Davis—resonated with Wilder, as it did with an increasing number of Democratic regulars.[32] In the spring party caucuses, Baliles narrowly trumped Davis in the competition for delegates. He secured the nomination amicably before the party's summer convention when Davis agreed to drop a threatened credentials challenge and endorse Baliles in exchange for Davis's return to the party chairmanship and the Baliles team's payment of some $150,000 in Davis campaign debts.[33] What had seemed just a few months earlier like a runaway train careening toward calamity pulled comfortably into station sporting the ultimate "rainbow" ticket—Baliles, Wilder, and, for attorney general, Delegate Mary Sue Terry of Patrick County—all nominated by the Democratic conventioneers without opposition.

The bitterly divided Republicans, meanwhile, had no similar success papering over their differences. Having excluded the Godwin-led Byrd fac-

---

29. Baker, *Wilder*, p. 175.

30. Yancey, *When Hell Froze Over*, p. 80.

31. Yancey, *When Hell Froze Over*, p. 81.

32. Gerald L. Baliles interview, November 30, 2004, and January 5, 2005; Wilder interview. Wilder later described his alliance with Baliles as one of "mutual necessity—my support was the key to his winning the nomination, and his support was the key to my winning the general election." Wilder interview.

33. Sabato, *Virginia Votes 1983–1986*, pp. 60–61.

tion from their 1981 ticket, Republicans proceeded to err at the opposite extreme in 1985 by fielding a ticket that appeared hand-picked by Mills Godwin and Roy Smith from top to bottom. Completely without representation on the 1985 slate headed by former Delegate Wyatt Durrette was any candidate with ties to the moderate mountain-valley faction of the Republican Party. With early public endorsements from Godwin and Smith, Durrette successfully quashed a gubernatorial boomlet in the Richmond-based business community for Roanoke's Caldwell Butler. Then, in the contest for the lieutenant governor nomination, forces aligned with Durrette overcame a comeback-minded Marshall Coleman and, in another hard-fought convention contest, gave the second spot on the ticket to state Senator John Chichester of Fredericksburg. Chichester, a former Democrat with ties to Godwin, had been attracted to the GOP in the late 1970s by then-Governor John Dalton.[34] He won the nomination for lieutenant governor on the fourth ballot by outpolling a field that included, besides Coleman, conservative fundraiser Richard Viguerie of Arlington, veteran Staunton Delegate A. R. ("Pete") Giesen, and Maurice A. Dawkins, an inspirational black minister whose stated aim was to attract more African Americans to the GOP. Rounding out the Republican trio as the candidate for attorney general was W. R. ("Buster") O'Brien, a former University of Richmond football standout who represented Virginia Beach in the House of Delegates.

Tailor-made to satisfy the Coalitionists, the 1985 Republican ticket excluded not only the party's western moderates, but also the Alderson-led New Right conservative faction. Fresh off another organization-building stint as chairman of Ronald Reagan's 1984 reelection campaign in Virginia, Alderson and GOP national committeeman William Stanhagen had hoped to repeat Nathan Miller's 1981 feat by forging another anti-Richmond coalition—this time behind the gubernatorial candidacy of Eighth District Congressman Stanford Parris. Durrette's very visible backing from former Governor Godwin and his close political ties to the controversial Judy Peachee supplied reason to think the Alderson-Stanhagen plan could work. Moreover, Durrette's back-to-back losses in 1977 and 1981 had dimmed the glow of his once-brilliant political star, and Parris had financial supporters in prosperous Northern Virginia who were prepared to bankroll an all-out bid for the gubernatorial nod. But Durrette's long labors and broad personal following in the GOP enabled him to gather grassroots support across the party's factional lines, and his record as an anti-abortion legislative leader as far back as the early 1970s enabled him to add significant support from

---

34. John H. Chichester interview, February 9, 2005.

the increasingly influential conservative churches across the state. Once again, the Virginia GOP in the spring of 1985 was the scene of bruising, hand-to-hand combat as the Durrette and Parris forces met in a long-running series of vitriolic mass meetings and district conventions. The simultaneous sparring in the race for lieutenant governor multiplied the infighting and intrigue.

In early May, Parris appraised his delegate count, conceded defeat, and withdrew from the race. His once-promising effort had never regained the credibility it lost in a strange February incident, when his campaign staff gave the news media a copy of a letter purportedly written by Durrette finance chairman Smith Ferebee. In the letter, later established to be a forgery, the irascible Coalition fundraiser Ferebee assured business leaders that the conservative Christian activists assisting Durrette's nomination campaign would be denied influence in a Durrette administration. For those familiar with Ferebee, the letter had a ring of plausibility, and to Parris's handlers it seemed the perfect device to drive a wedge between Durrette's business community backers and religious conservative supporters. The only flaw was that Ferebee never wrote it, and, being renowned for nothing so much as candor, protested his innocence convincingly. The Machiavellian hand that penned the phony missive, though widely suspected, was never publicly confirmed. And, although the letter had been released to the news media by Parris's staff and consultants in contravention of the candidate's instructions, Parris neither apologized nor took disciplinary action against any of his workers. His campaign limped from then to its early end.

At least since 1977, Wyatt Durrette's admirers in the Virginia GOP had deemed him the logical heir to Richard Obenshain as the state's inspirational conservative leader. A staunch Republican loyalist, intelligent and articulate, ever reluctant to return the blows of his GOP foes, philosophically motivated, reform-minded, and bent on broadening the party's base by adding converts, Durrette had struck insiders in both parties as an up-and-coming star likely to carry the banner for a new generation of Virginia Republicans. But for a handful of votes at the 1977 GOP state convention, he would have been the party's nominee for attorney general that year and its heir-apparent for governor in 1981. And, but for the strange turn of events at the 1981 GOP convention, which sent a debilitated Republican ticket into the fall campaign, he might well have been elected attorney general that year, positioning him strongly for a gubernatorial bid in 1985. But those opportunities had eluded him, and in 1985 the twice-defeated Durrette entered the contest as the wounded nominee of a hapless party riddled with internecine conflict.

In the first open breach of party loyalty in a decade, Parris campaign policy chief Joel W. Harris led a small group of angry GOP dissidents in announcing formation of a "Republicans for Baliles" organization. Though few partisans overtly followed the controversial GOP operative's lead, Harris complemented his public relations ploy with subterranean assistance to the Democratic camp in the form of "opposition research"—services deemed sufficiently important to earn the ex-Republican a subsequent appointment as Lieutenant Governor Wilder's counselor and de facto chief of staff.[35] While most others in the Parris camp did not openly repudiate Durrette and his ticket,[36] newspaper reports regularly featured anonymous Republican sniping at the GOP campaign and leaks of important Durrette data, including crucial polling, financial, and media advertising information. On several occasions, the staff of Democrat Gerald Baliles was so well informed about planned Durrette thrusts that it was able to issue rebuttals and to unleash counterattacks almost simultaneously with the Republican's volleys. A key Baliles decision to invest all available funds in a late August advertising blitz apparently was made after leaks revealed that the GOP campaign lacked the financial resources to respond quickly.[37] Beset from without and within, Durrette seemed unable to reach out convincingly to the disaffected elements in his party or to control the infighting in his own campaign. As the contest drew to a close, even the most sensitive deliberations and debates within his campaign's inner councils were being replayed in the newspapers, as top advisers Judy Peachee and Edward DeBolt waged an increasingly bitter public duel over campaign strategy and blame.

Though Harris's "Republicans for Baliles" group was the only overt breach of party loyalty, even more damaging to the GOP cause in 1985 was the deafening silence and threatened defection of former Governor Linwood Holton, the brooding personification of mountain-valley Republicanism. Long keenly interested in the progress of race relations in Virginia,

---

35. See Baker, *Wilder,* pp. 272–273. Harris parted with Wilder in the late 1980s and reemerged politically a few years later as an aide to Richmond Mayor Leonidas Young. His luck ran out shortly thereafter. Harris was convicted of cocaine distribution and racketeering in 1997, and was jailed; his patron Young pled guilty a year later to fraud, obstruction of justice, and a tax offense. *Richmond Times-Dispatch,* December 16, 1997, and January 30, 1999.

36. According to Baliles, John Alderson was the Republican leader who provided the most valuable assistance to his campaign. Baliles interview. Alderson did not participate in the Republicans for Baliles effort but secretly gave behind-the-scenes assistance to Baliles during the Democrat's general election campaign. Alderson interview.

37. Durrette's campaign found itself unexpectedly vulnerable financially in late summer after a planned high-dollar fundraiser featuring President Ronald Reagan was cancelled due to the discovery of cancerous growths in the colon of the 74-year-old chief executive.

Holton privately hoped for a Democratic victory in Douglas Wilder's ground-breaking contest for lieutenant governor, and he suspected that Mills Godwin and the Byrd men would mount a racially tinged campaign to thwart Wilder's bid. For that reason, he declined to support the Republican ticket and went even a step further, threatening privately to endorse the Democrats if the GOP campaign included racial appeals. A racial moderate himself, Durrette made it clear to Holton that he would brook no such tactic. In addition, his campaign was determined to avoid even a seeming play on racial passions because of the intense negative reaction that any such ploy inevitably would provoke among the younger, suburban voters who were the key to the election. Indeed, it was the Durrette camp's desire to give the GOP ticket a more progressive hue and broader appeal that motivated its persistent efforts to enlist Holton's active and visible support. But the former governor steadfastly refused to help, thereby exacerbating the estrangement of party moderates and the perception of the GOP ticket as a Byrd-era relic.[38]

It should have been apparent in July 1984, when Wilder formally launched his campaign beneath a portrait of Senator Harry F. Byrd Sr. that he and top Democrats, including Baliles, would be happy to make the 1985 election a referendum on the racial codes of the Byrd era versus the egalitarian promise of the Democrats' "New Dominion." But it certainly was clear when the Democrats assembled for their June convention shortly after the GOP trio was nominated. "Our candidate for lieutenant governor is not going to be a lackey for the overseer from Chuckatuck," declared an exuberant state Senator Virgil Goode of Rocky Mount to the enthusiastic Democratic delegates, making the first of several race-related references to former Governor Godwin at the party conclave.[39] Baliles signaled his intention to stoke suburban discomfort, not only with the Republicans' continuing links to the racially troubled Byrd era but also with the state GOP's growing ties to the social and religious conservative New Right. To the assembled partisans he declared:

---

38. In a 1990 interview, Holton explained that he had offered to break his silence and back Durrette if the GOP standard-bearer would issue a preemptive public repudiation of Godwin and the Byrd organization. Holton interview. It was an odd demand, since Holton himself had sought and received significant financial and other help from the Byrd establishment in his own 1969 gubernatorial race. In later years, as Holton routinely backed Democrats for elective office, he would ignore his own reliance on Byrd-faction support to win the governorship in 1969 and lecture Republicans at length for making common cause with conservative Democratic politicians, whom he often branded as racists. See, e.g., Linwood Holton, "An End to the Southern Strategy?" *New York Times*, December 23, 2002. In a move laden with irony, Durette himself crossed party lines two decades later to aid Holton's son-in-law, Democrat Timothy Kaine, in the gubernatorial election. See Chapter 9.

39. Yancey, *When Hell Froze Over*, p. 154.

The Republican Party [is a party] of closed minds and closed doors. . . . Our opponents offer a narrow and negative vision that looks backward and to the far right. . . . In this campaign, we will invite the refugees from the Mountain-Valley and the suburbs into our Party. We belong to no single group—whether it is the new right or any other narrow interest. We are beholden to no single issue. We will set no litmus test and we will reject the illusion that labels can solve problems. We are in the mainstream.[40]

Durrette and his team realized their ticket was vulnerable to the charge that it was too conservative even for right-leaning Virginia, but with everyone from the state's Democratic governor to respected commentators like Larry Sabato indicating that Wilder's long-shot candidacy put the entire Democratic ticket at risk, the Republican strategy seemed simple: They would make Baliles's liberal leanings and allies, including Wilder, the issue. Though the attorney general was largely perceived as a moderate in the Robb mold, he was not well known and his alignment with Wilder during the Democratic nominating process gave the Republicans an opening. They planned to paint Baliles into a corner by airing Wilder's liberal record on such key topics as law enforcement and labor policy, and then challenging Baliles to declare himself either in defense of or in opposition to his running mate's stands. If Baliles opted for the former course, he would forfeit normally Democratic conservative votes. If he chose the latter path, he would enrage Democratic liberals and blacks. Either way, the Robb coalition would be torn asunder, the GOP planners thought, and the Republican campaign would be in a position to pick up the pieces. There was a catch, however: Durrette campaign leaders knew the criticism of Wilder had to be completely devoid of racial content and innuendo, lest it trigger a backlash among youthful, suburban, and moderate white voters.

Durrette's handlers thought that their candidate's reputation as a racial progressive, coupled with efforts to keep Godwin and other Byrd organization figures mum on Wilder, would protect the GOP campaign against charges that its airing of Wilder's liberal record was a subtle appeal to racial prejudice among voters. Well before Wilder's place on the Democratic ticket was assured, Durrette had been cultivating ties in the African-American community, especially among the growing black middle class and the upwardly mobile black entrepreneurs who were less involved in Democratic Party activism than the entrenched black political and religious power structure. He targeted independent-minded African Americans with an opportunity-oriented appeal stressing economic growth, antidiscrimination enforcement, education reform, and an all-out attack on urban crime. Dur-

---

40. Text of speech on file with author.

rette's minority outreach efforts promised multiple benefits: broadening the Republican Party base by recruiting like-minded blacks; fortifying the GOP gubernatorial nominee's racially progressive image in a way that would enhance his standing among suburban whites; inoculating against portrayal of attacks on Wilder's record as racially motivated; and positioning Durrette to harvest African-American disaffection if and when Baliles moved to distance himself from Wilder. The Republican's intensive series of private meetings and public appearances before minority organizations bore fruit, as Durrette won notable endorsements from prominent African-American businessmen, conservative black ministers, and the usually Democratic Newport News Crusade for Voters. The GOP nominee even received one out of every four votes cast at the state Crusade for Voters endorsement meeting—an impressive showing for any conservative Republican, but especially one whose Democratic opponent was a moderate with an African-American running mate. Ultimately, however, none of those inroads mattered. A series of events ensured that Virginia's racial sins would be front and center in the 1985 election, and that only Douglas Wilder's election would supply a route to redemption.

The first such event came in early May when Durrette casually referred to Wilder as one of the most liberal candidates ever to seek statewide office in Virginia. It seemed like an innocuous enough statement; the "liberal" moniker had been routinely placed on Wilder by politicians, journalists, and just about everyone else who had observed the Richmond senator's sixteen-year political career. But Wilder immediately charged that Durrette had used "liberal" as a racial code word. The charge brought a vitriolic rejoinder from the GOP camp, an outpouring of editorial criticism directed at Wilder, and private expressions of chagrin from many of the Democrat's fellow partisans. To Democrats from Governor Robb on down, it seemed that their "worst fears were being realized—Wilder careening out of control, pointing his finger and shouting racism at the top of his lungs."[41] But, as Wilder aide Goldman later acknowledged, the code-word charge was a calculated move to head off racially motivated attacks on Wilder and to use race as a shield against attacks on Wilder's record. "Everybody was nervous because it was race," the Democratic strategist recalled; "[i]t was like a brush-back pitch. It looked like we were out of control, but we knew exactly where we were throwing it."[42] As he had done frequently during his remarkable political and professional career, Wilder was playing the game by his own set of rules.

"It is difficult to overstate the impact Wilder's attack had," according

41. Yancey, *When Hell Froze Over*, p. 150.
42. Yancey, *When Hell Froze Over*, p. 150.

to Yancey. "Wilder came out the loser in the short run. But incredibly, with one simple news conference, he made it virtually impossible for Republicans to do what Republicans do best—accuse Democrats of being liberals." He explained:

> Wilder's unexpected outburst terrified Virginia Republicans. The foul stench of being called racists—even when it was clearly untrue—was too much for Republicans to bear. Instead of holding their noses and flailing away at Wilder's voting record, from then on they went out of their way to avoid upsetting Wilder so he wouldn't call them that awful name.[43]

Like the charge leveled three years earlier against Owen Pickett, the allegation that Durrette was acting out of racial prejudice instantly struck most on the political scene as preposterous. The father of eight, including adopted children of other races, Durrette long had practiced what many others merely preached about racial fairness and color-blindness. The message from Wilder's attack was clear: If he could accuse a racial progressive like Durrette of bigotry and not be buried in an avalanche of political, press, and public indignation, there was not a Republican critic alive who would be beyond the reach of the Democrat's damning epithet.

Republicans backed off after Wilder's code-word allegation, in part because of the intended intimidation and in part because so many of them, like political observers generally, facilely believed that Wilder could not win the general election. In the Durrette camp, however, the desire to see Wilder's record challenged had little to do with concern about the contest for lieutenant governor; it was the cornerstone of the campaign's strategy for the governor's race. Baliles could not be linked to and called to account for Wilder's liberal record unless someone first illuminated it and held Wilder himself accountable. That duty necessarily would rest principally upon the shoulders of Wilder's Republican opponent, state Senator John Chichester. But the match-up between the affable GOP senator from Fredericksburg and his nimble, aggressive counterpart from Richmond's Church Hill proved to be a particularly glaring mismatch. Even if Chichester had been comfortable serving as the GOP ticket's point man in attacking Wilder— and he was not[44]—the Republican's ties to Godwin and the Coalition would have rendered his criticisms of Wilder almost inherently suspect on

---

43. Yancey, *When Hell Froze Over*, p. 151.
44. Chichester interview; see also John C. Goolrick, *A Life in the 'Burg* (Victoria, BC: Trafford Publishing, 2003), p. 99. Chichester had a lifelong aversion to negative campaigning, according to John Goolrick, a Fredericksburg journalist, community leader, and congressional aide who helped arrange Chichester's first run for the state Senate in 1978.

racial grounds.[45] The Durrette camp had overlooked this vulnerability in its zeal to keep former rival Marshall Coleman out of the second spot on their ticket.

The crucial event that framed the 1985 contest as a choice between forward-thinking racial inclusiveness and the discredited racial codes of Virginia's past occurred six weeks before election day in the heart of Harry Byrd's Southside. One of Wilder's key advisers, Senate Clerk J. T. ("Jay") Shropshire, hailed from the region and had watched its nuanced racial politics for decades. "One thing Shropshire always had in mind," reported Yancey, "was trying to bait former Gov. Mills Godwin into the campaign with some sort of racial statement that would help put the election in the stark contrast of the past vs. the future."[46] The Democratic dream came true, and the worst GOP fears were realized, on September 18 at Hampden-Sydney College in Prince Edward County, when Godwin spoke, ever so fleetingly, of the state song.

Written by an African American, James Bland, in 1875, "Carry Me Back to Ole Virginny" recalled the supposedly halcyon days of antebellum plantation life and slavery. As traditions go, the state song was much revered by older whites, but many black Virginians of the twentieth century did not yearn to be carried back even imaginatively to the days of the Peculiar Institution and understandably resented the notion that such offensive sentiments should be embodied in the Commonwealth's official anthem. In 1970, Wilder as a state senator had been among those African Americans harboring such resentment, and during his first month in the legislature he offered a bill in an unsuccessful attempt to remedy the situation. The episode had been little discussed since then and was not a subject of campaign comment until that sunny September day in 1985. Having dutifully refrained, at the Durrette campaign's vigorous urging, from broaching the subject of Wilder in any way during a daylong swing through Southside, Godwin strayed from his script only briefly during his final stop at conservative Hampden-Sydney. Unfortunately, the impromptu remarks concerned the state song, and therefore—inexplicitly but inescapably—the subject of

---

45. The only senior Durrette adviser who had dissented from the nomination of Chichester for lieutenant governor was Edward DeBolt, a former campaign consultant to Godwin, Harry F. Byrd Jr., and John Dalton. "I know what a race-baiting person Doug Wilder can be," said DeBolt. "The last person you want to run against someone as adept as that is someone who is seen as part of the Byrd Machine." Yancey, *When Hell Froze Over*, p. 154. Democrats understood that the Republican division again had helped their cause. "If the Republicans had nominated Marshall Coleman [for lieutenant governor] . . . , they might have beaten us," opined Wilder strategist Goldman. Yancey, *When Hell Froze Over*, p. 16.

46. Yancey, *When Hell Froze Over*, p. 226.

race. "I have a hard time seeing how Jerry Baliles could . . . espouse the record of this man (Wilder)," Godwin declared. "Why, he actually introduced a bill to repeal the state song."[47] The words were few, but they reverberated off the remote college campus like an atomic bomb.

The news media reaction was swift and severe. Godwin's speech at the close of the campaign four years earlier had received little attention outside of the African-American community, where the Robb campaign had used it to fire black voter turnout. But now the speech was recounted in myriad news articles, along with the former governor's prominent role in Virginia's Massive Resistance during the 1950s. In this context, the state song comment appeared not as an isolated, unfortunate reference to a sore subject, but rather as a calculated ploy to aid the GOP ticket by arousing racial passions. The reality, of course, was that the Democratic candidates were the only ones who could benefit from the remark and ensuing reaction, a fact that was immediately confirmed in campaign polling: Durrette's statewide standing slipped nine points virtually overnight, and the drop was even more precipitous in Northern Virginia. Though newspapers across the state "jumped on the state song controversy and rode it for days,"[48] the *Washington Post* appeared to give special emphasis to the details of Godwin's segregationist past while ignoring the 20-year interval since Massive Resistance when the two-term governor had achieved broad acclaim as one of the Commonwealth's most accomplished—and progressive—chief executives. The influential newspaper simultaneously declined to give any coverage to the surprise endorsement of Durrette—several days *after* Godwin's state song comment—by the black Newport News Crusade for Voters. Republicans watched the devastating developments with a mixture of anger at their own misstep and furious incredulity at the news media's treatment of the subject.[49] Only former Governor Linwood Holton seemed pleased; he had been under pressure to campaign on behalf of the GOP ticket, and the state song episode now "gave [him] an out."[50]

No one knew, when the campaign started, how Virginians really would react to a black statewide candidate. It was widely assumed that Wil-

---

47. Baker, *Wilder*, pp. 208–209.
48. Yancey, *When Hell Froze Over*, p. 266.
49. While Republicans faulted the *Post* for its coverage of the state song controversy and of the contest generally, defenders of the newspaper pointed to a particularly negative story about Wilder that ran in early September. The article by reporter Tom Sherwood highlighted a series of personal and professional problems that had plagued Wilder, including a reprimand by the Virginia State Bar, delinquent tax payments, and legal proceedings related to dilapidated residential property owned by the state senator. *Washington Post*, September 8, 1985.
50. Yancey, *When Hell Froze Over*, p. 269.

der was seriously disadvantaged because of his race, although most made no effort to distinguish the liabilities that were Wilder's because of his liberal record from those that accrued by virtue of his race. In both Republican and Democratic camps, astute tacticians recognized that race would aid Wilder's candidacy in two crucially related respects—one positive, the other negative. The positive side of the equation was the appealing opportunity to "make history" by electing the first African-American statewide official. Despite his frequent protestations that race was irrelevant, Wilder's own campaign slogan—"Let's Make History"—made it clear he thought his race not only was relevant but indeed was among the most compelling arguments for his election. The alluring appeal to history benefited not only Wilder but also his running mates; gubernatorial candidate Gerald Baliles found that his groundbreaking "New Dominion" ticket supplied excitement that his own candidacy and campaign otherwise lacked. At one rally late in the contest, Baliles proudly declared that his ticket was "part of Virginia's renaissance," and exclaimed, "I don't just read history, I make it."[51] In a race defined by little else, Baliles was happy to rest the case for his election largely on the achievements of his immensely popular predecessor, Charles Robb, and the "history-making" appeal of his eventual successor, Douglas Wilder.[52]

At least as potent as the call to "make history" was the negative flipside of that appeal—the challenge to reject Virginia's racially tinged past and "expurgate the stain of massive resistance."[53] From the beginning, Democratic strategists hoped that campaign events would make the election a referendum on racial tolerance, with voters presented a choice between a racially divisive past symbolized by the Republicans and a racially enlightened future represented by the Democrats. While members of the news media were expected to assist—wittingly or not—in that portrayal, few Democrats could have imagined how inept the Republicans would be in resisting the destructive characterization. The GOP not only failed to illuminate liberal aspects of Wilder's legislative voting record, thereby foreclosing their main avenue for forging another winning moderate-conservative statewide coalition, they made matters incalculably worse by allowing an issue with racial connotations—the state song—to dominate the discourse. Since most voters were never informed of Wilder's left-leaning stands on criminal justice, labor, and social services issues, many undoubtedly suspected that criticism of him was motivated primarily by racial prejudice, a

---

51. Yancey, *When Hell Froze Over*, p. 332.
52. In response to exit polling in 1985, fully 48 percent of voters favoring Baliles cited satisfaction with Robb's performance in office as the primary reason for their choice. Sabato, *Virginia Votes 1983–1986*, p. 103.
53. Yancey, *When Hell Froze Over*, p. 368.

suspicion that seemed warranted after the state song episode. In suburban Virginia, and especially in populous and cosmopolitan Northern Virginia, upscale white voters eschewed any association with the distasteful attitudes of the Massive Resistance era and voted Democratic in November less for policy reasons than because it had become the only socially acceptable thing to do. Indeed, Northern Virginia was the one area of the state in which Wilder's percentage of the vote often exceeded Baliles's share.

The past-versus-future imagery fashioned effectively by Virginia Democrats in 1985 was not limited to matters of race. Having capitalized on the support of Christian evangelicals to win the GOP nomination for governor, Wyatt Durrette quickly found himself on the defensive on the abortion issue in the general election contest, with Democrat Baliles charging in the candidates' first debate that the GOP wanted to reverse progress on women's rights. It was a charge Durrette never effectively answered. Even more damaging to the Republican's cause in the suburbs, however, were his campaign's missteps on education. In charging that Baliles had proposed new initiatives that would require tax increases, the GOP nominee primarily cited proposed education funding to support his claim; the Democrat promptly turned the tables and portrayed Durrette as stepping back from Robb-led progress on school funding. An October comment by Durrette that favored mandating inclusion of creationism in public school curricula made the candidate look not only offbeat on education but also thoroughly beholden to the religious right interests within his party. Another unplanned endorsement—this time by Virginia Beach–based television evangelist M. G. ("Pat") Robertson—further linked Durrette with the conservative religionists. Though Robertson's influential nod undoubtedly generated some additional support for Durrette and his running mates among social conservatives, it also cemented a generally negative perception of the Republican team among many socially moderate swing voters in the suburbs.

The Democratic ticket coasted to a surprisingly easy set of victories on election day, posting the party's second consecutive sweep of all three statewide offices and shattering, all at once, long-held assumptions about the attitudes of Virginia voters on the sensitive topics of race and gender. In capturing the governorship, Baliles ran up the biggest margin for a Democratic gubernatorial contender since the onset of serious two-party competition in the 1960s.[54] Terry ran even farther ahead of her foe in the race for attorney general, and Wilder's win, though by a lesser margin, was hardly a

---

54. The vote totals were: Baliles (D)—741,438 (55.2 percent); Durrette (R)—601,652 (44.8 percent). Sabato, *Virginia Votes 1983–1986*, p. 64.

nail-biter.[55] During a time of economic prosperity under a popular Democratic governor, Virginians unsurprisingly chose continuity.[56] Yet, they also confounded the political elite by issuing a decisive declaration about their state's determined move, culturally and politically, toward the aristocracy of ability envisioned by the Commonwealth's preeminent visionary, Thomas Jefferson. Just a year earlier, few people other than Douglas Wilder had sensed that Virginians might be ready and willing to make such a statement. Wilder spent much of the ensuing year traversing the state, mingling with ordinary Virginians, and proving to them, not so much that *he* was ready to govern them, but that *they* were ready to give him a fair shot. That was the message delivered by the candidate's 4,000-mile summer trek through sultry rural Virginia, by the white police officer from Southside who appeared in a Wilder television ad to lend support,[57] and by the people in countless places where Wilder campaigned in that first statewide race and *nothing racial happened.*

In a retrospective forum on his governorship convened by the University of Virginia Center for Politics in 2003, Wilder recalled the overarching importance of his 1985 breakthrough. There never was the incident that reporters all expected and were on constant alert to capture—the "we don't allow your kind in here" moment when a bigot rebuffed the candidate's outstretched hand. "There never was an incident," said Wilder, "not a single person ever refused to grant me an audience."[58] Although leading politicians, reporters, and pundits earlier had dismissed his chances—making what Wilder thought were outrageously prejudicial assumptions about the role of race in Virginia politics and necessitating his own intimidating, hardball tactics—the candidate found the people themselves were far more fair-minded than the press or politicians supposed. The groundbreaking candidate not only was heard; he started "listening and listening . . . learning and learning" from the diverse Virginians he encountered.[59] Among the most

---

55. The vote totals in the lieutenant governor's race were: Wilder (D)—685,329 (51.8 percent); Chichester (R)—636,695 (48.2 percent). In the contest for attorney general, the vote totals were: Terry (D)—814,808 (61.4 percent); O'Brien (R)—512,269 (38.6 percent). Sabato, *Virginia Votes 1983–1986*, p. 64.

56. In addition to retaining the state's three top offices, Democrats held on to their 65-seat majority in the 100-member House of Delegates.

57. The memorable advertisement also highlighted a key endorsement of the Democrat by the state's chapter of the Fraternal Order of Police (FOP), an embrace that went far in refuting persistent GOP criticism of state Senator Wilder's voting record on criminal justice issues.

58. L. Douglas Wilder, "When the Dream Became Reality," *Virginia News Letter* (Charlottesville: Weldon Cooper Center for Public Service, University of Virginia), August 2003, p. 2.

59. Wilder, "When the Dream Became Reality," p. 2.

important lessons apparently was the liberating discovery that racial fairness was not confined to people of any one race, party, region, political persuasion, or economic condition. If Virginia was transformed in the process, so was Wilder—from a conventionally liberal, inner-city politician focusing on minority interests to a populist "son of Virginia" who identified with the people he met all across the state, people who, like himself, had high hopes and had overcome adversity to fulfill them. "Truth is, my aspirations in life were no different than any Virginian's," Wilder said later,

> I wanted success for me and my family. I wanted to be able to enjoy all the best, and as the doors are opening, to stick a doorjamb in the way. My goal wasn't to be revolutionary, to preach to people that their values were wrong or that they should do things out of guilt or the goodness of their heart. All I asked for myself, and for everybody, is that anyone with ability and perseverance got a chance to walk through that door.[60]

Wilder added that, without his election in 1985 as lieutenant governor and his service in that post, he never could have been elected as the nation's first African-American governor four years later. "The people of Virginia needed to know that I could be a good lieutenant governor, and, more importantly, that I could reflect their values before they would give me the chance to be governor."[61]

Among those values was fierce independence, and Wilder soon revealed a penchant for displaying that Virginia virtue at times and in ways deemed inauspicious, if not downright disloyal, by those who counted themselves as his allies. The first such incident came about two weeks after the November election. Wilder's victory, and to a lesser extent Terry's, brought national attention and accolades to Virginia and the state Democratic Party, and the news media assigned much of the credit for the landmark election results to outgoing Governor Robb. There was no doubt that the popular Robb deserved ample credit for, as Baliles put it, "making it respectable, socially, politically, and economically, to be a Democrat"; Wilder himself readily acknowledged as much.[62] But neither Robb nor his political allies initially had been eager to help Wilder, and the specter of Robb getting much of the glory in the election's aftermath was too much for the self-made Wilder to bear. Less than two weeks after the election, he unleashed aide Paul Goldman to call reporters, complain about the excessive credit Robb was collecting, and point out deficiencies in the governor's

---

60. Wilder, "When the Dream Became Reality," p. 3.
61. Wilder, "When the Dream Became Reality," p. 3.
62. Baker, *Wilder*, p. 231.

campaign efforts.[63] Wilder also pointedly canceled an appearance with his running mates before the centrist Democratic Leadership Council, where its leading light Robb had planned to show off the successful trio.[64] Soon thereafter came the governor's (temporarily) private rejoinder, a startlingly frank, six-page, single-spaced letter in which the outgoing chief executive reviewed his own contributions to the Wilder effort and the pair's mutually beneficial past activities, lectured the black political leader about his ingratitude, and warned that some of Robb's supporters "just won't be there again for Doug Wilder" unless he and Goldman made amends.[65] Wilder did not reply.

Basking in his new status as a national celebrity and beginning immediately to lay the groundwork for his 1989 gubernatorial bid, Lieutenant Governor Wilder quickly found additional opportunities to display his independence, this time at Governor Baliles's expense. Only a few months into the new administration, Wilder took issue with the governor on a controversial decision to allow inmates on death row to have physical contact with their spouses and family members during visits. Under attack from Republicans for coddling criminals and making concessions to the American Civil Liberties Union, Baliles did not need his erstwhile running mate piling on and legitimizing the attack, but that was exactly the effect of Wilder's pronouncement. A far more serious breach occurred a few weeks later, in fall 1986, when Wilder took issue with a recently enacted sales tax increase that Baliles's handpicked blue-ribbon commission had advocated and Baliles had embraced as a funding mechanism for transportation projects.

In the gubernatorial contest the previous year, GOP nominee Durrette had made Baliles's extensive proposals for new state spending—and the attendant inevitability of higher taxes—a central campaign theme. Former Governor John Dalton had sharply assailed Baliles for not being "man enough to admit" that the Democrat's spending proposals would necessitate tax hikes,[66] and former Delegate W. Roy Smith, who served as chairman of Governor Robb's council of economic advisers, had publicly offered a simi-

---

63. Baker, *Wilder*, p. 232.
64. A few weeks later, Wilder ridiculed suggestions that the Democratic Leadership Council (and by implication its leader Robb) deserved a share of credit for his victory. "They had nothing to do with it, and I think that ought to be said rather abundantly," Wilder declared, adding that if the group's push to downplay the party's historic ties to blacks, labor, and liberals had prevailed, he likely would never have been elected lieutenant governor. Edds, *Claiming the Dream*, pp. 46–47.
65. Copy on file with the author.
66. Text of remarks on file with the author.

lar assessment. Baliles had responded to these charges through television advertisements and campaign pronouncements in which he gave increasingly firm, and eventually rock-solid, assurances that his administration would not propose any tax hikes. "I will not seek a tax increase to accomplish what I have set out as goals—period," Baliles declared impatiently during one mid-October campaign debate.[67] "If Jerry Baliles says he isn't going to raise taxes, you can bank on it," vouched Governor Robb.[68] But when Baliles convened a special legislative session to address a newly discerned "transportation crisis" during his first year in office, his proposals did not include the bond-financed initiatives he had initially suggested. Instead, the new governor touted a plan recommended by his prestigious bipartisan study panel that would hike taxes by nearly a half-billion dollars annually.[69]

Wilder, who had served on the panel as a nonvoting member, stayed mum about his objections to the new levies until after the proposals had passed with bipartisan support. The lieutenant governor then sounded an anti-tax theme that would become a recurring part of his new, more conservative and populist political persona, telling a Northern Virginia business group, "[W]e must stop piling regressive taxes upon those citizens and businesses least able to afford them."[70] Though some argued Wilder's anti-tax fervor was a political expedient, the lieutenant governor contended that opposition to regressive sales taxes had been among his basic tenets since entering public office nearly two decades earlier. During the 1985 campaign, he had responded to a query from the Crusade for Voters by making a specific pledge to oppose any sales tax hike. "I did not favor the tax increase," Wilder later explained.

---

67. Baliles's various campaign statements foreswearing tax hikes are recalled in Kent Jenkins Jr., "Baliles Contradicts No-Tax Pledge," *Virginian-Pilot & Ledger-Star*, September 14, 1986.

68. *Washington Post*, November 1, 1985.

69. For a detailed study of the Baliles transportation initiative, see Gary M. Bowman, *Highway Politics in Virginia*, (Fairfax, VA: George Mason University Press, 1993). As Bowman indicates, Baliles's initial suggestion to finance road-building primarily through bonds rather than new taxes represented a bold departure from Virginia's longstanding "pay as you go" orthodoxy on funding transportation infrastructure, a political mantra of the Byrd era that had survived long after Byrd himself and that clearly swayed the new governor's blue-ribbon panel. Baliles had toured the state in advance of the blue-ribbon commission's report, pledging to support its recommendations and encouraging others to do the same. When the commission ultimately recommended tax hikes instead of bonds as the primary funding mechanism, Baliles concluded that addressing transportation needs by capitalizing on the consensus forged by the commission was in the state's best interest and "took precedence" over the "personal campaign statement" he had made a few months earlier pledging opposition to higher taxes. Baliles interview.

70. Baker, *Wilder*, p. 235.

> But, in addition, Jerry Baliles had raised taxes after saying many times during the campaign that he wouldn't. If I had gone along with that, no one would have ever believed anything I said on taxes when I ran for governor. . . . I don't believe in using campaign slogans you don't mean. The things you say in the campaign are the things people should measure you by in office. . . . It was not a hard decision for me [to split with Baliles on taxes after his no-tax-hike promise during the campaign]. I just could not be in that same camp.[71]

The reaction to Wilder's move was bitter, especially from leading pols who had walked the plank to support the new taxes and hoped that a degree of bipartisan consensus on the topic would shield them from the wrath of taxpaying voters. Delegate C. Richard Cranwell of Vinton, a Democratic leader, blasted the lieutenant governor for "Monday morning quarterbacking," and another fellow partisan, Chesterfield Delegate N. Leslie Saunders Jr. branded Wilder a "coward" for his stance and timing on the issue.[72] Wilder contended he had withheld his criticism until after the plan was passed out of loyalty to Governor Baliles, but the bushwhacked governor, surprised and irked by the ploy, hardly seemed grateful. Republican Party spokesman Steve Haner immediately saw the method in Wilder's madness, noting that the lieutenant governor was intentionally distancing himself from the taxing governor and trying "to establish the conservative credentials he needs to be governor."[73] The episode and other affronts sent Wilder's newfound pen pal, Charles Robb, back to his legal pad to scribble out another angry, rambling missive, this one branding Wilder as untrustworthy and indicting him for "deliberate distortions and untruths, and the blindsiding of allies."[74]

The blistering Robb epistles might not seem so unusual today, since the advent of electronic mail ("e-mail") has increased the frequency of ill-tempered diatribes that in another era might have been discarded after calmer reflection. But in the 1980s, the frank letters were remarkable, and they became immeasurably more so when the usually circumspect Robb took the extraordinary step of making them public in December 1986. A firestorm erupted; Wilder marveled publicly at Robb's "act of incontinence" in releasing the letters and suggested they had racial overtones;[75] the former governor let his hundreds of harshly critical words speak for them-

---

71. Wilder interview. Wilder later parted ways with another Democratic governor, Mark R. Warner, over his breach of a similar no-tax-hike promise. See Chapter 9.
72. Baker, *Wilder*, p. 236.
73. Baker, *Wilder*, p. 236.
74. Copy on file with the author.
75. Baker, *Wilder*, pp. 247–248.

selves; and the long-suffering Virginia Republicans delighted in the seeming self-immolation of the state's Democratic leadership.

It would be folly to suggest that all of this was planned by Wilder— indeed, the release of the lurid Robb letters directly impugning his integrity was both a surprise and a serious setback—but much of the acrimony that transpired in the wake of the 1985 election was both purposeful and helpful to the brash African-American politician's strategy for capturing the Virginia governorship. In his biography of Wilder, Donald Baker of the *Washington Post* wrote:

> As Wilder neared the end of his first year as lieutenant governor, he was engulfed in controversy, nearly all of it of his own making. As a result of challenges, first to former Governor Robb and then to Governor Baliles, he had handed the Republicans sure-fire fodder for the 1989 gubernatorial campaign. He was denounced by fellow Democrats as a coward, a Monday-morning quarterback, a johnny-come-lately and a sandbagger. But Wilder didn't blink, because the attacks were part of a high-risk strategy to establish conservative credentials and show his independence from Robb and Baliles, who Wilder believed were likely to support Attorney General Mary Sue Terry against him if an intra-party fight developed for the gubernatorial nomination in 1989.[76]

In refuting the suggestion that Robb or anyone else deserved credit for his 1985 victory, Wilder was protecting his hard-earned image as a self-made man who had overcome obstacles and earned his political success on his own merit. His was no affirmative-action advance, no product of benevolence from the white power structure, and Wilder had no intention of letting such uncomplimentary notions creep into the public perception as he prepared to reach for the ultimate political prize in the conservative Commonwealth.[77] The swipes at Baliles somewhat served the same purpose, but his high-profile disagreements with the new governor had more to do with Wilder's plan to position himself squarely in the Virginia political center, and thus to the right of most of the Democratic Party, for the 1989 race. It was no accident that Wilder took on Baliles in two areas—criminal justice and taxes—where Democratic politicians often had been vulnerable in Virginia and other states. "Wilder's main goal," wrote Dwayne Yancey, "was to avoid getting painted [by Republicans in 1989] as a tax-and-spend

---

76. Baker, *Wilder*, p. 230.
77. Yancey, *When Hell Froze Over*, pp. 377–378.

liberal, and if that meant breaking with Baliles on the governor's most cherished initiative, so be it."[78]

Wilder had four years as lieutenant governor during which to complete his metamorphosis from liberal voice-in-the-wilderness to centrist insider, and he used the time wisely. Much in demand nationally as a speaker, he often advanced Republican-sounding anti-tax and anti-crime themes that distinguished him from other Democrats, including Jesse Jackson, whose liberal mantras and grievance-driven approach to politics Wilder routinely disparaged. Speaking at a benefit roast, the University of Virginia's Larry Sabato noted that Virginia now had a lieutenant governor with decidedly conservative stands on issues ranging from capital crime and drug dealing to taxes and mandatory seat belts. "Just as I predicted," Sabato deadpanned, "John Chichester won."[79] The self-deprecating line got laughs and helped put behind the hard feelings from the pundit's errant prognostications on Wilder, but it contained more than a little truth. In a note to Sabato a short time later, Chichester observed, "I believe that our governor is convinced that Wilder has adopted my philosophy and is becoming more of a thorn in his side than I would have been."[80]

With the notable exception of Wilder, Governor Baliles enjoyed excellent relations with the key players in the legislative process, and he proceeded to preside over one of the most accomplished legislative governorships since Mills Godwin's first term in the 1960s. A former member of the House of Delegates, Baliles and his lieutenants had close ties to the legislature's dominant Democratic leaders and to many in the GOP minority as well. His success in pushing through the transportation-funding tax package set his legacy his first year in office, but he added numerous legislative and administrative accomplishments thereafter, including increased funding for

---

78. Yancey, *When Hell Froze Over*, p. 382. Interviewed years later, Baliles downplayed his reaction to Wilder's moves, noting that he (Baliles) understood at the time that Wilder would have to move to the right if he were to gain election in 1989 as the nation's first African-American governor. Baliles interview.

79. Baker, *Wilder*, p. 237.

80. Baker, *Wilder*, p. 237. Chichester later observed that his 1985 loss was rightly characterized by some as a "blessing in disguise" for another reason. Remaining in the state Senate, he joined the powerful Senate Finance Committee in 1992 at the behest of his mentor and ally, Senator Hunter B. Andrews, the committee's chairman. By 1996, with Andrews defeated for reelection and Republicans sharing power in the equally divided Senate, Chichester became the committee's co-chair and de facto leader. "It began a whole new era in public service for me, even though I'd been in the Senate 14 years, when I was appointed to the Senate Finance Committee in 1992. It gave me the opportunity to really understand state government, and that was an experience and knowledge I never would have had if I had been elected statewide in 1985 and gone on to be governor after that." Chichester interview.

mental health, indigent healthcare, and child care services, a public-private initiative to restore the Chesapeake Bay, and development of the Governor's language academies and curricula on foreign languages and geography.[81] Leading a record eight foreign trade missions, Baliles made economic development and promotion of international trade a focus of his administration. In the wake of his tenure, Professor Robert Holsworth credited the Baliles regime with "chang[ing] the way Virginians looked at [trade missions and] establish[ing] the model of Virginia as an international state."[82] Fueled by surging economic growth and large tax increases, state spending soared on Baliles's watch; indeed, he presided over Virginia's only significant, albeit transitory, climb in the per capita spending ranking of American states during the century's closing decades.[83] A variety of worthy new initiatives were funded, but the sharply higher base budget left the state vulnerable when the economic bubble burst as he left office at decade's end.

Quiet, cerebral, and workmanlike, devoid of distracting charisma, more progressive in his core convictions than Virginia chief executives before and since, sandwiched between two celebrity governorships, and stalked politically by the shadow of his about-face on taxes, Baliles would return to the practice of law and never seek public office again. He would remain, however, a highly influential figure in the state's elite business and political circles, pressing successive state leaders for increased spending on programs and infrastructure and faulting his Democratic and Republican successors alike for promoting popular tax relief at the expense of needed investments in Virginia's future. "Major investments, especially in infrastructure, both intellectual and physical, require the spending of political capital in order to get financial capital," Baliles declared at a 2002 conference reviewing his governorship. "Somehow, in recent years, we have lost our way. . . . Instead of tax investments, we talk of tax cuts."[84]

As Wilder maneuvered for the pole position in the next governor's race and Baliles gritted his teeth and governed, other political figures were

---

81. Baliles interview. Baliles and his cabinet secretaries summarized their accomplishments in a 16-page news release presented at a December 1989 year-end meeting with reporters. See Commonwealth of Virginia, Office of the Governor, News Release, December 22, 1989.

82. *Richmond Times-Dispatch*, May 12, 1996.

83. JLARC December 2004 Spending Update, p. 51.

84. Transcript of Proceedings, "Virginia Governor's Project—The Honorable Gerald L. Baliles, Governor of Virginia, 1986-1990," Center for Politics and the Weldon Cooper Center for Public Service, University of Virginia, July 18–19, 2002, pp. 55–56. Baliles was a partner in the Richmond-based Hunton and Williams law firm from February 1990 to March 2006, when he became director of the Miller Center of Public Affairs at the University of Virginia.

getting in place for the next series of Virginia contests. In Washington, the Iran-Contra scandal beset the Reagan administration, propelling into the limelight and eventually into politics one Lieutenant Colonel Oliver North, an instant folk hero for some on the Republican right but eventually a pariah to the moderate middle. Senator Paul Trible likewise had his moment in the sun, serving on the high-profile congressional committee that investigated the scandal. But the youthful Trible seemed less than heroic to many in the Virginia GOP when he passed up a reelection bid in 1988 and surrendered the party's incumbency advantage in the face of formidable former Governor Robb's impending bid for the seat.[85] The man who enraged Virginia Republicans, however, was Senator John Warner, who seemed to kick President Reagan while he was down by opposing his celebrated but controversial Supreme Court nominee, Judge Robert Bork, in 1987. Reagan of course rebounded from the Iran-Contra and Bork nomination setbacks, and the ensuing years saw the momentous events that would place the 40th president prominently in the history books for the rest of the Republic's days—the dramatic summits with Soviet leader Mikhail Gorbachev, the refusal to bend on the Strategic Defense Initiative, the liberation of Eastern Europe, the fall of the Soviet Union, and the end of the Cold War. Virginia's Senator Warner would bounce back, too, and assume a major leadership role on the national stage in post–Cold War military matters.

While the 1986 federal mid-term elections saw the scandal-plagued Republicans surrender control of the United States Senate, the 1987 mid-term legislative contests in Virginia produced no comparable setbacks for the governor's party even after state Democrats' promise-breaking tax increase. With key GOP lawmakers having backed the Baliles tax hikes, Republicans gained two seats in the 100-member House of Delegates for a total of 35, and added just one, their tenth, in the 40-member Virginia Senate. Some changes were notable, however. In the increasingly Republican Richmond suburbs, former First Lady Edwina P. ("Eddy") Dalton, widowed a year earlier, narrowly topped the Senate president pro tempore, conservative Democrat William F. Parkerson Jr., to gain not only a seat but a platform for an imminent statewide bid.[86] In Virginia Beach, Republican Joe Canada, who waged unsuccessful bids for lieutenant governor in 1977 and Congress in 1986, lost his Senate seat as well. In Chesapeake, Republican Mark Earley assembled an unusual coalition that included organized labor,

85. Trible's decision to leave the Senate and his subsequent candidacy for the 1989 GOP gubernatorial nomination are described in chapter 4.

86. Two women had served in the Senate previously; Republican Eva Scott of Amelia County and Democrat Evelyn Hailey of Norfolk had both retired in 1983. Sabato, *Virginia Votes 1987–1990*, p. 13.

evangelical Christians, and suburban Republicans in ousting another incumbent senator, Democrat William T. Parker. And in Bristol, William C. Wampler Jr., son and namesake of the former Ninth District congressman, gained his political start by capturing an open Senate seat with a margin of just 32 votes out of 42,000 cast.[87] The 1987 voting also saw Virginians reject the advice of virtually every major state official and endorse creation of a new state lottery.[88] One political figure who benefited from the lottery referendum fight was Marshall Coleman, who used his vocal opposition to state-sponsored gambling to build grassroots support among social conservatives in preparation for a comeback bid for the GOP gubernatorial nomination in 1989.

The men who would actually gain the governorship in ensuing years labored in relative obscurity during this time. George F. Allen, the son of the future Hall of Fame football coach, got his political start as a statewide youth leader in Reagan's 1976 presidential bid and came to the House of Delegates representing Albemarle County in 1983; like Wilder, he staked out conservative ground on criminal justice issues while opposing the Baliles sales tax hike. James S. Gilmore III, a former classmate of Allen's at the University of Virginia and key cog in the GOP political machine of Third District Congressman Thomas J. Bliley Jr., was elected as Henrico County's top prosecutor in 1987 and began burnishing his credentials as a crime fighter. Mark R. Warner, a former Democratic National Committee staffer, paid his political dues as a party volunteer in Alexandria while parlaying his telecommunications investments into a personal fortune that would ensure his political formidability. Perhaps no one except the budding politicians themselves had any inkling that they were bound soon for positions of statewide leadership.

Virginia politicos typically look past the normally predictable presidential contests in the state to focus on the next year's gubernatorial showdown, but the 1988 battle to succeed outgoing President Reagan produced unusual activity and interest. State Democrats initially were somewhat enthusiastic about the prospects of their nominee, Massachusetts Governor Michael Dukakis, but the rosy early outlook for the liberal northeasterner and his moderate Texas running mate, United States Senator Lloyd Bentsen, quickly faded in the Old Dominion, as it did in the rest of the nation. Earlier in the year, Vice President George Bush dominated the GOP preliminaries in the state despite the candidacy of televangelist Pat Robertson of Virginia

---

87. Sabato, *Virginia Votes 1987–1990*, pp. 13–14.
88. Voters approved the state lottery ballot proposition by a vote of 791,518 (56.6%) in favor and 607,884 (43.4%) opposed. Sabato, *Virginia Votes 1987–1990*, p. 2.

Beach.[89] The other minister-turned-presidential candidate, Jesse Jackson, fared better in his party's Virginia competition; he garnered 45 percent of the vote to handily win the Virginia Democratic primary. The result was a setback—a thoroughly predictable one, in Wilder's view[90]—for the Democratic moderates, including former Governor Robb, who had championed the idea of a "Super Tuesday" primary across the South in hopes of positioning a white Southern centrist for the party's presidential nomination. Instead of rallying Virginians to the support of Tennessean Albert Gore Jr., whom Robb favored, the March 8 Democratic primary in the state produced a dismal turnout, and the few who participated in the balloting dominated by African-American and liberal voters awarded two-thirds of their votes to the two left-most candidates in the race, Jackson and Dukakis.[91]

Bush and his running mate, U.S. Senator Dan Quayle of Indiana, rolled to a decisive victory in November, polling nearly 60 percent of the general election tally in the state.[92] Also enjoying a cakewalk was the Commonwealth's newest contribution to the United States Senate, Charles Robb. Following incumbent Paul Trible's surprise retirement announcement in the fall of 1987, Republicans were unable to recruit a serious challenger to Robb; the GOP rank and file decided instead to use the party's nod to "make history" a year ahead of the Democrats by nominating the first African-American major-party candidate for the United States Senate in Virginia—sixty-seven-year-old Baptist minister Maurice Dawkins.[93] Dawkins's high point came in his mesmerizing convention speech, which enabled him to seize the nomination from the front-running former aide to Senator John Warner, Andrew Wahlquist. Against the experienced, well-financed, and heavily favored Robb, however, Dawkins did not have a

---

89. State Republicans chose their national convention delegates in district and state conventions as usual, but the Virginia GOP held a nonbinding "beauty contest" primary on March 8 as Democrats cast their "Super Tuesday" votes. Bush polled 53.3 percent of the Virginia vote on March 8, 1988, compared to Kansas Senator Robert Dole's 26.0 percent and Robertson's 13.7 percent. Sabato, *Virginia Votes 1987–1990*, p. 24.

90. Wilder later said he warned fellow Democrats that Jackson would be the unintended beneficiary of the "Super Tuesday" idea. *Richmond Times-Dispatch*, November 21, 1990.

91. The vote totals for the four principal contenders were: Jackson—164,709 (45.1 percent); Albert Gore Jr.—81,419 (22.3 percent); Michael S. Dukakis—80,183 (22.0 percent); Richard Gephardt—15,935 (4.4 percent). Sabato, *Virginia Votes 1987–1990*, p. 13.

92. The vote totals were: Bush (R)—1,309,162 (59.7 percent); Dukakis (D)—859,799 (39.2 percent); Lenora B. Fulani (I)—14,312 (0.7 percent); Ron Paul (Libertarian)—8,336 (0.4 percent). Sabato, *Virginia Votes 1987–1990*, p. 42.

93. The vote totals were: Robb (D)—1,474,086 (71.0 percent); Dawkins (R)—593,652 (28.7 percent). African-American voters gave approximately 84 percent of their ballots to Robb rather than to his black opponent. Sabato, *Virginia Votes 1987–1990*.

chance, and his disorganized campaign attracted few financial or grassroots resources. Signs of the serious problems to come for Robb—salacious news reports of raucous partying at sex- and drug-drenched Virginia Beach soirees that belied Robb's straight-laced, milk-drinking Marine image—first emerged during the campaign,[94] but the Dawkins campaign was too far in the hole to exploit the issue. Like the romps by Reagan and Warner four years earlier, Bush and Robb won landslide victories, carrying all ten of the state's congressional districts and reaffirming the decade's main dynamic: Republican hegemony in Washington and Democratic dominance in Virginia.[95]

With Robb's win, Democrats perfected their claim to parity in the state's congressional delegation. Two years earlier, they had achieved an even split in United States House of Representatives seats when Delegate Owen B. Pickett overcame the GOP's Joe Canada to claim the Second District seat of retiring 18-year Republican veteran G. William Whitehurst in Hampton Roads. While his first win was a narrow one, Pickett sailed to reelection in 1988, aided in both contests by support from his erstwhile antagonist, Douglas Wilder. Indeed, the moderate-conservative Pickett, accused by Wilder of making anti-black remarks in the infamous 1982 episode, garnered more than 85 percent of the African-American vote in his reelection bid despite facing a black Republican opponent, retired Army General Jerry R. Curry. Democrats also prevailed in conservative Southside Virginia after the death of Representative W. C. ("Dan") Daniel, the Fifth District's Byrd Democrat stalwart, prompted a June special election and then a November contest for election to the next Congress. Democrats recruited an attractive political novice, Wintergreen resort developer L. F. Payne Jr. to carry their standard; aided by GOP division, Payne delivered a narrow June special-election win and then an easy November reelection victory for Fifth District Democrats. The change marked a milestone in the realignment process: Daniel was the last of the conservative Byrd men to serve in Congress as a Democrat, while a majority of the state's then-serving Republican congressmen (Representatives Bateman, Slaughter, and Bliley) were conservative former Democrats who had switched parties.[96]

For Virginians, however, the most significant political development of

---

94. See *Virginian-Pilot & Ledger-Star*, August 28, 1988; *Washington Post*, August 31, 1988; *Washington Times*, October 7, 1988.

95. For the second straight year, Virginia voters endorsed legalized gambling. Reversing a decision made at the polls a decade earlier, voters approved pari-mutuel betting on horse races by a vote of 55.9 percent in favor and 44.1 percent opposed. Sabato, *Virginia Votes 1987–1990*, p. 49.

96. See generally Jack Irby Hayes Jr., *Dan Daniel and the Persistence of Conservatism in Virginia* (Macon, GA: Mercer University Press, 1997).

1988 did not involve that year's elections, but positioning for the next. Attorney General Mary Sue Terry, who had outpolled both of her running mates in 1985, announced in the spring that she would run for reelection to her lawyer's post the following year, thereby averting a mutually destructive clash with Wilder for the gubernatorial nomination. The danger to Democrats had been enormous and the source of it familiar, as reporter Margaret Edds explained in her chronicle of the 1989 campaign:

> [T]he memory of the 1982 Pickett affair hung over the quiet deliberations of Democrats as they looked toward 1989. The expected Wilder-Terry match was not a prospect to warm the hearts of the party faithful. If Wilder won, the moderate-conservative voters whose return to Democratic ranks had fueled the successes of the 1980s might well be disaffected by the defeat of Terry, a favorite of the group. And if Wilder lost, the fear of another 1982—massive defections by alienated black voters—might preclude any hope of victory in the fall.[97]

A year earlier, commentator Ray Garland had offered this similar take on the ruling Democrats' dilemma:

> These gimlet-eyed, itchy-palmed gentlemen may be divided and confused about a great many things, but one thing that unites them is a conviction that Doug Wilder is not a man with whom they can trifle. Behind him they perceive the power of the black vote and know that whatever else they may do, they dare not disturb the orderly tranquility with which blacks have resegregated themselves at the polling place to deliver overwhelming majorities to virtually all candidates of the Democratic Party.[98]

Not only did Terry's demurrer avoid a rending of the Democrats' winning coalition; it precipitated an outbreak of peace that extended to Wilder's sparring partners, Robb and Baliles. Wilder had again bullied and barged his way into a consensus nomination, and now that the coveted nod was his, it was time to extend an olive branch to the popular Democratic leaders and begin the process of presenting himself to Virginians as their predictable, logical heir. A rapprochement of sorts ensued; Wilder even joined Robb later for an appearance before the Democratic Leadership Council. And Governor Baliles moved to ensure there would be no repeat of the 1985 spectacle when hand-wringing Democrats had cast about in vain for a stop-Wilder candidate. In a graduation address at Norfolk State University in May 1988, Baliles signaled his support for Wilder's history-making candidacy, and the nomination issue effectively was resolved.

97. Edds, *Claiming the Dream*, p. 44.
98. Yancey, *When Hell Froze Over*, p. 384 (1990 expanded edition).

The deft grandson of slaves, *perseverando*, had accomplished the unimaginable. A Democratic Party that had begun the century by enacting constitutional changes to disfranchise African-American voters would now give Wilder its most prized possession, the nomination for governor, without opposition.[99]

---

99. With conservative Democrats firmly in control of Virginia's government, state constitutional amendments adopted in 1902 dramatically restricted those eligible to vote in the state. African Americans were the primary targets of the discrimination. See *The Dynamic Dominion*, Chapter 1.

# 4

## SWINGING SUBURBS: MAKING
## MONEY AND MAKING HISTORY

> Three years ago, Doug Wilder ran for lieutenant governor of Virginia. Many told him he could not win. He politely ignored them. . . . He talked not of the past, but of the future. And, he won. Now, Doug Wilder has his sights on a new office. . . . Again, he will address the future. And, again he will have a chance to make history in Virginia. Perhaps more to the point, Virginia will have the chance to make history [and to establish] that Virginia does not have time to waste on the old fears, the old habits, and the old divisions.[1]
>
> —Governor Gerald L. Baliles, May 1988

Virginia in the late 1980s was a portrait of mainstream America. Economically, the Commonwealth was diverse and dynamic; traditional manufacturing industries and agricultural enterprises, while generally prosperous, represented a declining portion of the state's overall economy, and were fast being eclipsed by the explosive high-technology and service-oriented business sectors. For two decades before 1980, the Commonwealth's policymakers had cultivated a social and legal climate conducive to business and industrial development, and the Virginia economy had remained relatively strong while the nation experienced recession and stagnation during the 1970s. With the sustained nationwide recovery in the 1980s, the state enjoyed unprecedented economic growth. Particularly significant was the major boost that the Reagan administration's defense build-up gave to the economies of Northern Virginia and the Hampton Roads area.

The corresponding population trends were away from the rural areas and central cities and toward the suburbs. The share of the statewide vote turned in by the suburbs grew from 39 percent in 1977 to 49 percent in

---

1. Baker, *Wilder*, p. 56.

1989.[2] The urban corridor extending from Northern Virginia through the Richmond metropolitan area to the Tidewater cities in the southeastern corner of the state was the locus of much of the suburban sprawl, with the fastest growth occurring at opposite ends of the corridor. It was in these vote-rich suburban areas that the prosperous baby-boomers—young, upwardly mobile, white professionals and business men and women—comprised the dominant population group and voting bloc. Also notable was the steady expansion of the suburban African-American middle class, an inevitable product of anti-discrimination measures and social and economic integration. While generalizations remained hazardous, a decade of polling data and social literature confirmed that the overriding concern of the upscale voters, white and black, was economic advancement. For most Americans and most Virginians, the decade of the 1980s was a very good time to make money—personal income in the state rose sharply—and making money made for good times. "Reaganomics"—the sweeping tax reduction initiative championed early by Republicans such as Virginia's Richard Obenshain and originally branded a "nightmare" by Democrats such as Virginia's Douglas Wilder[3]—was, by decade's end, synonymous with the unparalleled prosperity that Virginia and most of the nation enjoyed. While federal government budget deficits remained an ominous cloud on the horizon, the prosperous (and those who aspired to join them) were generally content with the handling of economic affairs, and few wanted to risk a return to the troubled times of the 1970s.

Though tax restraint and growth-oriented economic policies supplied common ground for the younger voters in the suburbs and the traditional conservatives throughout the state, the two groups' interests and social outlooks otherwise diverged markedly. The rapid growth of the suburbs, coupled with the influx of women into the workforce there, brought to the fore a host of special concerns—transportation systems, child-care services, land-use planning and restrictions on development, educational and recreational facilities, environmental safeguards—that were widely viewed by suburbanites as governmental responsibilities. To such suburban voters, stand-pat Republican conservatism seemed as outdated and out-of-touch as dogmatic Democratic liberalism. Moreover, the suburban perspective was characterized by youthful optimism, prosperity-fueled expectations of progress, and general nonchalance concerning evidence of cultural decline. Having come of age in the turbulent 1960s, many suburban dwellers retained

---

2. Sabato, *Virginia Votes 1987–1990,* p. 84. For historical data on the impact of suburbanization on state elections, see Sabato, *Virginia Votes 1983–1986,* p. 83.

3. *Richmond News Leader,* May 5, 1982.

individualistic, libertarian attitudes on social issues even as they exuberantly adopted their elders' passion for the fruits of capitalism. In contrast, the outlook of older conservatives tended to be more culturally focused and tradition-oriented and less sensitive to unfulfilled aspirations and social barriers to personal opportunity. The dramatic shift of political clout to the suburbs in the 1980s thus was accompanied by a precipitous decline in the influence of the aging conservative symbols of the rural-based Coalition. Virginia Republicans generally were slow to recognize that change, but GOP strategist Judy Peachee anticipated it in a 1980 interview:

> I think [support from the Coalition] is a diminishing factor. The younger crowd that is coming along does not use the same yardstick to measure the candidate. The litmus test is changing, and our party has to be very sensitive to the evolution that is taking place. . . . The candidates that we nominate have to represent traditional principles of conservative government, but they also have to have a vision for the future; they have to have new ideas. The newer crowd is measuring by the future and not by the past. The "Coalition," as we know it, is measuring by known quantities; the younger crowd uses those quantities as a bedrock, but they've added on to it what they want for the future. So I think you are dealing with a changing conservative base.[4]

Unfortunately for the Virginia GOP, the only lesson many partisans seemed to glean from Charles Robb's victory in 1981 was that the Republican Party had to act in concert with the Coalition in order to win. While that was largely true in the watershed Coleman-Robb race, it became markedly less so in the political climate that developed in that election's wake. Republicans nevertheless remained preoccupied during the 1980s with recapturing solid Coalition backing for GOP candidates, and that focus almost completely obscured the imperative of fashioning a forward-looking message for younger, moderate suburban voters. The situation bore striking similarities to the plight of the Byrd organization in the 1950s and 1960s. The aging Byrd leadership then had failed to accommodate state policies to the reality of urban growth, and the organization had lost the loyalty of many of its metropolitan adherents. Somewhat ironically, it was Democratic Governor Mills Godwin who broke with tradition in the mid-1960s and supplied the leadership that enabled the state to address an array of pressing urban needs. But by the 1980s, the pace of change had accelerated, and many suburban voters came to view Godwin and the Coalition as anachronistic symbols of an unflatteringly caricatured and unappreciated Virginia past.

---

4. Peachee interview.

Once in power with Robb's election as governor in 1981, Virginia Democrats were positioned to capitalize on the economic prosperity and the widespread contentment of voters throughout the decade. The Democratic demon of tax-and-spend liberalism was exorcised, not by spending restraint—state spending in Virginia, while still relatively low compared to a majority of states, outpaced the growth in federal spending and average state budget growth nationally during the 1980s[5]—but by the effects of economic growth, which consistently filled state coffers and yielded steady increases in the disposable incomes of most voters. The Robb Democrats also distanced themselves from the party's prior liberal stands on key business and labor issues, such as repeal of the Right to Work Law and support for public employee collective bargaining. Republican candidates attempted throughout the decade to make campaign hay out of Democratic fiscal policies, but the general economic satisfaction in the suburbs and the absence of a unified stance on taxes and spending among General Assembly Republicans impeded the attempts. GOP statewide contenders during the 1980s thus faced a frightful dilemma: the issues that had been principally relied upon to forge winning conservative Republican coalitions in the 1970s—taxing, spending, and labor policies—were generally unavailing; and the more GOP candidates assailed the Robb-Baliles fiscal policies in an effort to reassemble that coalition, the more they opened themselves up to Democratic charges that they were mired in the past and opposed to worthwhile public investments in education, transportation, and other "forward-looking" programs with suburban as well as central-city appeal.

In the wake of the 1985 Democratic sweep, introspective GOP partisans agreed with Professor Larry Sabato that a major shortcoming during the Robb administration had been the absence of a vocal Republican "loyal opposition" pointing out flaws in and suggesting alternatives to the incumbent Democratic governor's policies.[6] GOP chief Donald Huffman responded by creating a Republican Policy Committee, chaired by former delegate and party chairman George McMath, to formulate Republican policy positions on major state issues. GOP legislative leaders, however, generally saw the initiative as an encroachment upon their policymaking prerogative and lent little support. Despite the improving Republican num-

---

5. For comparative data on income and spending growth in Virginia and nationally during the last three decades of the twentieth century, see Crain, pp. 1–24, 82–95; see also JLARC December 2004 Spending Update, p. 51; Interim Report, "Review of State Spending," Joint Legislative Audit and Review Commission, Commonwealth of Virginia, January 2002; Report, "Review of State Spending: June 2002 Update," Joint Legislative Audit and Review Commission, Commonwealth of Virginia, January 2002.

6. See Sabato, *Virginia Votes 1983–1986*, p. 109.

bers in the Virginia General Assembly during the 1980s, the GOP legislative caucus generally failed to fashion and coalesce behind innovative initiatives in key areas, such as education, law enforcement, environmental protection or transportation, that might serve to contrast the loyal opposition with the party in power and thereby give voters a *partisan* reason to oust Democrats and install Republicans. Many GOP lawmakers backed some or all of the Baliles road-building program and tax increases in 1986, and it was 1991 before Republican legislators galvanized in opposition to a Democrat-sponsored budget bill. Virginia Democrats thus enjoyed a continual monopoly on state offices, a strong legislative majority, and a free ride from Republicans on state policies and administration for much of the 1980s.

It was against this adverse backdrop of Democratic incumbency, economic contentment, and Republican malaise that GOP candidates endeavored, ultimately without success, to break into the winning column in state elections during the 1980s. In a phenomenon that was not limited to Virginia, the liberal-conservative dichotomy that made GOP victories predictable in presidential elections was effectively erased in state elections. "[T]he common denominator of the New South generation of Democratic nominees has been their refusal to present themselves unambiguously as either national liberal Democrats or unreconstructed southern Democrats," wrote Professors Earl and Merle Black in 1987.

> Most victorious southern Democrats have waged campaigns that skillfully intertwine conservative postures (budgetary restraint, opposition to increased taxation, enthusiasm for school prayer and the death penalty) with progressive themes (support for equal opportunities, educational advancement, environmental protection). . . . By deliberately blurring distinctions between conservatism and progressivism [Southern] Democratic politicians have been able to appeal on different grounds to black (and liberal white) Democrats and to moderate and conservative white Democrats.[7]

In Virginia, where Republicans for a decade had forged winning coalitions around conservative precepts, blurring the ideological differences between the parties was the chief prerequisite for Democratic success in the 1980s. Once it was apparent that Virginia Democrats were not going to do anything to prevent upwardly mobile suburban voters from making money, the way was clear for Democrats to focus on other concerns that would satisfy the suburban appetite for progress and salve the suburban social conscience. Aided by the paucity of major policy differences between the parties in state contests, Democratic candidates successfully directed suburban

---

7. Black, Earl, and Merle Black, *Politics and Society in the South* (Cambridge, MA: Harvard University Press, 1987), p. 287.

voters' attention to the hot-button issues of race relations and abortion policy, and to the corresponding pejorative symbols of Massive Resistance and Moral Majority. Democratic tacticians used those issues and symbols to construct a thematic paradigm that repeatedly moved suburban voters into their column in the 1980s: the GOP as the intolerant, divisive party of the past; Democrats as the inclusive, unifying force for the future.

Probably the most accurate description of the prevailing political philosophy in the Virginia suburbs—and within the expanding Southern middle class generally—was supplied by the professors Black, who termed it "entrepreneurial individualism."[8] Shared entrepreneurial aims and economic outlooks linked the suburbs to more traditional conservative elements of society and the electorate, but in important respects the ethic of individualism separated suburban voters from traditionalists. No topics more dramatically divided younger suburban voters from older conservatives throughout the state than race relations and civil rights. Ironically, both of the decade's GOP gubernatorial standard-bearers (Marshall Coleman and Wyatt Durrette) were racial moderates whose conservative credo of individual liberty called for according every person opportunity based on individual worth rather than the happenstance of racial identity. In that belief, they were in harmony with the progressive sentiments of suburbanites. But, as they tried to forge conservative coalitions in the 1980s using the Byrd-era symbols that had so aided the realignment effort in the 1970s, they repeatedly found that the specter of past racial discrimination hung like a cloud over the state's politics. Partly through Republican fumbling, and partly as a result of skillful Democratic manipulation, the GOP's ties to the remnants of the Byrd organization were repeatedly used to link Republican candidates to the discredited segregationist policies of Virginia's past. Wilder's presence on the 1985 and 1989 Democratic tickets guaranteed that the issue of race relations would remain front-and-center throughout the decade. But, more than that, his candidacy gave voters a concrete opportunity to signal their repudiation of Virginia's legacy of discrimination, to purge their racial guilt, and to "make history" in a way that would capture both the attention and the admiration of the nation.

If race was the Scylla upon which Democrats dashed the GOP's comeback hopes, abortion by decade's end had become the Charybdis that drew Republicans into a perilous debate they rarely won before suburban audiences. Even before the United States Supreme Court's July 1989 *Webster*[9]

---

8. Black and Black, *Politics and Society in the South,* pp. 296–316.

9. *Webster v. Reproductive Health Services*, 492 U.S. 490 (1989). In the controversial ruling, the Supreme Court opened the way for additional state-imposed restrictions on access to abortions.

decision energized advocates of legalized abortion and thrust the issue temporarily to the fore, GOP candidates were often hampered in the suburbs by identification with the conservative social agenda of the New Right and its nationally prominent leaders, two of whom—Jerry Falwell and Pat Robertson—were Virginians. Of course, the morality-driven issues emphasized by the politically active conservative Christian community touched a receptive chord among many Virginia voters. School prayer, restrictions on pornography, parental rights in education, and parental consent for teenage abortions were policy positions that attracted large numbers of politically unaligned citizens to the GOP cause, especially in rural areas and among church-goers in all parts of the state. But many suburban voters reacted warily to politicians who seemed preoccupied with such issues, and the suburbanites' reticence typically focused less on the particular issues themselves than on the vocal televangelists' seeming moral imperiousness and intolerant-sounding mixture of religion and politics. The libertarian brand of conservatism prevalent in the suburbs and among younger voters throughout Virginia ran counter to the majoritarian methods of the culturally conservative New Right, and the disagreement represented another major fault line in the conservative coalition that had elected Republicans in the 1970s.[10]

The manifold reasons for the GOP's failures were not evident, however, to most partisans in the trenches. And after experiencing the debilitating GOP conventions in 1977, 1981, and 1985, a number of leading Republicans concluded their party might fare better in 1989 if it nominated its statewide slate by primary election rather than via a convention. It was a

---

10. In their 1996 study of the Christian Right's role in Virginia politics from the mid-1970s to the mid-1990s, Mark J. Rozell and Clyde Wilcox contend that the movement's leaders initially "took extreme positions on social issues, preferring purism to political compromise," but later became "more pragmatic" and "sought to build interdenominational alliances and to compromise when necessary to achieve their goals." Mark J. Rozell and Clyde Wilcox, *Second Coming: The New Christian Right in Virginia Politics* (Baltimore and London: The Johns Hopkins University Press, 1996), p. 4. The reflexive hostility of many moderate suburbanites to the religious conservative leaders reached its peak in the 1980s, during the first phase of Christian Right activism, and subsided thereafter. As discussed in chapters 6–8, attempts by Virginia Democrats to invoke symbols such as Falwell and Robertson largely failed to sway voters in the elections of the 1990s, partly because the tactics wore thin over time, and partly because the Christian Right organizations and leaders modified their methods, integrated themselves into GOP campaign efforts, and lowered their profiles to avoid serving perennially as whipping boys for the Democrats. For a description of the politically sophisticated "Christian Coalition" grassroots organization, which was formed by Robertson after his 1988 presidential bid and was led by GOP activist Ralph Reed in the 1990s, see Reed's *Active Faith: How Christians Are Changing the Soul of American Politics* (New York: The Free Press, 1996).

dubious notion. It had been four decades since the Virginia GOP last exper-
imented with a gubernatorial primary, and fewer had gone to the polls in
that 1949 contest than had attended the party's 1978 and 1985 state conventions as delegates and alternates. State Democrats had experienced a reversal
of their sagging fortunes in Virginia after abandoning primaries in favor of
conventions in the late 1970s. Nevertheless, the sentiment for change
among Republicans was strong, and it was reinforced by the immediate
political interests of two men who decided to seek the 1989 GOP nomination for governor—the just-retired Senator Paul Trible and Eighth District
Congressman Stanford Parris. Trible and Parris believed their prospects for
nomination would be enhanced in a primary because a third candidate in
the field, former Attorney General Marshall Coleman, had labored hard
since his last bid to cultivate support among the activists likely to decide the
nomination in a convention setting. In opposing the primary, Coleman's
backers and a few others on the party's governing committee argued that a
primary contest would damage the party's general election prospects by
draining precious campaign funds from GOP benefactors and applying them
toward television ads critical of the party's eventual nominee. In December
1988, however, the primary advocates aligned with Trible and Parris prevailed before the GOP central committee. A June 1989 primary was set, and
Trible, the most well known of the three among the general electorate, was
instantly the frontrunner.[11]

Trible was dogged, however, by a credibility problem. When he
announced his departure from the Senate in 1987, he cited as reasons his
frustration with the glacial pace of the Senate's decision-making processes
and his desire to spend more time with his young family—views he also
expressed in candid private conversations with others. Although running for
governor was an option that Trible and his advisers were actively consider-
ing, he had made no decision and declined to state any such plans in
announcing his retirement. Already criticized for abandoning the hard-won
Senate seat in the face of the impending Robb challenge, Trible found his
motives for leaving the Senate and his candor questioned even more directly
once he announced for governor less than a year later. To many, it appeared
that he had planned the gubernatorial bid all along, and his opponents for
the nomination openly derided him for the apparent dissembling as well as
fleeing in the face of the Robb threat. Interviewed a decade and a half later,

---

11. The nomination struggle began as a four-way contest, but Delegate Raymond
R. ("Andy") Guest of Front Royal, the Republican leader in the House of Delegates,
dropped out in March, three months before the June 13 primary. The lesser-known
Guest had favored nomination by convention because of his belief that the convention
delegates might turn to him as a compromise choice.

Trible, now president of fast-growing Christopher Newport University in Newport News, rebutted both criticisms. If he had resolved in his own mind to run for governor by the time he announced his Senate retirement, Trible noted, it would have been far smarter politically for him to have said so, since many Republicans were openly casting about for a strong gubernatorial candidate.[12] But the real determinant was Trible's growing concern about the impact that the demands of Senate life had on his ability to be involved with his children during their formative years. "I had come to Congress at age twenty-nine, and I wanted to be president of the United States," Trible said.

> And, by the 1980s, I had come pretty far. I was one of a hundred United States senators, a place from which a person could actually run for president. I had scaled way up the political ladder. But I decided the ladder was against the wrong wall. I wanted to be part of my children's lives, and I could not do that and stay in the Senate, on the political path I was on. To make that decision, when lots of people had invested their time and resources in my political career, was hard to do gracefully. I am not sure it can ever be done gracefully. But I decided other things were more important; I made that choice; and in more than a decade since I have never looked back.[13]

Acknowledging that many Republicans believed he left the Senate to duck a showdown with Robb, Trible added:

> Robb really was not the factor. Yes, Robb would have been the strongest opponent I ever had, but I would have been the strongest opponent he ever had. I would have been a well-funded incumbent United States senator running with a candidate for president who was popular in Virginia. Plus, anyone familiar with how I had gotten to that point knows that I was always an underdog and had difficult races, but I never shied away from them. And that was not the reason I decided against running in 1988.[14]

Whatever impact the Robb obstacle and more promising gubernatorial opportunity may have had on Trible's decisions to leave the Senate and to run for governor, it soon became apparent that he and his chief adviser, Judy Peachee, had underestimated the difficulty of winning the gubernatorial nomination against the relentless Marshall Coleman. The former attorney

---

12. Trible interview. Trible recalled that some advisers hoped he would run for governor and urged him to announce his intended gubernatorial candidacy when he made public his plans to retire from the Senate. Still undecided on the bid for governor, Trible rejected the advice.

13. Trible interview.

14. Trible interview.

general had used the time since his 1985 setback to court conservative party activists and to convince Boyd Marcus—the political mastermind aligned with Third District Representative Thomas J. Bliley Jr. and future governor James S. Gilmore III—to serve as his campaign manager. Coleman's aggressive primary campaign stressed a number of innovative policy initiatives, including far-reaching plans to combat crime and illegal drugs, as well as his extensive state government experience. As reporter Margaret Edds explained, "Through a discouraging decade for the state GOP, [Coleman] had been the party's vigilant intellectual voice,"[15] and many Republicans came to believe that his knowledge of state issues and his debating skills would be the best match for Douglas Wilder's. That impression was reinforced when the GOP contenders squared off across the state in a lengthy series of spring debates. While Trible played the cautious frontrunner trying to protect a lead, Coleman trumpeted his new ideas and flayed the former senator for not supporting President Reagan sufficiently during the Iran-Contra controversy and for abandoning the GOP-held Senate seat to Robb. The third candidate, Parris, had a strong political base in Northern Virginia and a creditable congressional record, but his focus on federal issues and regional concerns impeded his effort to appeal to downstate Republicans. In the end, however, Parris played an important role in the contest's outcome when his campaign and Coleman's simultaneously unleashed a withering, multimillion-dollar television ad assault on frontrunner Trible in the weeks just before the election.

The comeback-minded Coleman pulled off a stunning upset on June 13, aided not only by Trible's sudden collapse but by a sophisticated voter identification and turnout program that maximized Coleman's own ballot total.[16] Although the outcome surprised most observers, the primary bore out the varied predictions of its advocates and opponents. Though the GOP trio waged an intense struggle over many months, the battle was fought mostly over the airwaves and through the mail, and it produced little of the bitter personal animosity generated among Republican regulars during the rough-and-tumble convention fights of 1977, 1981, and 1985. Yet, the primary contest also produced many of the damaging side-effects that convention proponents had feared. Coleman spent $3.4 million to secure his victory—the three contestants together spent $10 million—and the Republican nominee entered the general election campaign against the well-funded Wilder with a $900,000 deficit. Moreover, while Wilder had been

---

15. Edds, *Claiming the Dream*, p. 64.
16. The vote totals were: Coleman—147,941 (36.8 percent); Trible—141,120 (35.1 percent); Parris—112,826 (28.1 percent). Sabato, *Virginia Votes 1987–1990*, p. 56.

carefully crafting a positive, upbeat image as the standard-bearer of a united Democratic Party, Coleman had been tarnished by the heated spring exchanges. The costly three-way battle for the 1989 GOP nomination prompted comparisons with the Democrats' divisive 1969 primary and run-off, which had set the stage for the election of Virginia's first Republican governor since Reconstruction.[17] Without the fierce spring 1989 clash for the GOP nomination, it is doubtful that Wilder would have eked out his narrow, history-making victory in November.

Coleman's surprise primary win averted the Wilder-Trible duel that most of the state's political establishment had been expecting. But in the wake of Coleman's primary win commentators suggested that the feisty former attorney general might well have been the best suited all along to take on Wilder.[18] A racial moderate, Coleman's politically problematic past clashes with the ex-Byrd men in his party now became something of an asset, freeing him to challenge liberal aspects of Wilder's record without risking a repeat of the "racial code word" rejoinder from the Democratic camp. Moreover, Coleman had never shied away from robust exchanges with political opponents—former foes considered him a "vicious campaigner," according to Edds[19]—and the belief that he would carry the fight unrelentingly to Wilder had much to do with his upset primary victory. The GOP nominee also had extensive state government experience and a reform-minded agenda for the new Republican administration he hoped to lead. But it was universally apparent to strategists in the Republican camp that the GOP would have to illuminate Wilder's record or face a third consecutive gubernatorial defeat. With the state economy seemingly strong, and with Robb and Baliles ostensibly back in his corner, Wilder had all the advantages of pseudo-incumbency. At the same time, his unique candidacy satisfied the electorate's appetite for excitement, change, and the perception of progress. There was the powerful pull of "making history," the opportunity to signal a new era of racial harmony, and—as Virginians were repeatedly reminded by national news accounts during the campaign—the chance to impress the nation with Virginia's surprising progressivism. Either the GOP would take the fight to Wilder and convince Virginians that he was a soft-on-crime liberal tarnished by personal controversies or the Democrat would glide into office on a wave of good feeling.

The Wilder stratagem in 1989 was not markedly different from his 1985 plan. He would present himself as the logical heir to his centrist Dem-

17. See *The Dynamic Dominion*, Chapters 17–18.
18. See Sabato, *Virginia Votes 1987–1990*, pp. 60–61.
19. Edds, *Claiming the Dream*, p. 72.

ocratic predecessors, a force for continuity and cautious progress. To capture a sufficient share of the suburban swing vote, he would run to the right of center thematically and minimize policy differences with his GOP foe (except on social issues). The fiscal storms of the late 1980s and early 1990s in Virginia and the nation were just over the horizon, safely out of view,[20] and Wilder had forestalled any fight on the GOP's favorite issue of taxes by taking a stronger stand against the 1986 Baliles levies than leading Republican lawmakers had taken. With economic concerns secondary in a third consecutive governor's race, Wilder was free to focus voter interest where he and his strategists wanted it. Racial pride and the novelty of his candidacy would be relied upon to keep black and liberal Democrats on board, and Wilder's legislative record and reassuring winks would keep organized labor's foot soldiers marching in his parade. The key to success, however, would be re-creating the past-versus-future dichotomy that had worked so well in the suburbs in 1981 and 1985. And the key to that, inevitably, was race. Governor Baliles set the theme early when, in a May 1988 speech credited with squelching any lingering Democratic opposition to Wilder's nomination, he declared:

> Three years ago, Doug Wilder ran for lieutenant governor of Virginia. Many told him he could not win. He politely ignored them. . . . He talked not of the past, but of the future. And, he won. Now, Doug Wilder has his sights on a new office. . . . Again, he will address the future. And, again he will have a chance to make history in Virginia. Perhaps more to the point, Virginia will have the chance to make history [and to establish] that Virginia does not have time to waste on the old fears, the old habits, and the old divisions.[21]

Baliles's remarks reflected the confidence in Democratic circles that Wilder's race would be a net benefit in the coming campaign. As Margaret Edds observed in her account of the 1989 contest, "Whatever else it might become, the 1989 race for governor would also be a referendum on racial tolerance. History to the contrary, Wilder and his strategists believed that was a winning proposition."[22]

---

20. Republican Marshall Coleman endeavored during the fall campaign to focus attention on the Baliles administration's tax and spending hikes and the evidence that a state fiscal crisis loomed, but the extent of the mounting budgetary problems was not apparent until after the election. Baliles himself dismissed Coleman's dire—though prescient—fiscal predictions as the politically motivated rhetoric of one who "knows very little about the budget process." *Virginian-Pilot*, October 24, 1989; see also Thomas R. Morris, "Virginia: L. Douglas Wilder, Governing and Campaigning," in *Governors and Hard Times*, ed. Thad L. Beyle (Washington, DC: CQ Press, 1992), p. 194.

21. Baker, *Wilder*, p. 56.

22. Edds, *Claiming the Dream*, p. 14.

Wilder's unique status as potentially the first elected African-American governor guaranteed immense favorable publicity for his "historic" candidacy; the symbolic importance of his potential achievement, when broadly advertised in the local and national news media, made his race a distinct political asset. Had the perceived racial barrier been broken before 1989, it may be safely ventured that Wilder's cause, like that of 1990 Georgia gubernatorial candidate Andrew Young,[23] would have attracted far less attention; in such a circumstance it is entirely possible (though by no means certain) that white votes forfeited because of racial bigotry might have outnumbered those gained through positive racial imagery. But that was not the case in Virginia in 1989.

Most of the literally hundreds of national and international reporters who streamed to the erstwhile capital of the Confederacy to report on the Wilder-Coleman campaign still were on the lookout for a racial incident— some dramatic confirmation of the widespread assumption that race remained a talisman to the Virginia electorate. News accounts typically portrayed the contest as a test of Virginians' integrity on matters racial; if Wilder won, the state's suspect citizenry would earn a passing grade, while a Republican victory would be taken as proof that the old attitudes persisted. Among the in-state news media there was much of the same. The State Capitol press corps had been the target of nonpartisan allegations of pro-Wilder bias four years earlier—"the most imbalanced and unfair picture of an election I've ever seen," Larry Sabato had charged[24]—and before the 1989 election a number of front-line state political reporters talked openly of subjecting Wilder's candidacy, record, and statements to closer scrutiny in his campaign for governor. As the contest unfolded, however, there was little evidence of increased journalistic aggressiveness. In the critical weeks immediately preceding the election, major news outlets in the state echoed many of the race-related themes beneficial to Wilder that permeated the national coverage.

Republican strategists assumed that Wilder's campaign for governor would feature a reprise of his 1985 "Let's Make History" theme. Indeed, his bid for the top spot in state government promised to make that message even more compelling. But one thing was certain to be different in 1989: Republicans this time were not going to let Wilder's race deter them from calling attention to his record. In addition to his liberal stances as a state

---

23. Young, a protégé of Dr. Martin Luther King Jr. had served as United Nations ambassador during the administration of President Jimmy Carter and later as mayor of Atlanta. Despite predictions that he would mount a formidable bid, Young was soundly defeated in the Georgia Democratic gubernatorial primary in 1990.

24. Yancey, *When Hell Froze Over*, p. 312.

legislator, Wilder's professional, business, and political wake was strewn with controversies—a state Supreme Court reprimand in 1978 for unprofessional conduct as a lawyer, a serious legislative conflict-of-interest scrape in 1979, successive citations for building code violations, insistence upon honoraria for speeches to constituents while lieutenant governor, deficient state financial disclosure submissions, and, perhaps most potentially damaging, two published letters from the popular Charles Robb directly indicting his integrity.[25] Wilder had explanations and excuses for some of these problems, but the reality was that the problems themselves had not been aired in any systematic way before 1989. Marshall Coleman served notice at the start of his campaign that the gloves would come off. While declaring that he would tolerate no subtle or overt racial appeals on his behalf, Coleman also stated that he would "not be intimidated or deterred by groundless charges that my discussion of Mr. Wilder's record and views is racially inspired."[26] Republicans would challenge Virginians to vote for the best person regardless of race, convinced that if Wilder's vulnerabilities were exploited he would not win.

Although standing against the tide of history, the Virginia GOP's strategy might have prevailed in 1989 if it were not for two decisive developments—both legacies of the spring nomination fight—that ran interference for the Wilder campaign throughout the fall contest. The first was the "negative campaigner" moniker that was fixed firmly—and unavoidably—on the Republican nominee after his savaging of GOP frontrunner Trible in May and June. Coleman emerged in early summer from a primary campaign in which he had played the aggressor, so when he turned his sights on Wilder in the fall he was particularly susceptible to the charge that he was an exceedingly negative and mean-spirited politician. Wilder's media consultants craftily exploited the Republican's vulnerability with ads that simultaneously blasted Coleman for waging a negative campaign and fired hard-hitting messages of their own aimed at discrediting him. Correctly anticipating a Coleman campaign fusillade on Wilder's ethical misadventures, the Democrats launched television spots that coupled a sweeping denial of the GOP

25. Robb, back on board with Wilder in the 1989 race, helped minimize the letters' political impact by sending word privately to Republicans that he would write a similarly hard-hitting letter to Coleman if the GOP invoked the missives in its anti-Wilder campaign advertising. Robb interview. It was a successful bluff; the Coleman campaign never used the letters in any concerted way, but Robb's endorsement nevertheless was featured prominently in Wilder campaign ads that were aired frequently during the contest's final weeks.

26. Marshall Coleman, *Agenda for the '90s: Fulfilling Virginia's Promise,* Coleman for Governor Campaign, November 1988, p. 26.

charges with the preemptive declaration that "you just can't trust Marshall Coleman." By October, newspaper polls indicated that voters were disproportionately blaming the Republican candidate for what they believed to be excessive campaign mud-slinging. "Coleman was hurt by a peculiar circumstance," ventured Larry Sabato. "[H]e was forced to run two negative campaigns back to back in the same year. That was probably one too many."[27]

The two Coleman campaigns in 1989 also exposed the Republican to another charge—that he was a "right-wing extremist" by virtue of his strong stance against legalized abortion. If, as Democratic lawmaker Richard Cranwell once noted, Republicans suffered in Virginia because President Ronald Reagan fared too well in managing the national economy, the same could be said of the president's judicial appointments. Until the United States Supreme Court dominated by Reagan appointees signaled greater deference to state-legislated restrictions on abortion in its July 1989 *Webster* decision, the preponderance of political energy stemming from abortion-related activism was on the pro-life side. But the threatened rescission of abortion rights created in the Court's sixteen-year-old *Roe v. Wade*[28] ruling suddenly energized the pro-choice activists in the summer of 1989, transforming the dynamics of the Virginia campaign for governor. Coleman had staked out firm anti-abortion ground in vying for the Republican Party's gubernatorial nomination during the spring, and that turf proved exceedingly treacherous in the post–*Webster* general election campaign.

As a result of the *Webster* decision and the intense national interest it generated, Wilder never had to answer for his legislative or personal record. While the "negative campaign" charge helped shield the Democrat from incoming Coleman missiles, the abortion issue supplied ammunition for a series of devastating Wilder counterattacks. When the Coleman camp—armed with support from the Fraternal Order of Police (FOP), which had endorsed Wilder four years earlier—launched a mid-September blitz focusing on Wilder's past opposition to capital punishment, the Democratic camp responded with advertisements assailing Coleman's abortion stance. And, when Coleman's handlers a month later launched the expected barrage focusing on Wilder's ethical lapses, the Democrat's handlers fired off another round of abortion ads. The highly effective Wilder missives were targeted to the youthful, GOP-leaning, libertarian audience in the suburbs. Against a backdrop of the American flag and Jefferson's Monticello, they stressed "keep[ing] the politicians out of your personal life," and warned

---

27. Sabato, *Virginia Votes 1987–1990*, p. 96.
28. *Roe v. Wade*, 410 U.S. 113 (1973).

that Coleman would "take us back" to the days of back-alley abortions when the procedure was illegal. Having cultivated pro-life backing in the nomination campaign by pledging opposition to abortion even in cases involving rape and incest—a commitment also made by Trible and Parris—Coleman now watched as his controversial position was plastered over the airwaves with devastating effect. Wilder, meanwhile, avoided being portrayed as an abortion-on-demand liberal by reiterating support for some abortion restrictions, including requiring parental notification whenever minors had abortions. The Wilder team's libertarian spin on the abortion issue resembled the line of attack used in the unprecedented national media campaign against Supreme Court nominee Robert Bork two years earlier—indeed, some Wilder advisers actually were veterans of that battle[29]—and it would become a mainstay of Democratic campaigns in the aftermath of Wilder's win.

In what would become the most frequently second-guessed tactical decision of the fall campaign, Coleman's handlers responded to Wilder's September media blitz on abortion, not with an abortion-related rejoinder, but with further attacks on the Democratic nominee's criminal justice record. Wilder had raised abortion as an issue in order to stem the erosion in his support resulting from the GOP's sharp attacks on his death penalty stance, and Republicans were loathe to let him change the subject before they pressed the point home. Reading the polls, the Coleman team concluded that abortion would be distinctly inhospitable—and expensive—ground on which to join an electronic battle with Wilder. Rather, they would keep the heat on the Democrat with attacks on his criminal justice record, including a controversial Wilder-patroned bill that would have subjected young rape victims to courtroom interrogation about their past sexual conduct; then, in the campaign's closing weeks, they would zero in on the so-called character issues on which Wilder was deemed most vulnerable. The Republicans would simply duck and let the abortion wave pass over, convinced that voters would tire of the issue and focus on other concerns by the time the November election rolled around.

Wilder's handlers thought they knew better—or at least they hoped so. They realized the abortion issue had moved front-and-center in people's minds after *Webster*, that it had produced a seismic shift in the political landscape, and that it had opened a chasm between elements of the moderate-

---

29. Michael Donilon and David Petts, who were polling and strategy consultants for the Wilder campaign, provided polling services to the anti-Bork coalition in 1987. They crafted a strategy for turning Southern senators against Bork's confirmation by emphasizing race relations and privacy rights.

conservative coalition on which Republicans relied. While some commentators doubted the staying power of the issue and thought its political power
for Wilder had been spent by October, events on the national stage con-
spired to keep abortion in the headlines all fall.[30] To an electorate increasingly disgusted with negative campaigning, Coleman's eventual blasts on
Wilder's ethics seemed not only shrill but impertinent and probably untrue,
while the Democrat's no-less-persistent but more artful pounding on abortion fit nicely with the national political focus on that evocative topic.
Months after the election, it would become "quite clear," according to a
prominent journalist who covered the campaign, that abortion had been
"debated to the exclusion of other important campaign issues."[31] But that
was all good news for Wilder. Locked in a close struggle as the election
approached, he now had arrived safely at the brink of "history," his single-
issue campaign on abortion having completed his capture of national news
media attention. Indeed, the abortion issue resonated well with Wilder's
racial theme and his campaign's past-versus-future imagery. The Democratic rallying cry, "Don't let Marshall Coleman take us back," was not tied
explicitly to race, but a reference to Virginia's segregationist past was clearly
implied. "You were saying it, but you weren't saying it," chortled J. T.
Shropshire, the Wilder intimate who later became his chief of staff.[32]

   The Coleman campaign had gone the extra mile, with success, to prevent a repeat of the 1985 debacle when Mills Godwin had obliviously
ignited a media frenzy by recalling Wilder's efforts to repeal the state song,
thereby making what many construed as a subtle racial appeal. The Republican candidate and his advisers well understood the Wilder strategy and its
power by this time, and they wanted to give the Democrats no opportunity
to cast the GOP again as a bunch of backward-thinking bigots. Coleman
and his aides thus watched in acute frustration in the 1989 contest's closing
weeks as a blizzard of race-focused news articles seemed to romanticize Wilder's impending "history-making" achievement while glossing over serious
questions raised by Coleman and others about the Democrat's record and
credibility. Coleman found especially galling the *Washington Post*'s treatment
on November 2 of revelations, confirmed in a tape recording disclosed by
the National Right to Work Committee, that Wilder had secretly promised
striking coal miners in southwest Virginia that he would assist efforts to
weaken the state's venerated Right to Work Law. Though Coleman's tele-

---

30. See, e.g., Margie Fisher, "Abortion Debate Fizzles," *Roanoke Times & World-News*, October 1, 1989.
   31. Jeff E. Schapiro, "Story Details Historic Contest for Governor," *Richmond Times-Dispatch,* June 10, 1990.
   32. Edds, *Claiming the Dream*, p. 125.

vision advertisements had indicted Wilder's trustworthiness, the Right to Work Committee's tape seemed to provide dramatic independent corroboration of the GOP's charge, and newspapers around the state gave the story devastating (for Wilder) front-page play. "Yet the *Post*," recounted Larry Sabato,

> buried the [tape] story on page A37, choosing to showcase on page A1 a positive Wilder piece and a very accusatory commentary about one of Coleman's "negative" phone bank operations—an article that even now appears to the lay reader to be utterly devoid of significant hard news.[33]

In a November 2 news conference, Coleman lashed out at the *Post*, and at the alleged news media bias generally, charging that reporters were applying a "double standard" to the gubernatorial candidates.

It was, according to author Margaret Edds, the Republican's most "controversial performance" of the campaign.[34] Coleman had in mind several reasons for the alleged bias, with the two most salient and emotive issues of the campaign—race and abortion[35]—obviously high on the list; but he refrained from explicitly identifying any particular motive for the perceived unfairness. News accounts in the wake of the Coleman allegation varied sharply. The *Washington Post*, apparently chastened by the criticism, juggled the reporters it had assigned to cover the campaign, with the result that its coverage during the final days of the contest became noticeably less hostile in tone to Coleman. The Norfolk-based *Virginian-Pilot*, however, blistered the GOP candidate in a front-page story that depicted his "double standard" remark as a flagrant appeal to racial resentment among whites;[36] the newspaper followed up two days later in its Sunday edition with another page-one article reporting that a desperate Coleman had "played the explosive wild card in his deck: the color of his opponent's skin."[37] By contrast, the *Richmond Times-Dispatch*'s report on Coleman's news conference and bias charge did not even hint at the possibility that the candidate had intended a racial appeal.

---

33. Sabato, *Virginia Votes 1987–1990*, pp. 94–95.

34. Edds, *Claiming the Dream*, p. 224.

35. Coleman campaign officials attributed pro-Wilder bias in in-state news coverage partly to the pro-choice sentiments of most reporters on the high-profile abortion issue. A similar view was expressed by Larry Sabato, whose analysis of the gubernatorial contest highlighted the "clear pro-choice tilt" of the news media. See Sabato, *Virginia Votes 1987–1990*, p. 92.

36. Bill Byrd, "Coleman Blasts Racial 'Double Standard,'" *Virginian-Pilot*, November 3, 1989.

37. Warren Fiske, "Wilder Looks Unscathed as Smoke Clears," *Virginian-Pilot & Ledger-Star*, November 5, 1989.

The divergent treatment of Coleman's eleventh-hour news conference demonstrated the volatility of race in the campaign and the sensitivity of the news media to allegations of bias, racial or otherwise. To the extent that Coleman was referring to a racial double standard, his focus was the positive publicity accorded Wilder because of the history-making nature of his candidacy and campaign—publicity that tended to overshadow questions about the Democratic nominee's ethics. "I for one am not going to stand by and watch a person who is unfit . . . glide into office with a 'feel good, make history' message," Coleman had bitterly declared to the assembled reporters.[38] An angry and aggrieved Wilder, who judged himself to be the "most ventilated candidate in Virginia history," heeded his advisers' advice and resisted the temptation to respond.[39] But his press secretary, Laura Dillard, saw an opening and unreservedly seized it. "[Coleman] is bumping up against a [racial] line that we in the Wilder campaign have assiduously avoided," she protested.[40] "If tapping racial sentiment was [Coleman's] intent, he had done so in a sophisticated, New South way," commented Margaret Edds, whose account suggested that Coleman's "double-standard" charge may have been designed to capitalize on white resentment of affirmative action programs.[41] Yet, even the even-handed Edds seemed to miss the plain point of Coleman's news conference; a few days after the GOP candidate's protest, her *Virginian-Pilot* report began: "Forty-eight hours away from a possible rendezvous with history, Democrat L. Douglas Wilder. . . ."[42]

For a while on election night and even thereafter, it appeared Wilder might not make that heralded rendezvous. Despite pre-election and exit polls suggesting a relatively comfortable glide into the governorship—and history—for the Democrat, Wilder's totals in the actual election returns fell well short of what the pollsters had predicted. The evening turned into one of the great nail-biters in Virginia political history, and it was weeks later after a recount before Wilder's win—by 6,741 votes out of nearly 1.8 million cast—was finally confirmed.[43] Political analysts, operatives, and commentators were then left to assess what had caused the unexpectedly close vote. Was there latent racism in the Virginia electorate after all, a bias suppressed throughout the campaign but revealing itself finally in Wilder's

---

38. Text of remarks on file with the author.
39. Edds, *Claiming the Dream*, p. 254.
40. *Virginian-Pilot*, November 3, 1989.
41. Edds, *Claiming the Dream*, p. 225.
42. *Virginian-Pilot*, November 6, 1989.
43. The vote totals were: Wilder (D)—896,936 (50.1 percent); Coleman (R)—890,195 (49.8 percent). Sabato, *Virginia Votes 1987–1990*, p. 66.

depressed totals on election day? Or, had the appeal to "making history" become so pervasive that some poll respondents had given surveyors the only socially acceptable response, and then cast an unbiased vote on the candidates' merits in the privacy of the polling place? Both explanations were plausible, and the truth presumably lay somewhere in between.

Wilder's thin victory was built in Northern Virginia and in Hampton Roads, where he ran up large margins that offset his losses in much of the rest of the state. He carried just twenty-two counties and twenty-two cities; Coleman prevailed in the other seventy-three counties and nineteen cities. Turnout was relatively high all over the state, but African-American voters went to the polls in record numbers, and it made the difference for Wilder. He rolled up nearly 69 percent of the urban vote, and the urban turnout increased more compared to previous elections than did the voting rate in the suburbs. Also important was the Democrat's strong showing among females, younger voters, and those with the highest level of education. Wilder prevailed among the richest and poorest voters; the middle went to Coleman. The voting patterns differed markedly from other Virginia gubernatorial elections, a reflection of the impact of the contest's two hot-button issues, race and abortion, which cut across the electorate's traditional liberal-conservative lines.[44] While Wilder's landmark candidacy drove record numbers of Virginians to the polls—some to vote for him and others to stop him—Coleman's losing effort also accomplished a significant feat: his organizationally proficient campaign identified 520,000 supportive voters, made follow-up contact with 200,000 of those deemed undecided or favorable to his candidacy, and boosted the GOP vote total toward the million-vote mark, easily dwarfing all previous vote performances by a Republican candidate for governor.[45] Coleman's large margins in normally Democratic rural areas were especially impressive—a breakthrough that subsequent GOP statewide contenders would exploit in their winning bids in the 1990s. The two candidates also broke all previous fundraising records for a Virginia gubernatorial campaign; of the total spent ($16 million), Coleman had an edge, but he had spent much of it winning the GOP primary, and the two candidates were evenly funded in the fall.

The 1989 governor's race was the election of superlatives in Virginia— the one that attracted the most national attention; the one with the biggest vote totals and thinnest margin of victory; the most expensive; the most

---

44. Sabato, *Virginia Votes 1987–1990*, pp. 65–88.

45. The Coleman campaign's organizational efforts were spearheaded by veteran GOP organizer Michael E. Thomas of Chesterfield, who would go on to play key leadership roles in future successful Republican statewide campaigns.

hard fought and negative; and, of course, the most groundbreaking and historic—so it was unsurprising that the simultaneous races for lieutenant governor, attorney general, and the House of Delegates received scant attention. In the race for lieutenant governor, Democratic nominee Donald S. Beyer Jr., an urbane Volvo dealer from suburban Northern Virginia who had contributed generously to Democratic candidates, made his political debut against the heir to the Dalton name and legacy, recently elected state Senator Edwina P. ("Eddy") Dalton of Henrico County. Beyer touted his business experience and used his family's considerable resources to pummel Dalton over the airwaves on abortion and her lack of business or governmental experience. Dalton could not match the Democrat's campaign spending, nor could she offset the sizeable vote advantage he amassed in Democratic strongholds and in his native Northern Virginia.[46] The other female statewide candidate fared much better. In her reelection bid, Attorney General Mary Sue Terry polled more than a million votes and carried every congressional district and all but a handful of counties and cities in trouncing the GOP's Joseph B. Benedetti, an affable state senator from the city of Richmond.[47] The evening's only positive news for Republicans came in the House of Delegates contests, where the GOP achieved the net addition of four delegates and reached a century-high total of thirty-nine seats in the 100-member body.[48]

Though news organizations and reporters are frequent targets of criticism by dissatisfied political partisans, journalistic objectivity became a serious issue in the wake of the 1989 Virginia elections. The *Washington Post* received the lion's share of the attention—and unsurprisingly so, since its own ombudsman, Richard Harwood, joined in the criticism. Harwood recited a string of actions by the *Post*'s news department that were, in his considered judgment, "enough to raise non-paranoid questions about the disinterested nature of the coverage."[49] Professor Sabato agreed, observing in his post-election analysis that the *Post* was among those who could take "credit (or blame, depending on one's viewpoint) for Coleman's defeat" in

---

46. The vote totals in the contest for lieutenant governor were: Beyer (D)—934,377 (54.1 percent); Dalton (R)—791,360 (45.8 percent). Sabato, *Virginia Votes 1987–1990*, p. 66.

47. The vote totals in the race for attorney general were: Terry (D)—1,096,095 (63.2 percent); Benedetti (R)—638,124 (36.8 percent). Sabato, *Virginia Votes 1987–1990*, p. 66.

48. Sabato, *Virginia Votes 1987–1990*, p. 75. Republicans polled nearly half—49.3 percent—of all legislative votes cast statewide. In the legislative races contested by both major parties, GOP candidates received 44.8 percent of the vote.

49. Richard Harwood, "Tilt! Tilt!" *Washington Post,* November 19, 1989.

the close contest.[50] To the Republicans, though, the most egregious reflection of the *Post*'s bias was not the newspaper's reporting but its polling. Four years earlier its October surveys had shown Democrats Baliles and Wilder sporting twenty-percentage-point leads that did not materialize when the actual ballots were cast on election day. The wildly errant surveys had sapped GOP activists of their motivation and, according to Dwayne Yancey, supplied "a powerful cue [for] Northern Virginia voters, who may have had no real feel for how ridiculous [the inflated poll numbers] seemed downstate."[51] Four years later, Republicans assured themselves that it could not happen again; after all, the *Post* had its reputation to protect, and the newspaper hardly had enhanced its credibility in the polling trade by forecasting a 1985 Wilder margin that was overstated by a factor of six. But on Sunday, October 29, 1989, Northern Virginians awakened to survey results that showed Wilder with an insurmountable fifteen-point lead little more than a week before the election. Though the *Post*'s survey was skeptically received by political and journalistic insiders—no other poll showed anything close to that kind of Wilder lead—the tone of news coverage around the state nevertheless changed perceptibly in the wake of its release. After that, wrote Sabato, "[v]irtually no story on Coleman was written without the obligatory, deflating qualifier, 'trailing badly in the latest *Post* poll,' with much of the prose that followed suggesting desperation and impending doom."[52]

The misleading survey results published by the *Washington Post* in 1989, like those four years earlier, discouraged the GOP's volunteer organization and depressed turnout by Coleman supporters on election day. The impact, though not objectively verifiable, may well have exceeded Wilder's paper-thin statewide margin of victory. In Fairfax County alone, Wilder trounced Coleman by 27,000 votes, a figure nearly four times the Democrat's cumulative statewide advantage. There were, of course, multiple explanations for the avalanche of Wilder votes in pivotal Northern Virginia. Among them were Coleman's failure to capture the potent transportation and tax issues in the region, the GOP candidate's anti-abortion stance, fallout from "negative" Republican media advertising, large financial contri-

50. Sabato, *Virginia Votes 1987–1990,* p. 94.
51. Yancey, *When Hell Froze Over,* p. 297. In the 1985 voting, Baliles outpolled Durrette by 10 percent, and Wilder's winning margin was less than 4 percent.
52. Sabato, *Virginia Votes 1987–1990,* p. 99. Though sharply critical of the newspaper's slanted news coverage, Sabato suggested that flawed methodology rather than pro-Democratic bias was primarily responsible for the wayward *Post* polls in 1985 and 1989. See Sabato, *Virginia Votes 1987–1990,* pp. 97–99; Sabato, *Virginia Votes 1983–1986,* pp. 93–97.

butions to the GOP campaign by developers who then became targets in Wilder television ads, and the enthralling appeal of the Democrat's history-making, guilt-purging candidacy. But Republican strategists came away from the 1989 campaign convinced that their most formidable institutional obstacle in the politically powerful region was not the Democratic Party, but the region's heavyweight newspaper. With television advertising exceedingly expensive in the Washington area, the widely read *Post* possessed unusual influence over the flow of campaign information. The experiences of the 1980s suggested to Republicans that whenever the *Post* failed to restrain its "liberal intellectual predisposition," as ombudsman Richard Harwood bluntly termed it,[53] GOP statewide candidates would have great difficulty getting their message across in the region.

The Democratic and Republican campaigns both had complaints with particular journalists covering the intense battle, just as reporters had grievances of their own with campaign operatives who endeavored to "spin" them with dubious contentions and partial truths. Who got the better of it in 1989, as in the other campaigns during the 1980s, is ultimately in the eye of the beholder, and political beholders are rarely objective. The larger political truths of the 1980s, however, were to be seen not in isolated or occasional events, but in the sweeping trends and recurring themes. Once in power, Democrats benefited throughout the decade from a prosperous national and state economy and their steady stewardship of state government. Virginia voters seized opportunities in the 1980s to make a symbolic statement about racial fairness; unfairness to particular candidates was an unfortunate by-product of that exercise, but at least it arose out of the most laudable of intentions. By decade's end, controversial social issues—most notably abortion—produced cross-cutting coalitions that reinforced the contemporary tendency toward partisan de-alignment. And, from Reagan to Wilder, personality remained an intangible but often compelling force on the political landscape.

The varied facets of Douglas Wilder's intriguing personality would be in full flower during his rocky governorship, but on January 13, 1990, it was Wilder the magnanimous winner, Wilder the transcendent statesman, Wilder the enduring symbol of America's opportunity society and Virginia's racial redemption, that stood before a record crowd in Virginia's historic Capitol Square to become the Commonwealth's 66th governor. Proudly proclaiming himself a "son of Virginia," Wilder outlined few initiatives or policy goals; the moment itself was accomplishment enough.[54] From the soil

---

53. *Washington Post*, November 19, 1989.
54. *Richmond Times-Dispatch*, January 14, 1990.

in which both American liberty and American slavery were first planted nearly four centuries earlier at Jamestown, a political life had sprung, the issue of enslaved Virginians and a survivor of state-imposed segregation, yet nurtured by the Old Dominion's otherwise wholesome cultural and political traditions and validated ultimately by its fair-minded people. The usual fare of politics—issues, qualifications, voting records, tactics, methods and details of every kind—could be set to the side this day. Virginians had bestowed their highest elective honor on a grandson of slaves, and the rest of the nation, having never elected any African-American citizen as governor, could only watch in wonder. As Supreme Court Justice Lewis F. Powell Jr. administered the oath of office and proclaimed it a "great day for Virginia,"[55] the stately Capitol envisioned by Thomas Jefferson provided a compelling backdrop and seemed to say, "My designer's egalitarian promise finally has been fulfilled."

Four years later, when Wilder's gubernatorial portrait was hung on the third-floor balcony of the Capitol's rotunda where likenesses of the sixteen most recent Virginia governors reside, Wilder's portrait would be the newest and Governor Harry F. Byrd's would be the oldest on display. The chief executives from Byrd to Wilder had been witness to and participants in a period of profound social, cultural, and economic change. While the nation trudged through turbulent times from Roosevelt to Reagan, Virginia had been at work reconciling its conservative governmental traditions and cultural values with new realities: the transformation of the Old Dominion's once-rural economy and society, the emergence of the federal leviathan and modern social welfare state, the rise of the Cold War defense establishment, the political ascendancy of suburbia, and the advent of competitive two-party politics. If the question of race seemed to highlight the long distance traveled between the two historic Virginia figures, the issue of fiscal policy showed that the Commonwealth had not strayed all that far on the Byrd-to-Wilder odyssey.

Faced upon taking office with an acute economic downturn that soon produced a billion-dollar-plus budget shortfall, Wilder proceeded to accomplish what few other governors in the recession-plagued America of the early 1990s were able: he balanced the budget by cutting spending rather than raising taxes. And, to prevent the budgetary calamity from repeating itself, he convinced the legislature and then Virginia voters to take out an insurance policy, successfully promoting a pay-as-you-go plan that set aside a share of surplus dollars each year in a new constitutionally protected "rainy day" fund. The fiscally conservative moves had political bene-

---

55. *Washington Post*, January 14, 1990.

fits for Wilder, just as Harry Byrd's tight-fisted ways served his purposes during a half-century-long political career. "[M]any state lawmakers and other Wilder watchers say the dark financial clouds have a silver political lining for the incoming governor," wrote veteran reporter Bill Byrd. Noting that Wilder had "spent much of his career as a liberal," the journalist Byrd observed, "Tight money will let Wilder wear the time-honored mantle of fiscal conservative, further enhancing his stature as a mainstream politician."[56] Wilder seemed to relish his role as cutter-in-chief. The economic hard times made it "the perfect time to be governor," he told one interviewer. "You can take the scalpel out and cut where you need to cut. Ignore the pain. People will grumble and gripe, but they know it has to be done. So then, when the economy turns around, that unneeded fat is gone forever."[57] "The state budget shortfall . . . precluded the possibility of an achievement or activist [Wilder] administration," wrote political analyst Thomas Morris in 1992, but it "allowed Wilder to define himself politically as different from his progressive predecessor and the Republican president, both of whom reneged on pledges of no new taxes."[58]

Writing at the conclusion of Wilder's tenure four years later, *Virginian-Pilot* reporter Warren Fiske wrote, "If Doug Wilder hadn't been so confrontational, he might be spending his final weeks as governor enjoying the praise Virginians traditionally reserve for fiscal conservatives instead of the barbs that go with being the most unpopular chief executive in memory." But then, Fiske added, "[I]f Doug Wilder hadn't been so confrontational, he never would have been governor."[59] The astute reporter seemed to sum up the whole story of the Wilder governorship in a single statement. The afterglow of Wilder's election victory, the magical moments of the inauguration, and the traditional gubernatorial honeymoon were quickly past, and the feisty politician was soon immersed in the often-mundane task of governing. Confrontations and pitfalls followed in rapid succession: the full effects of the unprecedented budget crisis, for which Wilder unabashedly blamed his predecessor Gerald Baliles; seemingly petty score-settling at the expense of Robb and Baliles partisans; unflattering news stories about Wilder's refusal to disclose the disposition of excess inaugural funds; a dust-up with powerful state Senator Hunter B. Andrews; and frequent out-of-state travels trumpeting his political success in the conservative Old Dominion

56. *Virginian-Pilot*, January 7, 1990. Bill Byrd, a longtime political reporter for the Norfolk-based newspaper, was not related to the political Byrd family.
57. "Interview with L. Douglas Wilder," *Playboy*, September 1991, quoted in Morris, "Virginia: L. Douglas Wilder, Governing and Campaigning," p. 197.
58. Morris, "Virginia: L. Douglas Wilder, Governing and Campaigning," p. 201.
59. Edds and Morris, pp. 142–143.

and prompting speculation that the new governor was already running for national office. Wilder's in-state political standing was damaged further by his opposition to the Persian Gulf War effort in December 1990, and by his endorsement of federal civil rights legislation that President George H. W. Bush charged would result in racial hiring quotas. But it was the specter of Wilder's self-serving political travel during a time of economic travail that swiftly drove a wedge between him and the previously supportive Virginia electorate. With a 32 percent approval rating after only eighteen months in office, Wilder had earned the unfortunate distinction of being one of the least popular Virginia governors since Lord Dunmore fled to England in 1775.[60] And the numbers would only get worse.

Two political appointments by the new governor were especially noteworthy. Upon taking office, Wilder tapped Paul Goldman to be the new state Democratic Party chief, a move that installed an experienced strategist but also ensured a renewed round of sparring with Charles Robb. One political reporter who later joined Robb's Senate staff derided Goldman as "the first vegetarian, the first political campaign consultant, the first New Yorker, and the first unregistered Virginia voter to hold the party's top spot, at least in this century."[61] The reporter, Steven D. Johnson of the *Charlottesville Daily Progress*, wrote that when Goldman called Robb to report his impending elevation, the senator bluntly observed that "Goldman hardly was an appropriate symbol for the party and that, while he had many sterling qualities, being chairman was not one of them."[62] Meanwhile, the new governor gave Mark Warner—the Alexandria businessman and politico whose mid-stream addition to the candidate's team had been "widely credited with turning around Wilder's floundering campaign for governor"[63]—a comparatively safe, resumé-enhancing assignment as a member of the prestigious Commonwealth Transportation Board. Warner was able to ride out the political storms of the next twenty-four months in that role before being tapped in 1993 to help mend the party as chairman.

Egged on by Goldman, Wilder was convinced that his mainstream message of fiscal conservatism combined with the racial barrier-breaking character of his candidacy could carry him not just to the Virginia Executive Mansion but to the White House.[64] He thus moved inexorably—and, he

---

60. *Virginian-Pilot* & *Ledger-Star*, June 18, 1991.
61. *Daily Progress*, January 28, 1990.
62. *Daily Progress*, January 28, 1990.
63. *Richmond Times-Dispatch*, April 7, 1990.
64. The pivotal role of Virginia Democratic Party chairman Paul Goldman in Wilder's decision to run for president was highlighted by *Washington Post* reporter Donald Baker in a March 1991 report on the formation of Wilder's presidential exploratory committee. "If Doug Wilder is elected president or vice president, many [in Richmond]

would concede later, mistakenly—toward a presidential candidacy during 1990 and 1991. The dual duties of managing a troubled state and launching a history-making presidential bid soon proved overwhelming. In August 1990, Wilder delivered the bad news that Virginia's two-year budget shortfall would reach $1.2 billion; he reiterated his opposition to new taxes and declared the need "to determine what are the necessities and what are the niceties that we . . . can do without."[65] The message was reasonably well received, but his method of delivering the news—via a television address during a brief break in a six-state speaking tour—was less so. "Wilder's apparent preoccupation with national politics was dramatized," wrote Jeff Schapiro, "when, in defending his planned TV speech, he said he had a responsibility to 'be candid with the American people.' Catching himself as the room erupted in laughter, Wilder said, 'uh, the people of Virginia.' "[66]

The fiscal crisis at home continued to deepen during the remainder of 1990 and most of 1991 (the deficit ballooned to $2.1 billion), but still Wilder kept adding to his frequent-flyer miles and moving toward a presidential run. While the governor received increasingly unflattering press back home, he encountered the opposite as he stumped around the country. Commentators as diverse as conservative Paul Gigot of the *Wall Street Journal* and liberal Mary McGrory of the *Washington Post* seemed fascinated with the Wilder phenomenon and sang his praises.[67] It was all too much for Virginia Commonwealth University political scientist and commentator Robert Holsworth. "The national press has acted irresponsibly—there's no other way to describe it," complained Holsworth. "They've promoted him as a national candidate with almost no regard for his record back home."[68] Pollster Brad Coker weighed in with evidence of a similar reaction on the part of the voting public; his December 1990 survey found that, if the election were held then, incumbent President Bush would trounce sitting Governor Wilder in his home state by twenty percentage points.[69]

Though Wilder's national moves angered Virginians, Republicans around the country were impressed with his stand against higher taxes, and leading Democrats were delighted—"jubilant" is how the *Philadelphia*

---

think he will have Paul Goldman to thank," wrote Baker. "If Wilder falters, he could have Goldman's risky strategy to blame." *Washington Post*, March 29, 1991.

65. *Richmond Times-Dispatch,* August 2, 1990.

66. *Richmond Times-Dispatch,* August 2, 1990.

67. *Wall Street Journal,* March 24, 1990; *Washington Post,* April 12, 1990.

68. *Richmond Times-Dispatch*, August 5, 1990.

69. *Virginian-Pilot,* December 19, 1990. The survey was conducted by Mason-Dixon Opinion Research, Inc., of Columbia, Maryland. Ten months later, another survey by the same polling organization found Wilder trailing Bush in the state by the astounding margin of 72 percent to 14 percent. *Virginian-Pilot,* September 18, 1991.

*Inquirer* described them[70]—to have a moderate new black leader on the scene as an antidote to liberal, two-time presidential candidate Jesse Jackson. Mary McGrory explained:

> To Democrats, Wilder represents the hope that they may one day soon escape from the Jacksonian bondage. Wilder, a no-sweat, no-threat black politician, is no match for Jackson in oratory. Jackson is a volcano of words and passion, spewing forth fiery challenges about rivers of justice, rainbows of mercy, and his unappreciated efforts to "keep hope alive" in the country. Jackson, a towering, lowering presence, fills many Democrats with apprehension. In two presidential campaigns he has proved implacable. Wilder, of medium height, with silky white hair and amiable mien, they find infinitely reassuring. He is the grandson of a slave. It is not a point that needs belaboring. He has only to mention it to show his rise is just as dramatic as Jackson's assent from South Carolina squalor. . . . [Wilder] does not presume to speak for black people. He presents himself as a success story who happens to be black. The sense of grievance that Jackson presents is absent.[71]

In his speeches around the country, Wilder proclaimed a "New Mainstream" of racially progressive, fiscally conservative, politically practical stewardship accountable to and in tune with the broad American middle class. His targets were clear, and it was not long before Jackson and other liberal black leaders responded to his challenge. "For those who are not in the mainstream," Jackson asked derisively at an assemblage of African-American mayors, "does that mean backwater? Does that mean cesspool? We want justice to roll down like a mighty stream, not a narrow mainstream."[72] Having once disparaged the Democratic Leadership Council (DLC) and its efforts to move the party toward the political center, Wilder was fast becoming the chief purveyor of its centrist message and winning new friends, foes, and a lot of national attention because of it.

"It must gall [Senator Charles] Robb," wrote the *Times-Dispatch*'s Schapiro, "that Wilder . . . seems to be getting all the credit for the moderate message that the Governor-turned-Senator has been peddling for nearly six years—and that Wilder once gleefully demeaned."[73] It was not just the moderate message Wilder appeared to have purloined; it was the mantle of

---

70. S.A. Paolantonio, "Iowa Crowns Democrats' Newest Star," *Philadelphia Inquirer*, June 25, 1990; see also Robert Shogan, "Wilder's Political Travels Stir Talk of '92 Ambitions," *Los Angeles Times*, June 25, 1990.
71. Mary McGrory, "Wilder's Way of Winning," *Washington Post*, April 12, 1990.
72. John Dillin, "Jackson, Wilder Vie for Turf as Top Black Leader," *Christian Science Monitor*, April 13, 1990.
73. *Richmond Times-Dispatch*, April 22, 1990.

Virginia-Democrat-Running-for-President. As the 1990s opened, Robb's apparent presidential ambitions seemed intact and attainable. Appearing at the state party's annual Jefferson-Jackson Day dinner in February 1990, the Democrats' highest profile national figure, Senate Majority Leader George J. Mitchell of Maine, flatly declared, "Chuck Robb ought to be on the next ticket of the Democratic Party."[74] Within months, however, any hope for a Robb presidential bid had been dashed, not because of the Wilder rivalry (at least, not chiefly so), but because of Robb's own prior misconduct and ongoing attempts to contain its disclosure.

Rumors about Robb's activities on the Virginia Beach party scene while governor had been circulating for several years, and, beginning in 1988, reports on the subject had appeared in numerous newspapers. But in 1991, a soap opera–like succession of scandalous revelations engulfed the senator, shifting his focus from possible inauguration to potential indictment. The year's salty surprises were succinctly recapped by the University of Virginia's Sabato, a vocal Robb critic:

> Robb's serious past indiscretions began to catch up with him in 1991 as television shows, books, and newspaper and magazine reports began to focus on his attendance while governor (the state's chief law enforcement officer) at dozens of Virginia Beach parties where cocaine was openly displayed and used. Attention was also given to sexual encounters Robb had with women other than his wife as well as the senator's and his staff's efforts to intimidate some of those who were willing to come forward to tell the truth about Robb. The senator compounded his difficulties with an inept damage-control operation that resulted in the public disclosure of still more specific allegations about Robb's behavior. Finally, Robb admitted that he had kept for two and a half years an illegally recorded cellular telephone conversation of then-Lieutenant Governor Wilder during which Wilder had told a financial supporter that Robb was "finished" politically. Upon being questioned by a reporter for the first time about the tape, Wilder erupted in fury, and the entire nation was soon treated to a tit-for-tat brawl between Robb and Wilder more appropriate to the free-wheeling precincts of Texas or Louisiana than of staid Virginia. The resignations of Robb's top staff, a brief Wilder-inspired state police investigation, and lengthy grand jury proceedings . . . followed the tape's disclosure. A further humiliation for Robb was a *Playboy* cover article and pictorial on former beauty queen Tai Collins, a special friend who Robb agreed gave the fully nude governor a "massage" in a New York luxury hotel in 1984.[75]

74. *Richmond Times-Dispatch*, February 11, 1990.

75. Larry J. Sabato, *Virginia Votes 1991–1994* (Charlottesville: Weldon Cooper Center for Public Service, 1996), p. 17; see also Larry J. Sabato, *Feeding Frenzy*, 2nd edition (New York: The Free Press, 1993), pp. 110–111, 193–195, 290–295. The wave of disclosures regarding Robb was triggered in part by publication of controversial findings and allegations by Billy Franklin, a Virginia Beach private investigator hired by Rich-

Robb forcefully denied awareness of the cocaine usage at parties he attended, but he eventually conceded to "peccadilloes" and conduct "not appropriate for a married man," and his apparent presidential aspirations were, as Wilder had said, "finished."[76] Although three Robb aides pled guilty to criminal offenses related to their handling of the illegal telephone conversation recording, a prolonged federal grand jury investigation of Robb's own actions in the matter concluded in early 1993 without an indictment, leaving the severely wounded senator to linger in office for what most assumed would be just the two remaining years of his term.[77]

Having occupied national attention with Wilder's landmark gubernatorial win, Virginia politics was again center stage in 1991 and 1992 as national news organizations rushed to cover the Robb scandals and the ensuing pitched battle between the two Virginia Democratic titans. Aggrieved and angry over the surveillance and Robb's denials of culpability in it, Wilder lashed out unsparingly at the senator and his allies. With Robb already fatally debilitated, however, the renewed sparring between the two politicians served mainly to damage Wilder, who still was pursuing the presidency and who, because of numerous past quarrels, was vulnerable to portrayal as an incorrigible pugilist who was willfully perpetuating the pair's long-running "feud." An indication of the controversies' devastating political effects on Virginia Democrats came in November 1991, when voters went to the polls in state legislative elections. A strong "Republican tide" was running; the surge swept away more than a half-dozen Democratic incumbents and nearly brought in a GOP majority in the state Senate.[78] Republicans even increased their strength in the House of Delegates despite the effects of aggressively partisan redistricting by the Democratic majority.[79]

---

mond-area Republican Lewis Williams and other GOP activists several years earlier to look into persistent and sometimes sensational rumors regarding Robb's activities. See Billy Franklin and Judy Tull, *Tough Enough: The Cocaine Investigation of United States Senator Chuck Robb* (Virginia Beach, VA: Broad Bay Publishing Co, Inc., 1991).

76. *Virginian-Pilot & Ledger-Star,* March 11, 1994.

77. Robb twice appeared before a federal grand jury in Norfolk investigating the matter, the second time forgoing a planned twenty-fifth wedding anniversary trip to Bermuda in December 1992 in a last-ditch—and apparently successful—effort to avoid indictment. *Washington Post,* December 18, 1992.

78. Sabato, *Virginia Votes 1991–1994,* pp. 3–16. For the first time in the twentieth century, Republican candidates outpolled Democratic candidates statewide in the two-party contested legislative races. The GOP increased its representation in the forty-member state Senate from ten to eighteen seats, and narrowly missed capturing three additional seats, and thus a majority, in the upper chamber.

79. The net change in the House of Delegates was a one-seat gain for the GOP, bringing the party's representation to a century-high forty-one seats, but the net effect masked the underlying significance of the Republicans' accomplishment. Pursuing a more partisan redistricting course than their Senate counterparts, House Democrats had

"A bomb went off in Virginia politics Tuesday," reported the *Washington Post* after the election.

> Few Democrats heard the ticking until it was too late, and the explosion of voter discontent left office holders from Governor L. Douglas Wilder on down contemplating a future that suddenly includes the Republican Party as a powerful force in the General Assembly. . . . Politicians and analysts said the fuse was lighted by a combination of general anti-incumbent sentiment among voters and their anger at Wilder and other Democrats.[80]

One event with significant political implications received little attention in the election post mortem assessments focusing on the GOP's sudden legislative gains. Delegate George Allen of Albemarle County was elected to Congress to fill the unexpired term of Seventh District Representative French Slaughter, who stepped down because of illness.[81]

Wilder had formally entered the presidential race in September, "[flinging] himself into the arena for the Presidency with the fury and zest of an unleashed gamecock, feathers flying, bright spurs flashing, crowing, laughing" as Guy Friddell described the scene at the Virginia Capitol.[82] His speech on that occasion had contained the "New Mainstream" themes the governor had been testing around the country for months, but it also had a racial edge that Donald Baker, the *Washington Post* reporter who authored a

---

lumped fourteen Republican incumbents together in new districts, effectively cutting GOP strength by seven seats before the elections began. The Republican tide in November more than offset the party's redistricting-related losses.

80. *Washington Post*, November 7, 1991. Adding to the change was the death in September 1991 of House of Delegates Speaker A.L. Philpott of Henry County, who succumbed to cancer after battling it for twenty of his thirty-four years in the legislature. See Barnie Day, "Remembering A. L. Philpott," in *Notes from the Sausage Factory,* ed, Barnie Day and Becky Dale (Lawrenceville, VA: Brunswick Publishing, 2005), pp. 145–149. An era ended in the state Senate as well, with the retirement of two of the last Byrd stalwarts from Southside, Democratic Senators Elmon Gray and Howard Anderson.

81. The unexpected Republican legislative gains in 1991 contrasted sharply with the strong Democratic performance in the previous year's midterm federal elections, when a budget stalemate in Washington and economic woes helped Democrats gain a majority in the state's congressional delegation for the first time in a quarter century. In the 1990 contests, Eighth District Representative Stanford Parris succumbed to Democrat James P. Moran Jr., the mayor of Alexandria, and First District Congressman Herbert Bateman narrowly survived a strong challenge from Democrat Andrew H. ("Andy") Fox, a former television news reporter. Senator John Warner faced no Democratic opponent—the first time in the twentieth century that Virginia Democrats had foregone the opportunity to nominate a Senate candidate. Warner polled 80.9 percent of the vote in defeating Nancy Spannaus, an independent candidate linked to fringe political figure Lyndon LaRouche. Sabato, *Virginia Votes 1987–1990*, pp. 102–103.

82. *Virginian-Pilot & Ledger-Star*, September 14, 1991.

1989 book on Wilder, found significant. Wilder bashed Bush for "going out of his way to raise the phony and divisive issue of racial quotas in hopes of turning back the clock on civil rights," for "pitting one group against another," and "for deliberately attempting to take us backward."[83] Baker noted that Wilder had downplayed race in his statewide bids in 1985 and 1989 but now was making it a central part of his presidential campaign in an effort to appeal to the liberal Democratic rank and file. As the fall wore on, Wilder stressed racial pride and racial reconciliation as key reasons for his candidacy; he savaged President Bush and even his Democratic rivals for racial insensitivity, at one point comparing the welfare reform position of his rival, Arkansas Governor Bill Clinton, to that of ex-Klansman David Duke of Louisiana.[84] None of it served to attract much support, however, and Wilder was hampered by a political calendar that featured early primaries in states with few African-American voters.[85] The months of unflattering stories from back home—the "feuding" with Robb, the November election setbacks, the loud complaints that the governor was neglecting his duties—all took their toll.

Bowing to the inevitable, Wilder announced his surprise exit from the presidential race during his address to the General Assembly on its opening day in January 1992. The applause triggered by the announcement, Wilder recalled, "was the loudest I ever got" during a speech before the legislature.[86] The governor justified his exit from the presidential sweepstakes by stressing the need to attend to the fiscal and other controversies back home, but the rhetoric could not mask the failure. Wilder's national bid had not succeeded well enough or lasted long enough even to position him for a hoped-for spot on the ticket as the vice presidential nominee.[87]

---

83. *Washington Post*, September 14, 1991.

84. *Daily Progress*, November 17, 1991. Duke, a former state legislator and former grand wizard of the Ku Klux Klan, generated national attention for his extreme views when he ran unsuccessfully for governor of Louisiana in fall 1991.

85. Jack W. Germond and Jules Witcover, *Mad as Hell: Revolt at the Ballot Box,* 1992 (New York: Warner Books, Inc., 1993), p. 108.

86. Wilder interview.

87. According to the authors of one book on the 1992 presidential race, "It was understood by [Wilder's aides]—and, friends said, by Wilder himself—that he was in fact running for the vice-presidential nomination this time around. The plan was a reprise of the long game he had played in Virginia, where he had first put in four years as lieutenant governor and let white people get used to seeing a black man in high state office." Peter Goldman, Thomas M. DeFrank, Mark Miller, Andrew Murr, and Tom Mathews, *Quest for the Presidency* (College Station: Texas A&M University Press, 1994), p. 62. In a 2005 interview, Wilder acknowledged that he "never thought [he] would be the nominee for president." His goal instead was to gain "a national voice" through his presidential candidacy, thereby "putting [him] in a position to be considered for a role in the national administration, in the cabinet or as [the vice presidential] ticket mate." Wilder interview.

"Obviously I was wrong. . . . [Y]ou can't do both things well," Wilder told Donald Baker just before his withdrawal announcement, finally acceding to the widespread wisdom that deemed it folly to run for president as a brand-new governor, especially in a state grappling with a fiscal crisis.[88] It was a rare admission of error by the proud Wilder, but one he would restate freely and frequently thereafter. "People felt I should have had more gratitude for being elected, the first elected African American in the country, and before I could even settle into the job, I [was] talking about running for another job," Wilder observed later.[89] The disastrous effects of his ill-advised presidential bid on his standing with the Virginia electorate would shadow the history-making politician for the remainder of his tenure as governor and long thereafter. The final two years of his gubernatorial term would bring accolades for sound fiscal management and a few legislative wins, including surprising success on a measure to stem illegal handgun trafficking by limiting handgun purchases to one per month. But it would also see continual conflict with Robb and his allies, including the woman who hoped to succeed him as governor, Attorney General Mary Sue Terry.

In May 1992, following a newspaper's disclosure of a year-old strategy memorandum by Robb aide Christine Bridge explicitly outlining ways to sabotage Wilder's presidential candidacy, the livid governor directly blamed his in-state rival's "smear campaign" for the failure of his national bid.[90] Wilder also lashed out at reporters for harming his candidacy by frequently suggesting that he bore equal or greater responsibility for the so-called feud with Robb. John Harris of the *Washington Post* found merit in Wilder's criticism. Reciting a litany of episodes in which Robb had been the aggressor, Harris wrote that "[a]lthough Wilder has made his share of verbal digs and minor protestations, Robb has been responsible for the most dramatic breaks in their relationship."[91] Political analyst Robert Holsworth agreed, concluding that Wilder had gotten "a bad rap at a critical time in his career."[92] The blame game aside, the reality was that both Wilder and Robb—or at least their respective supporters—had their hearts set on commanding center stage nationally at the same time, and that stage was not big enough for both of them. "Virginia is a large state, increasingly populous and wealthy, and often put in the ranks of the nation's dozen or so 'megastates,'" wrote Drummond Ayres of the *New York Times*. "But a case could probably be made that it is not big enough to contain the political personas

88. *Washington Post*, January 10, 1992.
89. Germond and Witcover, *Mad as Hell*, pp. 107–108.
90. *Washington Post*, May 23, 1992.
91. *Washington Post*, May 23, 1992.
92. *Washington Post*, May 23, 1992.

of both Mr. Robb and Mr. Wilder."[93] The high-stakes battle for national preeminence left both politicians mortally wounded; a summer 1992 poll found that only 19 percent of Virginians approved of Robb's performance as senator, surpassing the previous record low approval rating for a Virginia statewide official—23 percent—which Wilder had earned the preceding December.[94]

At the root of the continuing Robb-Wilder contretemps remained those damning missives that Robb had penned to Wilder several years earlier and then released to the news media. In an interview after his Senate tenure ended, Robb rebutted suggestions that conflicting presidential ambitions were at the heart of their conflict, insisting that he, unlike Wilder, never harbored any such ambitions.[95] But, like Wilder, Robb blamed the two politicians' aides and allies for intensifying the conflict.[96] The former senator candidly acknowledged the damaging letters' acute and lasting impact on relations between the two Democratic leaders and their respective supporters. "I never viewed Doug Wilder as a potential rival for national office. . . . I had no intention of ever running for national office, and it never occurred to me [until later] that he would, either," Robb recalled.

> I think a few members of my staff simply did not trust Doug and thought he was out to do me in because of the letters I had written to him in late 1985 and mid-1986. It was a supposed rivalry or feud that I spent a great deal of time, effort and capital trying to eliminate. I was naive in not recognizing the depth of it—both in perception and reality—much sooner. Once [Governor Wilder] decided to get into the presidential race, he knew that something would have to be done to offset or diminish the impact of those unanswered letters. I had been able to pretty well quarantine their use in his [1989] gubernatorial campaign, but they represented a major obstacle to a viable presidential bid, and he knew it. I assumed that [Wilder] and/or his advisers

93. *New York Times,* June 14, 1991.
94. *Richmond Times-Dispatch,* June 12, 1992.
95. Robb had been touted as a potential presidential candidate for more than a decade, with many news articles reporting on his presidential aspirations as if they were a confirmed fact. In 2005, however, Robb averred that he

> never fell into the trap of taking talk about being presidential timber too seriously. I had been close to too many presidents and presidential candidates to underestimate the challenge. And I never felt I had enough reasonably well-thought-through concepts and workable answers to the most pressing national and international challenges to ever seriously consider going down that path. There were qualities and strengths I looked for in presidential candidates that I did not believe I had.

Robb interview.
96. Robb interview; Wilder interview.

thought if they could not get me to recant on the letters, the next best thing was to discredit me.[97]

Robb viewed Wilder, or at least his supporters, as behind-the-scenes purveyors of the scandal-related stories that oozed to the surface as the 1992 presidential campaign approached. Especially after disclosure of the unambiguous anti-Wilder memorandum by a senior Robb aide, Wilder blamed the senator, or at least his supporters, for actively working to torpedo his presidential candidacy. It was a political rivalry of epic proportions, with destructive consequences for both men.

In November 1992, that *other* Southern governor, Bill Clinton, captured the presidency after waging the centrist Democratic campaign that Robb and Wilder had recommended to their party and appeared to covet for themselves.[98] Virginia once again had been ahead of its time; even Robb's personal peccadilloes and strained, word-parsing denials oddly presaged the new president's tarnished tenure.[99] After an active campaign that included a presidential debate at the University of Richmond[100] and numerous visits to the state by Bush administration luminaries, the Bush-Quayle ticket prevailed in the surprisingly competitive Old Dominion, continuing the state GOP's post–1964 winning streak in presidential elections. But elsewhere, the country's stagnant economy—and resentment over a Bush-backed federal tax increase that belied his adamant no-tax-hike campaign pledge in 1988—obscured the Republican administration's notable foreign policy successes and created a tide for change that swamped the GOP ticket. Bush had carried on the Reagan mission, presiding over a remarkable period that saw the liberation of Eastern Europe, collapse of the Soviet Union,

97. Robb interview.
98. James Carville, a key Clinton strategist, observed that Wilder's withdrawal from the 1992 presidential race decisively aided Clinton's bid by removing the major obstacle to the Arkansas governor's harvest of African-American votes in key Southern primaries. Mary Matalin and James Carville, *All's Fair* (New York: Random House, Inc., 1994), pp. 97–98.
99. President Clinton was impeached by the House of Representatives in 1998 and acquitted by the Senate after testifying inaccurately in a sworn deposition regarding his sexual activities with White House intern Monica Lewinsky. In his deposition testimony and public statements about the Lewinsky relationship, Clinton appeared to draw fine distinctions similar to Robb's in characterizing—and denying—certain types of sexual activity. See Walter Kirn, "When Sex Is Not Having Sex," *Time*, February 2, 1998; see generally John Harris, *The Survivor: Bill Clinton in the White House* (New York: Random House, 2005), pp. 222–229, 298–316.
100. The debate, which featured questioning of the candidates by audience members, is most remembered for the moment when President Bush was captured on camera glancing at his watch, seemingly eager for the tedious encounter with his opponents and the participating citizens to be behind him.

removal of the Berlin Wall, and the stirrings of democracy, though crushed brutally, in China's Tiananmen Square. He had assembled an impressive international coalition to forcibly expel Saddam Hussein's invading Iraqi army from neighboring, oil-rich Kuwait. But most American voters were preoccupied with economic concerns and seemed to lose confidence in a GOP administration that, while sure-footed on foreign affairs, lacked both passion and a plan for reigniting America's economic engine. Bush's re-election bid also was damaged, probably decisively, by the independent candidacy of Texas billionaire Ross Perot. Leading the nascent "Reform Party," Perot siphoned off independent swing votes—many of them cast by male voters—that otherwise might have gone to the incumbent.[101]

Virginia's Democrats had more to celebrate in the congressional race returns. Having gained a six-to-four majority in the state's congressional delegation two years earlier, Democrats added to their advantage in 1992 with the election of Leslie Byrne, the first female elected to Congress from the state, in the newly formed Eleventh District. The composition of Virginia's team in the House of Representatives reflected the changes wrought during a decade of Democratic successes in the Old Dominion. A dozen years earlier, when the Reagan tidal wave lifted Republicans to their high-water mark, GOP candidates had won in nine Virginia congressional districts. In 1992, Republicans captured only four congressional seats, while Democrats raised their total to seven.[102]

Making money had been easy and making history had been therapeutic for Virginia voters in the 1980s. With few economic concerns, Virginians—especially the swing voters in the state's swelling suburbs—had been free to focus on social concerns and the powerful, positive imagery of barrier-shattering political sagas. But as the Commonwealth entered a new decade,

---

101. The vote totals in Virginia were: Bush (R)—1,150,517 (45.0 percent); Clinton (D)—1,038,650 (40.6 percent). Independent Ross Perot received 348,639 votes, or 13.6 percent of the statewide total. Larry J. Sabato, *Virginia Votes 1991–1994* (Charlottesville: Weldon Cooper Center for Public Service, University of Virginia, 1996), p. 26.

102. Virginia was allocated an eleventh House district as a consequence of population growth that outpaced the nation's as a whole. In addition to Byrne's noteworthy "first," state Senator Robert ("Bobby") Scott's victory in the reconstituted, majority-black Third District made him the first African American elected to Congress from Virginia in the twentieth century. In other changes, Seventh District Representative George Allen did not stand for reelection after the General Assembly adopted a redistricting plan that paired him with Third District incumbent Thomas J. Bliley Jr. Republican Robert W. Goodlatte of Roanoke defied the pro-Democratic national trend in capturing the open seat of retiring Democratic Congressman James Olin of the Sixth District. Byrne's victory in the Eleventh District race came against Henry Butler, a George Mason University law professor and son of former Sixth District Representative M. Caldwell Butler. Sabato, *Virginia Votes 1991–1994*, pp. 44–45.

the sagging national economy created renewed fiscal and economic concerns in the Old Dominion. And though the history-making achievements of Douglas Wilder had been a source of spine-tingling pride for many citizens in the state, voters across the political spectrum seemed to have had their fill of symbolism as the 1990s opened and were ready for leaders offering substantive, practical solutions to vexing problems. An increasingly irritated electorate had watched as several of the state's most prominent elected officials seemed to engage in interminable infighting over matters having more to do with their political self-interest than the public interest. Few political observers sensed it at the time, so numerous were Terry's seeming advantages in the impending 1993 gubernatorial race, but the winds of change were beginning to blow briskly again in the dynamic dominion.

*Part II*

GEORGE ALLEN AND THE
"VIRGINIA RENAISSANCE,"
1993–1999

# 5

# REAGAN POPULISM AND THE
# POSITIVE POLITICS OF REFORM

> George Allen is most like Ronald Reagan in his ability to relate to
> people and to express his conservative philosophy in optimistic,
> encouraging, and understandable terms. Like Reagan, his extraordi-
> nary talent as a leader first became apparent during his exceptionally
> active and successful tenure as governor.[1]
>
> —Edwin Meese III

R onald Reagan had ended his Presidency, and so his storied political
career, in 1989. But any overview of the Virginia political developments of the 1990s, when Republicans rebounded and capped the state's
long-running political realignment with a stunning string of election victories and policy reforms, must begin with the inimitable "Gipper."

Reagan had redefined what it meant to be a Republican and, in the
process, reordered American politics. Where once had been a center-right
Republican Party aligned with the interests of big business and most comfortable among country club elites, he forged a bread-and-butter GOP that
stressed individual empowerment and the needs of working families and
appealed to independent voters and blue-collar Democrats (the so-called
"Reagan Democrats"). Where once had been a Republican balanced-
budget orthodoxy that treated spending restraint and revenue increases as
value-neutral and economically indifferent options for achieving fiscal stability, he substituted the core idea of "Reaganomics"—the belief that a
lower tax burden and less regulation on individuals and businesses would
unleash the creative capacity of the free marketplace and spur economic
growth, resulting over time in more rapidly growing government revenues.

---

1. Edwin Meese III interview, November 16, 2004. Meese was counselor to the
president and then attorney general of the United States during President Reagan's
administration, and he also served as one of Reagan's most trusted advisers during his
tenure as California governor.

Where once had been an internationalist party bothered by Soviet expansionism but reconciled to coexistence with the Communists and obeisance to international apparatuses like the United Nations, he forged a forward force for freedom—for individual liberty, free enterprise, and democratic institutions—and made the advancement of those fundamental human rights his party's crusade. And, where once the Republican Party had differed only in subtle hues from its Democratic counterpart on morality-laden social issues, he painted a new traditional-values GOP in bright colors and made it a rallying point for Americans across the political spectrum who were convinced that something had gone terribly wrong with the nation's moral compass.

"Populism," a term burdened with the baggage of colorful demagogues from Huey Long to George Wallace (and many others before and since), often is employed pejoratively to describe the methods of rabble-rousing politicians who advance their political fortunes by playing on popular passions, making insincere promises, and peddling snake-oil remedies. Reagan's persistent detractors might say that his appeal for popular support for his dramatic ideas during the 1980s deserved the same pejorative characterization. But most observers would acknowledge—especially with the aid of hindsight—that Reagan and the voters who supported him were right about many of the big things on which the political and cultural elite of his day were proven wrong. Reagan's "populism" was an appeal for grassroots support in the face of that flawed conventional wisdom and the entrenched political order that perpetuated it. His message stressing economic empowerment, recurrence to traditional values, and the moral imperative to advance freedom internationally struck a chord with voters that cut through the din of partisan politics and the naysaying chorus of political insiders. The political establishment in the nation's capital felt the true power of Reagan-style populism, not only in the three successive GOP presidential landslides of the 1980s but also in Reagan's effective rallying of broad-based popular support to push his sweeping policy changes through a reluctant, Democrat-controlled Congress.

During the 1990s, Democrats and Republicans around the country accommodated themselves to many of the post-Reagan realities. Two long-standing minority traditions within the political parties—liberal Republicans in the Northeast and conservative Democrats in the South—eroded precipitously. As the GOP remade itself largely in Reagan's image, the opposing party's responses varied. On some issues Democrats moved toward the center to close a gap that had widened as the electorate shifted rightward behind the GOP's lead. But on other issues, especially values-laden social issues, many Democrats hardened their stances on the political left, producing an even more acute partisan polarization. Beginning in 1993, Clinton's first two years as president saw a series of missteps and flirtation with a liberal policy agenda on health care and other issues, but thereafter the Clinton-led Democrats found space at the political center where the uncanny skills of their presidential leader kept them in control of the White House. The Clinton revival came too late to save the Democratic majority in Congress, however. Democratic leaders there continued to espouse the big-government mantras that echoed from the New Deal and Great Society, and they surrendered their decades-old grip on the House of Representatives as a result.

Clinton's party suffered the most stinging setbacks in statehouses across the country: from a 29–21 Democratic advantage in governorships in 1990 to an 18–30 deficit to the Republicans in 1998; and from thirty states in which Democrats controlled all legislative chambers in 1990 to just twenty in 1998.[2] A new generation of Republican leaders adhering to tenets popularized by Reagan took control at the state level, their responsibilities enhanced markedly by "devolution"—the transfer of government responsibilities back to the states, whose constitutional role as sovereign partners and possessors of plenary powers had been much diminished through federal initiative during the first three-quarters of the twentieth century. The effects of Reagan's tenure remained palpable at the national level, but the big political story of the 1990s became the spread of his "revolution" to the state capitals, where Reagan's own career had been launched a quarter-century earlier.

Cutting a striking figure atop the first wave of Republicanism that rolled onto the statehouse beaches in the 1990s was the eldest son of a football legend, a native of Reagan's California who came east, then south, and made his stand in the agreeable environs of Virginia's Albemarle County. Young George Allen's ambitions initially focused on football—he occasionally got the call to direct the downtrodden Cavaliers as quarterback—but he spent more consequential time soaking up the rich Jeffersonian ethos of the University of Virginia and forging his political philosophy. In the early 1990s, a smiling fortune seemed to reward the uncanny work ethic that Allen, ever his father's son, had exhibited in professional and political life. His winsome way combined with his oft-underestimated abilities to catapult him—in two years' time—from the obscurity of a Charlottesville-area state legislative district to Congress, and from there to the Virginia governor's mansion.

---

2. Despite Clinton's southern roots, much of the state-level change that advantaged the Republicans during his tenure occurred in the South. See David Lublin, *The Republican South: Democratization and Partisan Change* (Princeton, NJ: Princeton University Press, 2004), p. 1, 33–65.

Allen's 1993 gubernatorial victory and activist tenure shook the Commonwealth's political foundations. Like Charles Robb's election as governor a dozen years earlier, it redirected the flow of state politics for a decade. But it did more than that. Just as Ronald Reagan's transforming campaigns and administration remade the American political landscape, George Allen's distinctive persona and message and his productive tenure decisively reoriented Virginia politics during the 1990s. On the heels of the nationally renowned Wilder breakthrough in 1989, Allen's reform-driven governorship added substance to the symbolism and seemed to complete Virginia's return to the vanguard of American politics.

Virginia's Democratic leaders had governed steadily but unexceptionally during the 1980s. Major expenditures had been made, especially in elementary and secondary education and in transportation, and some notable improvements had followed. But on the whole the state's Democratic governors and legislative leaders had been content to stay the course, attempting few significant reforms in the way the Commonwealth served its citizens or conducted its affairs. The state's Republicans had not pressed the majority party to do more or to do better.[3] Indeed, during the Reagan-Bush years, Republicans at the state level in Virginia had seemed almost wholly devoid of a policy-related mission. The GOP's attraction to the Commonwealth's conservative-leaning electorate in the 1960s and 1970s—and the driving motivation for the ardently conservative activists who had propelled the party since the 1964 Goldwater campaign—had been the great national debates: free markets versus government planning as the way to prosperity; private institutions versus the welfare state as the engine of social improvement; individual liberty and responsibility versus government paternalism as

---

3. See the epilogue, entitled "Why Stand We Here Idle?" in *The Dynamic Dominion*, first edition, pp. 487–500. Viewing the Virginia landscape as of 1991, the author wrote:

> If the Commonwealth's competitive system works well in the 1990s, it will yield at least one party of genuine reform—Republican or Democratic—whose mission will be to apply Virginia's traditional values innovatively to the state's rapidly changing and ever more complex conditions. For Republicans, the challenge will be to promote principled reform rather than lapsing into reflexive resistance to change; for Democrats, the challenge will be to temper change with tested values rather than blithely promoting the indiscriminate displacement of tradition. Neither the passive sentimentality of the conservative Old Dominion nor the aggressive technocracy of the Balilesian "New Dominion" offers real promise for resolving the great social and political dilemma of our time: how to realize the potential of this dynamic new age while preserving the character, culture, shared values, and sense of community among our people. . . . Because both parties generally have failed to offer a distinctive vision worthy of the Commonwealth's heritage and potential, Virginia voters in the 1990s will seek reform-minded leaders—Republican or Democratic—who advocate creative approaches grounded in proven principles and common sense.

*The Dynamic Dominion*, first edition, pp. 491–492.

the means to personal fulfillment; military strength versus disarmament as the path to peace; state prerogatives versus federal mandates in governmental policymaking; judicial restraint versus judicial activism in enforcing the law; assertiveness versus passivity in promoting capitalism over communism and democracy over dictatorship on the world stage. That a clear majority of Virginians preferred the conservative Republican vision to the liberal Democratic view on these issues had been apparent from the GOP's presidential victories, which continued uninterrupted with a single exception through the five decades after Eisenhower carried the state in 1952. Only when the Cold War had been won, Eastern Europe had been liberated, and the politically galvanizing Soviet threat had been removed had the presidential elections in Virginia become somewhat more competitive. But, with the exception of the 1970s, when the Henry Howell–led state Democrats embraced their national party's most liberal nostrums, the defining national issues rarely had differentiated the parties at the state and local levels. Democrats had succeeded in the 1980s in Virginia and much of the South by blurring philosophical distinctions and using the fruits of an expanding economy to fund increased spending on popular state programs.[4]

The GOP's long drought as the party of reform in Virginia ended in 1993 when two new ingredients in state politics converged in the groundbreaking gubernatorial candidacy of forty-one-year-old George Allen. One new element was the advent in Virginia of Reagan-style populism,[5] and the other was the introduction of a far-reaching agenda of dramatic state-level policy reforms. Allen's tenure was on the leading edge of a wave of Republican governorships in the 1990s that featured these elements. In tone and substance, the Allen candidacy and governorship provided a model that was frequently replicated in ensuing statehouse races and gubernatorial administrations around the country. As noted by Reagan confidant Edwin Meese, the 1995–2000 governorship of Texan George W. Bush shared this attribute with Allen's, and both bore similarities to Reagan's gubernatorial tenure in California.[6]

---

4. Black and Black, *Politics and Society in the South*, p. 287.

5. Reagan's pivotal impact on Southern politics is described in Earle Black and Merle Black, *The Rise of Southern Republicans* (Cambridge, MA: The Belknap Press of Harvard University Press, 2002). "Reagan's presidency," wrote the professors Black, "was the turning point in the evolution of a competitive, two-party electorate in the South. The Reagan realignment of the 1980s dramatically expanded the number of Republicans and conservative independents in the region's electorate." The authors detail the positive response of moderate and conservative Southerners to Reagan's themes and policies. Black and Black, *The Rise of Southern Republicans*, pp. 25, 205–240.

6. Meese interview; see also Stuart Rothenberg, "Are Republicans Ready for Another George?" *Roll Call*, March 28, 2005.

With the exception of Richard Obenshain, whose service was cut short by tragedy, George Allen was the first Virginia politician to embody Reagan populism and employ it at the state level. "Tall, dark-haired, and ruddy, Allen has drawn widespread comparisons with Ronald Reagan," wrote reporter Warren Fiske in 1998. "Like the former president, Allen exudes immense personal charm, is dogmatic in his approach to governing, and shares inner thoughts with almost no one."[7] "Essentially undoubting" is how William F. Buckley Jr. earlier had described then-Governor Ronald Reagan, and the phrase well captured the self-certain Allen.[8] Personal comparisons highlighting their sunny dispositions and western ways also were common, but the substantive similarity between the two reformers was less often remarked.[9] That comparison rested on this: Like Reagan before him, Allen unreservedly championed a set of conservative principles and policy ideas denigrated by the then-reigning political elite, generated a groundswell of public support for those tenets, and then scrupulously endeavored to keep his promises and enact the reforms despite an imposing array of forces bent on preserving the status quo.

Allen's worldview, like Reagan's, ultimately was rooted in a Jeffersonian ideal.[10] Jefferson had planted Locke's theory of liberty in the fertile soil of the new nation, and a republic had flourished.[11] Fundamental to its flowering had been the proposition that governmental institutions were created and offices occupied through the *consent of the governed*. The success of representative democracy thus depended on informed consent and a bond of trust between the elected and the electorate. To Allen, this meant that a principled politician should place his guiding philosophy and policy ideas candidly before the voters, make the case and seek a mandate, and then keep

---

7. *Roanoke Times & World News*, January 12, 1998.

8. Lou Cannon, *Governor Reagan: His Rise to Power* (New York: Public Affairs, 2003), p. 206.

9. *Washington Post*, October 10, 1993.

10. Allen's first foray into politics occurred in 1976 while in law school at "Mr. Jefferson's University" (the University of Virginia) when he was recruited to lead Virginia youth efforts for Ronald Reagan's campaign for the GOP presidential nomination. See *The Dynamic Dominion*, Chapter 28.

11. The English liberal John Locke's influence on Jefferson and Jefferson's central role in the evolution of American ideas on liberty are beyond dispute, but it may be argued persuasively that Calvinist doctrine and the Scottish Enlightenment were earlier and highly important contributors to the emergence of America's democratic philosophy and institutions. See, e.g., Jeffrey H. Morrison, *John Witherspoon and the Founding of the American Republic* (Notre Dame, IN: University of Notre Dame Press, 2005), pp. 78–88. George III famously referred to the American Revolution as "a Presbyterian Rebellion," an appellation that was "not far wrong," according to historian Paul Johnson. Paul Johnson, *A History of the American People* (New York: Harper Perennial, 1999), p. 173.

his promises once in office—or go down fighting.[12] Later dubbed the "Reagan of Monticello" by a prominent commentator,[13] Allen subscribed wholeheartedly to Jefferson's "populist" notion about the inevitable emergence of two parties in politics. "Men by their constitutions are naturally divided into two parties," Jefferson wrote to Henry Lee late in his life,

(1) Those who fear and distrust the people, and wish to draw all powers from them into the hands of the higher classes. (2) Those who identify themselves with the people, have confidence in them, and cherish and consider them as the most honest and safe, although not the most wise depository of the public interests. In every country these two parties exist; and in every one where they are free to think, speak, and write, they will declare themselves.[14]

When it came to trusting "ordinary, hard-working, taxpaying folks," Allen saw the world like the Sage of Monticello—in just two tones. He placed himself emphatically among those willing to defer to popular wisdom and common sense, and he lumped together and gleefully derided as "monarchical elitists" those with contrary opinions.

Virginian Woodrow Wilson—a leader, like Reagan and Allen, who possessed a Jeffersonian affinity, Presbyterian heritage, and gubernatorial mantle—perceived a covenant relationship between the electorate and the elected, asserting often that a politician with integrity should make just a few promises and keep them all religiously.[15] Allen apparently agreed with Wilson as to the quality but not the quantity. As a candidate for governor in 1993, Allen pledged state policy changes in everything from criminal justice and social services to education and economic development, and under Virginia law he would have to accomplish it all in one four-year term. Armed with an apparent mandate from the largest landslide victory in a Virginia gubernatorial contest since the onset of serious two-party competition, the youthful chief executive proceeded to rally public support and muscle or cajole most of his agenda through a wary legislature controlled by the

---

12. The promise-keeping mantra had been a feature of Allen's political persona from his earliest campaigns. When he first ran for the Virginia House of Delegates seat occupied centuries earlier by Albemarle County's Thomas Jefferson, Allen's campaign posters bore the slogan, "He Keeps His Word." George Allen interview, April 5, 2005.

13. Howard Fineman, "The Virginians," *Newsweek*, December 26, 2005—January 2, 2006.

14. Jefferson to Lee, August 10, 1824.

15. See Josephus Daniels, *The Life of Woodrow Wilson* (Philadelphia: Will H. Johnson, 1924), p. 118. Wilson, like Allen, was governor of an adopted state. Born in Staunton, Virginia, Wilson attended law school at the University of Virginia and later served as president of Princeton University and then governor of New Jersey before becoming the eighth Virginia-born American president.

opposing party. The pace of legislative activity exceeded even that in the most prolific of prior administrations. "George is making Jerry Baliles's term seem like a somnolent four years," cracked Democratic Lieutenant Governor Donald Beyer.[16] To an electorate skeptical of promising politicians and recently reminded why by the sight of a Democratic governor and then a Republican president reneging on firm no-tax-increase pledges, the "honest change"[17] delivered by Allen was a tonic. Virginia voters evidently had tired of politicians absorbed with symbolism, score-settling, negative campaigning and scandal-dodging more than developing practical ways to make life in the Commonwealth tangibly better. Now, as if on cue, came young George Allen, upbeat, optimistic, innovative, and positive, with a seemingly endless string of ideas he claimed would help "make Virginia the best place to live, learn, work and raise a family."

All of Allen's ideas could be aptly characterized as "conservative," and his rhetoric frequently was described as "populist," but what Virginians saw was an energetic agent of change whose pronouncements seemed sensible, creative, and genuine. Writing during Allen's first year as governor, *Richmond Times-Dispatch* reporter Michael Hardy observed:

> For a self-described conservative, Governor Allen has been nothing less than radical. He's actually doing what he promised voters he would. With an electorate jaundiced about politicians' promises, the Republican governor has stuck to the script of his campaign promises. Less than a year into his term, Allen has pushed major initiatives ranging from abolition of parole to a refund deal for illegally taxed federal pensioners. He has launched the biggest prison-building program in state history, proposed a record tax cut, and plans a record scaling down of state government. To boot, he's also promising statewide welfare and school reform. The agenda of his first year in office is among the most far-reaching of any Virginia governor this century, many legislators and analysts agree.[18]

While some commentators were comparing Allen's young regime to the two twentieth-century Virginia governorships most noted for sweeping reforms—Harry F. Byrd Sr.'s in 1926–1930, and Mills Godwin's first term in 1966–1970[19]—others, such as Professor Mark Rozell of Mary Washing-

---

16. *Washington Post*, December 11, 1994.

17. Allen and his political operatives used the two-word slogan to summarize his dual message stressing candor in public life and adoption of wide-ranging policy reforms. As governor, Allen formed a political action committee called the "Campaign for Honest Change" to support his program.

18. *Richmond Times-Dispatch*, December 5, 1994.

19. Among those making such comparisons were veteran Virginia political scientist Thomas R. Morris of Emory & Henry College and longtime political reporter Donald Baker of the *Washington Post*. See *Washington Post*, December 11, 1994.

ton College,[20] were describing Allen as "Reaganesque" and noting that he seemed to possess a number of Reagan-like attributes, including a willingness to set ambitious goals and the advantage of being continually underestimated by his foes. "The great problem for Democrats is that George Allen is the most popular figure in Virginia politics," opined Rozell. "He's exploited his personality and made it risky to oppose him."[21] Everyone seemed to recognize that Reagan's "revolution," or something akin to it, had swept into Jefferson's Capitol in the person of George Allen.

Allen's populist themes and extensive reform agenda swiftly revised the substance of policy discourse in the Commonwealth and rearranged the decade-old political alignments that had kept Democrats comfortably in power since the beginning of the Robb administration. A new set of popular issues placed front-and-center by the telegenic Allen changed the subject almost overnight in the suburbs and produced a cascade of GOP votes, forging a working majority there in statewide elections for roughly a decade and fueling a now-inevitable Republican capture of the General Assembly. With his down-home manner, conservative values, and tobacco-dipping orneriness, Allen also reinforced and expanded GOP gains throughout rural Virginia. Perhaps most important for a Republican Party whose factional fault lines had produced yawning chasms that stymied the party's candidates throughout the 1980s, Allen's persona and positions surmounted factional differences and largely reunified the strife-torn state GOP. The agile young governor proved adept at appealing simultaneously to traditional Republican activists, business leaders, the party's growing corps of Christian Right enthusiasts, rural conservatives, and the younger, more moderate and more independent voters in the suburbs. The secret to Allen's success, often masked by his aw-shucks demeanor and penchant for football-laced, partisan rhetoric, was his uncommon blend of intellectual rigor, philosophical motivation, and political ingenuity. Only those working most closely with him or against him came to appreciate fully those attributes. His unusual talents won grudging praise even from his legislative nemesis, House of Delegates Majority Leader Richard Cranwell. "[George Allen is] one of the best politicians we have had in the governor's office in the twenty-seven years I've been around. Maybe the best," said Cranwell as Allen's governorship drew to a close.[22]

In the 1990s, a durable new winning coalition was forged around the populist themes, popular reforms, and promise-keeping ethic espoused by

---

20. The college, located in Fredericksburg, Virginia, later became the University of Mary Washington.

21. *Richmond Times-Dispatch*, December 5, 1994.

22. *Washington Post*, January 9, 1998.

Allen, his successor James S. ("Jim") Gilmore III, and the Republicans who followed their lead. The coalition was held together mainly by ideas and values, and it bore remarkable fruit: two Republican gubernatorial landslides; an unprecedented GOP sweep of statewide offices led by Gilmore in 1997; Republican majorities in both houses of the General Assembly by 1999; a restored GOP majority in the state's congressional delegation; and a ticket to the United States Senate for Allen himself in 2000. Even the Democratic recapture of the governorship in 2001 led by the well-heeled Mark Warner reflected the broad consensus that developed around the GOP's policy initiatives. Candidate Warner embraced virtually all of those major reforms and won office by downplaying substantive policy differences with Allen, Gilmore, and state Republicans.[23] The evidence became compelling that, as political analyst Robert Holsworth asserted, George Allen "presided over a realignment of state politics."[24]

While the ensuing chapters chronicle the electoral developments of the 1990s and first years of the new century, the next few pages focus on the policy initiatives—mainly during the Allen gubernatorial tenure—that both sparked and sustained the period's remarkable Republican resurgence.[25] While a discussion of legislative activity may seem a digression in a work mainly about political dynamics, the interrelation between the GOP-led policy initiatives and the decade's electoral developments is inescapable. As candidates and then governors in the 1990s, Allen and Gilmore built on the Reagan philosophical and rhetorical foundation with popular and practical state-level reform measures. Without that popular reform agenda, Allen likely would not have overcome exceedingly long odds to capture the governorship in the watershed 1993 contest. And if Allen as governor had not followed through on that agenda and achieved widely acknowledged success as the first GOP chief executive in a dozen years, his party likely would not have sustained its gains throughout the decade.

At no point did the sweeping Allen policy proposals seem *less* likely to be enacted into law by the Democratic politicians who controlled the Virginia General Assembly than on Inauguration Day 1994. On one of the most frigid days in state history, Allen icily served notice that he meant to deliver on his promises of wide-ranging change and was prepared to run over anyone who stood in his path. To the consternation of the legislative leadership assembled in the shadow of the stately, Jefferson-designed capitol, he declared:

---

23. Rozell, "Virginia: The New Politics of the Old Dominion," p. 149.

24. *Washington Post*, January 15, 1998.

25. The author had firsthand involvement in some of the events chronicled here, having served in Allen's cabinet during 1994–1996 as counselor to the governor and director of policy. In that role, he oversaw the administration's legislative initiatives.

·

> The people of Virginia have a clear understanding of the change that is needed. They have given us a clear mandate to make that promise of change a reality. And, though some here may doubt their insight, this much is clear: The problem in Virginia is not that the people have lost touch with reality; it is that our government has lost touch with the people. . . . [T]his great house that Jefferson designed was meant to be the people's house, not the citadel of special interests.[26]

Few insiders applauded the tone of the speech, but Allen's blunt declaration was calculated. He was entering the Capitol, transitioning from candidate to governor, and he wanted his new audience inside the hallowed halls to hear the same commitment he had expressed to the people outside who sent him there. His agenda was the people's agenda, Allen believed, and those who stood in its way were not just wrong; they were obstructionists defying the manifest will of the owners of Virginia's government. Allen's effort had begun as an insurgency, and an insurgency it would remain, even though he now had at his disposal the considerable powers of the Virginia governorship.

As events unfolded over his four-year term, Allen surprised and impressed observers with his skillful mobilization of public pressure on lawmakers and his resilience as a legislating governor. Less than a year into his new administration, he already had three sessions of the General Assembly (including two special sessions) under his belt, and commentators were referring to his Midas touch in dealing with the solons. Among other first-year successes, he and lawmakers had enacted new tax incentives for businesses to locate or expand major plants in Virginia, restricted college tuition growth to the rate of inflation, passed legislation imposing mandatory life imprisonment on violent three-time felons (the "three strikes" law) and allowing sentencing juries to be informed of convicted criminals' prior offenses (the "bifurcated trials" law), resolved an $800 million dispute with retired federal employees who were illegally taxed in the 1980s,[27] repealed

---

26. *Washington Post*, January 16, 1994.

27. The costly tax dispute arose from the decision of the United States Supreme Court in *Davis v. Michigan*, 489 U.S. 803 (1989), which struck down differential state income tax treatment of federal and state retirement benefits. Prior to the Allen administration, the Commonwealth, acceding to the recommendation of Attorney General Mary Sue Terry, refused any repayment to wrongly taxed federal pensioners in hopes the Supreme Court would deny retroactive enforcement of the law. The Supreme Court's subsequent decision in *Harper v. Virginia Department of the Treasury*, 509 U.S. 86 (1993), confirmed the wisdom of settling the claims; it held the *Davis* ruling had retroactive application and, in so doing, precipitated serious state budget crunches in numerous nonsettling states. The settlement enacted in 1994 was a modified version of a proposal developed by Attorney General James Gilmore and refined in negotiations between Democratic Delegate Richard Cranwell and retiree group representatives.

the implicit state income tax on Social Security benefits, and enacted several ethics reform measures, including legislation to make the controversy-plagued Virginia Retirement System an independent agency. Though many of these initiatives had been emphatically rejected by the state's ruling Democrats in the months and years before Allen arrived, they now garnered bipartisan support.

The highlight of the new governor's first year came with adoption of his landmark legislation to abolish parole and reform sentencing. Nothing had aroused voters more in Allen's 1993 campaign than his indictment of Virginia's sentencing laws, under which violent criminals served on average only a fourth of their sentences. With statistics showing that 75 percent of violent criminals in Virginia were repeat offenders, Allen had little difficulty convincing alarmed citizens that prematurely released criminals were the primary culprits in the sudden violent crime rise Virginia experienced in the late 1980s and early 1990s. Allen chose the spotlight of a special legislative session in September 1994 as the venue for action on his parole abolition initiative. A bipartisan gubernatorial commission headed by former United States Attorney General William Barr and former United States Attorney Richard Cullen oversaw preparation of the detailed plan with assistance from Attorney General Gilmore and his staff and senior Allen administration officials. It called for the complete abolition of parole, adoption of a truth-in-sentencing system, and non-mandatory sentencing guidelines that increased by as much as 700 percent the average time served by violent repeat criminals.[28]

Allen recruited bipartisan chief patrons in both legislative chambers for his dramatic proposals, but he encountered resistance in the House of Delegates. Some Democrats preferred a rival plan that would retain discretionary early release—parole by another name—and the wily House Democratic leader, Richard Cranwell, actively maneuvered to defuse public support for Allen's plan by delaying action until the 1995 regular legislative session on the ground that Allen's prison construction cost projections were unreliable.[29] House Speaker Thomas W. Moss Jr. of Norfolk saw Democratic

---

28. Barr served as attorney general under President George H. W. Bush from 1991 to 1993, and prior to that was deputy attorney general. Cullen, a Richmond lawyer, was United States attorney for the Eastern District of Virginia from 1991 to 1993. Both men enjoyed crime-fighting notoriety in Virginia because Barr had targeted crime-plagued Richmond for his "Weed and Seed" anti-drug and anti-crime initiative. Cullen also had assisted Governor Wilder in passing legislation restricting handgun purchases in 1993.

29. Shortly before the special session voting on the Allen plan, the staff of the Democratic-controlled House of Delegates Appropriations Committee produced a report suggesting the Allen administration had severely underestimated the number of new prisons that would be needed if parole were abolished. The legislative staff suggested that prison construction needs would reach $2 billion under the Allen plan, a

opposition to parole abolition as both futile and politically dangerous, however, and he heatedly prevailed on Cranwell to desist. The opposition collapsed, and an Allen plan derided earlier by Democrats as radical and unworkable was enacted with only sixteen dissenting votes in the entire 140-member legislature.

Not surprisingly, Allen's remarkable string of first-year successes left Assembly Democrats frustrated and fearful of losing their thin Virginia Senate and House of Delegates majorities in the November 1995 elections. Determined to take the GOP chief executive down a peg before the critical election contests, opposition leaders hired a political consultant and pollster in late 1994 to help craft a legislative strategy for thwarting the governor and his agenda. "I was the principal hawk," said Cranwell of the Democratic strategy sessions that continued through the 1995 elections. "I said you have to take Allen on. If you don't he'll come back to haunt you at every turn."[30] As Democrats quietly organized their forces for legislative resistance, the Republican governor and his allies blithely prepared to advance along a broad policy front—too broad, in fact, for success against concentrated opposition. The governor's agenda for the 1995 session included a sweeping welfare reform proposal, education reform measures, funding for the new prison construction required to implement the just-passed parole abolition program, and—most controversial—a large multiyear tax reduction proposal.

After enacting tax relief for senior citizens and tax incentives for large-scale business investment in 1994, Allen turned his attention to tax relief for lower- and middle-income working families and small businesses. Although there had been no promise of tax cuts in his 1993 campaign, Allen saw a multiyear phased tax reduction plan as a way to achieve two of his major policy objectives: spurring economic growth and imposing discipline on a legislature he thought was too prone to spend every available dollar. The Allen tax cut plan included income tax relief for individuals and families (by raising the personal exemption) and help for small businesses through elimination of the locally levied business, profession, and occupation licensing ("BPOL") tax, with the state reimbursing localities for the lost revenue. Cumulatively over a five-year period, Allen's proposed income and BPOL tax reductions would reduce state coffers by $2.1 billion.

The size of Allen's tax cut plan and its timing—in the middle of the state's two-year budget cycle, with revenue growth still lagging due to a

---

figure more than twice the governor's projections. Ironically, the crime rate fell so fast in the years after parole was abolished in Virginia that Allen's critics later faulted him for *overbuilding* new prisons.

30. *Virginian-Pilot*, October 11, 1996.

recent recession—stunned many lawmakers. But with state spending having tripled in the preceding fifteen years, Allen argued that the Virginia budget could easily withstand the less than 3 percent reduction his plan would accomplish when fully implemented after five years. Privately, the governor and his finance secretary, Paul Timmreck, viewed his proposal as an opening bid; they expected Democrats and moderate Republicans to whittle down the size of the final tax cut package to preserve more funds for favored programs.[31] Indeed, that was the initial response from the state's top-ranking Democrat, Lieutenant Governor Beyer, who quickly seconded the governor's tax-cutting idea while suggesting that the legislature would modify and reduce the proposals. But two Democratic legislative power-brokers, often at odds with one another but now united in opposition to Allen's tax-cutting scheme, had other ideas.

No tax cut could emerge from the legislature unless it was approved by the Senate Finance Committee chaired by Senator Hunter B. Andrews of Hampton and the House of Delegates Finance Committee chaired by Delegate Cranwell. While Cranwell had made it clear he hoped to thwart the new governor at every turn, Andrews was another matter. The Senate Democratic leader had helped Allen pass other first-year initiatives and—until blindsided by the unexpected release of the governor's sweeping tax proposal during a Senate Finance Committee retreat in late 1994—he seemed a potential ally on some of the tax measures. Shortly after the legislative session began, however, the two powerful chairmen peremptorily signaled they would oppose *any* tax cut and would bottle up all tax legislation in committee. That effectively settled the issue. Beyer and other Democrats supportive of tax relief quickly reversed field and joined in decrying the hardships that would be inflicted by the resulting revenue reductions. "I'd like to see some form of tax cut pass," candidly acknowledged Senator Charles Colgan, a Democratic moderate from Manassas, "but you've got to stick with your party. . . . [T]his thing has just gotten too political."[32]

On the Republican side, sticking with the party was a lesser priority. A nominally bipartisan coalition of business leaders led by Northern Virginia developer John T. ("Til") Hazel stepped forward to criticize the Allen tax plan's likely impact on higher education, which was still recovering from the recession-driven cuts administered under the Wilder administration. Former Governors Baliles and Holton, joined (to Allen's surprise and cha-

---

31. George Allen interview. Timmreck, a career state government employee, became secretary of finance during the Wilder administration and was reappointed to that cabinet post by Allen.

32. *Washington Post*, February 4, 1995.

grin) by former Governor Godwin, provided Hazel with an open letter critical of the tax cut proposals. The Republican governor's ultimate embarrassment came when Cranwell and House Democrats put his proposed budget reductions up for an unexpected floor vote. With the tax relief portion of Allen's budget now dead, even most Republican delegates abstained rather than go on record in support of the governor's unpopular spending reductions.

The chief executive who had dominated legislative deliberations just months earlier now found himself complaining bitterly of the once-pliant Democratic majority's "obstructionist" tactics. And his problems did not end with the tax cut initiative. One of the most polarizing sessions of the Virginia legislature in memory ensued, as both sides turned their attention from legislating to posturing for the fall election showdown. In the melee, many of the governor's other legislative proposals were shredded with his tax cut recommendations, including an alternative proposal to allocate the state's lottery profits to local governments for education, law enforcement, or tax relief. While insisting that his tax reduction initiative had been sound as a matter of public policy, Allen would later acknowledge that its timing was all wrong. The miscalculation, and the serial legislative setbacks that followed, represented the low point of his legislating governorship.[33]

The contentious 1995 legislative session entered its final week with just one major issue unresolved—welfare reform. Democratic lawmakers led by Beyer were pushing for a modest welfare proposal they hoped would satisfy the general public's appetite for reform without sheering off the party's liberal wing. The Allen-led Republicans remained firmly behind the governor's far-reaching plan, which included a strict work requirement for able-bodied recipients, a two-year time limit on benefits, denial of assistance to welfare mothers who refused to identify the fathers of their children, and a "family cap" that denied additional benefits for children born to a mother on welfare.[34] Slim Democratic majorities in both houses held, and the weaker bill advanced to the governor's desk. Democrats assumed Allen's embarrassing defeats on tax cuts and other legislative proposals would make him eager to compromise to obtain passage of some welfare reform bill. But

---

33. George Allen interview.

34. The governor's welfare reform plan was developed during 1994 by a bipartisan Commission on Citizen Empowerment chaired by Allen's human resources secretary, Kay Coles James. Two leading GOP lawmakers and eventual attorneys general—Senator Mark Earley of Chesapeake and Delegate Robert McDonnell of Virginia Beach—were chief patrons of the legislation. A commission led by Lieutenant Governor Beyer crafted most elements of the Democrats' competing proposal; Delegate David Brickley, a Prince William County Democrat, was its chief legislative proponent.

they were mistaken. The governor was insistent on what he regarded as fundamental reform, and despite the grueling session and its ignominious setbacks, he was determined to go to the mat for his vision and version of welfare reform. It was a gamble, but Allen doubted that moderate Democrats were willing to face voters having ditched both his tax cut initiative and his popular welfare reform plan. He thus announced he would veto the Democratic welfare bill because it did not represent "real" welfare reform.

The dramatic veto announcement set off a flurry of last-minute negotiations that consisted almost entirely of a succession of grudging concessions by the Beyer-led Democrats. In the closing minutes of the legislative session, the Allen welfare reform plan passed, with all its essential provisions in place, as a wholesale substitute for the Democratic bill. Allen's 1995 legislative agenda resembled a trash heap, and there was a near-universal sense he had overreached with a tax cut plan that strayed from his campaign-promise script. But Allen's eleventh-hour win on welfare helped salvage the otherwise disastrous session, and it kept his ambitious reform program on track. The stunning breakthrough gave Virginia the first comprehensive statewide welfare reform program in the country—a measure much broader in scope than Wisconsin's, which was usually cited at the time as the national model, and ahead of federal welfare reform legislation eventually agreed upon by President Clinton and the GOP-controlled Congress.

In the wake of the polarizing partisan battles of the 1995 legislative session, Allen and his GOP allies set out to claim a majority in one or both houses of the General Assembly in the November elections. They decried the legislative majority's obstructionism and appealed for election of Allen allies who would support his reform agenda. Assembly Democrats just as resolutely plotted their defense, focusing on the negative impact they charged Allen's ill-conceived tax cut ideas would have on education funding and other pressing needs. The governor campaigned personally for more than fifty Republican legislative candidates and raised more than $1.2 million in campaign cash. In the end, however, the entrenched majority Democrats still outspent the GOP and prevented the governor's party from achieving its stated objective of capturing control of at least one legislative chamber. Although Republican contenders won a majority of the votes cast statewide in both the House and the Senate contests, Democrats maintained their 52-seat majority in the 100-member House of Delegates and held the GOP to a two-seat gain in the Senate.

The Senate results nevertheless were historic. The net addition of two Republican seats produced a 20-20 tie in the 40-member body, and among the defeated incumbents was the Democrats' kingpin, Hunter Andrews. For more than three decades, the inimitable Andrews had been a fixture in the

Senate—its intellectual heavyweight and unsurpassed orator, its foremost expert on state government and the labyrinthine budget, and, in later years, its irascible and strong-willed majority leader. So pervasive had been the impact of his brilliant intellect and deft hand on Virginia's government that his friend and colleague, state Senator Elmon Gray, once aptly labeled him "Virginia's Alexander Hamilton."[35] With the possible exception of Governor Godwin, no one in his era had been more active or instrumental in supporting the cause of public education, including higher education, in the Commonwealth. But the seventy-three-year-old Andrews had stayed long—he himself joked that he was the official state fossil—and his Republican-leaning Peninsula district was ready for a change. More than any other development in the 1995 election contests, Andrews's departure from the Senate scene signaled a political changing of the guard.

Allen had set the takeover goal and cast the legislative contests as a referendum on his reforms, so when his party fell short news reports immediately cast the outcome as a stinging defeat for the governor. Reporters and pundits hastened to write Allen's political obituary, predicting that he would be relegated early to lame-duck status. "Not only is George Allen a lame duck," asserted Virginia Tech political communications professor Robert Denton, "he's a dead duck when it comes to legislative initiatives."[36] Few observers anticipated that the combative governor would prove as adept at legislative fence-mending and horse-trading as he had at rounding up voters in 1993 and stampeding lawmakers in 1994. But when the General Assembly convened in early 1996, it quickly became apparent that the net effect of the midterm elections had been to strengthen the governor's legislative hand.

Although the vituperative campaign had further damaged Allen's standing in the Democratic-controlled House of Delegates, the governor and his agenda now benefited from a working conservative majority in the Senate that regularly included nineteen or twenty Republicans and two or three right-of-center Democrats. The most dramatic developments occurred on the first day of the 1996 session as Democrats attempted to organize the Senate. Lieutenant Governor Beyer eagerly offered to use his tie-breaking vote as Senate president to tip the balance so Democrats could retain control, but one of their number, conservative Senator Virgil Goode of Rocky Mount, refused to go along. Instead, Goode joined Republican

---

35. George W. Grayson, "Virginia Senator Hunter B. Andrews's Impact on the Nation," in *Notes from the Sausage Factory,* ed. Day and Dale, p. 333; see also Jeff E. Schapiro, "Hunter Andrews's Spirit Lives On, Loud and Clear," in *Notes from the Sausage Factory,* ed. Day and Dale, pp. 141–145.

36. *Washington Post,* November 9, 1995.

senators in insisting on a "power-sharing" arrangement that neutered Beyer and awarded Republicans parity on most legislative committees and five of twelve committee chairmanships.[37] In a flash—almost unnoticed by the general public—more than a century of Democratic hegemony in the Virginia Senate was broken.

The 1996 legislative session proved pivotal for Allen's governorship. His two-year budget blueprint called for achieving savings through privatization, state employee workforce reduction, and other efficiency initiatives, and for shifting the freed-up resources to education, public safety, and economic development. Building on many of the recommendations issued by a citizen "Strike Force" he had assembled,[38] the governor instructed budget director Robert Lauterberg to institute a new "performance budgeting" and strategic planning process in which every existing state program would be reappraised. The resulting Allen budget plan contained the smallest increase in overall spending of any nonrecession Virginia budget in the last quarter-century, and honored the governor's campaign promise to direct more of the budgeted dollars to education, law enforcement, and job creation. The new investment in elementary and secondary schools—more than $600 million—was especially significant. The increase dwarfed that in any prior Virginia budget, and even an inveterate Allen foe, Democrat Robley S. Jones of the Virginia Education Association, publicly conceded that the governor's blueprint was the "best budget we [in education] have seen for a number of years."[39] At the same time, the Allen spending plan restored dedicated funds for transportation and local school construction financing that had been tapped to balance the recession-battered budget in preceding years. Bowing to overwhelming opposition in the Democratic-controlled House of Delegates, however, the governor offered no reprise of his failed tax reduction initiative.[40]

Allen's substantive education recommendations were where the greatest controversy centered. There was virtually no dissent in the legislature to

---

37. Under the agreement, Democrats chaired six committees, Republicans chaired four, and the powerful Senate Finance Committee was led by Republican and Democratic co-chairs.

38. In his first official act as governor, Allen established a fifty-citizen Commission on Government Reform (also known as the "Blue Ribbon Strike Force") to conduct an exhaustive examination of state government organization, programs, and practices. In late 1994, the commission issued a lengthy report identifying more than 400 cost-saving and efficiency-enhancing reforms.

39. *Washington Post*, January 7, 1996.

40. Although no action was taken on individual income tax relief, legislators and the governor reached a compromise in 1996 on the business prong of Allen's earlier tax plan. The measure provided small businesses some relief from the local BPOL tax.

Allen's recommendations for increased spending on classroom technology, full funding of the state's Standards of Quality, and incentives for smaller class sizes in the early grades. Democrats had advocated similar proposals during the fall election campaign. The debate was over the centerpiece of Allen's education reform agenda: his plan to link the increased spending on schools with accountability through regular testing geared to specific, rigorous statewide academic standards in English, math, science, and history. Such academic reforms would become common around the country in ensuing years, and would receive a nationwide boost from federal passage of the "No Child Left Behind Act" in 2001 under President George W. Bush. But in the early 1990s the Allen-led initiative was groundbreaking and controversial.

The new, measurable Virginia "Standards of Learning" had been developed during the first two years of the Allen administration through an arduous process that included the Governor's Commission on Champion Schools, the State Board of Education, and more than 5,000 teachers, administrators, parents, and other citizens. Though the bipartisan Board of Education approved the new standards unanimously in June 1995, the initiative was opposed by many educators, especially professors at university-based schools of education, because the concept of content-rich academic standards and corresponding accountability measures ran contrary to the "progressive" theories of education then fashionable in much of the educational establishment.[41] The active opposition in the professional education community suffered a key setback in January 1996, when the state Board of Education president, influential former Democratic Senator James P. Jones of Abingdon, strongly endorsed the governor's proposal to put teeth in the new academic standards through development of a comprehensive Virginia-based testing program geared to the standards.[42]

---

41. See Mark Christie, "Virginia's Education Reform Works," *The Virginia News Letter* (Charlottesville: Weldon Cooper Center for Public Service, University of Virginia), August 2001, p. 4; Mark Christie, "Virginia's Education Reform Works—II," *The Virginia News Letter* (Charlottesville: Weldon Cooper Center for Public Service, University of Virginia), January 2004, p. 2.

42. The development of the academic standards was led by Dr. William Bosher, the Allen-appointed superintendent of public instruction, under the direction of Dr. Beverly Sgro, Allen's education secretary. From its inception, however, the development, refinement, and implementation of the state's educational accountability program benefited from crucial bipartisan support. A decade-long succession of State Board of Education presidents—Democrat James Jones, Republicans Michelle Easton, Kirk Schroder, and Mark Christie, and Democrat Thomas Jackson—played instrumental though very different roles in keeping the program on course, preventing it from becoming the subject of partisan debate, and resisting inevitable pressures to water down the requirements to make it easier for students to progress and graduate. One of Bosher's successors as state superintendent, Jo Lynne DeMary, also played a key role in implementation of the

Allen made educational accountability the focus of his "State of the Commonwealth" message as the 1996 session opened, holding aloft in the House chamber a chart showing that student test scores had remained static despite huge education spending increases over the preceding decade. As various education establishment groups urged legislative committees to delay or derail the testing proposal, Allen kept up public pressure and lobbied lawmakers of both parties behind the scenes. In the end, Allen received only meager funding for his proposal in the budget that passed the House of Delegates. But in the Senate, where the Finance Committee was now co-chaired by Republican John Chichester of Stafford and Democrat Stanley Walker of Norfolk, the governor's testing program emerged somewhat reduced but largely intact. In the closing hours of the legislative session the Senate approach prevailed, and the governor emerged with a major legislative victory. The new budget also included Allen-backed measures for increased funding for higher education, a two-year freeze on tuition for Virginia students at state-supported institutions, and a 33 percent hike in tuition assistance grants for students attending the state's independent colleges.

With landmark changes underway in the core state policy arenas of criminal justice, welfare, and education, Allen in 1996 also achieved legislative success in a fourth major area—economic development. Having devoted substantial time and energy to recruiting new business facilities to the state, the governor received accolades for a strong performance that included record-shattering investment announcements by some of the nation's largest technology companies. The biggest prizes were huge facilities for the manufacture of computer memory chips; first enticed to Virginia during Allen's tenure, their output was so voluminous and valuable that, less than a decade after their arrival, computer memory chips had replaced cigarettes as the state's leading manufactured export.[43] "While some Democrats in Richmond may squirm and withhold their applause," wrote the editorial writers of the usually critical *Washington Post*,

> the fact is that Governor Allen has been markedly successful in generating business investment in the state. His scorecard, which he cited during his budget presentation to the legislature's money committees on Monday, was

---

program during a 1999–2005 tenure that spanned Republican and Democratic gubernatorial administrations. See Kirk T. Schroder, "Standards, Accountability and Education Reform . . . from the President of a State Board of Education," *Southern Regional Education Board*, September 2003; Christie, "Virginia's Education Reform Works—II," pp. 1–4; Thomas Jackson, "Students and the SOLs Ended Year Successfully," *Richmond Times-Dispatch*, July 9, 2004; Mark Emblidge, "SOLs Prove Their Value with Higher Scores," *Richmond Times-Dispatch,* February 13, 2005.

43. *Richmond Times-Dispatch*, March 23, 2006.

rich with eye-popping numbers. With the governor for his report were executives of 28 corporations that have announced expansion plans in the state. The value: $2.3 billion; number of jobs: 7,659. "Just in the last two and one half years, companies large and small have announced investments totaling nearly $10 billion," Governor Allen said. "Now, to put that in perspective, the old record for [new business investment in Virginia in] any one year prior to 1994 . . . was a little over $1 billion."[44]

During his first two years in office, Allen and his team had completed a statewide economic development planning effort, formed regional economic development councils, enacted new job-creation tax credits, revamped the rural and urban enterprise zone program and doubled the number of zones, conducted a series of international trade missions, and initiated comprehensive regulatory reform, including legislation mandating economic impact analyses before imposition of new state regulations. Legislators in 1996 approved the central recommendation of Allen's planning panel: creation of an independent authority, the Virginia Economic Development Partnership, to enhance and provide continuity for the state's economic development marketing and recruitment programs. The General Assembly also endorsed most of the governor's spending proposals for economic development programs and incentives.[45]

The final half of Allen's busy term produced additional successes and some disappointments. The most significant success was passage in 1997 of legislation requiring parental notification for minor-age abortions. Aided by senior adviser Anne B. Kincaid, a leading Virginia social conservative and anti-abortion activist, Allen had made the issue a focal point of his 1993 campaign and had pressed for the measure each session since taking office, only to be thwarted by a resolute coalition of Democrats and Republican moderates that dominated the Senate Education and Health Committee and routinely bottled up pro-life measures. The Allen team and its legislative captain on the issue, state Senator Mark Earley of Chesapeake, unsuccessfully tried a variety of parliamentary gambits to get the parental notice bill to the floor of the Senate where it enjoyed majority support. At one point, a compromise measure that allowed notification of relatives other than parents emerged from committee, passed the legislature, and arrived on the governor's desk, only to be vetoed by Allen, who concluded after much

---

44. *Washington Post,* August 22, 1996.

45. Allen announced nearly $14 billion in new business investment during his gubernatorial tenure despite post–Cold War defense-industry downsizing during the period. *Washington Post,* January 15, 1998. The Allen economic development initiatives were spearheaded by Robert Skunda, a Democrat and former president of the Virginia Chamber of Commerce, who served as his cabinet-level secretary of commerce and trade.

soul-searching that the compromise would diminish public pressure and thwart eventual passage of a "real" parental notice requirement. The veto decision, derided by Allen critics at the time as evidence of stubbornness, was vindicated by passage of the original Allen-backed notification bill in 1997—a major victory that prompted two veteran reporters to write that the persistent governor resembled a "Mighty Duck" more than a "lame duck" as his term drew to a close.[46]

Compromise was more acceptable to Allen in another key context— juvenile justice reform. A bipartisan plan to address a rising tide of juvenile violence was forged from the recommendations of rival executive and legislative branch study commissions. The governor's panel led by Attorney General Gilmore stressed trial and incarceration of violent juvenile criminals as adults, while the legislative Commission on Youth chaired by Democratic Delegate Jerrauld Jones of Norfolk emphasized new state resources for prevention and rehabilitation programs. The second half of the Allen tenure also brought implementation of legislation providing for innovative public-private partnerships to build and finance transportation infrastructure projects.[47] After several years of intense criticism of his administration's policies by environmental advocates, Allen late in his tenure successfully proposed creation of a new water quality improvement fund to provide incentives to improve the condition of the Chesapeake Bay and its tributaries. But each of the governor's proposed constitutional changes—to provide for initiative and referendum, to explicitly recognize parental rights in the upbringing of children, and to require a super-majority for enactment of tax hike legislation—were rejected. Democratic lawmakers also rebuffed successive Allen attempts to pass legislation authorizing local school systems to establish privately owned and operated charter schools. And, although he presided over a period of rapid economic and revenue growth, the most successful legislative governor in at least a generation in Virginia never succeeded in convincing lawmakers to send a portion of the new revenues back to citizens in the form of income tax relief. Instead, as he prepared to leave office, Allen assembled a record-shattering budget that allocated large new sums to

---

46. Michael Hardy and Jeff E. Schapiro, "Allen Successful in His Last Session," *Richmond Times-Dispatch*, February 23, 1997.

47. The legislation, known as the "Public-Private Transportation Act of 1995" (PPTA), had been developed by Senator Walter Stosch of Henrico and refined at the suggestion of Allen's transportation secretary, Robert Martinez. A similar statute applicable to school facilities and other public infrastructure, also patroned by Stosch, was adopted by the General Assembly in 2002, and was extended to procurement of technology infrastructure in 2003. The measures made Virginia a "national model" for the use of such approaches, according to Richard Norment, executive director of the National Council for Public-Private Partnerships. *Richmond Times-Dispatch*, April 19, 2004.

increased spending on programs and infrastructure and to a car tax relief program advocated by his successor.

As he concluded his tenure in 1998, a satisfied Allen told legislators his administration had "kept faith with the people who sent us here."[48] Virtually every review of his governorship by the state's political reporters agreed that the young chief executive had made sweeping promises as a candidate and fulfilled most of them, placing him in the top rank of influential Virginia governors.[49] Sharing credit with lawmakers, Allen contended that "four years of hard-charging effort" had produced "a flourishing Virginia Renaissance—a rebirth of expanding hope, opportunity, jobs, and prosperity."[50] The effort had not been without its ups and downs, as Allen freely admitted, and he had employed a mix of tactics to get his program adopted. Where he enjoyed a strong popular mandate, as with parole abolition and welfare reform, the governor had taken a hard line, demanded action, and essentially dared lawmakers to stand in his way.[51] After his midterm election setbacks, when his mandate was clouded and entrenched interests threatened his education and juvenile justice initiatives, Allen had stressed conciliation and compromise. The young governor and his team had made mistakes, admitted some of them, learned and adapted. Once a buckaroo on a western ranch, Allen compared his varied tactics to breaking horses. "There is the western way—hard and fast. The eastern way is slower and gentler—pat them on the side a few times and encourage them," he said. "I've done it both ways. Either way is fine so long as the result is the horse gets broken."[52] The people of Virginia seemed to agree. Allen's change-oriented tenure was often tumultuous, but he left office with some of the nation's highest gubernatorial approval ratings.[53] And the lopsided victory of his ally, James Gil-

---

48. *Washington Post*, January 15, 1998.

49. See Spencer S. Hsu, "The Transformation of Governor Allen—And Virginia," *Washington Post*, January 9, 1998; Michael Hardy and Jeff E. Schapiro, "Allen Fulfilled Most Promises," *Richmond Times-Dispatch*, January 11, 1998; Warren Fiske, "A Legacy of Reform; Allen Rekindled GOP by Picking, Winning His Fights," *Virginian-Pilot & Ledger-Star*, January 11, 1998; Bob Gibson, "One Full Term," *Daily Progress*, January 11, 1998.

50. *Washington Post*, January 15, 1998.

51. Allen wielded his veto pen ninety-nine times—a record number—and all of his vetoes were sustained in the General Assembly.

52. See the author's "George Allen's 1,000 Days Have Changed Virginia," *University of Virginia News Letter* (Charlottesville: Weldon Cooper Center for Public Service, University of Virginia), September 1996, p. 8.

53. Allen's approval rating was 69 percent, according to the Mason-Dixon polling organization. It was the highest approval rating of any Virginia political figure at the time and made him one of the five most popular governors in the nation. *The Daily Progress*, January 11, 1998.

more, in the 1997 governor's race was partly viewed as a strong expression of voter satisfaction with Allen's performance.

Constitutionally barred from a second term, Allen necessarily entrusted implementation of his wide-ranging policy initiatives to Governor Gilmore. The task was not a glamorous one, but in controversial areas—most notably the implementation of educational accountability measures, including new Standards of Accreditation—Gilmore's less flashy but steady stewardship was crucial to the fulfillment of the goals that Allen and Gilmore had both championed as candidates. Gilmore also succeeded in some areas where his predecessor had failed. His 1998–2002 tenure saw the GOP complete its capture of majorities in both houses of the state legislature, and with that came passage of various measures, including charter schools legislation, that senior Democratic lawmakers had repeatedly blocked. Gilmore convinced the legislature to cut college tuition by 20 percent and allocate lottery profits to public schools, instigated reform of the state's mental health system, pushed through a series of groundbreaking information technology initiatives, and appointed the nation's first state cabinet secretary of technology. He also successfully appropriated several themes and issues previously championed by Democrats, including increased state aid for local school construction and relief from the sales tax on food, and pressed for significant new funding for Virginia's historically black colleges and universities.

Gilmore's signature initiative, however, was a multibillion-dollar plan to roll back and largely eliminate the local personal property tax on cars and trucks, with the Commonwealth reimbursing local governments for the decrease in revenue. Along with his call for hiring 4,000 new school teachers, the Gilmore proposal to cut the unpopular "car tax" became the rallying cry of his 1997 gubernatorial campaign and the centerpiece of his agenda as governor. Democratic lawmakers who had blocked Allen's comparatively modest tax cut plan three years earlier, including House Majority Leader Cranwell, were powerless to prevent passage of Gilmore's sweeping tax relief measure, which voters had resoundingly endorsed. By late spring during his first year in office, the new governor had made good on his whopping campaign promise and had secured passage of legislation providing for a five-year, phased "car tax" rollback, subject to the availability of increased state revenues produced by the state's growing economy. Gilmore would spend much of his remaining term struggling to preserve that legacy.

As the end of Gilmore's tenure approached in 2001, a state economy that had surged during the second half of the 1990s began to sag significantly, creating budget shortfalls that threatened the governor's "car tax" initiative and the state's reputation for sound fiscal management. The shortfalls and what to do about them led to a high-decibel budget impasse in

2001 between the state's Republican chief executive and the GOP-controlled legislature he had helped to elect, and the legislative meltdown helped pave the way for Mark Warner to capture the governorship for Virginia's Democrats in 2001. Importantly, however, Warner campaigned more as a candidate of continuity than of change. He faulted the GOP's management of state finances and promised to prevent any repeat of the state's unseemly budget deadlock, but otherwise he went out of his way not to challenge the popular policy reforms that had fueled Republican electoral successes during the Allen-Gilmore years. He would, Warner promised, complete the "car tax" phase-out, implement the next stage of the state's educational accountability program, and continue successful reforms in areas ranging from criminal sentencing to welfare programs. He even sounded Allenesque on the subject of voter referenda, pledging to oppose tax increases but arguing that politicians should "trust the people" and let them decide by referendum whether to embrace regional transportation initiatives funded by higher taxes.[54] A decade after George Allen had earned derision from the state's dominant Democrats with calls for dramatic changes in most major areas of state policy, the once-revolutionary measures had become a matter of bipartisan consensus and part of the Commonwealth's accepted wisdom.[55]

The Republican electoral successes of the 1990s in Virginia were inextricably linked with the GOP's major policy initiatives under Allen and Gilmore. Once in office with Allen's election as governor in 1994, the incumbent Republicans were buoyed politically by a state economy that outperformed the national economy throughout the decade. In this, the situation resembled the prosperity-fueled successes of the Virginia Democrats after Charles Robb's election in the watershed 1981 gubernatorial race. But, as political scientists had observed, the absence of philosophically polarizing issues in state races had tended to favor centrist Democrats in two-party

---

54. *Washington Post,* October 10, 2001.

55. The most politically controversial of the Allen-initiated reforms was the state's Standards of Learning and educational accountability program, which generated strong criticism from the education establishment. Reflecting the initiative's success and bipartisan acceptance a decade later, Governor Mark Warner used his annual address to the General Assembly in 2005 to tout his administration's success at helping students meet the academic requirements without watering down the standards. "With your support," Warner told legislators, "we have remained steadfast in our commitment to the Standards of Learning. . . . All across the Commonwealth the story is the same. By almost any measure, Virginia's schools continue to improve. Thanks to your support—and Virginians' strong commitment to standards-based education—our schools are on the right track and moving forward!" Text of 2005 State of the Commonwealth Message, Governor's Press Office, January 12, 2005.

competitive states like Virginia. Republicans overcame that dynamic in the Old Dominion by combining Reagan-style populism with a practical problem-solving agenda that addressed voters' priorities and reflected their right-of-center perspective and values. The GOP's state-level successes and gains in legislative and local races also were bolstered continually during the 1990s by evidence suggesting that the party's broad-based policy initiatives were working. That evidence came in varied forms, including statistics showing a 26 percent decline in the crime rate,[56] state welfare rolls cut in half,[57] record levels of new business investment in the state (especially in the high-technology sector), reductions in the number of state government employees, falling college tuition costs, lower taxes, and, most significant, the first marked improvement in student educational performance in more than a generation.[58] The evidence of success also came in the form of imitation, as delegations from other states and even the federal and foreign governments came to the Commonwealth to investigate and replicate aspects of Virginia's successful criminal sentencing, educational accountability, welfare, and other reforms.[59]

The Virginia Republican administrations of the 1990s and their wholesale embrace of Reagan populism also set the stage for the controversies of the next decade. A fault line appeared on issues of taxes and spending that would become a widening divide when economic challenges emerged just after the turn of the century. On one side were Governors Allen, Gil-

---

56. By 2002, the overall serious crime rate in Virginia had fallen to its lowest level since 1970. Virginia Criminal Sentencing Commission, *A Decade of Truth-In-Sentencing in Virginia* (Richmond: Commonwealth of Virginia, 2005), p. 7; see also Daniel F. Wilhelm and Nicholas R. Turner, "Is the Budget Crisis Changing the Way We Look at Sentencing and Incarceration?" *Issues in Brief*, Vera Institute of Justice, June 2002.

57. Leaving office in 1998, Allen reported that the state's welfare rolls had declined 42 percent since the enactment of welfare reform and were at the lowest level in a quarter-century, *Washington Post*, January 15, 1998; see also *Richmond Times-Dispatch*, October 16, 2004 (reporting on accolades received by Virginia for its successful welfare reform program and noting that the state's welfare caseload had declined from 70,000 households before welfare reform to about 35,000).

58. See Christie, "Virginia's Education Reform Works," pp. 1–2, 4; Christie, "Virginia's Education Reform Works—II," pp. 4–6.

59. After evaluating sentencing systems throughout the United States, a British team decided in 2004 to use Virginia's truth-in-sentencing system as a model for a redesigned sentencing system for the United Kingdom. In 2006, Chinese officials studying sentencing reform focused on the Virginia model after being encouraged to do so by the China Law Center at the Yale University Law School. Richard P. Kern, Ph.D., interview, April 21, 2006. Virginia's use of jury sentencing and nonmandatory sentencing guidelines also made its sentencing system one of the few state systems to avoid constitutional defect in 2004 under the sweeping United States Supreme Court decision in *Blakely v. Washington*, 125 S.Ct. 21 (2004), and related cases.

more, and their Democratic predecessor Wilder—all proponents of tax reduction for working families, and all committed foes of higher taxes even as a remedy for recession-driven budget shortfalls. On the other side were all of the living former governors, Republican and Democratic, who preceded Wilder, as well as the first two Virginia governors elected in the twenty-first century, Mark Warner and Timothy Kaine.[60] Tending to side with Governors Wilder, Allen, and Gilmore in favor of lower taxes were the new generation of younger conservatives elected to the General Assembly and Congress, many of the up-and-coming small businessmen and -women in the state, and a large share of upwardly mobile suburbanites, white and black. Siding with Governors Warner and Kaine and their pre-Wilder predecessors in support of higher taxes were the older, more moderate leaders of the General Assembly and members of Congress, the larger and more well-established business interests in the state, many civic and educational elites, and voters in the state's economically distressed rural and urban areas. Examples would abound to contradict these generalizations, but they reflected an economic, generational, and cultural divide that would emerge several times in the 1990s before becoming a dominant dynamic early in the new century. The political mantras would become familiar, too. Opponents of higher taxes would stress the need to reform government operations, better prioritize state expenditures, and keep taxes low to enhance the state's economic competitiveness and protect the pocketbooks of working families. Supporters of more spending—and thus higher taxes—would contend the state's tax burden was already relatively low and would emphasize the greater need to make forward-looking investments in education, transportation, social services, and public infrastructure.

While the state-level Allen "revolution" that began in 1993 became the top Virginia political story of the 1990s, dramatic developments also occurred on the federal scene. The decade's dominant national figure, President Clinton, appealed to many younger suburban voters, and their temporary addition to the Democratic base assured the president's reelection in 1996. But, despite his Southern roots, Clinton's politics and personal foibles—culminating with his impeachment in 1998—helped complete the Southern partisan realignment by driving away most traditional and cultural conservatives who had remained in the Democratic Party there.

---

60. As described in Chapter 9, Warner in 2004 successfully pushed through an omnibus tax package that produced a $1.4 billion net biennial increase in state revenues. The 2004 tax legislation was touted affirmatively as an accomplishment in Democratic Lieutenant Governor Timothy Kaine's winning bid in 2005 to succeed Warner. Kaine in turn proposed a billion-dollar annual tax increase to fund transportation initiatives. Both revenue measures were backed by the moderate Republican leadership of the state Senate but were opposed by the conservative GOP captains of the House of Delegates.

Meanwhile, the most prominent Virginian on the national stage, Senator John W. Warner, became a transcendent political figure in the state. After spurning his party and its most conservative nominees in 1993 and 1994, he embraced the GOP again and helped fortify its winning moderate-conservative coalition in several state elections thereafter. The senior senator thus personified and perpetuated the Commonwealth's disposition toward independence from political parties, a Byrd-era attribute that retained salience even as realignment progressed and the two major political parties in the state became consistently competitive. Senator Warner's most significant impact, however, was governmental, not political. After flirting seriously with a career-capping bid for the governorship in 1993, he turned all his energies to the Senate and went on to play a major role on the national scene as chairman of the powerful Senate Armed Services Committee. He was the most senior member in a Virginia congressional delegation that gained considerable legislative and political clout in the nation's capital, rivaling even that enjoyed by the state's venerated congressional delegation during the heyday of the Byrd organization.

With decisive Republican gains at the local and legislative levels, the 1990s saw the consummation of Virginia's half-century-old partisan realignment. The journey had begun in the ruins of the Civil War and Reconstruction, when only the Democratic label had been deemed socially acceptable in much of Virginia and the South. Memories had faded as generations passed; loyalties had been shaped and reshaped by defining events such as the Great Depression, the New Deal, and two great wars; and momentous demographic, economic, legal, and political changes had rearranged the state's landscape. The changes accelerated after World War II. A series of "first Republican wins"—Dwight Eisenhower's Virginia victory in 1952; Linwood Holton's gubernatorial breakthrough in 1969; William Scott's upset win for the United States Senate in 1972—had marked realignment's path and allowed observers to trace the advance of two-party competition from the presidential level to races for state posts. The transition took longer to reach the local level, where ties between politicians and voters typically are strong and often personal, and where party affiliation traditionally has been far less relevant. But in the 1990s, most of the remaining influential Byrd Democrats passed from the scene, and Virginia became a two-party competitive swing state, leaning Republican, from the courthouse to the statehouse to contests for the White House. A four-year period of bipartisan power-sharing in each of the state's legislative chambers helped ease the transition from Democratic to Republican rule in the General Assembly. With a final electoral surge led by Governor James Gilmore and Delegate S. Vance Wilkins of Amherst in 1999, Wilkins became the first Republican since Reconstruction to serve as speaker of the Virginia House of Delegates. The GOP achieved its long-sought majorities in the General Assembly and thereby marked the final milestone on the long realignment march.

While some of the decade's historic changes might have happened regardless of the outcome of the pivotal 1993 contest for governor, none would have been predicted as that race opened. For the first time since 1965—before the two-party competitive era began—Virginia Republicans would nominate a candidate for governor who had never before waged a race for statewide office. The Democratic nominee, by contrast, was an experienced two-term attorney general, the consensus nominee of her party, poised to become the state's first female governor, her campaign coffers bulging with donations from those who wanted her to win and from "smart money" players who were convinced she could not lose. "There's almost a sense the Democrats are entitled to the governorship," observed Emory & Henry College's Thomas R. Morris, "and that she is the next person in line."[61] Nothing seemed less probable than a Republican resurgence. But that was before the voters got into the act.

---

61. *Richmond Times-Dispatch*, September 7, 1993.

*6*

# FROM INSURGENT TO INSIDER: THE 1993 ALLEN LANDSLIDE

> At the outset of our journey, only a handful of insurgents came forward to join our cause for a new direction for Virginia's government. But as the journey continued, this insurgency grew, and it took root in cities and counties across our Commonwealth. By election day, the insurgency had become a revolutionary army that was victorious in taking back Virginia's government for Virginians—not for stolid, *status quo*, monarchical elitists. It was a victory for the people who own Virginia's government . . . the most dramatic call for change we have seen in modern times in Virginia.[1]
>
> —Governor George Allen, 1994

George Allen won the Virginia governorship in 1993 with 58 percent of the vote, amassing more than a 300,000-vote advantage over his opponent, and rolling up the largest gubernatorial winning margin in numerical or percentage terms since Democrat Albertis Harrison's 1961 cakewalk for the Byrd organization.[2] It was a landslide by modern Virginia standards, so far unsurpassed, and it appeared even more impressive when considered in light of the 27-point lead in polls[3] and the vast financial advantage that Democrat Mary Sue Terry enjoyed as the race got underway earlier in the year. Whether the outcome had more to do with Allen's resourceful and resilient "insurgency" or Terry's "spectacularly inept" cam-

---

1. *Washington Post*, January 16, 1994.
2. In the 1961 contest, which preceded the modern competitive era in Virginia politics, Harrison amassed more than 63 percent of the vote against Republican Clyde Pearson. See *The Dynamic Dominion*, Chapter 11.
3. A published poll in January 1993 found Terry with the support of 55 percent of voters and Allen with 28 percent. *Virginian-Pilot*, January 22, 1993. A similar poll seven months earlier showed Terry with a thirty-four-point lead, 54 percent to 20 percent. *Daily Progress*, June 14, 1992.

paign, as one neutral commentator called it,[4] would be a source of continual debate. For her part, Terry would place primary responsibility not on either person on the ballot, but on two unpopular fellow partisans who were constantly in the newspapers, Senator Robb and Governor Wilder. So consistently did the GOP's television ads lump her name with theirs that Terry wryly noted at the end of the contest that most Virginians knew her, not as "Mary Sue Terry," but as "Robb Wilder Terry." As in 1969 and 1981—two earlier gubernatorial elections that had produced a partisan changing of the guard in competitive Virginia—the divisions and controversies that embroiled the incumbent party created a strong appetite for change in the Virginia electorate in 1993. But the vivid contrast in the personalities of candidates Terry and Allen, the GOP's skillful use of its limited resources, and a series of stunning tactical errors by the front-running Democrat and her handlers also were crucial factors in the lopsided outcome.

How the forty-one-year-old George Allen even came to be the GOP nominee for governor in 1993 is a strange story. Barely two years before the gubernatorial election, Allen was a five-term member of the Virginia House of Delegates whose immediate ambitions ranged only as far as a possible bid for attorney general in 1993. But when an ailing French Slaughter announced retirement from his Seventh District congressional seat in mid-1991, Allen quickly jumped into the special election contest to succeed the popular conservative. He overcame two Slaughters to win the heavily Republican seat in the heart of Virginia's Piedmont, besting the retiring congressman's son and namesake in an abbreviated GOP nomination contest, and then trouncing Democrat Kay Slaughter, an environmental activist and cousin of the congressman, in the November special election.[5]

Even as Allen was winning election to Congress, however, General Assembly Democrats were crafting a redistricting plan that would deprive the new federal lawmaker of his district by pairing him with one of the state's Republican incumbents. Outwardly unfazed, Allen initially signaled his readiness to battle for reelection in the newly formed district or move to another more hospitable one. "I'm going to fight in whatever territory they give me . . . [or] load up the truck and move, like the Beverly Hillbillies," he declared. "They are not going to get rid of me easy."[6] When the plan was finalized, Allen had been lumped with Richmond-area incumbent Thomas J. Bliley Jr. in a new Seventh District that ran west across the full

---

4. Rozell, "Virginia: The New Politics of the Old Dominion," p. 145.
5. Allen won the November 5, 1991, special election with 62 percent of the vote. Sabato, *Virginia Votes 1991–1994*, pp. 21–22.
6. *Washington Post*, November 6, 1991.

breadth of the Piedmont from the capital city. By the time state Republicans assembled in early December 1991 for their annual party leadership conference, the congressman-elect had decided on a different course. Instead of challenging Bliley or changing his residence to run in an adjacent congressional district, Allen opted to aim higher—he would run for *governor*. The Democratic partisans who had masterminded his ouster were openly derisive.

Allen had the opportunity to make the jump into the governor's race because of the slow start by the other two expected contestants, Delegate Clinton Miller of Shenandoah County and Northern Virginia businessman Earle C. Williams. Miller had a reputation within the General Assembly as an effective if sometimes maverick lawmaker, but he failed to excite significant grassroots GOP support mainly because his stands on hot-button issues, such as abortion and gun rights, were at odds with the views of many Republican activists. In Williams's case, the problem was chiefly one of timing. Before Allen's sudden entry, many influential Republican leaders had begun to warm to the idea of fielding a political newcomer and seasoned businessman for the top job in state government. Voters in Virginia and across the country seemed dissatisfied with the performance of traditional politicians in both parties, and state Republicans were eager for a fresh face after the multiple attempts and failures by party nominees Coleman and Durrette in the 1980s. An Alabama native, Williams had led McLean-based BDM International, a fast-growing defense contractor with a payroll of 4,000 employees, for three decades. Not only was he free of scars from the GOP's persistent factional infighting; Williams's impressive record as a business executive promised to close the stature and experience gap that was sure to plague Republicans in a contest against two-term Attorney General Terry. But Williams hesitated to throw his hat into the ring, and when he finally committed himself to the race in the spring of 1992, Allen's headstart had given him a virtually insurmountable advantage in the jockeying for nominating convention support.

Williams was already assured of strong support in vote-heavy Northern Virginia, where he was backed by influential Fairfax County Board of Supervisors chairman (later, congressman) Thomas M. Davis III, a relentless political organizer who enjoyed strong GOP grassroots support in the region. Williams probably could have effectively clinched the Republican gubernatorial nomination in mid-1991 (before Allen's entry) by also locking down the backing of Representative Thomas Bliley, Bliley's potent political organization in central Virginia, and his allies in Richmond's business community. In March 1991, Davis adviser and longtime GOP consultant Kenneth Klinge urged Williams to signal his gubernatorial intentions and reach out to Richmond financier Lawrence Lewis Jr., Congressman Bliley, and Bliley's key lieutenant, Boyd Marcus, for support. Bliley and Marcus were then preparing to run the Bush-Quayle reelection campaign in Virginia, and they had the opportunity to give Williams the ideal platform for a maiden gubernatorial bid. In an ensuing series of verbal and written discussions with Williams and his advisers, Marcus and veteran GOP organizer Michael Thomas outlined a proposed strategy that would preempt most opposition, avoid a divisive intraparty battle, and sew up the 1993 nomination for Williams well in advance. The key, they advised, was to move decisively early. Williams's advisers Edward DeBolt and Todd Stottlemyer concurred with the political advice, but the noncommittal business executive declined to move. Obligations to his company, Williams felt, precluded any such announcement or overt political steps for some months—months that proved crucial.[7] Williams's intentions were still undeclared when, in late 1991, Allen was gerrymandered into the seat with Bliley and suddenly opted to run for governor. Among the first and most influential supporters of Allen's gubernatorial bid were Congressman Bliley, Boyd Marcus, and Michael Thomas, who became campaign manager. Also on board early with Allen was Lawrence Lewis Jr., who became the financial mainstay of the Albemarle Republican's campaign.[8]

A most unlikely potential GOP candidate for governor—but also seemingly the strongest—surfaced in late 1991, when Senator John Warner let it be known that he was being urged to consider a 1993 gubernatorial bid. Warner's party was out of power in the Senate, and his long-sought goal of chairing the powerful Armed Services Committee seemed out of reach, so the senior senator gave serious consideration to a career-crowning bid for the governorship.[9] Privately he commissioned a legal analysis to determine whether, if elected governor, he would be able to appoint his successor, and thus keep his Senate seat in GOP hands—a question that was

---

7. Todd A. Stottlemyer interview, December 15, 2004. Interviewed a decade later, Congressman Davis agreed that Williams's late start doomed his bid, noting the difficulty of communicating to a businessman who lacks political experience the importance of early grassroots effort in a party nomination contest. Thomas M. Davis III interview, March 17, 2005.

8. In addition to Bliley's appreciation for Allen's decision to cede the new Seventh District seat to the Richmonder, the stage had been set for the Bliley-Allen alliance two years earlier. After Congressman Slaughter's resignation in 1991, Bliley had endorsed Allen for the GOP nomination to succeed him, and Marcus and Thomas had assisted Allen's 1991 congressional campaign. Thomas J. Bliley Jr. interview, March 15, 2005; M. Boyd Marcus Jr. interview, July 8, 2003; Michael E. Thomas interview, July 16, 2003.

9. *Richmond Times-Dispatch*, February 9, 1992.

answered in the negative. The thought of surrendering his Senate seniority, which benefited Virginians, as well as the prospect that the outgoing Governor Wilder would be able to choose a Democrat to succeed him, weighed heavily on Warner.[10] Yet, as he pondered the race over a five-month period, opinion polls showed that he likely would defeat Terry in a contest for governor. While Terry enjoyed big leads in hypothetical match-ups against Allen, Williams, and Miller, she trailed Warner by a 14-point margin in a January 1992 survey by the Mason-Dixon polling organization.[11] Warner was still undecided on the race two months later when George Allen announced formation of his own campaign exploratory committee, chaired by Bliley. Allen earlier had described Warner as the party's strongest candidate for governor, and before announcing formation of his campaign committee, he called Warner and pledged to step aside if the senator entered the race.[12] The problem for Allen and his likely competitors was that Warner's prolonged flirtation with a possible gubernatorial bid was hampering their own efforts to attract campaign support and financing. Acceding to their urgings that he promptly make a decision, Warner announced in April 1992 that he would remain in the Senate. Relieved state Democrats applauded the news; Lieutenant Governor Donald Beyer chortled that Warner's decision deprived Republicans of their "dream ticket" and made a Democratic victory even more certain.[13]

The dizzying events of late 1991 and 1992 were like a roller-coaster ride for Allen. As he served out his single year in the House of Representatives and simultaneously launched his gubernatorial bid, it seemed that the most improbable, rapid-fire succession of events were conspiring to put him in position to represent his party against the seemingly formidable Terry. Although the nomination contest among Allen, Williams, and Miller was often contentious, Allen was the frontrunner from the time he formally kicked off his campaign in November 1992, and his nomination was never seriously threatened. He benefited from his own strong personal appeal among rank-and-file party activists, an effective grassroots mobilization effort led by experienced GOP organizers Michael Thomas and Ray Allen Jr., and the desire of many Republican partisans to settle on a candidate early so as to avoid another long-running intraparty nomination fight. Williams stressed his business experience and made the most of his Northern Virginia political base, which included support from regional GOP luminaries like

---

10. John W. Warner interview, June 27, 1980, May 17, 1990, and December 8, 2004.
11. *Richmond News Leader*, January 14, 1992.
12. *Daily Progress*, November 17, 1991; *Washington Post*, March 17, 1992.
13. *Washington Post*, April 10, 1992.

Davis and wealthy developer John T. ("Til") Hazel. But outside the populous northern region, the Williams candidacy never caught on. "Many downstate Republicans," wrote John Harris of the *Washington Post* early in the race, "sensing a chance to recapture the governorship after twelve years of Democratic rule, are eager to avoid a debilitating nomination battle like the GOP had in 1989 and are rallying around Representative George F. Allen of Charlottesville."[14]

If Allen had an Achilles' heel in the nomination contest, it was money. In contrast to the well-heeled Williams, the frontrunner had no significant base of financial supporters in any of the business centers of northern, western, central, or southeastern Virginia. Yet, this circumstance may have been a key factor in Allen's eventual triumph over Terry, because it forced Allen and his team to focus on building a broad-based, highly active political organization. They responded to their financial disadvantage creatively— "living off the land," as Allen put it,[15] and surviving, even thriving, primarily through grassroots effort. Since the campaign had few large contributors, finance director Betsy Davis arranged literally hundreds of low-dollar fundraisers all across the state, capitalizing on the enthusiasm of party activists and reinforcing the esprit de corps within Allen's happy band of "insurgents." The innovative financial approach succeeded in keeping the campaign's coffers full enough to be competitive. A similar method was used to gain news coverage. Since major media outlets were not covering the longshot Republicans' stumping closely, the Allen camp relied on hundreds of visits to small town newspaper offices, appearances on radio shows, and other opportunities for local exposure.

The Allen campaign's ubiquitous recreational vehicle took the candidate over much of the state's terrain, conjuring up recollections of the many miles logged by Douglas Wilder's station wagon in his famous rural tour eight years earlier. The difference was the volunteer army that supported the Allen effort. His legions soon were showing up everywhere from county fairs to shopping centers, handing out campaign materials, putting up signs, and waging a political campaign the exhilarating way it was done before the advent of high-dollar fundraisers, automated phone calling, and massive television buys. The grassroots emphasis was hardly a stroke of tactical genius; it was a necessary response to the absence of alternatives. Yet, its success depended on the convergence of two crucial elements: a candidate able to excite and motivate volunteer workers, and a seasoned campaign staff schooled in the techniques of grassroots politics. The scarcity of money,

14. *Washington Post*, May 2, 1992.
15. *Richmond Times-Dispatch*, November 3, 1993.

recalled Allen campaign manager Michael Thomas, had a salutary effect that was felt all the way through to the general election contest:

> We had literally thousands of people out in the streets, passing out fliers, putting on bumper stickers, going to every county fair, talking to their neighbors, doing all kinds of things. And it always seemed we had just enough money to keep doing those things. So, by the time Mary Sue Terry started taking George Allen seriously, there was all this momentum behind us. The lack of money, which caused such a struggle over a year, really two years, actually turned out to be a blessing, because if we had had more money, we would never have set out to do things that way and probably would not have been able to build that kind of spirit in people. Folks got on board and rose to that challenge because they really wanted to prove it could be done—that "people power" really could win. . . . The struggle for money was the key in making us build a strong grassroots and overwhelming volunteer effort that really was unlike anything we have seen to date.[16]

"If ever there was a well-run organization that used its . . . limited resources to greatest advantage," agreed Larry Sabato, "it was Allen's."[17]

All of this activity was occurring under the radar, however, and the conventional wisdom remained dismissive of Allen's chances throughout the 1993 preliminaries. As Terry formally launched her bid in May 1993, reporter Margaret Edds wrote that she brought "a treasure trove of assets to the race [for governor]: $1.5 million in the bank, well-wishes from much of the state's corporate and civic elite, and the politically correct virtue of being female."[18] "Since 1965, when Mills Godwin ran as a Democrat," commented Sabato, "no candidate has started out with as many advantages as Mary Sue Terry."[19] Yet, Edds, Sabato, and other commentators also understood the electorate's increasingly negative disposition toward incumbents and the resulting chance that political fortunes could shift suddenly; Edds cited President Bush's rapid fall from popularity and power the previous year as an example.

Among the slowest to perceive Allen's potential and his growing grassroots momentum were some of the most prominent Republican-leaning business and professional leaders around the state. Some strayed to back Terry, while others huddled privately—even after Allen had largely corralled the delegate support needed for nomination—to see if some stratagem could

---

16. Thomas interview.
17. Sabato, *Virginia Votes 1991–1994*, p. 74.
18. *Virginian-Pilot*, May 9, 1993.
19. *Virginian-Pilot*, May 9, 1993.

be developed for pressing the frontrunner to step aside in favor of Williams.[20] The supposedly secret discussions quickly made their way back to Allen. "It would certainly have been understandable if George Allen had been discouraged by the poll numbers, the lack of resources, the negative attitude and conspiring by some in the business community, and the skepticism of the press during that time," observed deputy campaign chief Jay Timmons, who later became Allen's gubernatorial chief of staff. "What kept him going was his intense competitive spirit, the extraordinary energy he drew from people on the campaign trail, and his passion for ideas. The adversity only made him more determined to see his 'insurgency' succeed."[21]

Ironically, it was one of the oldest and wealthiest business titans in Virginia who embraced the youthful Allen candidacy with the most fervor and provided him with crucial financial backing as the election year contests got into full swing. The irascible Lawrence Lewis Jr. was heir to part of the enormous Flagler fortune and had been an institution in Virginia's conservative coalition politics at least since he led a group of Byrd Democrats calling themselves "New Republicans" to back Linwood Holton's 1969 gubernatorial bid.[22] His legendary generosity extended not only to political pursuits but to a wide range of civic, educational, and charitable causes as well. Frustrated with the serial setbacks suffered by GOP gubernatorial candidates in the 1980s, Lewis had taken the initiative in convening more than 100 thirty- and forty-something business and professional colleagues in 1991 to explore ways to get the party back on its feet and back in power. When he embraced the Allen candidacy, Lewis brought not only financial backing but also legitimacy in the social and political circles in which he moved.

As the contest got underway, Allen's persona and campaign could not have contrasted more vividly with Terry's. And it was not just the gender difference or the fact that Allen's campaign cupboard was often nearly bare while Terry was continually awash in resources. Allen reveled in challenging the establishment, and he positioned himself as a champion of change, the standard-bearer for an "honest new generation of Republican leadership." The groundbreaking nature of her candidacy also gave Terry the ability to present herself as a change agent; she began the campaign by asserting that "[our] great state . . . was named after a woman [and] will finally be led by

20. Cullen interview; *Washington Post*, February 17, 1993.
21. Jay W. Timmons interview, July 16, 2003.
22. Henry Morison Flagler founded the Standard Oil Company with John D. Rockefeller in 1867. The role of Lewis and the New Republicans in the 1969 election is described in *The Dynamic Dominion*, Chapter 18.

one."[23] But she instead chose to stress her credentials as a governmental insider and a card-carrying member of the political club that had controlled Virginia for more than a decade.[24] Her installation after Wilder's tenure, observed commentator Robert Holsworth, would constitute "not so much a changing . . . as a resuscitation of the Old Guard."[25] While Allen was most comfortable mixing with ordinary folks at country stores and Friday night football games, Terry seemed to recoil at the thought of unscripted interaction with the voting public. The spontaneous Republican would plunge gleefully into a crowd, while the reticent, methodical Terry would rarely show up in public settings unless surrounded by a protective cocoon of aides and allies.

The major differences of image and style—Allen as the exuberant populist; Terry as the aloof establishmentarian—were somewhat belied by the reality of the candidates' backgrounds. While the forty-five-year-old Terry was the daughter of school teachers and traced her roots to hardscrabble Patrick County, Allen had enjoyed a comparatively privileged youth as the elder son of a famous professional football coach. And though Allen derided Terry as an elitist—he dubbed her "Mary Sue Antoinette"[26]—the Republican candidate was a millionaire while Terry possessed no comparable personal wealth. Terry's legendary prowess as a campaign fundraiser became such a dominant part of her political persona that it defined her as a friend of the rich and famous, while Allen's down-home appeal succeeded in Virginia—in spite of his West Coast roots—because it reflected his genuine disposition toward "ordinary working folks" more than moneyed interests. When voters eventually tuned in to the contest, what they saw was probably the starkest contrast in personal styles and image ever projected in a Virginia gubernatorial election, and that contrast decidedly favored Allen.

The other major contrast that began to emerge during spring 1993 centered around the candidates' very different approaches to campaign issues. While Terry took an exceedingly cautious tack, stressing her experience and rarely stepping out with new policy recommendations, Allen and his campaign became a veritable font of proposals for substantive change,

---

23. *Washington Post*, May 9, 1993.

24. Terry was more comfortable running as an experienced insider than as a female trailblazer, but she and her handlers also perceived that voters were not in the mood for another history-making candidacy after Wilder's rocky gubernatorial tenure. "If Governor Wilder's approval ratings had been at 60 percent, people might have been more in a mood to make history again," she observed. "But the previous campaign had been positioned as history-making, and the incumbent was not popular. Plus, it was not my style or who I am to lead with that." Mary Sue Terry interview, March 22, 2005.

25. *Washington Post*, October 31, 1993.

26. *Washington Post*, October 10, 1993.

sometimes unveiling several new ideas and initiatives in a single week. The Allen proposals ranged from prescriptions for major reforms, such as over-hauls of the welfare and educational systems, to more narrow and specific suggestions for correcting vexing problems that plagued ordinary citizens. So commanding was Terry's lead in the polls that the cascade of Allen ideas was largely ignored by media and political insiders during the spring prelim-inaries. The exception came in May 1993, when Allen unveiled his plan to abolish parole and replace it with a truth-in-sentencing system that would keep violent and repeat criminals behind bars significantly longer. The plan was modeled on the federal sentencing system, which had eliminated parole and instituted a sentencing guideline regime.[27] To give the seemingly radical proposal credibility, Allen was joined for the announcement by two well-known crime-fighting alumni of the just-ousted Bush administration, for-mer Attorney General William Barr and former federal prosecutor Richard Cullen. Democrats nevertheless dismissed the plan, and it received little positive comment in newspaper coverage and commentary. Even some Republicans publicly doubted it. But Allen stuck with the issue, castigating Terry for presiding over a violent crime spike as attorney general and for supporting a "dishonest, lenient, liberal parole system" that allowed mur-derers and rapists to get out of prison early and claim more innocent victims. It would prove to be the pivotal issue of the campaign.

Much of the intraparty fighting that had plagued the Democrats over the preceding several years seemed to have been quelled by spring 1993. The Democrats' new party chairman, Mark Warner, observed half-jokingly that he was selected for the post because he "was the only Democrat who was on speaking terms with Wilder, Robb and Terry all at the same time."[28] Warner worked hard to put the divisive genie back in the bottle after several years of tumult. "The Democratic Party of Virginia entered the 1990s with tremendous optimism," he explained.

> We had just set Virginia and national history with the election of Wilder. Our margins in the General Assembly were still fairly strong. Wilder was the third leg of the Robb-Baliles-Wilder [gubernatorial] chain. That almost immediately began to break down as the governor and legislature had their series of battles, and from a party standpoint, institutional inner tensions in the party, papered over in 1987 and 1989, all sort of broke open in 1991.[29]

---

27. A similar proposal advanced four years earlier by GOP gubernatorial nominee Marshall Coleman had failed to gain traction in the history-making, abortion-focused climate of the 1989 election.

28. Mark R. Warner interview, March 21, 2005.

29. Margaret Edds and Thomas R. Morris, "Virginia: Republicans Surge in the Competitive Dominion," *Southern Politics in the 1990s*, ed. Alexandra P. Lamis (Baton Rouge: Louisiana State University Press), pp. 143–144.

In addition to the notorious Robb-Wilder clash, which intensified again as the governor moved toward challenging Robb for his Senate seat in 1994, Attorney General Terry had sparred with Wilder over several matters, including her decision to investigate actions by the governor's appointees overseeing the Virginia Retirement System and her withdrawal as counsel defending the all-male admission policy of Virginia Military Institute. It had become increasingly apparent that Terry was out to distance herself from the unpopular governor, and Wilder was not about to step willingly into the shadows. He felt, with considerable justification, that his success at managing the state's finances during the recessionary period, and the resulting accolades from respected publications such as *Financial World* magazine, represented a record that Terry could and should defend.[30] The rift between the governor and attorney general was not repaired, but it was glossed over as the 1993 campaign got underway. Wilder endorsed Terry for governor, and that, combined with Lieutenant Governor Beyer's decision to wait his turn and seek reelection rather than challenge her for the gubernatorial nod, allowed Terry to claim that she had not only a superior resume and resources but also a united party that was poised to retain the governor's mansion.

Virginia Democrats nominated Terry and Beyer in an early May convention that Larry Sabato described as "a carefully orchestrated and exquisitely dull event."[31] Joining them on the ticket as the attorney general candidate was Arlington lawyer William D. Dolan III, who had not held public office but had served creditable stints as chairman of the state's community college board and as president of the Virginia State Bar. A month later, Republicans finalized their ticket in a raucous conclave attended by more than 13,000 delegates and alternates—a number that eclipsed even the party's "Great Indoor Primary" of 1978, which had set the previous record for free-world political assemblages.[32] After endorsing a resolutions committee video that laid down a wide-ranging indictment of the scandal-plagued ruling party, the exuberant conventioneers gave Allen the expected nomination victory with 64 percent of the delegate vote. The Albemarle Republican carried every congressional district except the Eighth and Eleventh in Northern Virginia, which stuck with its favorite son, Earle Williams. In the race for the attorney general nomination, James Gilmore, the Henrico

---

30. *Financial World* named Virginia the best fiscally run state in the nation twice during Wilder's administration, and Virginia was one of only two states to refrain from raising taxes during the recession of the early 1990s. Edds and Morris, "Virginia," p. 146.

31. Sabato, *Virginia Votes 1991–1994*, p. 51.

32. For a description of the tumultuous 1978 Republican state convention, dubbed the "Great Indoor Primary" by newspaper columnist Charles McDowell, see *The Dynamic Dominion*, Chapter 31.

County prosecutor, prevailed with more than 60 percent of the vote over Delegate G. Steven Agee of Roanoke.[33] The biggest GOP fireworks were reserved for the cultural clash between Michael P. Farris and Bobbie Kilberg in the contest for lieutenant governor. Farris, a resident of Loudoun County and leader of the national home-schooling movement, was a political newcomer who galvanized the party's expanded rank of Christian Right activists, while Kilberg was a longtime moderate, pro-choice GOP activist from McLean who served in the Bush White House. Though the contest for the second spot on the ticket was contentious and presented the party's economically conservative faction with something of a Hobson's Choice, Farris joined Allen and Gilmore in amassing more than 60 percent of the delegate vote.[34]

While the GOP conventioneers were enthusiastic about their ticket, Democratic strategists seemed even more pleased with the Republicans' handiwork. "We were delighted [by the outcome of the Republican convention]," said Mary ("Mame") Reiley, a member of the Democratic National Committee and aide to Eighth District Representative James P. Moran Jr. "We couldn't ask for a better ticket to run against."[35] Party chairman Mark Warner agreed, branding the Allen-led ticket "the most extreme, right-wing, radical ticket" in the state's history, as he zeroed in on Michael Farris's strong anti-abortion position and his past statements critical of the public schools.[36] With a remarkable $2.3 million in cash sitting in Terry's campaign kitty—in contrast to Allen, who had spent nearly all of his limited resources in winning the nomination—operatives in both parties now expected Terry to launch a preemptive television attack defining the Allen-Farris-Gilmore ticket as too extreme for suburban, moderate-conservative Virginia.[37] Democrats wanted the well-heeled Terry campaign to give the Allen ticket "a ride on the Farris wheel," as they put it, by using the strongly conservative positions of the GOP nominee for lieutenant governor on education and cultural issues to portray the entire Republican ticket as outside the Virginia mainstream.[38] But the expected post-convention attack

---

33. Agee was a well-regarded member of the House of Delegates from 1982 to 1994. He joined the state Court of Appeals in 1997, and, in 2003, was elected by the General Assembly—newly under Republican control—to a seat on the Virginia Supreme Court.

34. Sabato, *Virginia Votes 1991–1994*, p. 51.

35. *Richmond Times-Dispatch*, June 7, 1993.

36. *Washington Post*, June 26, 1993.

37. While Terry had $2.3 million in her campaign coffers, Allen had raised only about a third of that amount, and had spent virtually all of it on the GOP nomination race. *Washington Post*, June 7, 1993.

38. *Richmond Times-Dispatch*, October 4, 1993.

never came, in part because their study of other female candidates' campaigns convinced Terry and her advisers that she could not fire the first negative salvos in the contest without incurring voters' wrath.[39] In a move that made the legendarily reticent Union General George McClellan seem adventurous, Terry and her team chose to husband their enormous resource advantage, making only a modest ad purchase on cable television stations in June that stressed her credentials and invited viewers to call a toll-free number to get a copy of her "agenda for action."[40]

Terry's failure to capitalize decisively on Allen's cash deficit as the general election contest commenced in June would prove to be the most colossal blunder of a flawed Democratic campaign that seemed hobbled throughout by overconfidence.[41] Of all the improbable events that had suddenly propelled George Allen toward the governorship, the decision by Terry to hold her fire in the wake of the GOP convention ranked as the most curious. The Republican nominee's flank actually was even more exposed in June than the Democrats, or even Allen's own campaign team, had anticipated. Having emptied its kitty in winning the party's nod, the Allen campaign expected that the nomination would bring a prompt infusion of campaign cash from the usual Republican corporate contributors as well as the Republican National Committee and the state GOP, which had raised significant funds through convention delegate fees. They planned to use the new resources to pay for a June advertising blitz that would introduce Allen, his attractive young family, and his reform-minded agenda to voters for the first time. But, doubting their own nominee's chances, state and national Republican Party sources resisted Allen's requests for post-convention funding, and support barely trickled in from the GOP-leaning business community. It was only the intervention of the independent-minded Lawrence Lewis Jr. that permitted the Allen campaign to execute its strategy and exploit the opportunity created by the Terry blunder. Lewis threw the Allen team a $175,000 lifeline, making it possible to fund the early-summer ad campaign through which the Republican candidate introduced himself

---

39. Terry interview. "That was commandment number one—that we could not go negative first," Terry recalled.

40. *Washington Post,* June 8, 1993.

41. In a 2005 interview, Terry challenged the widespread view that her campaign exhibited overconfidence. Her campaign's internal polling showed that the political climate was very adverse for Democrats and that Allen would be competitive if able to raise sufficient campaign funds. "There never was overconfidence. In fact, there was surprise at how strong I was in the polls at the start," she declared. "We knew the race would be close, and the only question was whether the Republican nominee would be able to raise the money." Terry interview.

positively to Virginia voters before Democrats branded him an "extremist."[42]

Terry's missed opportunity would be much-remarked in the wake of Allen's upset victory, and though some doubted its significance in light of the Republican's ultimately lopsided win, experienced operatives and observers viewed it as the campaign's turning point. Terry had begun the race with a 27-point lead in polls, and in the wake of the June convention, her lead had narrowed to 18 points.[43] Allen used the narrowing poll gap to make the case to skeptical party leaders and funders that his long-shot campaign could succeed—a contention that began to gain traction as internal polls showed Terry's lead shrinking still further after Allen's June media buy.[44] A major ad campaign by Terry in the same time frame would almost certainly have undercut the Republican's bid for credibility as a challenger. "It would have been very hard for us to raise money if those poll numbers, after closing somewhat, had widened again as a result of a major TV buy by Terry," said Allen manager Michael Thomas. "It wasn't that people wanted to give money to Mary Sue Terry; they just thought she was going to win."[45] "Had [Terry] gotten out early and defined [Allen negatively], I don't think we would have ever been able to recover," ventured Allen campaign aide Christopher LaCivita.[46]

If Terry missed a fleeting chance to bury Allen early, she did so, according to Larry Sabato,

> because of her cautious nature, her previous, conventional campaign experience and her consultants' advice. Like state attorney general Andrew P. Miller before her, she incorrectly believed that two landslide victories in down-ballot statewide races gave her the formula for success in a contest for governor. . . . Terry herself had run two high-dollar "stealth" campaigns for attorney general, with little coverage or controversy, and lots of paid television advertising.[47]

Allen's campaign pollster, John McLaughlin, suggested the Democratic campaign also was fooled by their candidate's big lead in the polls, which was largely a reflection of Terry's higher name identification among voters.

---

42. Thomas interview; Betsy Davis (Beamer) interview, July 16, 2003.
43. *Virginian-Pilot*, June 15, 1993.
44. The gap between the candidates had closed to approximately twelve percentage points after the Republicans' June television advertising. John McLaughlin interview, July 8, 2003, and July 16, 2003.
45. Thomas interview.
46. Christopher LaCivita interview, July 16, 2003.
47. Sabato, *Virginia Votes 1991–1994*, pp. 72–73.

McLaughlin's surveys for Allen showed that, of those familiar with both candidates (only about 20 percent of all voters as of the time of the GOP convention), Allen fared the best. McLaughlin explained:

> The Terry people apparently looked at their lead in the polls and thought they did not need to attack and define George Allen. They thought Terry was stronger than she was. But at the time, only one in five voters knew George, and he was winning among them; Terry was only winning among those who did not know George. Terry's advisers probably did not give her the analysis that said, "Hey, you have got to use your money to go out and rearrange this guy, because if he gets equally known as you, you will lose." On the other side, those of us working for Allen knew we had an unusually good candidate with the right message, and the only question was whether we would be able to get the resources to get him known.[48]

The June advertising decisions were not the only ones that showed the underdog Allen campaign team was more seasoned and had a better conceived strategy and message than its Democratic counterpart. Terry's campaign was directed by a coterie of her longtime confidants and a lead consultant, Tom King, who had assisted Terry's earlier bids but never advised a Virginia statewide candidate in a competitive race. In contrast, the team assembled by Allen consisted of a close-knit group of battle-tested GOP operatives and advisers who had learned valuable lessons from their work together in the tumultuous 1989 Coleman gubernatorial campaign and other hard-fought Virginia contests in the 1980s. As events played out in the summer and early fall, the GOP's superior strategy on the crime issue, its preparation to head off any reprise of the 1989 abortion debate and other social-issue controversies, and its plan for exploiting Terry's links to the unpopular President Clinton and the controversial Robb and Wilder, all bore fruit. The Terry camp's mishandling of each of these key matters deepened her campaign's descent until she found herself in an October free-fall unparalleled in two-party competitive Virginia.

As a two-term attorney general, Terry had been expected to dominate the law enforcement issue in the race for governor. An unmarried female, the Democrat planned to establish her gubernatorial bona fides with skeptical male voters by positioning herself as a tough and successful crime-fighter. Although Virginia had experienced a significant increase in violent crime in the late 1980s during her tenure as attorney general, Terry had compiled a generally conservative seven-year record as the state's top lawyer, and there was reason to believe she could prevail on the issue. In June, she and her

---

48. McLaughlin interview.

handlers moved to make law enforcement the focus of the race by holding a news conference with sixty-four local sheriffs, mostly Democrats, at which she put forward one of her few new policy proposals: a five-day waiting period for handgun purchases. The Terry plan resembled the "Brady bill" then pending in Congress,[49] but the General Assembly controlled by Terry's party had only recently rejected a less-stringent, three-day waiting period requirement, and the attorney general herself had not even supported that more modest measure. It had been rejected in part because the state already had in place one of the nation's first laws requiring a computerized criminal record check before handgun purchases. The Terry team was persuaded, however, by campaign polls showing strong public support for the waiting-period idea. On the heels of Governor Wilder's surprising success at building bipartisan support for a one-handgun-purchase-per-month restriction to stem illegal firearms trafficking, moderate and suburban Virginia seemed to have a new appetite for combating crime with gun restrictions—or so the Democratic planners thought.

In the Allen camp, the waiting-period proposal was greeted with some surprise, but more satisfaction than alarm. John McLaughlin's polling revealed that Terry's waiting-period proposal and Allen's parole-abolition plan both enjoyed broad support in an electorate anxious to get violent crime back under control by any reasonable means. But McLaughlin posed a question to his survey respondents that his Democratic counterpart apparently never asked. When queried about which of the two proposals would do a better job of reducing violent crime, Virginians by a margin of roughly 70 percent to 20 percent cited ending liberal parole policies as the more effective crime-fighting technique.[50] Terry's brain-trust thus had committed a threefold error: they had tethered her campaign to a remedy for violence that most suburban swing voters perceived as weak compared to Allen's decisive parole reform plan; they had embraced gun control in a way that jeopardized Terry's longstanding support in rural areas where gun restrictions were intensely unpopular; and they had played into the Republicans' hands by making crime the central issue in the contest, inviting a focus on the violent crime surge that had occurred on Terry's watch as attorney general.

By advocating the gun purchase waiting period, the Democrat gave her erstwhile supporters in the National Rifle Association the back of her

---

49. After White House press secretary James Brady was severely wounded in the 1981 assassination attempt on President Reagan, he and his wife Sarah became leading advocates of proposed federal legislation, dubbed the "Brady bill," that would require a five-day waiting period prior to the purchase of a handgun.

50. McLaughlin interview.

hand, and they responded with an avalanche of campaign ads and grassroots activities assailing her position. Terry hoped the shift at least would help her among law enforcement advocates. But in late August, the state's 7,100-member Fraternal Order of Police (FOP), which had backed Terry in her successive bids for attorney general, strongly endorsed Allen, along with Democrat Beyer and Republican Gilmore in the down-ballot races. FOP president Garth Wheeler acknowledged that the organization agreed with Terry's waiting-period plan, but said its members were more interested in "taking criminals off the street and keeping them off" through Allen's no-parole plan than in adopting gun-purchase waiting periods.[51] Terry sought to dismiss the union's endorsement as a product of "pandering" by Allen on police officer benefits, but Lieutenant Governor Beyer undercut his running mate by touting the group's verdict in his favor as an authoritative expression by "the law enforcement officers who are on the front lines every day."[52] In September, Allen and Terry took to the airwaves with their contrasting remedies for the state's crime woes. The Republican's evocative ads featured Allen personally recounting the horrific story of an actual killing in homicide-wracked Richmond, along with references to the rise in violent crime during Terry's tenure and Allen's endorsement by the state FOP. Terry's less effective television missives, which were punctuated by a discharging handgun rather than words from the candidate, portrayed Allen as a "reckless" politician who opposed sensible gun restrictions because of subservience to the National Rifle Association. Remarkably, Terry's handlers aired the gun control ads in rural parts of the state where support for gun rights was particularly strong.

In addition to coming out on the short end of the dominant crime debate, Terry was dogged all summer and fall by the unpopularity of fellow Democrats Clinton, Wilder, and Robb. Allen continually linked Terry to all three, and he implicitly referenced the scandal-plagued Democrats' misdeeds in calling for an "honest new generation" of leadership for the state. Terry could never figure how to distance herself from those disliked party leaders without alienating the Democratic base groups that still supported them. "Always lurking in the background for Terry," wrote Larry Sabato,

> were the three unpopular leaders of her party. The Terry campaign was successful in keeping Senator Robb virtually out of sight, and President Clinton never crossed the Potomac to make an appearance with the Democratic nominee for governor. But Governor Wilder was in the headlines almost daily, as was news of his impending challenge for Robb's Senate seat. And

---

51. *Richmond Times-Dispatch*, August 31, 1993.
52. *Richmond Times-Dispatch*, August 31, 1993.

Clinton's wildly disliked policies on defense and the economy dominated the airwaves in a way that was difficult for Terry to surmount.[53]

In a mid-summer debate before the Virginia Bar Association, moderator Sabato characterized President Clinton and Allen's running mate, Michael Farris, as "twin millstones," and he challenged the gubernatorial candidates flatly to "endorse or repudiate" their respective fellow partisans. Allen largely ducked the question, asserting only that he and Farris did not agree on every issue and that meant the GOP had a "strong and diverse ticket."[54] But Terry's response reverberated loudly from the quiet mountain resort where the debate was held, as the *Times-Dispatch*'s Mike Allen reported:

> Democratic gubernatorial candidate Mary Sue Terry gave President Clinton the Heisman Trophy straight-arm, cementing the independent course of a campaign that has shunned the word "Democrat." Asked to endorse or repudiate her fellow Democrat's policy on gays in the military and his proposed tax increases, Ms. Terry said without missing a beat: "I repudiate." The Virginia Bar Association audience of four hundred and fifty was stunned for a few seconds, then laughed.[55]

The problem for Terry was noted by an unnamed Democratic activist quoted in *Washington Post*: "It's a Catch-22 problem with Clinton. Clinton is killing [Terry] downstate, but when she criticizes him up here [in Northern Virginia], she turns off a lot of loyal party people."[56] Governor Wilder, who remained an immensely popular icon in the African-American community, posed a similar problem for Terry. The more she appeared to avoid association with the controversial governor, the more she dampened enthusiasm for her candidacy among black voters.[57]

"A summertime surge of support for Republican George Allen," wrote Dale Eisman of the *Virginian-Pilot* on the first day of September,

> has all but wiped out Mary Sue Terry's big lead as the campaign enters its final two months, according to a new poll. Allen, now backed by 40 percent

53. Sabato, *Virginia Votes 1991–1994*, p. 53.
54. *Richmond Times-Dispatch*, August 1, 1993.
55. *Richmond Times-Dispatch*, August 1, 1993.
56. *Washington Post*, August 19, 1993.
57. Reflecting doubts about Terry among traditional Democratic constituencies, the state AFL-CIO declined to endorse her candidacy. The candidate seemed to approve of organized labor's abstention, since its nod might have hampered her efforts to attract moderate and conservative swing voters, but it also deprived her of the group's voter mobilization efforts. *Richmond Times*-Dispatch, September 7, 1993.

of state voters, trails Terry by only six percentage points in the survey by Mason-Dixon Political/Media Research, Inc.[58]

The startling new poll results, soon corroborated by other published surveys showing the race to be a statistical dead heat, pierced the aura of invincibility that had been the Terry campaign's chief asset since before the race began, and they triggered a long-delayed flow of campaign contributions into the GOP coffers. That Allen had narrowed the gap that far, despite being heavily outspent on television advertising during the summer months, suggested that the campaign's underlying dynamics were irretrievably negative for the Democrats. "We knew based on our internal polls around Labor Day that we were not where we needed to be to win the race," recalled Terry. "We had a stiff head wind, and George had a strong tail wind. Virginians' attitude toward the Democratic Party and Democratic elected officials was such that we could see we were not going to get above 49 percent of the vote without shaking up the race."[59]

With the contest clearly slipping away, the Terry camp in October launched a strident attack portraying Allen as an "extremist" allied with the Christian Right. "Look behind the [Allen] smile; is this the kind of change Virginia needs?" intoned the Terry television ad, as ominous photos of religious broadcaster Pat Robertson and Lynchburg fundamentalist Jerry Falwell filled the screen and the narrator charged that Allen and his "right-wing allies" would undermine public education and "take us back and to the right on a woman's right to choose."[60] Terry's running mate, Lieutenant Governor Beyer, launched an even more pungent diatribe against his outfunded GOP opponent, Michael Farris, while Democratic attorney general candidate William Dolan attacked his counterpart James Gilmore by linking him to Farris. Introducing the attacks, party chief Mark Warner lamented at a Richmond news conference that Terry and her allies had not launched the fusillade earlier. The Republican team, he said, practiced the "politics of hate and fear," would dismantle the public schools and eviscerate abortion rights, and was "the most extremist, most right-wing [ticket] this state has seen in thirty years."[61]

Similar attacks, albeit more artful, had been the mainstay of Democratic campaigns in the 1980s, but by 1993 the tactic had worn decidedly thin, and Terry's volleys had the sound of desperation. Terry had "watched a huge poll lead evaporate," wrote reporter Mike Allen, and now she was

---

58. *Virginian-Pilot*, September 1, 1993.
59. Terry interview.
60. *Richmond Times-Dispatch*, October 20, 1993.
61. *Richmond Times-Dispatch*, October 14, 1993.

"gambl[ing] on a high-risk strategy of trying to make Republicans sound like stormtroopers."[62] The problem with the new Terry line was not only that it came late—after the GOP's Allen had established a folksy, reassuring image with voters—but that it self-evidently stretched the truth. On abortion, Allen had couched his pro-life stance and limited exceptions as a position of "reasonable moderation" and had branded Terry as "extreme" on the issue because she opposed all abortion restrictions, including Allen's widely supported call for a law requiring notification of parents when abortions were performed on minors. Even the attacks focusing on Robertson and Falwell sounded like cookie-cutter criticism that did not fit Allen.[63] Republicans responded to the Democratic counteroffensive by dismissing the attack and reminding voters why they were ready for a change. "Isn't it pitiful?" shrugged Allen over the airwaves. "Mary Sue Terry and the Democrats will say or do anything to stay in office. Their distorted, negative attacks prove the Robb-Wilder-Terry politicians have been in Richmond too long."[64] At the same time, Allen strategists cheered privately as the combined effect of Terry's harsh attacks and Farris's grassroots campaigning energized evangelical Christian voters and set in motion an avalanche of culturally conservative votes for the GOP ticket on election day.[65]

The mid-October Democratic assault produced a temporary halt in the Terry slide, but the attack did not stick, and within days internal polls showed Allen's momentum had resumed. "It's analogous to Ronald Reagan running for president in 1980," observed pollster Scott Keeter of Virginia Commonwealth University after Terry's first attacks seemed to miss their target. Reagan's opponents portrayed him as a crazy right-winger, "but then when people saw him, he was very unthreatening."[66] "It was hard to demonize George Allen," agreed Mark Warner years later, "because he was so good with people."[67] Veteran Democratic fundraiser Alson Smith, part

---

62. *Richmond Times-Dispatch*, October 17, 1993.

63. Although Robertson had made a contribution to Allen's campaign, he had assumed no active role in the GOP effort, and Allen had supported George H. W. Bush, not home-stater Robertson, in the presidential primary five years earlier. Falwell had no apparent connection to Allen's campaign.

64. Copy of campaign advertisement on file with the author.

65. "We knew we were taking a big risk with those spots [portraying Allen as an extremist ally of the Christian Right]," recalled Terry. "We had to make a choice between taking the risk and trying to shake up the race or playing it safe, in which case our best estimate was that we would lose narrowly. So we tried to shake things up. We knew [the attacks] could blow up on us, and that is what they did. That accounted for the size of George's margin in the end." Terry interview.

66. *Richmond Times-Dispatch*, September 18, 1993.

67. Mark Warner interview.

of Terry's inner circle, complained in frustration that Allen "isn't the kind of candidate Republicans are used to running"; he obviously meant that the attractive Allen and his populist campaign were not the kind of GOP effort Virginia Democrats were accustomed to running against.[68] Reflecting a widespread consensus among campaign observers, political scientist Mark Rozell gave the credit not only to Allen's disarming manner but to his talented ad-maker, Greg Stevens, whose television spots "created a feeling of warmth that [paid] off" for Allen while veteran Democratic consultant Robert Squier's ads for Terry were "as bland as . . . white bread."[69]

Whether due to her own failings, the errors of her advisers, the adverse political environment, or all of the foregoing, the 1993 campaign simply was not Mary Sue Terry's finest hour. Her storybook rise to power as a protégé of House of Delegates Speaker A. L. Philpott, her strong statewide campaigns in 1985 and 1989, and her solid tenure as the state's attorney general had given no hint that her high-flying star could fall so fast. Asked after the campaign what she might have done differently in order to win, she answered, "Run for governor four years ago"—a reference to her having stepped aside to clear the way for Wilder's bid in 1989.[70] The disappointed candidate and her supporters would complain later that Republicans had unfairly exploited her status as an unmarried female and had waged a subterranean campaign of innuendo against her, but there was little evidence—other than the Allen camp's frequent display of their candidate in the company of his attractive spouse and children—to support the charge.[71] One Terry critic, former Democratic chairman Paul Goldman, charged that

68. *Richmond Times-Dispatch*, October 4, 1993.

69. *Richmond Times-Dispatch*, October 4, 1993.

70. *Washington Post*, November 5, 1993.

71. Terry interview; Claire Guthrie Gastanaga interview, March 16, 2005. Several of the Allen campaign's television advertisements showed the candidate with his wife Susan and young children. In the only overt mention of the marital status topic by either campaign, Allen's treasurer, James C. Wheat III made an offhand observation in August that Allen would be more sensitive to family concerns because he was married and had children. The Terry campaign pounced on the statement as evidence of intolerance in the GOP camp, and Allen convened a news conference to distance himself from the errant remark. *Richmond Times-Dispatch*, August 25, 1993. The *Washington Post* editorially complained in late October that Allen had successfully "[used] his ill-considered plan to abolish parole and the mere fact that he is married and has children" to gain advantage in the gubernatorial contest. *Washington Post,* October 20, 1993. The "issue" of the candidates' differing marital status was little discussed other than behind the scenes, but it was sufficiently pertinent that exit pollsters asked voters about it on election day. According to Sabato, the exit poll results indicated that 35 percent of voters agreed with the assertion that Allen had "unfairly attacked Terry for being unmarried and not having any children," while 50 percent disagreed. Sabato, *Virginia Votes 1991–1994*, p. 53 n.6; see also Sabato, *Virginia Votes 1991–1994*, p. 73 n.23.

the Democratic nominee's unparalleled collapse was due to her own "culturally extreme campaign," which was unabashedly "pro-abortion, . . . pro-gun control, . . . anti-Christian . . . and impl[ied] that evangelical Christians were a dark force manipulating George Allen's puppet strings." These "out-of-the-political-mainstream values" had alienated rural and suburban areas, Goldman argued, while at the same time Terry was

> stiff-arming labor and minorities in order not to appear tied to these key Democratic groups. This unprecedented strategy produced the worst of both worlds. She scored a weak win in key Democratic areas, while suffering record losses in bellwether rural and suburban precincts.[72]

"We must recognize we have a tidal wave of change that has swept across Virginia," said the defeated Terry in a gracious election-night speech.[73] Indeed, the Allen wave had continued to build right through election day, fueled by a flood of campaign contributions—much of it so-called make-up money from corporate givers who had lavished donations on the front-running Terry earlier in the year—that came so fast Allen campaign chief Michael Thomas and finance director Betsy Davis were challenged to collect and spend it all.[74] The magnitude of the Allen tidal wave was not fully apparent until the waters receded.[75] In the election's wake, analysts marveled that the GOP nominee had captured a majority of the female vote against his better-funded and more experienced female opponent,[76] had held Terry to a smaller share of the white vote than that received by African-American Wilder in 1989, and had polled a majority of votes even among

---

72. Paul Goldman, "Ms. Terry Must Accept Responsibility for Loss," *Richmond Times-Dispatch*, November 5, 1993. Larry Sabato's post-election analysis similarly faulted Terry for allowing herself to be painted as a "cultural liberal" while simultaneously failing to "activate[e] two liberal subgroups of her own party, African Americans and professional women." Sabato, *Virginia Votes 1991–1994*, p. 74.

73. *Washington Post*, November 3, 1993.

74. Davis (Beamer) interview.

75. The vote totals were: Allen (R)—1,045,319 (58.3 percent); Terry (D)—733,527 (40.9 percent). Sabato, *Virginia Votes 1991–1994*, p. 55.

76. Terry's failure to rally women voters was especially disappointing to some of her female advisers. Claire Guthrie Gastanaga, Terry's chief deputy in the attorney general's office but not a member of her campaign's inner circle, observed that the Democratic candidate and her advisers appeared to take the votes of women for granted. Issues that might have appealed to female voters, such as Allen's opposition to family leave legislation, were never used by Terry's campaign. "There never was a [Terry campaign] strategy for appealing to women voters other than that she wore a skirt," Gastanaga complained. Gastanaga interview.

those who cited abortion as a key campaign issue.[77] Allen had carried all but two congressional districts, including the moderate Northern Virginia areas that backed Wilder in 1989 and supported Allen's GOP opponent in the spring nominating contest. The Republican had prevailed in 120 of 136 counties and cities, won a 63 percent majority of the rural vote, captured 60 percent of suburban ballots, and held Terry to a slim, 53 percent majority in the central cities.[78] Allen's appeal for "honest change" and his ambitious reform agenda, anchored by his pledge to abolish parole for violent criminals, had appealed to a broad cross-section of voters and had even helped garner Allen roughly a fifth of the African-American vote.[79] Sizeable majorities not only had agreed with the Allen prescription on issues from crime-fighting to education and economic development; they also had tended to blame Terry for the negativism in the campaign.[80] It had been, by all measures, the most complete rout in a Virginia gubernatorial election since the advent of viable two-party democracy in the Old Dominion and one of the most decisive gubernatorial wins by a nonincumbent in any competitive state.

Elected with Allen were James Gilmore as attorney general and a record number of GOP candidates for the House of Delegates. Gilmore's win was nearly as broad as his ticket leader's.[81] The Henrico commonwealth's attorney, the first prosecutor to seek the attorney general post in modern times, stressed a crime-fighting agenda that appealed across demographic groups and regions and enabled him to carry more than half of the state's cities and all but eight of its ninety-five counties; he even battled William Dolan to a draw in the Democrat's home region of Northern Vir-

---

77. Terry's campaign spent $6.5 million; Allen's combined nomination and general election campaign spending totaled $5.47 million. Sabato, *Virginia Votes 1991–1994*, pp. 49–50, 71.

78. Sabato, *Virginia Votes 1991–1994*, pp. 67–68. The suburbs supplied 58 percent of the total statewide vote in 1993, nearly ten percentage points more than its share of the statewide vote in the 1989 gubernatorial contest.

79. Exit polls placed Allen's share of the black vote at 17–22 percent. In predominantly black precincts examined by Larry Sabato, however, Allen received only 11 percent of the vote. The most striking evidence of Allen's inroads and Terry's failure among African-American voters came in the turnout data; only 51 percent of registered voters in predominantly black precincts came out to vote, compared with an overall statewide turnout rate in excess of 61 percent. By contrast, African-American turnout had exceeded the participation rate of the electorate as a whole in the four preceding gubernatorial elections. Sabato, *Virginia Votes 1991–1994, pp. 49, 68–69.*

80. Sabato, *Virginia Votes 1991–1994*, pp. 55–56.

81. The vote totals were: Gilmore (R)—958,982 (56.1 percent); Dolan (D)— 749,565 (43.9 percent). Sabato, *Virginia Votes 1991–1994*, pp. 55–56.

ginia.[82] For the first time in the twentieth century, Republican candidates captured a majority (51.2 percent) of all votes cast statewide in House of Delegates races, resulting in a century-high forty-seven seats for the GOP in the hundred-member body. The Republicans' net gain of six seats was impressive enough, but even more stunning to the ruling legislative Democrats was how close the Allen-led GOP surge had come to dispossessing them of their seemingly permanent lower-house majority. Democrats won four of their House seats with less than 52 percent of the vote; if Republicans instead had been the ones to eke out those narrow wins, the GOP would have captured control of the chamber. "The Democratic Party is going to have to do some soul-searching after this election," commented Gordon C. Morse, a former aide to Democratic Governor Gerald Baliles. "Democrats in the legislature take a lot of things for granted, and they are going to have to conduct themselves responsibly. Arrogance permeates the Democratic Party; [it] happens to any organization that's been successful over time."[83]

The only statewide Democrat to survive the Republican landslide was Lieutenant Governor Donald Beyer, and his reelection margin over meagerly funded, first-time candidate Michael Farris was the thinnest of the three statewide winners.[84] In fact, Farris's losing effort garnered more total votes than Terry's or Dolan's. Farris's bid was hampered by his lack of a political resumé, his ties (though greatly overstated) to religious conservative lightning-rods Jerry Falwell and Pat Robertson, and his history of sometimes provocative statements on education, health and social issues.[85] In a barrage of electronic attack ads, Beyer used that ammunition to portray the home-schooling advocate as far outside Virginia's moderate mainstream.[86] Given the predilection of media and academic elites against candidates with Farris's conservative social views, the degree of criticism that Beyer's attack

---

82. Sabato, *Virginia Votes 1991–1994*, p. 57. Dolan protested that the office had little to do with law enforcement, but Gilmore broke new ground by convincing voters that fighting crime should be the attorney general's focus.

83. *Richmond Times-Dispatch*, November 3, 1993.

84. The vote totals were: Beyer (D)—947,837(54.5 percent); Farris (R)—791,593 (45.5 percent). Sabato, *Virginia Votes 1991–1994*, p. 55.

85. In one often-cited statement, Farris had once called the public school system a "godless monstrosity." Sabato, *Virginia Votes 1991–1994*, p. 74.

86. Recalling the race years later, Farris cited his lack of prior elective office as the key impediment to his candidacy. He had been encouraged by friends and supporters to run for the state Senate in 1991, and his decision not to do so proved pivotal two years later when he ran for lieutenant governor. Had he served in the General Assembly prior to running statewide, Farris observed, it would have been far more difficult for his critics to create "a caricature of me as some kind of crazy nut." Michael Farris interview, March 15, 2005.

ads received during and after the contest was striking. The consensus among commentators of all stripes was that Beyer's negative salvos were wildly exaggerated and, in some cases—such as the often-repeated claim that Farris had advocated banning certain popular books from school libraries—flatly untrue.[87] Unfortunately for Farris, he lacked the campaign funds to respond to the bogus charges, and the Democratic effort to portray him as a right-wing extremist received a major boost in early October when moderate Senator John Warner pointedly declined to endorse his fellow Republican's candidacy.

Coming from the state's most prominent elected Republican official, the Warner refusal to endorse Farris seemed to lend credence to Beyer's theme that the GOP candidate for lieutenant governor had bizarre and unacceptable social views.[88] It was, recalled Beyer, "a powerful signal to Republicans. . . . The only way I survived in that election was through a big defection from Allen-Gilmore voters."[89] A race that polls showed was a dead heat a month before the election turned in Beyer's favor by election day, as moderate suburban voters shifted in his direction. With the advantages of incumbency, a largely unrebutted propaganda campaign, and bipartisan assistance, Beyer managed to withstand the Republican onslaught, though at evident cost to his previously pristine political reputation. The widespread criticism of his negative campaign tactics "did dim the glow . . . and made it easier for the Republicans four years later to say 'there he goes again' when I ran contrast ads [in the 1997 race for governor]," Beyer acknowledged. But, he added, "it would have dimmed the glow a lot more if I had lost."[90]

Although George Allen had resuscitated the Virginia GOP and delivered the governorship for his fellow partisans in a convincing manner, that feat did not assure him control of the state Republican Party apparatus. Frustrated by what he and aides regarded as tepid support from party chairman Patrick McSweeney even after the state GOP convention, Allen called McSweeney a few weeks after the election with the request that he step down so the governor could suggest a more supportive replacement. When

---

87. See Rozell and Wilcox, pp. 128–130; Sabato, *Virginia Votes 1991–1994*, p. 74.

88. In explaining his decision not to back Farris, Warner cited the candidate's devotion to "a very narrow field of interests and issues," which, the senator said, left him unsure of Farris's "breadth of experience" and location "in the mainstream of a lot of issues in Virginia." Rozell and Wilcox, p. 131. Also damaging to Farris was a "Republicans for Beyer" campaign effort led by Virginia ("Jinx") Holton, wife of former Governor Linwood Holton.

89. Donald S. Beyer Jr., interview, March 18, 2005.

90. Beyer interview.

the angry chairman refused, Allen operatives and supporters reacted by pushing for a Republican central committee vote calling on him to resign. The contentious move garnered more than two-thirds of the committee vote, but the tally fell short of the three-fourths vote that would have been needed to force the chairman's ouster. McSweeney remained—and so did an estrangement between the new governor and the state GOP operation—until 1996, when McSweeney's term ended and Delegate J. Randy Forbes of Chesapeake, an Allen ally, was tapped as chairman at the party's state convention. In the meantime, the governor's team organized its own political action committee—called the "Campaign for Honest Change"—to mobilize grassroots support for Allen's governmental reforms and to help elect GOP legislative candidates.

Allen had better success seizing the reins of state government. The full dimension of the "creative conservatism" promised in his January 1994 inaugural address was soon apparent, and it transformed the once-staid State Capitol. At the end of his frenetic, often tumultuous, and undeniably productive tenure as governor, the charismatic Allen would emerge as an intensely popular political figure in the state. Though voters in Virginia never have the chance to render direct verdicts on gubernatorial administrations because of the constitutional bar to reelection, Allen's success as governor would prove to be a key factor in the choice of his successor in 1997 and in his own successful bid for the United State Senate in 2000. In the meantime, however, the GOP factional fault lines that Allen successfully surmounted in his 1993 campaign would be jarred open again, making the landscape exceedingly treacherous for some Virginia Republicans and creating new paths of opportunity for state Democrats. At the center of these seismic shocks was Senator John Warner, who seemed to relish his role as the man in the middle.

# 7

# JOHN WARNER AND THE POLITICS OF INDEPENDENCE

I could have slapped on a sticker of someone I didn't support . . .
and I would be unopposed this time. I'm not cut out to do that. I
wasn't raised by my parents to do that. I learned under the honor
system at [the University of Virginia] not to do that. . . . I felt I
should put the interests of my country and of my state ahead of politics.[1]

—Senator John W. Warner, 1995

Whether political parties are a blessing or curse for American democracy is a question as old as the Republic. In his Farewell Address in
September 1796, President George Washington left no doubt as to his view
on the subject, which had been a source of painful contention during and
within his administration. "Let me now . . . warn you in the most solemn
manner against the baneful effects of the spirit of party," the preeminent
American famously declared.[2] Another Virginian founder displayed the
contrary conviction with equal vigor. Thomas Jefferson regarded the philosophically based division of people into parties as a natural, indeed inevitable, phenomenon. When, in 1796, he found himself elected as vice
president in an administration to be captained by his friend and rival John
Adams, Jefferson spurned the Massachusetts Federalist's overture to set aside
their differences and govern together for the good of the country. Instead,
the Virginian charted a distinctly partisan course and, in so doing, set in
motion events that would yield a quarter century of political success for him

1. *Richmond Times-Dispatch*, April 17, 1995.
2. George Washington, Farewell Address to the People of the United States, delivered September 17, 1796, U.S. Government Printing Office, 1991.

and his Republican allies.[3] Evidence abounded in the ensuing two-plus centuries to support a verdict of virtue or vice on the question of partisanship. The American two-party system has provided a useful vehicle for the orderly presentation of contending choices to the electorate, yet it has fostered behavior that sometimes subordinated the larger public good to partisan political self-interest.

In recent generations, the long-running discussion of partisanship has been accentuated, in Virginia and much of the South, by the dominant dynamic of party realignment. The nation's ingrained two-party system ensured the continual relevance of parties, but in the South the residual political effects of the great sectional conflagration of the nineteenth century were still felt well into the twentieth, and so the state-level parties in that region bore little resemblance to their national counterparts. This dichotomy was gradually erased in the second half of the twentieth century, as the Republican and Democratic parties in the Southern states transitioned to an alignment generally reflective of national party positions and interests. But the transition was not a tidy one, and in the process many voters and some elected officials found it beneficial to place themselves outside the uncertain confines of the shifting political parties. Beginning in the 1950s, Virginia's leading Democrat, Harry F. Byrd Sr., employed "golden silence" as an artful way of lending tacit support to GOP presidential candidates. In 1970, his son, Senator Harry F. Byrd Jr., formalized that independence by leaving the Democratic Party and standing for reelection without party affiliation. With Virginia's political parties dramatically in flux in the early 1970s, liberal Democrat Henry Howell similarly took an independent tack in his successful populist bid for lieutenant governor in 1971 and in his near-miss for governor two years later. Many political and business elites in the state likewise embraced an independent stance in response to partisan transition, working through loose-knit "Virginians for" groups and positioning themselves as conservative-leaning coalitionists.[4]

While a penchant for independence from parties among voters plainly has been an effect of Virginia's partisan realignment, it would be a mistake to attribute the appetite for independence wholly to that state and regional phenomenon. Many "realignments" of varied character and dimension have occurred in American politics, as diverse events, issues, and movements—among them, FDR's New Deal, the civil rights movement, Reagan's "revolution," and emergence of the politically influential Chris-

---

3. Adams's invitation and Jefferson's rejection is described in Joseph J. Ellis, *Founding Brothers* (New York: Alfred A. Knopf, 2001), pp. 177–186.
4. See *The Dynamic Dominion*, Chapters 6, 20–22, 27.

tian Right—have dramatically reshaped the political landscape. As the two major political parties have refined their messages and redefined themselves in response to such issues and movements, they inevitably have attracted some new adherents and forced others away, with the departing loyalists often assuming an independent posture. Add to that effect the widespread popular frustration with "politics-as-usual" (a euphemism for the tendency of dedicated partisans to bicker continually, lob shrill negative volleys at one another, and jockey for partisan political advantage in seeming disregard of the greater public interest), and you have a formula for increasingly independent behavior by voters.

With the two major national parties evenly matched and contending for the political middle in recent decades, the independent tendency has been reflected in a growing number of "swing" voters who vote more for the person than the party at election time. While no new political party has taken hold institutionally, potent "protest" candidacies from outside the two major parties have been generated across the political spectrum and occasionally have had an important impact in individual elections.[5] Political "reforms" designed to stem or channel the flow of campaign contributions have weakened party loyalties still further.[6] All of these factors have contributed to a contemporary context in which this irony pervades: as party passions run hottest among Democratic and Republican loyalists, the level of disenchantment with the two parties in the moderate middle of the American electorate seems to boil as well.

In the 1990s, the person who best exemplified, reinforced, and capitalized on Virginia voters' independent tendencies was the state's senior United States senator, John W. Warner. The Middleburg aristocrat had come to the Senate in 1979, winning his first bid for elective office by the narrowest of margins in the aftermath of Richard Obenshain's untimely death, and owing his political berth largely to Obenshain's visionary party-building efforts.[7] By the 1990s, however, the twice reelected Warner had

---

5. In presidential campaigns, for example, Ross Perot's independent bid in 1992 received roughly 19 percent of the vote, much of it at the expense of incumbent president George Bush. Ralph Nader's bid as the nominee of the "Green Party" in 2000 garnered only about 3 percent of the national vote, but it negatively impacted Vice President Al Gore's candidacy in the razor-thin contest. Other significant independent candidacies for president were waged by segregationist Democrat George Wallace in 1968 and by liberal Republican John Anderson in 1980.

6. See generally Larry J. Sabato, *PAC Power: Inside the World of Political Action Committees* (New York: W. W. Norton & Co., 1984); T. Preston Lloyd Jr., "Endangered Guardians: Campaign Finance Reform and the Embattled Two-Party System," unpublished undergraduate thesis, University of Virginia, April 20, 2004.

7. See *The Dynamic Dominion*, Chapters 31–33.

become a political titan in the competitive Old Dominion and seemed to transcend the political parties. His senatorial diligence and aplomb had refuted early detractors' predictions that he was a dilettante who would merely warm the seat, and Warner began the decade as the state's most popular Republican (indeed, the only one serving in statewide office). Easily reelected to a second term in 1984, he did not even face a Democratic opponent when that term expired. Former Governor Gerald Baliles, the only significant potential foe, demurred in 1990, making Warner the first Republican senator to get a pass from the party of Byrd Sr. and Robb in the twentieth century. As the ranking Republican member on the Senate Armed Services Committee, Warner had seniority and influence in an area of tremendous importance to the Virginia economy: national defense. The senator thus had every reason to believe he was larger than the state Republican Party, and that it needed him far more than he needed the party.

Warner's electoral success and congressional clout did not assure him of widespread affection within the conservative-leaning state GOP. A variety of stances taken by the moderate senator irritated Republican regulars, but it was his 1987 vote against confirmation of President Reagan's nominee for the Supreme Court of the United States, Circuit Judge Robert Bork, that produced the first major rupture in Warner's conservative base. The event was the start of a very rough patch in the relationship between Warner and his fellow partisans, as politician-turned-columnist Ray Garland observed in a newspaper commentary several years later:

> When we last left him . . . John W. Warner flirted with the national spotlight in his last-minute declaration against Judge Robert Bork for the U.S. Supreme Court. At that time we said, "It wasn't Warner's vote against Bork that conservatives should mind so much—the cause was lost in any case—it was the odiousness of the company he joined." We stand by that. Whenever the likes of Ted Kennedy, Joe Biden and Alan Cranston are singing in an unholy choir of moral indignation, decent people should run—not walk—to the nearest exit.
>
> While the general public has long forgotten Warner's vote against Bork, it has stuck in the craw of some Republicans. But more as a symptom of the senator's persistent refusal to be a point man for the conservative agenda. . . . Still, Warner is now the Republican Party's sole surviving statewide officeholder, and criticism of him has been carefully muted. Repeated helpings of disappointment have served to curb the appetite of the Virginia GOP for such rash adventures as pulling the rug out from under their few remaining sure bets.[8]

---

8. *Chesterfield Gazette*, May 3, 1990.

Warner's vote against Bork and the intense negative reaction to it among GOP partisans were but precursors to the major controversy the independent-minded senator generated in 1993–1994. Warner parted ways with his party in two successive statewide contests, declining to endorse Allen running mate Michael Farris in the 1993 race for lieutenant governor and then actively opposing GOP nominee Oliver North in the 1994 contest for the United States Senate. Both races were close enough that Warner's high-profile, party-defying actions may have decided the outcomes, and the fallout among Republican regulars, especially the party's most ardently conservative activists, guaranteed the senior senator would face an intraparty challenge to his own renomination for the Senate in 1996. As it turned out, Warner not only had to deal with that internal challenge; he also found himself in a tough general-election battle in 1996 against Democratic Party leader (and future governor) Mark Warner. The senator prevailed in both hard-fought contests, and he silenced most of his Republican critics in the process. He also earned a new corps of strong supporters among centrist Democrats and moderate independents who appreciated his apparent placing of principle over party in opposing the controversial North. But Warner's difficult experience in 1996—engaging successive expensive and exhausting battles against two vigorous opponents—stood in marked contrast with his unopposed glide to reelection in 1990 and gave the senator renewed interest in getting along with GOP partisans in the future.

Warner's 1993–1994 straying from partisan fidelity was, as he later explained, a product of circumstance and conviction, not political positioning.[9] But even if Warner's unusual steps had been motivated by political self-interest, the full implications of his actions for Virginia politics would have been difficult to forecast. The negative impact of Warner's non-support on the Farris and North candidacies was of course foreseeable, as was the consequent hostility toward the senator on the part of their jilted supporters. Many of the Farris and North backers had reluctantly continued to back the centrist senator even after his vote against Judge Bork and other lesser heresies, and his failure to reciprocate their loyalty was profoundly upsetting to many. But what neither Warner nor state GOP leaders anticipated was the extent the senator's part-time party loyalty would enhance his influence among swing voters in the Old Dominion and redound to the benefit of those Republican candidates he later did support.

When Warner returned solidly to the Republican fold in the 1997 election, his credibility among independent voters and moderates in both parties, especially in the vote-rich suburbs of Northern Virginia and Hamp-

9. John Warner interview.

ton Roads, made his endorsement exceedingly valuable to gubernatorial nominee James Gilmore and his GOP running mates. The senior senator played a similarly important role in the 2000 Senate election, helping former Governor George Allen rebut attempts by incumbent Senator Robb to portray the Republican as too far right for moderate suburbanites. John Warner had shown voters that he did not endorse candidates automatically out of party loyalty, but advisedly after scrutiny of their individual merits—or so he could convincingly maintain—and that seemed to make a big difference to independent-minded moderate voters in the competitive Commonwealth. The Warner endorsement became like a seal of approval confirming a Republican's presence in the moderate-conservative Virginia political mainstream. Like the two senior Senators Byrd who preceded him, Warner asserted his transcendent right to decide whether and when he would remain true to his party. His displays of independence became a source of indignation for many party loyalists and a license and benefit for some others.

Virginia, which had been in the national limelight with the groundbreaking election of Governor Wilder in 1989, and again with the titillating revelations about Senator Robb in 1990–1991, found itself once more the focus of the national news media with the Senate candidacy of polarizing Iran-Contra figure Oliver North in 1994. North did not firmly decide to vie for the Senate until after George Allen's breakthrough win in 1993. But almost immediately after a federal appellate court overturned his Iran-Contra convictions in late 1990, North plunged into Virginia politics, using his celebrity status and national conservative donor base to attract crowds and raise funds for Republican candidates and party committees. Robb had been so wounded by the succession of unflattering revelations and piecemeal admissions in the interrelated sex, drugs and taping scandals that most observers in Virginia and elsewhere assumed that anyone, even the controversial North, could capture his seat. In a two-man race against Robb, that conventional wisdom might well have been proven correct when the ballots were cast in November 1994. But North and Robb were not destined to wage a conventional two-person, two-party race. Each first faced a nomination challenge—North's proved the more formidable—and then each had to cope with the defection of fellow partisans to an independent candidacy. After their respective parties nominated Robb and North in late spring 1994, the general-election field soon included a second Democrat, former governor Douglas Wilder, and another Republican, former attorney general Marshall Coleman, both running as Independents. And behind the Coleman candidacy lurked the resolutely anti-North John Warner.

It was ironic, given some of their similarities, that John Warner would mount such fierce opposition to Oliver North's effort to join him in the Senate representing Virginia. They were both Marines; both boasted careers that gave them strong military credentials in the pro-military Old Dominion; and both made their electoral debuts as candidates for the lofty position of senator, able to forego the usual political apprenticeships because of their celebrity status (Warner's came from marriage to actress Elizabeth Taylor) and resulting crowd-drawing, fund-raising star appeal. But North's star had shined at the expense of the Senate, and that was an offense, among others, that Warner could not countenance.[10] As the 1994 Senate contest got underway, Kent Jenkins Jr. of the *Washington Post* recalled the odd circumstances that had propelled North to stardom eight years earlier during his Senate testimony concerning the Iran-Contra scandal:

> It looked that morning as though North was a goner for sure. The dozens of lawmakers and hot-shot investigators fanned out in front of him had the goods. They had proof that he had flat-out lied to Congress about his scheme to sell missiles to Iran and divert the profits to arm Nicaraguan guerillas. They had proof that he had staged a "shredding party" to destroy documents detailing what he had done. . . . So what did this outnumbered and surrounded Marine do? He attacked. He stuck out his chin and steeled his gaze, and said, yes, sir, he had "misled" Congress and might have done wrong, but he was serving his President and defending democracy. . . .
>
> His spit-and-polish demeanor and commanding military presence hit the nation's televisions like a power surge, blowing the herd of pols around him completely off the screen. . . . By the end of the first day, the Congressional posse was itself on the run; the hunted had taken charge of the hunt. Polls show that before North took the witness stand, about half the country knew who he was, and most of that half didn't care for him. After four days of testimony, 80 percent of Americans recognized him and two-thirds liked what they saw. Like Jesse James, Oliver North had transformed himself into an Outlaw Hero.[11]

While a broad majority of Americans cheered North's bravado at the time of the Iran-Contra hearings, and many enthralled conservative GOP

---

10. Warner later recalled that he also had been concerned about North's potential reaction to the stress of life in the Senate, citing North's autobiographical account of emotional turmoil in the aftermath of his military service in Vietnam. John Warner interview; see Oliver L. North, *Under Fire: An American Story* (New York: HarperCollins Publishers, 1991), pp. 120–149. For his part, North found Warner's opposition inexplicable even years later. Warner, recalled North, had twice assured him that, although he would not support North's candidacy, he would not campaign against the colonel. Ultimately, Warner helped recruit Marshall Coleman as an independent candidate for the seat and took to the hustings vigorously on Coleman's behalf. Oliver North interview, April 5, 2005.

11. *Washington Post*, March 20, 1994.

activists became loyal followers of the charismatic colonel, the problem for North eight years later was that many leading lights of the Reagan administration were openly critical of him and were supporting his GOP rival for the Senate, former Reagan administration budget director James C. Miller III. The list of North detractors and/or Miller supporters included Reagan cabinet luminaries Edwin Meese III, Caspar Weinberger, and George Shultz, General Colin Powell, former National Security Advisor Robert McFarlane, and influential conservative columnist George Will. Will lavished praise on Miller as a bona fide Reaganite and bashed North as a threat to the conservative movement. "Identifying conservatism with this loose cannon on the deck of American politics," said Will of North, "is a recipe for recurring embarrassments on the right."[12] The Reagan loyalists' main rap against North, however, was the colonel's apparent disloyalty to Reagan. Five years after the Iran-Contra scandal, North had alleged in his autobiography that "President Reagan knew everything," a statement that seemed to directly rebut the president's often-stated denials in the matter.[13] Then, in February 1994, North asserted on the nationally televised *Face the Nation* interview program that he had not advocated the sale of arms to Iran and that Reagan had ordered the sales "over the objections of a number of us."[14] This statement appeared to contradict even North's own autobiography and to lend credence to his critics' charge that the colonel not only had misled Congress and President Reagan but also exhibited a pattern of exaggeration and dissembling that called his credibility generally into question.

In March 1994 came the bombshell that many in the Miller camp believed would win them the nomination. In a letter to Senator Paul Laxalt of Nevada, which Laxalt elicited and Miller's campaign distributed to the news media, former President Reagan declared that he was "pretty steamed" by North's "false statements," regarding which the former president offered a point-by-point rebuttal.[15] Reagan's letter even denied that a private meeting North claimed to have had with him took place. North hastened to pen a public response to the former president, sarcastically noting that "a letter you sent to a friend has found its way into the media," and disclaiming having ever made the charges that the letter purported to rebut. Reagan, North asserted, had been "seriously and intentionally misinformed" about the colonel's statements by his detractors.[16]

Fortunately for North, and to the great consternation of his rival

---

12. *Richmond Times-Dispatch*, February 3, 1994.
13. North, pp. 12–13; *Washington Post*, March 18, 1994.
14. *Washington Post*, February 21, 1994.
15. *Richmond Times-Dispatch*, March 18, 1994.
16. *Richmond Times-Dispatch*, March 18, 1994.

Miller, the potent Reagan missive was first disclosed by Senator Warner, who strode onto the Senate floor to deliver an uncharacteristically vitriolic attack. "Oliver North has betrayed President Reagan, he has betrayed the American people, and now he is trying to betray the people of Virginia," declared Warner. "If his oath of duty, honor and country have any meaning to Oliver North, he will withdraw from the race."[17] North could not win a fight with the revered former president, but if he could change the subject and make Warner's attacks the focus, many party regulars would side with the victimized colonel. A couple of weeks after release of the Reagan letter, Warner made explicit what he had hinted broadly before: he would not support North for the Senate even if he were to prevail in his GOP nomination battle against Miller. Instead, said the senator, he would be prepared to support an independent alternative to the scandal-tarnished Marine. Rumors were then abounding that Marshall Coleman was preparing to make such a bid.

Coming on the heels of his non-support of Farris during the preceding fall's campaign, the Warner declaration against North triggered a barrage of denunciations from angry partisans ranging across the GOP spectrum. Republican state chairman Patrick McSweeney observed that Warner had "obviously forgotten what it means to be a Republican" and suggested that "perhaps it is time for him to reconsider his party affiliation."[18] Seventh District Representative Thomas Bliley, though actively backing Miller against North, joined in the criticism. "The party supports us," said one-time Democrat Bliley, "[and we] have an obligation to support the party."[19] Even moderate Flo Traywick of Roanoke, the GOP's national committee-woman, was publicly critical of Warner: "We've been friends forever, and I'm very fond of him, but I'm sort of dismayed. He's certainly straining everybody's loyalty in the party."[20] State GOP executive director David Johnson reported that a deluge of passionate calls from Republican partisans had flooded the Obenshain Center, the party's statewide headquarters in Richmond. "People are furious [with Warner]. They want to know how they can get in touch with him and tell him how much they hate him."[21] Warner's Senate office confirmed that it, too, had received over a hundred calls on the subject, and the majority were critical of the senator's statement.[22] Seizing the opportunity, North spokesman Mark Merritt charged

17. *Washington Post*, March 18, 1994.
18. *Richmond Times-Dispatch*, March 31, 1994.
19. *Richmond Times-Dispatch*, April 1, 1994.
20. *Virginian-Pilot*, April 1, 1994.
21. *Richmond Times-Dispatch*, April 1, 1994.
22. *Richmond Times-Dispatch*, April 1, 1994.

that Miller was complicit in Warner's disloyal actions, a charge the Miller camp attempted to answer with a vigorous denial and release of a Miller letter to Warner criticizing the senator's stance.[23]

The harsh battle continued until the Republican state convention two months later, and reached a low point when a Miller news conference intended in part to raise questions about North's mental steadiness devolved into queries and responses regarding Miller's own history of mood swings. For the remainder of the contest, Miller sought to portray North as an unelectable, unstable, scandal-dogged wild-man who had been disloyal to President Reagan; North sought to portray Miller as an egg-headed tool of John Warner and the self-interested Washington establishment that was anathema to true conservatives. Warner remained invariably at the center of the controversy. "To the extent the convention becomes a vote for Warner, Miller loses," observed commentator Robert Holsworth on the eve of the GOP balloting. "Many Republicans hate John Warner more than they love Ronald Reagan."[24] To the Miller camp's relief, Warner stayed away from the early June convention, instead attending a ceremony in Normandy, France, commemorating the fiftieth anniversary of D-Day. But the hearts of the delegates, and so the day, belonged to North anyway. After a series of speeches punctuated by a high-decibel video that identified North as the true conservative choice and challenged delegates to answer the question, "Whose Side Are You On?" the colonel captured 55 percent of the delegate vote. Miller's solid campaign had prevented the contest from becoming the runaway many had predicted earlier; he carried central Virginia, where he was backed by Congressman Bliley's potent political organization, and the more moderate GOP bastions of Hampton Roads and Northern Virginia. But North carried seven of eleven congressional districts, and he rolled up such large margins in the Southwest, Southside, and other rural areas that he overwhelmed Miller's suburban edge.[25]

Miller's intellectual credentials and reputation for integrity were impeccable; his philosophical conservatism could not be questioned; and he enjoyed high-profile support from influential fellow Reaganites. But what rookie-candidate Miller could never overcome in the GOP nomination contest was North's head-start in lining up grassroots support and the yawning charisma gap between the two candidates. The colorful colonel's soaring rhetorical flights would prove an Achilles' heel in the general election cam-

---

23. *Richmond Times-Dispatch*, March 31, 1994.

24. *Richmond Times-Dispatch*, June 2, 1994.

25. The convention delegate vote totals were: North—4,858 (55.3 percent); Miller—3,924 (44.7 percent). Sabato, *Virginia Votes 1991–1994*, p. 96.

paign, but they gave him a decisive advantage in vying for the nomination. Nothing set GOP party regulars' hearts pounding like North's passionate, flag-waving, liberal-thumping speechmaking. Signaling his general-election campaign themes, North's victory speech took aim at both the Clinton administration and the congressional establishment he had faced down eight years earlier. "Virginians," he said, "are sick and tired of a Congress run by back-slapping good old boys and a White House governed by a bunch of twenty-something kids with an earring and an ax to grind."[26]

The most memorable line from the convention, however, was not North's but George Allen's. The new governor had remained neutral in the nomination contest, adhering to the position he took in all such "intra-squad scrimmages," as he called them.[27] Analogies to football were as common for Allen as nautical allusions in a Navy family, but they had their limits, as he would soon discover. With the nomination decided, the governor roared off the sidelines with a fiery pro-North speech that ended with the graphic exhortation, "[L]et's enjoy knocking [the Democrats'] soft teeth down their whining throats."[28] The statement, though used "figuratively," was more appropriate for a football locker room than a governor's public platform, as Allen would often acknowledge later.[29] Democratic Lieutenant Governor Donald Beyer reacted swiftly to the high-testosterone GOP gathering, denouncing the governor's "violent imagery" as setting a bad example for young people. With the hard-edged convention display and nomination of the controversial North, quipped Beyer, Republicans had "fired the shot in the foot heard round the world."[30]

The Democrats hardly seemed in better shape as the general election approached. Senator Robb had formally launched his campaign in March, prompting veteran political commentator Thomas R. Morris to contrast the much-diminished candidate with the political figure who had been so dominant for Virginia Democrats a decade earlier. "The glow is off his persona," observed Morris. "I remember being in rooms when [Robb] was running for governor in 1981, and there was excitement and anticipation at his

---

26. Rozell and Wilcox, *Second Coming: The New Christian Right in Virginia Politics* (Baltimore and London: The Johns Hopkins University Press, 1996), p. 147.

27. Edds and Morris, "Virginia," p. 163.

28. *Daily Progress*, June 5, 1994.

29. The "soft teeth" statement, as it became known, would be cited as an example of Allen's occasional rhetorical excess as a youthful governor, and Allen himself would routinely concede its inappropriateness. He had improvised the line—an inspiration while in the locker room of the Richmond Coliseum awaiting his turn to address the GOP faithful—and included it as the punctuation mark at the end of his convention exhortation despite contrary advice from his wife Susan and chief of staff. "I had no one to blame but myself for it," he recalled later. George Allen interview.

30. *Daily Progress*, June 5, 1994.

entrance. He was a legitimate celebrity. That's all gone."[31] Yet, Robb was an incumbent United States senator with all the attendant advantages and a political hide toughened by adversity. Few appreciated at the time how formidable a political figure he remained.

Shortly before his formal campaign launch, Robb released a letter to fellow Democrats in a bid to put behind him, once and for all, the philandering, eavesdropping, and infighting controversies that had killed his presidential prospects and posed the main threat to his reelection. In a genteel reference to his sexual activities and party-going exploits in Virginia Beach while governor, the embattled senator awkwardly acknowledged that he was "clearly vulnerable on the question of socializing under circumstances not appropriate for a married man," asserted that he had "never denied" that fact, then added he would say no more on the subject because "with Lynda's forgiveness, and God's, I put that private chapter behind me many years ago."[32] He stoutly denied personal use of drugs or knowledge of drug use in his presence even though allegations still abounded that he frequented parties hosted by a drug-dealing Virginia Beach jet set where cocaine was used widely and openly.[33] And he said his only involvement in the eavesdropping matter involving Wilder was his "mistake" in not ordering the illicit recording promptly destroyed when he learned that a member of his Senate staff possessed the tape. On the subject of his troubled relationship with Wilder, Robb waxed lyrical, wondering how "something that began so well could have gone so wrong."[34] Contradicting past statements that had tended to downplay Wilder's contributions to his 1981 campaign,[35] the senator said, "In truth, Doug Wilder had at least as much to do with getting me elected as I had to do with getting him elected. In the early days of 1981, when there was skepticism in the African-American community about me, Doug Wilder was one of my staunchest defenders."[36]

Robb's highly nuanced mea culpa and attempt to curry favor with his old foe apparently did not sit well with Wilder. In an effort to keep the volatile governor inside the Democratic tent, the party's governing committee the previous year had agreed to choose its Senate nominee via a primary election rather than by mass meetings and convention. Wilder had gone on Black Entertainment Television in mid-summer to declare his intention to run, and Democratic state Senator Janet Howell of Reston had

31. *Washington Post*, March 14, 1994.
32. *Virginian-Pilot & Ledger-Star*, March 11, 1994.
33. *Virginian-Pilot & Ledger-Star*, March 11, 1994.
34. *Virginian-Pilot & Ledger-Star*, March 11, 1994.
35. See Baker, *Wilder*, p. 120.
36. *Virginian-Pilot & Ledger-Star*, March 11, 1994.

predicted the two would wage the "primary from hell."[37] A July 1993 endorsement of Robb by President Clinton had appeared to strengthen the incumbent's standing within his party, but also had seemed to fortify Wilder's resolve. Then, in a reprise of his January surprise two years earlier when he ended his presidential bid, the departing governor had used his final address to the General Assembly on January 12, 1994, to announce he would not seek the Senate nomination or mount an independent bid for the seat. A bevy of other potential Robb foes, including party chief Mark Warner, Third District Representative Robert ("Bobby") Scott, state education secretary James Dyke, and Northern Virginia attorney and Democratic leader Daniel Alcorn, likewise had decided not to challenge the senator for the Democratic nod. Now, in March, with release of Robb's letter and another spate of scandal stories, Wilder let it be known that he was reconsidering his exit and might still run as an Independent.

The on-again, off-again Wilder Senate candidacy was, technically at least, still off-again when state Senator Virgil Goode announced his candidacy for the Democratic nomination in late spring. There was speculation that the state senator from Rocky Mount was only a stalking horse for Wilder, but the independent-minded Goode made his motivation clear in a late May debate with Robb. "Do we want a senator," Goode asked, "whose judgment is so flawed that, despite warnings, he continued to hang out with cocaine users and drug doers? I cannot condone and cannot accept [Robb's] example any longer."[38] Despite Goode's direct attack on Robb and endorsements of Goode's candidacy by Eighth District Representative James Moran and former Attorney General Mary Sue Terry, the folksy Southside state senator made little headway. Aided by his incumbency and head-start, Robb amassed a campaign war chest ten times the size of Goode's and posted a decisive victory in the sparsely attended June 14 primary.[39] That same day, former Governor Wilder showed up at the State Board of Elections with two cardboard boxes full of petitions qualifying him for a spot on the November ballot as an Independent.

---

37. *Washington Post*, June 25, 1993.

38. *Washington Post*, May 23, 1994. Goode's campaign also attacked Robb in a television ad that referred to the incumbent's earlier "parties with prostitutes and drug criminals" and "sexual activity with young girls." To support the charges, Goode's campaign released copies of memoranda prepared by Robb staffers outlining the sordid facts they uncovered while investigating allegations about their boss's conduct in Virginia Beach while governor. Edds and Morris, "Virginia," pp. 148–149.

39. The vote totals were: Robb—154,561 (57.9 percent); Goode—90,547 (33.9 percent); Sylvia Clute—17, 329 (6.5 percent); Nancy B. Spannaus—4,507 (1.7 percent). Robb raised $2.2 million compared to Goode's $212,000. Sabato, *Virginia Votes 1991–1994*, p. 98.

That the two major parties in Virginia had selected scandal-plagued nominees was national news, and the Mother of Presidents was lampooned from coast to coast. Typical of the coverage was an editorial cartoon in the *Kansas City Star* that converted the state's tourism slogan, "Virginia is for Lovers," into "Virginia is for Liars."[40] (An earlier offering had suggested "Virginia is for Losers."[41]) Late-night comic Jay Leno chimed in that Oliver North was the perfect Senate candidate because "he comes pre-indicted."[42] In this company, the well-worn Marshall Coleman, who announced his independent bid in June with Warner's backing, actually seemed like something of a fresh alternative. "Coleman may not be an exciting leader at the top of his game," wrote the *Washington Post*'s Kent Jenkins Jr., "but he never dallied with young women in Virginia Beach like Robb, never lied to Congress like North, and never became a world-class political bickerer like Wilder."[43] Coleman took his share of ribbing, too. "The difference between Lazarus and Marshall Coleman," quipped former Congressman Caldwell Butler, "is that Lazarus admitted he was dead."[44] Three-time loser Coleman seemed very much alive, however, when a June poll showed him starting out near the top in the looming four-person mud wrestle. The statewide Mason-Dixon survey found Robb with 27 percent support, Coleman with 25 percent, Wilder with 22 percent, and North with 21 percent. Of the four candidates, only Coleman was rated favorably by more respondents than rated him unfavorably.[45]

The summer months, however, belonged to North. Key Reagan allies who had opposed him for the GOP nomination, including Edwin Meese and Paul Laxalt, lent their endorsement. His national fund-raising machine hummed like none other, headed toward a total take of $20 million by campaign's end that would dwarf the amount collected by all of his opponents combined.[46] And North's energetic, magnetic campaigning seemed to

40. *Richmond-Times Dispatch*, June 1, 2004.
41. Joel Garreax, "Virginia Is for . . . Losers?" *Washington Post*, March 28, 1994.
42. *Richmond-Times Dispatch*, June 1, 2004.
43. *Washington Post*, June 2, 1994.
44. *Daily Progress*, June 8, 1994.
45. *Daily Progress*, June 8, 1994.
46. North's campaign collected $19.76 million, and, although direct mail fund-raising costs consumed a significant share of the total, the figure shattered all previous donation records in Virginia contests and placed the North effort among the most expensive United States Senate campaigns in the country's history. Robb's $5.5 million total, though small by comparison to North's, also exceeded that in any prior Senate campaign in Virginia and was nearly twice what Robb had spent to win the seat six years earlier. Wilder and Coleman each raised less than $1 million. Sabato, *Virginia Votes 1991–1994*, p. 115.

recapture the aura generated by his dramatic Senate testimony years earlier. Clad in what became his signature blue-plaid shirt, the candidate loosened up with reporters and seemed more folksy than threatening on the stump. Seldom mentioning his opponents—he dismissed them as "three professional politicians who have held every statewide office"[47]—North's populist, anti-Washington message placed him squarely on the side of "the honest, hard-working, God-fearing, law-abiding, tax-burdened and over-regulated people of the Old Dominion."[48] Rural voters, blue-collar workers, and young people seemed especially moved by North's appeals. A long-time observer of the Virginia political scene, conservative editorialist Ross Mackenzie of the *Richmond Times-Dispatch*, had seen nothing like "the North phenomenon," and he took pains to describe it:

> In nearly thirty years of observing Virginia politics, rarely have I seen performances equaling his. Gap-toothed and pug-nosed, the man has an undeniable star quality; this could as easily be up there, Springsteen or Stallone. Crowds crush against him. Men and women want his gaze, want to touch him and talk to him, want his signature on their shirt. There's an intensity in these people, an energy. They believe. . . .
>
> North voters are angry about the direction in which those set in authority over us are taking the country. For years they have been doing their best, but for years they have regarded so many of their politicians as having taken their tax money and spent it stupidly. They don't like paying ever more to combat crime while crime ever increases; they don't like paying ever more for quality education while educational performance ever declines. They don't like decimating defense to pay people not to work and stay home and have out-of-wedlock kids. They don't like penalizing accomplishment and rewarding sloth. They manage too little sleep and see too many pols stymieing their dreams. . . . These people passionate for North are angry populists who vehemently oppose the pols and institutions long in power. They believe—in liberty, individualism, America. They do not rejoice in government taking more of their money, sapping more of their energy, telling them what to do. And they detect in North a shared belief. . . .
>
> Maybe it's a class thing: the sophisticates versus the toilers, the comfortable condescenders versus the people in the trenches, the self-appointed intellectuals versus those who do the work . . . . [The] hearts of these people beat passionately for Ollie.[49]

Largely forgotten in the fervor—or, more aptly, disregarded as an invention of the liberal news media—were the actions in Iran-Contra that had earned

---

47. *Richmond Times-Dispatch*, July 31, 1994.

48. *Richmond Times-Dispatch*, July 31, 1994; *Richmond Times-Dispatch*, November 17, 1994.

49. *Richmond Times-Dispatch*, October 30, 1994.

North reprobation from prosecutors, a former president, and fellow partisans. Aided by media overreaching, North cultivated the notion that the press, hopelessly under the spell of a liberal bias, was simply making up bad things about him. "We thank the Lord for Oliver North," said the pastor during an invocation at one large North rally, "and we pray . . . the citizens of Virginia will not be guided by a liberal press."[50]

The 1994 congressional contests—the first midterm elections of the Clinton presidency—would produce historic Republican gains, especially in the South, and would effect a dramatic shift to GOP leadership in both houses of Congress.[51] Like other Republican candidates around the country, North trained his rhetorical sights on the intensely unpopular administration of President Clinton, who had already succeeded in raising taxes and was pushing for a sweeping new federal health care plan. This posed a particular problem for Robb. He had voted for the Clinton tax increase—an action sharply criticized by fellow Democrat Wilder—and had been singled out for endorsement by Clinton a year earlier. Although Robb had generally supported Clinton and the Senate Democratic leadership on key votes, the senator now sought to portray himself as a contrary centrist, pointing out that he voted with President Bush rather than fellow Democrats in supporting the Persian Gulf War resolution in 1991, had been booted off the Senate's budget-writing committee by the Democratic leadership because of his opposition to deficit spending, and had helped win large defense contracts for Virginia employers. By September, it was apparent that North had been surging during the summer and that support for the two independent candidates was slipping as voters increasingly perceived the contest as a North-Robb duel. Polls showed North had moved from last place into first, and the main reason was his effective drumbeat against the stumbling president.[52] "Clinton has done for North what North could never do for himself," observed Larry Sabato.[53]

If the summer belonged to North, Robb—ever the strong closer—owned the fall. The first decisive break for the Democrat came with the withdrawal of Douglas Wilder from the race in mid-September, ending what an observer termed his "thinly disguised quest for revenge," and soon thereafter endorsing Robb's reelection.[54] Concerned about the growing

50. *Richmond Times-Dispatch*, July 31, 1994.

51. See David Lublin, *The Republican South: Democratization and Partisan Change* (Princeton, NJ: Princeton University Press, 2004), pp. 1, 33–65.

52. Sabato, *Virginia Votes 1991–1994*, p. 120.

53. *Daily Progress*, September 26, 1994.

54. The characterization was by Donald Baker, Wilder's biographer. *Washington Post*, September 18, 1994. Wilder met with President Clinton before embracing Robb, leading to GOP charges—roundly denied by the Democrats involved—that a deal had been

prospect of a North victory, key African-American leaders, including legendary civil rights lawyer Oliver Hill and Congressman Robert ("Bobby") Scott, had bailed on Wilder and endorsed Robb days earlier. Wilder's sagging poll numbers and depleted campaign coffers afforded little hope for a rebound, and—his feelings about Robb aside—the former governor had no desire to be blamed for splitting the Democratic vote and sending an arch-conservative like Oliver North to the Senate.[55] "I am a realist. I know when to hold them and when to fold them," said Wilder, adding that he had seen firsthand that "the two-party system in Virginia is strong and the difficulty of financing independent candidacies is real."[56] Wilder's withdrawal was crucial, but Robb's long-shot bid to keep his seat would require more. With polls showing him still trailing in mid-October, the combative senator went on the offensive.[57] Nancy Reagan weighed in, and the news media pounded away relentlessly at the much-maligned colonel. But the biggest reason the GOP effort went south down the stretch was North—and his implacable foe, John Warner.

As the campaign entered its final phase, Warner and his hand-picked but poorly funded independent candidate, Marshall Coleman, seemed less and less relevant. The senior senator had clearly hurt North's bid by opposing his candidacy and by declaring him unfit for the Senate. But the "Outlaw Hero" had absorbed those blows and many others, and was still standing. The fight was now between North and Robb, and opinions varied about which major-party candidate was helped or hurt more by Coleman's persistence in the race. As with so many other independent candidacies, Coleman's eventually was squeezed from both sides as his mostly suburban supporters jumped ship to choose among the major-party contenders who had a real chance to win. Coleman's campaign did provide one final service,

---

cooked up by Clinton and Robb to gain Wilder's support. In August 1995, however, Clinton and Robb co-sponsored a high-dollar fund-raiser to help Wilder retire debts from his 1994 senatorial bid and his run for the White House in 1992. "All the principals denied there was any connection between the event and Wilder's life-saving endorsement of Robb ten months earlier," wrote Larry Sabato, "but only the naïve believed them." Sabato, *Virginia Votes 1991–1994*, p. 123.

55. Wilder interview.

56. *Washington Post*, September 16, 1994. In exiting the race, the sixty-three-year-old Wilder stated he was through with politics, at least as a candidate. "I will fight no more, forever," he declared. In 2004, however, Wilder was again elected to public office, winning a contest for mayor of the city of Richmond with roughly 80 percent of the vote.

57. Heading into the final three weeks of the campaign, a Mason-Dixon survey found North with 37 percent of the expected vote, Robb with 33 percent, Coleman with 16 percent, and the rest undecided. North led in all regions of the state except Northern Virginia. *Daily Progress*, October 20, 1994.

though. Neither North nor Robb wanted to be the first to unleash harsh attacks on the "character issue" over the airwaves, lest voters blame them for the negativism. Coleman obliged by picking the fight for them. "This is a picture of a Virginia senator who wants to be re-elected," intoned the Coleman television ad narrator as an unflattering black-and-white photo of Robb filled the screen. "He's a Clinton clone, been investigated by a grand jury, and admits to improper social conduct." A similarly ominous photo of North followed: "Here's the picture of a man who wants to replace him: convicted felon, confessed liar, and, according to Senator John Warner, unfit to serve in any public office." Next came a color photo of the toothy, upbeat Coleman: "Here's a much brighter picture: Marshall Coleman. When you think about the others you know he's the one for Virginia."[58]

Theoretically at least, Robb and North could have engaged in a robust debate on the issues, so far apart were they on major questions of national policy. But October was all about scandals and gaffes. After Coleman's negative volley, Robb followed quickly with a withering series of electronic attacks on North's Iran-Contra misdeeds and credibility, and the North camp drew a direct bead on Robb's personal scandals. "All that sensational talk of shredded documents and nude massages has obscured what otherwise might be the country's sharpest ideological battle this fall," observed reporter Peter Baker.[59] Also preventing a more illuminating discussion was a series of controversial misstatements by North, who seemed to buckle finally under the late barrage of Democratic attacks and nonstop media criticism.[60] In one damaging off-hand remark, North said President Clinton was "not my commander in chief."[61] In another, he opined that the nation had a "hollow military" under Clinton and would be unable to turn back Iraqi dictator Saddam Hussein's army if it again invaded Kuwait.[62] Democrats

58. *Washington Post*, October 5, 1994.

59. *Washington Post*, October 30, 1994.

60. In his post-election report, nonpartisan analyst Larry Sabato concluded that media coverage had decidedly favored the Democratic candidate in the contest. Noting that "[e]ven some liberal commentators were taken aback at the ferocity with which the news media hammered . . . [and] virtually demonized" North, Sabato cited an independent content analysis showing a lopsided anti-North slant in the extensive national news coverage of the race. Sabato found the reporting by in-state media outlets similarly unbalanced, concluding that "the usual pretense of media objectivity was openly suspended for this race." Sabato, *Virginia Votes 1991–1994*, p. 122. As the election approached, North's team figuratively threw up its hands in frustration. Reporters calling the campaign press office on election day did not get an answer but instead received this sarcastic recorded message: "Thank you very much for your fair treatment and wonderful coverage, and we look forward to working with you in the future." *Richmond Times-Dispatch*, November 8, 1994.

61. *Richmond Times-Dispatch*, November 10, 1994.

62. *Washington Post*, October 10, 1994.

were especially pleased by North's suggestion on October 28th that he might support making Social Security voluntary in the future; the Robb campaign immediately highlighted that statement in its closing mail and television ad blitz. Citing comments by unnamed North aides, *Richmond Times-Dispatch* reporter Mike Allen wrote after the election that the Republican candidate had "finished himself off with a string of gaffes that reminded Virginians why he scared them before he remade himself this summer."[63] "This," said one North adviser, referring to his candidate's self-inflicted wounds, "was a suicide."[64]

North's advisers seemed eager to blame the candidate, and certainly the series of gaffes hurt the GOP effort. One especially damaging event that neither North nor his campaign team could control, however, was Nancy Reagan's much-publicized statement twelve days before the election that North had "lied to my husband and lied about my husband"; it produced a three-point drop in North's support, as measured by the campaign's internal polls.[65] But the most fateful misstep—a tactical error rivaling the cash-flush Terry campaign's failure to define George Allen early in the previous year's gubernatorial contest—was the North campaign's decision to cease its electronic attacks on the vulnerable Robb and instead "go positive" in the campaign's final days.[66] If ever there was a race driven by negatives and bound to be decided by negatives, it was the battle of the two sullied soldiers who were seeking Virginia's junior Senate seat in 1994. But despite his passion for the rough and tumble of politics, North and his wife Betsy shared an aversion to negative campaign ads, and they hoped that if the GOP campaign pulled its ads attacking Robb and substituted a positive message about the Republican nominee, voters would respond affirmatively.[67] Com-

---

63. *Richmond Times-Dispatch*, November 10, 1994.

64. *Richmond Times-Dispatch*, November 10, 1994.

65. *Richmond Times-Dispatch*, November 10, 1994; Edds and Morris, "Virginia," p. 150.

66. The controversial decision was described by campaign operatives in a 1996 documentary on the North-Robb Senate contest. R. J. Cutler and David Van Taylor, *A Perfect Candidate* (New York: First Run Features, 1996); see also *Richmond Times-Dispatch*, November 9, 1994.

67. Interviewed years later, North took full responsibility for rejecting campaign advisers' recommendation to hit back in the contest's closing days. "It was the candidate's call," he said. "Almost everybody urged me to go negative in the ads, and I refused." North interview. Most of the campaign's internal debate, recalled North, focused on an especially evocative electronic rejoinder that ad man Mike Murphy had prepared in rebuttal to the constant Robb refrain that North was a "convicted felon." The spot showed news footage of an interview with a member of the all-black, mostly female jury that had convicted North; in the interview, the juror bluntly cited racial reasons for the jury's guilty verdict. See North, p. 398. "That spot would have forever branded me as a racist," North recalled. "Betsy and I talked about it, and it was just not

pounding the mistake, North's handlers mainly chose to put their candidate on the air making his own case, and they made only belated, sparse use of a strong endorsement taped by popular Governor George Allen that might have helped counter some of the North-bashing by Nancy Reagan, John Warner, and other Republicans.

It was, to say the least, a strange time to try to sell Oliver North positively to the Virginia electorate. Polls had shown for months that Virginians had a firmly fixed, negative view of the Republican candidate, and weeks of Democratic attacks and bad news stories had made matters worse. The Robb camp's transparent plan was to launch every imaginable missile at North in the campaign's closing days, and they did so with an intensity rarely matched in the state's politics. Robb himself led the Democratic assault in his public speeches, offering what undoubtedly will stand for some time as the ultimate negative diatribe in a Virginia campaign. North, thundered Robb in the shadow of Jefferson's Capitol and at other rallies, was a "document-shredding, constitution-trashing, commander-in-chief-bashing, Ayatollah-loving, arms-dealing, drug-condoning, Noriega-coddling, Swiss-banking, law-breaking, letter-faking, self-serving snake oil salesman."[68] With Robb firing everything in his arsenal while the North campaign engaged in unilateral disarmament, a Democratic surge was inevitable.

Two days before the election—and the day after former President Reagan first revealed his Alzheimer's affliction in a poignant letter to "my fellow Americans"—a *Richmond Times-Dispatch* poll showed that Robb had "opened a last-minute, [eight-point] lead after trailing or running even with the Republican" most of the campaign.[69] "In Virginia's mud-slinging battle of the ex-Marines," wrote Peter Grier of the *Christian Science Monitor* after the election, "incumbent Senator Charles Robb triumphed by convincing

---

who I am and what I am about. You wonder sometimes whether that or some other strong ad might have turned the close race—the pollster told us that ad would—but I have never regretted the decision not to use it." North interview. For his part, Robb rejected contentions that a negative ad blitz by North would have changed the outcome of the contest. "The kind of negative ads North's campaign had been running were hurting North more than they hurt me," he said. Robb interview.

68. *Richmond Times-Dispatch,* November 3, 1994.

69. *Richmond Times-Dispatch,* November 6, 1994. The survey results showed Robb at 39 percent, North at 31 percent, and Coleman slipping to 12 percent and "apparently surrendering votes to Robb." In his post-election analysis, Larry Sabato noted that the *Times-Dispatch* poll, published 48 hours before the election, showed a much bigger Robb lead than appeared in other surveys or in the actual election results. Comparing the Richmond newspaper's errant survey to similarly late and lopsidedly inaccurate polls by the *Washington Post* in the 1985 and 1989 statewide contests, Sabato renewed his call for media organizations to refrain from publishing last-minute horserace surveys that may unduly influence election-day voting. Sabato, *Virginia Votes 1991–1994,* pp. 116–118.

many moderate voters that his ethical problems were less serious than those of GOP challenger Oliver North."[70] Grier cited exit polls showing that North's Iran-Contra involvement was a factor affecting the ballot choice of 60 percent of voters, while Robb's personal controversies influenced only 40 percent. In the campaign's crucial days, with many undecided votes on the line, Robb had effectively driven home the message that North was ethically unacceptable; the GOP had failed to counter with a recitation of the incumbent's misdeeds that might have evened the score.[71] "You're right," said North to his campaign chairman, former Republican Party chief Donald Huffman, after his concession speech, "I'm not mean enough."[72]

"How sweet it is!" crowed Robb at his McLean victory party, wife Lynda at his side and his remarkable political resuscitation now achieved.[73] The thick-skinned senator had not only redeemed his political name and won another six years in the Senate; he had bucked an unusually strong national tide that swept Republicans to majorities in both houses of Congress for the first time since Eisenhower's day. Yet, the race was not mainly about Robb; North had become the central issue. "For Virginians, the choice came down to the devil they knew and the devil they knew better," wrote journalist Jeff Schapiro. "They didn't as much return scandal-stained Democrat Charles S. Robb to the U. S. Senate for a second term as prevent Iran-Contra figure Oliver L. North from getting there."[74] Agreed Larry Sabato: "The Virginia GOP could easily have caught the countrywide conservative wave in an anti-Clinton state, especially in a contest with the weakened Robb. But instead, the party indulged itself ideologically and badly over-reached by nominating Oliver North."[75] Conservative Michael Farris, who, like North, had lost amid a Republican landslide, rejected the notion that North's ideology was to blame for his defeat: "I don't think anybody thinks Ollie lost because he was too conservative. Iran-Contra was

70. Peter Grier, "Robb's Moderate Image Wins Out," *Christian Science Monitor,* November 10, 1994.

71. See Marc Short, "How the North Campaign Went South," unpublished paper, University of Virginia, December 17, 2003, pp. 18–21.

72. *Richmond Times-Dispatch,* November 11, 1994.

73. *Washington Post,* November 9, 1994.

74. *Richmond Times-Dispatch,* November 9, 1994.

75. Sabato, *Virginia Votes 1991–1994,* p. 95. Though pundits suggested North might have been the only candidate unable to oust Robb, the embattled senator deemed North to be a stronger foe than his GOP rival, James Miller. Interviewed after leaving the Senate, Robb ventured that he would have been reelected by a more comfortable margin if Miller had been nominated. "The turnout on both sides would have been much smaller," said Robb. "Jim [Miller] is very bright and knowledgeable, particularly on fiscal and monetary policy, but he [did] not have a political persona." Robb interview.

the driving force with Ollie." Plus, added Farris, "the one thing in common with our two races was John Warner."[76]

The loud and ugly Senate race embarrassed Virginians—nearly two-thirds of respondents told pollsters the contest put Virginia in a bad light nationally[77]—but it did not keep them away from the polls on election day. To the contrary, the turnout was among the highest in any non-presidential contest in the state.[78] Robb's plurality victory—he became the first United States senator from Virginia elected without a majority of the vote—was built in urban areas. While losing 73 of 95 counties to North, he prevailed in 26 of 41 cities. The Democrat trailed North in seven of 11 congressional districts and ran even in the swing-voting suburbs, but Robb more than offset North's geographically broad but thin rural advantage by winning decisively in densely populated Northern Virginia and Hampton Roads. Reflecting the partisan cross-currents, North failed to capture 26 percent of the Republican vote while only 13 percent of Democrats abandoned Robb. North, however, led Robb among independents by a margin of 46 percent to 38 percent.[79]

Throughout the campaign, North and GOP leaders seemed to have largely written off the African-American vote, while Robb actively endeavored to energize that traditionally Democratic voting bloc. The results—an 86 percent share of the black vote for Robb—showed how important Wilder's withdrawal and endorsement had been.[80] Remarkably, for the second year in a row, the white Democratic standard-bearer received a smaller share of the white vote than Wilder had received in his 1989 campaign.[81] Robb was helped significantly by female voters; a substantial gender gap was evident, as the Democrat enjoyed a 48 to 41 percent advantage among women (55 to 36 percent among working women) while trailing North 46 to 43 percent among male voters. North benefited from 60 percent support from the third of voters who identified themselves as "born-again Christians." Contrary to conventional wisdom, which late in the campaign had held that Coleman would draw as many votes from moderate Robb as conservative

76. *Richmond Times-Dispatch*, November 10, 1994.

77. *Richmond Times-Dispatch*, November 6, 1994.

78. The vote totals were: Robb (D)—938,376 (45.6 percent); North (R)—882,213 (42.9 percent); Coleman (I)—235,324 (11.4 percent). Sabato, *Virginia Votes 1991–1994*, p. 107.

79. Sabato, *Virginia Votes 1991–1994*, p. 107.

80. Sabato, *Virginia Votes 1991–1994*, p. 107.

81. Robb received 37 percent of votes cast by whites. Gubernatorial nominee Mary Sue Terry had received 33 percent of the white vote in 1993, while Wilder had received 41 percent of ballots cast by whites in the 1989 gubernatorial race. Sabato, *Virginia Votes 1991–1994*, p. 106.

North, exit polls revealed that Coleman's votes had come disproportion-ately at North's expense. Without Coleman's presence in the contest, Robb and North would have ended the race in a dead heat.[82]

Declaring winners and losers was not difficult in the aftermath of the tumultuous 1994 contest. Senator Robb's ability to breathe again after a seemingly interminable stint on political life-support made him the big win-ner. President Clinton, who suffered a shellacking from sea to sea—in fact, almost everywhere *except* Virginia—seemed a clear loser at the time. But the severe setback provided a wake-up call and produced a foil (the GOP congressional leadership), precipitating a Clinton move toward the center that would position him successfully for a reelection win two years later. Oliver North had his electoral aspirations doused at least temporarily by the loss to Robb, and he soon turned to radio and television commentary, argu-ably making him a long-term winner despite the near-term loss. Former Governor Wilder seemed more loser than winner, since his apparent swan song in politics had not yielded success and his rival had survived; yet, Wil-der could take credit for delivering crucial black votes to Robb, and he would continue to be a force in state and local politics for years to come. Except for the "soft teeth" crack at the GOP convention, which would bedevil him for years, Governor Allen was the other big winner. He had done everything North and his team had asked, yet the reelection of Robb set the stage for Allen's own opportunity to gain the Senate six years later. Also a winner was moderate Fairfax Republican Thomas M. Davis III, whose strong local persona and arms-length support for his party's Senate candidate enabled him to overcome the North downdraft in Northern Vir-ginia and oust incumbent Leslie L. Byrne in the Eleventh District congres-sional race.[83] Marshall Coleman came out a loser—again, and for the last time. His patron, Senator Warner, was neither a loser nor winner yet. War-ner's fight had only begun.

In the end, the 1994 contest stood as a testament to the dominance of the two major political parties and, as Wilder noted in finally exiting the

---

82. Sabato, *Virginia Votes 1991–1994*, pp. 106–108, 121.

83. Davis's comfortable win in the acrimonious contest was the only bright spot for Virginia Republicans in the 1994 congressional races. Democrats maintained a major-ity—now six of 11 seats—in the state's House of Representatives contingent, and they posted a decisive win (54 percent to the GOP's 45 percent) in the popular vote cast in the Virginia congressional races. Reflecting how far out of line the Old Dominion strayed from national trends in 1994, Republican candidates nationally polled more than 51 percent of all congressional ballots—the first such GOP majority since 1946. In con-trast, the 45 percent of the vote garnered by the GOP's congressional candidates in Vir-ginia constituted the state party's second worst showing in three decades. Sabato, *Virginia Votes 1991–1994*, p. 126.

contest, to the difficulty of waging an independent campaign even in independent-minded Virginia. Non-aligned swing voters plainly held the political power balance in the evenly divided Commonwealth, but the days of partisan transition—when a conservative like Harry Byrd Jr. in 1970 or a liberal populist like Henry Howell in 1971 could win as an Independent— were past. If the two major parties could force on voters an unwelcome choice like Robb versus North and not experience mass defections to credible independent alternatives like Wilder and Coleman, then it seemed pretty clear the two-party system would remain the controlling political dynamic in Virginia for the foreseeable future. For that reason, and perhaps that reason alone, John Warner announced shortly after the 1994 contest that he would seek reelection in 1996 as a Republican. There had been considerable speculation he would do otherwise, fostered by a loud chorus of GOP recriminations that were aimed at the senior senator in the aftermath of North's defeat.

That Warner would face a challenge in 1996 from his party's right wing was a foregone conclusion, and the talk was not confined to the Right. Former Governor Mills Godwin, no die-hard party loyalist, had seemed to capture the prevailing mood at the June 1994 GOP convention when, in conversation with reporter Bob Gibson, he expressed the hope that Virginia would have two Republican senators representing the state in Washington. In a jab at Warner, he quipped, "Two years from now is not very long to elect a second Republican from the state of Virginia."[84] Michael Farris, still stinging from the senator's non-support in 1993, passed out "Is it 1996 yet?" bumper strips at the convention and encouraged speculation that he would challenge Warner. In the wake of their 1994 defeats, James Miller and Oliver North also were frequently mentioned as possible candidates. Regardless of who ran against him, Warner understood that his future would depend on the method of nomination. To win in the current climate, he would need the contest to be decided in a primary election open to Democrats and independent voters rather than at a convention controlled by conservative Republican activists.[85] Eager to avoid forcing Warner into an independent candidacy that likely would split the Republican vote and elect another Democratic senator, GOP leaders generally were prepared to accede to Warner's primary preference.[86] More to the point, a state law permitted the

---

84. *Daily Progress*, June 5, 1994.

85. Virginia election laws do not provide for voter registration by party, and voting in primary elections is not limited by party affiliation. For a description of previous instances of "crossover" voting by rival partisans in Virginia's primary elections, see *The Dynamic Dominion*, Chapters 2, 4, 17, 29.

86. Warner later confirmed that he likely would have sought reelection as an Independent if the state party had not acceded to his preference for a primary election as the nomination method. John Warner interview.

incumbent to choose the nomination method, and Warner exercised his right to select a state-sponsored primary contest.[87]

All the post-election talk about the challenge to Warner in 1996 greatly concerned Governor Allen. He wanted partisans to concentrate on his sweeping legislative initiatives and, on a political level, to gear up to push for a Republican majority in the General Assembly in the 1995 midterm legislative elections. He therefore summoned about two dozen party officials and prospective candidates, including Warner, to the Executive Mansion in late November 1994 for a private session in which he admonished them to make sure "our immediate goal of Republican control of the General Assembly is not overshadowed or circumvented by a premature fascination with the presidential and . . . senatorial elections of 1996."[88] Speaking to reporters after the meeting, Allen was asked and declined to say whether he supported Warner's renomination; he declared only that he would support the GOP nominee. Perceptions of the meeting's success depended on the beholder. The governor seemed satisfied, and reporter Mike Allen cast the conclave as productive, writing that "Virginia's Republican leaders, who make the Hatfields and McCoys seem downright neighborly, called a one-year truce after coffee, Cokes, and a lecture in Governor George Allen's dining room."[89] Already considered his party's likely nominee for the Senate seat, Democratic chairman Mark Warner was predictably unimpressed. "Governor Allen is trying to put Humpty Dumpty back together again," said the Democratic chief. "He can't. The issues go much beyond personality, to whether the heart and soul of the Republican Party will remain with the Radical Right, or if there is going to be a moderate Republican Party." Allen, said Democrat Warner, was merely struggling to "postpone the blood bath."[90]

As it turned out, Allen's party did have a rocky time during his sophomore year as governor, but mainly because of sparring with the General Assembly's dominant Democrats, not because of internal GOP strife. In Richmond, Allen and Republicans battled Democratic lawmakers over

---

87. The Republican State Central Committee voted in December 1995 to nominate the party's Senate candidate via primary and to require the candidates to ascribe to a loyalty pledge. The action came after Attorney General James Gilmore opined that the state laws giving incumbent Warner the choice of nominating method and providing for an open primary were constitutionally defensible. GOP state chairman Patrick McSweeney and Republican Delegate Robert Marshall then filed a federal lawsuit challenging the two statutes. In April 1996, Federal District Judge Richard L. Williams dismissed the McSweeney-Marshall case, citing the GOP governing committee's earlier action in setting a June primary as the nominating method.

88. *Richmond Times-Dispatch*, November 29, 1994.

89. *Richmond Times-Dispatch*, November 29, 1994.

90. *Richmond Times-Dispatch*, November 29, 1994.

taxes, education, prison-building, and welfare early in 1995, and then sought to cast the fall legislative elections as a choice between the governor's reform agenda and Democratic obstructionism. Democrats countered that the fight was over support for education, and cast the GOP as tax-cutters first and school-funders second. In Washington, new House of Representatives Speaker Newt Gingrich, the Georgia firebrand, moved to implement his GOP majority's ambitious "Contract with America."[91] The political fall-out among moderates from the aggressive, Gingrich-led "revolution" on Capitol Hill, including new lines of attack opened by Democrats on hot-button issues such as the future of the Medicare program, was beginning to be felt as Virginians went to the polls in the fall of 1995.[92] Allen and GOP lawmakers nevertheless tried to replicate the political success of the "Contract with America" by assembling on the State Capitol steps and offering their own policy agenda, called the "Pledge for Honest Change." A majority of Virginians responded affirmatively: GOP legislative candidates received 55.3 percent of the total vote in races for the state Senate and 50.7 percent of the total in contests for the House of Delegates.[93] The modest Republican gain produced a tie in the 40-member Senate. But Allen had attempted to fire up GOP activists and donors by declaring capture of at least one legislative chamber as the party's goal. When the results fell short, post-election reports cast the outcome as a significant setback for the Republican governor and his fellow partisans.

Virginia Republicans understood they had little chance to improve their fortunes in 1996. They assumed they would carry the state for an eighth consecutive GOP presidential nominee, expected this time to be Senate Majority Leader Robert Dole of Kansas. But there was little passionate support for Dole, and his prospects for unseating President Clinton seemed increasingly dim, especially after Democrats spent millions in the

---

91. The Republican takeover on Capitol Hill thrust two Virginians into key leadership roles. In the House of Representatives, Seventh District veteran Thomas Bliley—in contrast to Gingrich, "a careful, quiet revolutionary," according to former aide David Mason—became chairman of the powerful House Commerce Committee. *Richmond Times-Dispatch*, January 1, 1995. In September 1995, a leadership shuffle caused by the sex-scandal-impelled resignation of Senator Robert Packwood of Oregon elevated John Warner to the chairmanship of the Senate Rules and Administration Committee.

92. A November 1995 voter survey conducted for state Democrats by Cooper and Secrest Associates found that House Speaker Gingrich was viewed unfavorably by 47 percent of Virginians and favorably by only 37 percent, while President Clinton was viewed favorably by 44 percent and unfavorably by 44 percent. Larry J. Sabato, *Virginia Votes 1995–1998* (Charlottesville: Weldon Cooper Center for Public Service, University of Virginia, 1999), p. 18.

93. Sabato, *Virginia Votes 1995–1998*, pp. 1, 10–13.

spring of 1996 on nationwide television ads linking Dole unflatteringly with his controversial House counterpart Gingrich. John Warner's reelection bid provided an opportunity for some GOP partisans, but that opportunity had little to do with advancing the party's electoral fortunes. Warner's detractors were out to replace him if possible, but, if not, at least teach him a lesson, in the interest of future party solidarity and purity. The senator's supporters were determined to defend his honor and his seat.

The anti-Warner forces galvanized around James Miller, the Reaganite who had waged a creditable race against North in 1994. But Miller became the choice to challenge Warner only after the party's most prominent social conservative, Michael Farris, opted out of the race. Farris had initially determined to take on Warner and had moved decisively to lay the groundwork for a 1996 Senate bid. He studied international affairs, lined up grassroots backing and financial support, and conducted a poll that showed him running almost even with Warner among likely GOP primary voters. But when he met with former Senator Paul Trible to ask Trible to chair his Senate campaign, Farris was stunned by the former senator's description of life in the Senate and its impact on his young family. The father of nine, Farris concluded—as had Trible eight years earlier—that the hurly-burly and demanding Washington scene was not right for his family.[94] When Miller formally kicked off his second Senate campaign in December 1995, Farris quickly signed on as one of his campaign co-chairmen, and Oliver North gave his informal nod to Miller a few weeks later.[95] With high-profile backing from the conservative leaders who had been wronged by the incumbent senator, the Miller challenge looked like payback for Warner's partisan lapses. But the challenger sought to cast the campaign more as a philosophical showdown. Citing statistics indicating the senior senator had sided with President Clinton on 60 percent of Senate votes the previous year, Miller called Warner "one of the Clinton administration's favorite Republicans" and said the choice in the primary contest was between a "Reagan Republican" and a "Clinton Republican."[96]

Acknowledging he was "in the fight of his life—politically," a feisty John Warner took to the hustings early, aided in April 1995 by a strong endorsement from former President Bush, who headlined a Richmond fundraiser that benefited both Warner and GOP legislative candidates.[97] But the

---

94. Farris interview.
95. North was also spoiling for a fight with Warner, but in the wake of the bitter 1994 battle he had promised his wife Betsy that he would not run for office again until their children had completed college. North interview.
96. *Richmond Times-Dispatch,* December 6, 1995.
97. *Richmond Times-Dispatch,* July 10, 1995.

event also highlighted the incumbent senator's vulnerability. "So unpopular is Warner among party regulars," wrote Tyler Whitley of the *Richmond Times-Dispatch*, "that none of the four potential candidates for statewide office in 1997 dared to show up for the [fund-raising dinner featuring the former president]. All said they were engaged elsewhere."[98] Warner, undaunted, stressed his influence in the Senate and his ability to retain the seat for the GOP. "I tell them what it means to hold the conservative seat and who is best qualified to go to Virginia's three million voters. I am making steady, gradual progress. An overwhelming majority want to hold this seat for Virginia," he said.[99] Regarding Farris and North, Warner was unapologetic. Visiting Professor Larry Sabato's government class at the University of Virginia, he declared:

> I could have slapped on a sticker of someone I didn't support . . . and I would be unopposed this time. I'm not cut out to do that. I wasn't raised by my parents to do that. I learned under the honor system at this University not to do that. . . . I felt I should put the interests of my country and of my state ahead of politics."[100]

The combative Warner hoped to goad another conservative into the race, the better to split the vote on the Republican right. He used his University of Virginia appearance to publicly needle GOP state chairman Patrick McSweeney, often mentioned as a possible candidate. "I said [to McSweeney] the other day, 'Come on, . . . show some guts and get in.'" Warner said. "I welcome everybody to get in, including the chairman of the party, Mr. McSweeney, who is one of my constant critics."[101]

In December 1995, weeks after a published opinion survey showed the once-invincible senator in a statistical dead heat with the never-elected Miller among likely GOP primary voters, Warner effectively declared war on his Republican primary opponent.[102] The senator touted his own role on defense legislation and appropriations—he was then second in seniority among Republicans on the Senate Armed Services Committee—and highlighted his opponent's lack of military service. Warner had volunteered at age seventeen to serve in the Navy during World War II and then had

98. *Richmond Times-Dispatch*, April 17, 1995.

99. *Richmond Times-Dispatch*, April 17, 1995.

100. *Richmond Times-Dispatch*, April 17, 1995.

101. *Daily Progress*, April 13, 1995.

102. The statewide poll by Mason-Dixon Political/Media Research showed Warner leading Miller, 41 percent to 39 percent. Another survey reported in the *Richmond Times-Dispatch* a few days later showed a more comfortable, double-digit lead for Warner. *Washington Post*, November 9, 1995.

served again with the Marines in Korea; Miller had received student defer-
ments while at the University of Virginia during the Vietnam War—
though, Miller quickly pointed out, he also had applied to the Air Force
Academy and was turned down due to colorblindness.[103] Military service
was again emphasized when Warner held a State Capitol news conference
in February 1996 to launch his campaign. But another theme also was
stressed—*money*. Multimillionaire Democrat Mark Warner had lent his Senate campaign $500,000, and had made it clear more would be forthcoming.
Senator Warner, whose campaign coffers already included $2 million,
argued that his proven fund-raising ability would be needed to match the
Democrat's personal wealth. Beyond that, the election was a test, said the
embattled sixty-nine-year-old senator, of whether "an elected leader [who
voted] his conscience, putting principle before politics, [could] win." He
predicted: "The Virginia I know . . . the Virginia I love, will say yes."[104]

The GOP contest played out all spring as Warner battled not only
Miller but his past and implemented a difficult, twofold strategy: counter
Miller's appeal to the Republican right and simultaneously attract Democrats and independents into the party's open primary in June. The Warner
bid for conservative GOP backing was aided by endorsements from former
Vice President Dan Quayle, a family-values champion on the Republican
Right, and from de facto presidential nominee Robert Dole, who campaigned with Warner as the duo promised repeal of Clinton-sponsored tax
increases. The senator's television ads used the word "conservative" repeatedly, stressed his military experience, and featured photos of him with
Quayle, former President Reagan, and former British Prime Minister Margaret Thatcher. Late in the season, Warner assailed Miller in radio and television ads that savaged the former Reagan lieutenant for, among other
things, avoiding military service and spending taxpayer dollars to redecorate
his Washington office. Miller suffered from a comparative lack of campaign
cash, but he attacked Warner's Senate record on taxes, abortion, gun control, and other issues, branded him a Washington-establishment elitist, and
countered with an array of conservative endorsements. The Miller backers
included the National Rifle Association, retired Judge Robert Bork, various
Reagan and Bush administration luminaries, former Governor Mills Godwin,
former Congressman Joel Broyhill (who had chaired Warner's first Senate
campaign), and the first family of Virginia Republicanism, the Obenshains.
The influential Christian Coalition weighed in shortly before the GOP primary with "voter guides" showing Miller in a positive light. Sticking to his

---

103. *Richmond Times-Dispatch,* December 14, 1995.
104. *Richmond Times-Dispatch,* February 23, 1996.

Reagan-like policy of noninvolvement in GOP nominating contests, Governor George Allen stayed neutral.

While contending for Republican support, Warner also appealed openly for Democrats and Independents to participate in the GOP primary and support his candidacy. "Everybody's got a right to participate [in the primary]," said Warner. "You do not win [general elections] unless you attract hundreds of thousands of other Virginia voters who do not share some of these extreme views."[105] One reason to expect so-called crossover voting in the GOP primary by Democrats and independents was what *Washington Post* reporter Peter Baker dubbed the "gratitude factor": they had strongly opposed Oliver North's bid two years earlier and appreciated Warner's seemingly courageous role in torpedoing it.[106] State Democratic leaders, including Mark Warner and new party chair Sue Wrenn, did little to mask their hope for a Miller win in the primary, and they urged fellow partisans to stay out of the GOP voting. Saying that Republicans Warner and Miller were both too far right—"Tweedledum and Tweedledee," she called them—Wrenn encouraged Democrats to save their votes for the fall election. If they felt the need to express gratitude to Senator Warner, they should call or write his Washington office, she suggested, and then "go to work, take care of the family, or enjoy the summer weather" on primary day.[107] Many Democratic loyalists—state Senator Edd Houck of Spotsylvania County was one example[108]—ignored the advice and entered the June 11th GOP primary to say "thank you" to Warner anyway. It looked like the incumbent senator would need those votes: a straw ballot at the Republican state convention in early June found that 76 percent of the GOP delegates favored Miller.[109]

It was a far different story on primary election day. Propelled by an advertising blitz that his underfunded opponent could not match, and assisted by Democrats and independent voters who invaded the GOP primary to express solidarity with the maverick moderate, Warner rolled to a lopsided victory.[110] One in seven registered Virginia voters went to the polls, and the number—nearly half a million—exceeded the turnout in nearly every other party primary held since the advent of two-party compe-

105. *Washington Post*, May 23, 1996.
106. *Washington Post*, May 23, 1996.
107. *Richmond Times-Dispatch*, May 24, 1996.
108. *Washington Post*, July 4, 1996.
109. *Roanoke Times*, June 2, 1996.
110. The vote totals were: Warner—323,520 (65.6 percent); Miller—170,015 (34.4 percent). Warner spent $2.5 million compared to Miller's $900,000. Sabato, *Virginia Votes 1995–1998*, p. 33.

tition in the Commonwealth. The University of Virginia's Sabato estimated that a third of the primary ballots had been cast by persons other than Republicans, and 77 percent of those votes had gone to Warner. But the senator also had received 59 percent of the GOP ballots and would have won a decisive victory even without the "crossovers," according to Sabato's analysis.[111] On primary night, Warner "savored his conquest of the right-wing Republicans who had taunted, tormented and—most of all—underestimated him [for] months," wrote reporters Peter Hardin and Mike Allen. The proud senator obviously did not like being "forced to go practically door-to-door, begging for his job," they noted, but he had "sucked it up, campaigned like he was running for his first office, and won overwhelmingly."[112] The completeness of Warner's victory stunned even his most virulent GOP critics, and it impressed and silenced most of them. Republicans appeared to emerge more unified and reconciled to Warner as their senatorial standard-bearer than they had been before the contentious nomination battle began a year earlier. The newly elected GOP state chairman, state Senator Randy Forbes of Chesapeake, quickly signaled the reconciliation by inviting the Warner campaign to take up residence in the party's Obenshain Center in downtown Richmond.[113]

Virginia Democrats had hoped all the Republican infighting would yield a badly bruised nominee and, ideally, an opponent more beatable than John Warner. It yielded neither. But what Democrats did get was a sixty-nine-year-old GOP nominee whose campaign coffers and personal vigor had been seriously depleted by the long-running nomination fracas. Energy and cash, by contrast, were two things Democratic nominee Mark Warner, forty-one, possessed in abundance. With an estimated net worth of $150 million from early cellular telephone franchise purchases and subsequent investments in mostly technology-related enterprises, the Democratic Warner

---

111. Sabato, *Virginia Votes 1995–1998*, p. 40.

112. *Richmond Times-Dispatch*, June 12, 1996.

113. Outgoing party chief Patrick McSweeney completed his four-year term at the party's June convention, but remained a prominent commentator and conservative spokesman thereafter. Delegates elected Forbes as his successor with strong support from Governor Allen and Attorney General Gilmore, the party's nominee-apparent for governor in 1997. Forbes had been among the most vocal and effective legislative advocates for the governor's agenda, and his installation ended the thirty-month-old estrangement between the GOP state party apparatus and governor's office. Allen's secretary of administration and former campaign manager, Michael Thomas, had enjoyed broad grassroots support for the chairmanship, but he declined to seek the post after a state-employee group raised concerns about a possible conflict between the party chairmanship role and Thomas's responsibilities for supervision of the state workforce. Thomas became a GOP vice chairman instead.

was ready, even eager, to stroke the big personal checks necessary to drive home his message over the airwaves.

When his campaign began in March, Mark Warner's political message seemed unusual, even novel. Gone were the strident attacks that Warner, as party chairman, had leveled at then-candidate George Allen in 1993. Instead, the Democratic Senate candidate's position papers complimented Governor Allen's reforms in areas such as social services and criminal justice, and stressed forward-looking economic themes. He touted, glowingly but often vaguely, the benefits and potential of the "new economy," and urged a modernizing of state and federal policies to fit the new, high-tech era and service-based economy.[114] His remarks often so closely tracked GOP themes that his Democratic rival, former Congressman Leslie Byrne, derided him as "Republican-lite."[115] Warner also sought to identify himself with middle-class working families. "I know what hard work and a dream can do," he declared to his party's thinly attended convention in Hampton. "I will earn this Senate seat the same way I've earned everything that's important to me—I'll work my tail off for it."[116] To prove the point, he launched a whirl-wind statewide tour, pledging to visit every Virginia county by election day.

The Democrat's early bipartisan themes and "new economy" rhetoric aside, what Mark Warner's campaign quickly focused on was creating a new, unflattering persona for John Warner. Outspending the Republican Warner by a massive $5.2 million to $350,000 between the June convention and October home stretch, the Democratic candidate's speeches and advertising sought to define the moderate senator as a closet ally of the "far-right, Gingrich-Dole" congressional Republicans who were said to be recklessly endangering Medicare and other vital federal services. "What you see in Virginia with John Warner is not what you get in Washington," declared Mark Warner. "John Warner comes to Virginia and says he's a moderate. . . . [T]he record reveals he's a different John Warner—one that talks like Mr. Independent but votes like Mr. Gingrich."[117] Indeed, charged the Democrat, Senator Warner was "a more dependable vote for the Gingrich agenda than [arch-conservative North Carolina Senator] Jesse Helms was."[118] A blizzard of negative TV ads drove home the indictment. "[John Warner] voted for Newt Gingrich's plan to cut Medicare by $270 billion, and double Medicare premiums on seniors," said one Democratic spot. "He

---

114. *Richmond Times-Dispatch*, March 12, 1996.

115. Byrne unsuccessfully challenged Warner for the Democratic nomination for the Senate. *Virginian-Pilot*, June 8, 1996.

116. *Richmond Times-Dispatch*, June 9, 1996.

117. *Richmond Times-Dispatch*, September 3, 1996.

118. *Richmond Times-Dispatch*, September 3, 1996.

voted to cut funding for higher education, cut the student loan program, and cut funding for school lunches for children."[119]

Democratic missives aimed at elderly citizens were especially evocative; one direct-mail piece charged that a vote by John Warner "could make your spouse have to sell the family home to pay for nursing home care under Medicaid."[120] Though attacked in the GOP primary for not being pro-life, John Warner was now blasted in Northern Virginia for opposing abortion and failing to "trust the women of Virginia to make their own decisions."[121] For good measure, the Democratic campaign also assailed the GOP incumbent for voting for a $23,000 congressional pay raise "in the dead of night" and voting "for a $2 million pension plan—paid for with our taxes."[122] The unprecedented assault was funded directly from Democrat Warner's personal resources—he poured in more than $10 million—and it proved stunningly effective.[123]

Mark Warner's lines of attack on his Virginia opponent were essentially indistinguishable from those used effectively in 1996 by the Clinton-led Democrats in the presidential race and congressional contests across the country. That John Warner had established a record and reputation as a centrist was no particular obstacle. Nor was association with Clinton, the onetime pariah, any longer viewed as a negative by Virginia Democrats. The president had rebounded from his 1994 midterm debacle by stressing a balanced budget, middle-class tax relief, welfare reform and mainstream values—and by contrasting his renewed centrism with the excesses of the Gingrich-led Republicans.[124] For much of the presidential contest, Clinton sported a healthy lead over GOP presidential nominee Robert Dole even in Virginia, and late in the campaign he visited the state in an effort to boost the candidacy of Mark Warner and Democrats running for Congress. "For decades, the law of Old Dominion politics was that local Democrats tried to keep their national ticket out of sight and out of state," wrote the *Washington Post*'s John Harris and Ellen Nakashima. "Just three years ago, Clinton

119. *Richmond Times-Dispatch*, October 27, 1996.

120. *Richmond Times-Dispatch*, October 30, 1996.

121. *Richmond Times-Dispatch*, October 5, 1996.

122. *Richmond Times-Dispatch*, October 31, 1996.

123. In the millionaire-versus-super-millionaire contest, Republicans tried in vain to make an issue of Mark Warner's lavish campaign expenditures from his personal wealth. The lesser millionaire, John Warner, complained that trying to "buy an election" was not "the Virginia way." Black and Black, *The Rise of Southern Republicans*, p. 289. The irony was palpable to those familiar with the start of John Warner's political career. Republican Warner's large contributions to his own first campaign for the Senate in 1978 had triggered virtually identical criticism of election-buying from his Democratic opponent, Andrew Miller. See *The Dynamic Dominion*, Chapter 31.

124. John Harris, *The Survivor*, pp. 230–258.

was so unpopular that the Democratic candidate for governor, Mary Sue Terry, prominently repudiated his policies. This year, Mark Warner . . . is not repudiating Clinton but embracing him."[125] "Bill Clinton is simply less threatening to Virginia voters than Democratic presidential nominees of the recent past," explained political scientist Thomas Morris. "What Clinton has done is nationalize the Virginia Democratic model, emphasizing fiscal responsibility and moderation on social issues."[126]

John Warner's campaign, which had ruthlessly dispatched James Miller in the summer by investing its superior resources in negative advertising, seemed to falter when the shoe was on the other foot. At first, the GOP team shrugged off the avalanche of electronic attacks, reassured by polls that showed perceptions of the moderate senator holding firm and the GOP still enjoying more than a 20-point lead over Mark Warner after Labor Day despite weeks of incoming negative volleys. "I just ran a primary where my opponent said I was the most liberal Republican . . . a *Clinton* Republican," said the confident GOP candidate. "Now [Mark Warner] is saying the opposite. Well, guess what? . . . Somewhere in the middle you'll find John Warner."[127] Even in early October the Republican's lead seemed secure. "Mark R. Warner is finding that it's not easy to knock off the king of the mountain," wrote reporter Tyler Whitley. "[D]espite an unprecedented advertising blitz, which has seen the young entrepreneur reach deep into his deep pockets, John W. Warner sits above the fray in Washington, holding onto a huge lead in the polls."[128] Democrat Warner was undeterred; he juggled his campaign staff weeks before the election, infused his campaign kitty with more personal cash, and pressed the assault. Only Larry Sabato seemed to think he had a chance. "Never count out a gazillionaire!" he warned.[129]

The long-awaited GOP counterattack came in the second week of October, and things quickly went awry. The hard-hitting Republican television spot highlighted Mark Warner's links to Clinton, Wilder, and prominent Democratic liberals such as Senators Edward Kennedy of Massachusetts and Christopher Dodd of Connecticut. It charged that the former Democratic operative on Capitol Hill had "spent his life as a political insider, raising millions to elect the country's most liberal politicians," and suggested that in the process Warner had gained advantage in the government's sale of cellular telephone franchises, resulting in his great personal wealth.[130] The

125. *Washington Post*, October 28, 1996.
126. *Washington Post*, October 28, 1996.
127. *Richmond Times-Dispatch*, September 3, 1996.
128. *Richmond Times-Dispatch*, October 6, 1996.
129. *Richmond Times-Dispatch*, October 27, 1996
130. *Richmond Times-Dispatch*, October 9, 1996.

big problem with the highly personal attack ad, though, was not its verbiage. Democrats soon noticed that a photo used in the spot had been electronically altered by the Republican ad maker: Mark Warner's face has been pasted over Senator Charles Robb's to create an image that appeared to show Democrat Warner shaking hands with Douglas Wilder as a smiling President Clinton looked on. A media mini-frenzy erupted, and Senator Warner was soon before news cameras apologizing for the seeming deception and announcing that the culpable media consultant had been dismissed.[131] The Democratic camp, smelling blood, was not about to let the senator off so easily. Former Governor Wilder suggested a possible racial motive for the ad. "Why include me?" he asked. "Is it the way I look?"[132] And the Democratic campaign launched a new round of attacks using the bogus photo episode to indict the incumbent's credibility and puncture his image as a man above politics. "What has happened to John Warner?" the Democratic ad began.

> He made us proud—once—but now he takes millions of dollars from special interests. He votes to cut Medicare, hurting our seniors. He votes to cut education for our children's schools. He votes to roll back our clean air and water protections. And now he's stooped to the lowest form of politics, running attack ads that fake a photo. A photo so doctored even a sleazy tabloid would not run it. John Warner. After eighteen years in Washington, you know what he's become? A typical politician.[133]

John Warner had resisted "going negative" against his Democratic opponent; he had acceded only reluctantly to his campaign staff's repeated entreaties that they be allowed to do so.[134] Now, with the attempted countermeasures backfiring badly, the Republican senator firmly directed that his campaign launch only positive missives for the remainder of the battle. It was a decision—ironically reminiscent of the Oliver North campaign's unilateral stand-down late in the 1994 contest—that almost cost the incumbent

---

131. The ad was produced by the company of veteran GOP media consultant Greg Stevens. The Dole campaign, which also was using Stevens's services, declined to follow Warner's lead and dismiss him. The consultant's defenders pointed out that Mark Warner's image had been in the original photo, and thus the only effect of the electronic manipulation had been to eliminate Robb's image and move Warner's directly adjacent to Clinton's and Wilder's. Stevens had enjoyed a positive reputation in the state prior to the incident; his ads in the 1993 governor's race were widely credited with conveying George Allen's upbeat personality to voters, and Stevens would again assist Allen in his 2000 Senate bid against Robb.
132. *Richmond Times-Dispatch*, October 11, 1996.
133. *Washington Post*, October 21, 1996.
134. John Warner interview.

his seat. The Democratic campaign bombarded Republican Warner relentlessly in the campaign's final fortnight, and the unanswered attacks took their toll. A healthy, double-digit Republican lead vanished, and the heavily favored senator staggered across the finish line on election day. An error by the Voter News Service, which confused the Warners' Fairfax County totals, made it appear for a while on election night that Virginia voters indeed had narrowly chosen "Mark not John," as a Democratic slogan urged.[135] But, once the error was corrected, the returns confirmed a thin Republican win. The once-indomitable Senator Warner, whom Democrats did not dare oppose six years earlier, survived by polling 52.5 percent of the vote against a challenger who, while wealthy, had never held public office.[136] Two years after the North episode, and after weeks of bashing by his Democratic foe, it appeared the "gratitude factor" still had worked in John Warner's favor, and may have saved him. Lieutenant Governor Beyer worked the polls all day in heavily Democratic Charlottesville and reported hearing fellow partisans say, "I like Mark . . . but I have to say thank you to John."[137] Republican Warner captured 17 percent of Democratic ballots and decisively won among independents.[138] Mark Warner, who had spent more than ten dollars per vote only to lose, had this solace: his more-than-respectable showing left him well-positioned for a future statewide bid.[139]

In addition to John Warner's reelection, Virginia stayed, by a thin margin, in the GOP presidential column. Although the Clinton-Gore team

135. The error was first discerned by freshman Congressman Thomas M. Davis III, whose encyclopedic knowledge of Fairfax County voting patterns enabled him to deduce the mistake before the transposed numbers were discovered.

136. The vote totals were: John Warner (R)—1,235,744 (52.5 percent); Mark Warner (D)—1,115,982 (47.4 percent). Sabato, *Virginia Votes 1995–1998*, p. 56.

137. *Richmond Times-Dispatch*, November 6, 1996. Mark Warner later seconded the view that Democratic "gratitude" votes for John Warner had decided the election. "If I had one, I had a hundred Democrats who told me the week after the election that if they had known how close the race was going to be, they would have voted for me," recalled Democrat Warner. "But most people never made a choice between voting to elect me and using their vote to say 'thank you' to John Warner because they just did not believe I had a chance of beating John. The media was convinced that he (John Warner) was comfortably ahead and kept saying so. We knew the race was close, but we could not convince anyone of it." Mark Warner interview.

138. John Warner's share of the independent vote was 58 percent. Some GOP activists obviously were still smarting over the senator's refusal to back Farris and North, as 14 percent of Republican votes went in protest to Democrat Warner. Sabato, *Virginia Votes 1995–1998*, p. 64.

139. Mark Warner's campaign spent $11.5 million, and $10.4 million of it was from his own resources. His Republican opponent spent only $2.7 million on the general election, slightly more than he invested to win the GOP primary. Sabato, *Virginia Votes 1995–1998*, pp. 72–73.

posted an easy plurality victory nationally, the Republican ticket consisting of Senator Dole and former Bush cabinet secretary Jack Kemp of New York managed a 47.1 percent plurality win in the state.[140] Exit polls suggested the Old Dominion's somewhat more positive attitude toward the Republican-led Congress may have been the difference; Virginians had a 52 percent favorable view of the congressional leadership while nationally 52 percent were *un*favorable.[141] Democrats, however, retained their majority in the state's congressional delegation. All ten Virginia members of the United States House of Representatives who sought reelection—five Democrats and five Republicans—were reelected easily. The sixth Democrat-held seat, the Southside Fifth District, went by a comfortable margin to conservative Democrat Virgil Goode Jr. He replaced popular incumbent L. F. Payne Jr., of Nellysford, who stepped down in anticipation of running for lieutenant governor the following year.

When the curtain rang down on 1996, it marked the end of a two-year drama in which John Warner had been the protagonist. "It has not been easy these two years," he said candidly after the election. "I hope that I emerged from it a much stronger senator."[142] His foray into political independence had come at a price, and the divergent response to his actions—accolades from across the aisle; arrows from his own side—had shown the perils of party disloyalty even in independent-thinking Virginia. Warner was satisfied that he had done his duty by putting principle above politics; others had sharply varying views. But this much was undeniable: he had taken a stand, placed his own political position in more jeopardy than he ever imagined possible, won fervent new supporters and detractors, defended his ground like a senator half his age, and prevailed in two difficult fights—a hard-fought party primary and an expensive general-election battle. He emerged from the 1994–1996 crucible stronger yet chastened, and he generally would find a way thereafter to live in harmony with GOP partisans and hew to the party line at election time.

Upon gaining the long-coveted chairmanship of the Senate Armed Services Committee, the senior senator made a rare visit to the state GOP's annual leadership conference in December 1998 to thank party activists for their support and acknowledge that his party's and his own fortunes had been linked. "Never let us forget, it is the Republican Party of Virginia that put in the Chairman of the Armed Services Committee," he told the

---

140. The vote totals were: Dole (R)—1,138,350 (47.1 percent); Clinton (D)—1,091,060 (45.1 percent); Ross Perot (Virginia Reform)—159,861 (6.5 percent). Sabato, *Virginia Votes 1995–1998*, p. 56.

141. Sabato, *Virginia Votes 1995–1998*, p. 62.

142. *Richmond Times-Dispatch*, November 6, 1996.

assembled partisans.[143] With the world then largely at peace in the post–Cold War era, the significance of the committee chairmanship was not fully apparent. But America would soon be at war again, and the young sailor who volunteered in World War II would, more than a half-century later, find himself back on the front lines in a new struggle to defend American freedom and values.

Although Senator Warner would fall in line behind GOP nominees after 1996, some other notable Virginians would follow his earlier example and take temporary leave of party when it suited them. The very next year, former Governor Wilder would essentially do to fellow Democrat Donald Beyer what Senator Warner had done to GOP nominees Farris and North, and, in so doing, Wilder would help Republican James Gilmore reach the governorship. Four years after that, a group of Republicans led by John Warner's (and Richard Obenshain's) 1978 campaign manager, Judy Peachee Ford, would abandon Republican nominee Mark Earley and organize a group of GOP-leaning notables to help Democrat Mark Warner gain the governorship. Partisanship would remain as it had been since the days of Washington and Jefferson: a matter of passionate commitment for loyal partisans, but far less relevant for the broad cross-section of Virginia voters who often decide election outcomes.

---

143. *The Washington Post*, December 12, 1998.

# 8

# NEW WORLD: AMERICA'S OLDEST
# LEGISLATURE TRANSFORMED

Free at last, free at last, free at long last! Democracy has finally come
to the Commonwealth![1]

—Governor James S. Gilmore III, November 1999

R epresentative government began in America in 1619 at Jamestown.
The current Virginia General Assembly traces its lineage directly to
the assembly of elected burgesses with the colonial governor and his coun-
cilors in that red letter year, making it the oldest continuous legislative body
in the New World.[2] During the twentieth century, as change of all sorts
swept the state, the thing that seemed most "continuous" about America's
oldest legislature was its domination by the Democratic Party. Barriers to
registration and voting by African Americans, women, and Republicans had
been removed; malapportionment had been remedied; the two political
parties had been realigned; GOP statewide candidates had achieved a series
of breakthroughs—but still the General Assembly remained a Democratic
bastion. By the late 1990s, it was the venerated Virginia party's last redoubt

---

1. *Washington Post*, November 3, 1999.
2. The inception and development of the General Assembly in early colonial Virginia is detailed in Warren M. Billings, *A Little Parliament* (Richmond: The Library of
Virginia, 2004). A leading seventeenth-century colonial historian, Billings describes how
the "Great Charter" of 1618 promulgated by the Virginia Company of London sought
to restructure the affairs of the struggling Jamestown colony for administrative efficiency,
not to transplant representative government in the New World. "When the orders to
convene the first assembly went out in 1618," wrote Billings, "no one anticipated how
it would grow from an administrative appendage into a representative legislature." Warren M. Billings, *A Little Parliament*, p.3. But that is what happened. Newly arrived Governor Sir George Yeardley issued a writ for "freemen and tenants" to elect burgesses in
the summer of 1619, and the twenty-two burgesses so elected convened with Yeardley
and his Council of State in the first "general Assemblie" on July 30, 1619. Billings, *A
Little Parliament*, pp. 5–23.

and the prize most coveted by the state's resurgent GOP. The latter-day Democrats who manned those ramparts, led by the tenacious and skillful House of Delegates majority leader, Richard Cranwell, were holding on for their dear political lives.

Many observers and activists on both sides expected the change of control to come in 1995. With George Allen's landslide in 1993, Republicans had come tantalizingly close to a majority—just four seats shy—in the hundred-member House of Delegates. In 1995, the whole House and the Senate, where Democrats enjoyed a similarly thin, 22–18 edge, were up for grabs. So high were the stakes and so heated were the partisan passions that a procedural dispute on the first day of the 1995 legislative session prevented Allen from delivering his "State of the Commonwealth" address to the traditional joint assemblage in the House chamber. Instead, the folksy chief executive spoke directly to Virginians via television from his office in the State Capitol. The fractious legislative session seemed to go downhill from there, as harsh words flew and the Cranwell-led Democrats successfully stymied Allen and the GOP on nearly every issue. The two sides then carried their angry argument to the voters in the fall, and fought almost to a draw. In the wake of the 1995 elections, the count in the House of Delegates remained unchanged while, in the forty-member Senate, Republicans added two seats to achieve a 20–20 tie.

The events that ensued in the 1996 legislative session shook the ruling Democratic legislative establishment to its foundation. With Lieutenant Governor Donald Beyer ready to cast tie-breaking votes as the Senate's presiding officer, Democratic senators believed they had retained control of the upper chamber for another four years by battling the GOP to an electoral draw. But shortly before the legislature convened in January 1996, Democratic Senator Virgil Goode, the Southside conservative, let it be known that such an arrangement was unacceptable. He had been meeting secretly for weeks with the Senate's key Republican leader, John Chichester, to discuss strategy for a power-sharing arrangement.[3] With the session's organizational vote looming, Goode suddenly announced that he would not vote with Democrats to organize the Senate unless the plan provided for sharing power with the equal-sized GOP contingent. Senator Charles Waddell of Loudoun County privately sided with Goode, but most of their fellow partisans deemed it outrageous that the maverick Democrat would use his decisive vote to force the unnecessary surrender of power to the rival Republicans. He has "gone nuts!" exclaimed Senator Louise Lucas of Portsmouth. She described the scene as Goode entered an after-hours reception

---

3. Chichester interview; Virgil Goode interview, March 14, 2005.

attended by Assembly Democrats: "It was like somebody sprayed Raid. As soon as he walked in, everyone scattered. It was the same everywhere he went. They treated him like a pariah."[4] "A lot of people want me to punish him," acknowledged Senator Richard Saslaw, the chamber's Democratic leader, at the time, "but I am not going to do that. We can't afford to do that."[5]

The man who occasioned all the controversy was defiant. "The Democratic Party has got to change its image. It's out of touch with mainstream Virginia," declared Goode. "I've seen it go from [a Senate Democratic majority] of 36–44 to 20–20, so that ought to tell somebody something."[6] Plus, he emphasized, no one in Virginia would be well served if the state Senate were to become bitterly polarized along party lines like the United States Congress.

Goode's action triggered a procedural impasse and two days of contentious, morning-to-night negotiations as the General Assembly convened. The senators, wrote Peter Carlson in the *Washington Post*,

> faced . . . a situation they'd never confronted before, a situation so foreign that nobody could figure out how to deal with it. The situation was called the "two-party system." For as long as any living human can remember, Democrats have controlled the Virginia General Assembly. For a century, as soon as the legislature convened, the Democratic leaders met behind closed doors and appointed themselves and other Democrats to all the best positions on all the best committees. The Republicans—those godforsaken, perennially outnumbered infidels—inevitably got the worst positions on the worst committees. This came to be seen as the natural order of things, sort of like heat in the summer and tobacco in the fields.
>
> But last November, Virginia voters upset the natural order of things. They elected twenty Democrats and twenty Republicans to the Senate. This was the nastiest, thorniest, gnarliest thing the People could have done. . . . This 20–20 split meant the Democrats and Republicans would have to work things out like rational adults. This proved very difficult for the Senate.[7]

"This is a totally unique experience," commented veteran Democratic Senator Joseph V. Gartlan Jr., explaining the prolonged behind-the-scenes maneuvering. "It takes a while to tell who will be bought. And it takes an infinite amount of time to see if they will stay bought."[8]

---

4. *Washington Post*, January 22, 1996.

5. *Washington Post*, January 22, 1996. Compounding the chagrin of Goode's fellow Democrats, the Rocky Mount lawmaker had chaired the Senate Democratic Caucus during the four years prior to the 1996 controversy.

6. *Washington Post*, January 22, 1996.

7. Peter Carlson, "State's Rites," *Washington Post*, February 25, 1996.

8. *Washington Post*, January 11, 1996.

After two days of marathon jawboning in which Goode, the swing vote, shuttled between the two partisan camps, senators emerged at 1:30 a.m. on January 12, 1996, with a power-sharing deal and passed it unanimously. The arrangement gave Republicans near-parity on committees, made some GOP senators committee chairs, and created a bipartisan co-chairmanship for the powerful Senate Finance Committee. Goode gave up his own committee chairmanship to close the deal, but he emerged as an influential "budget conferee" through the bipartisan bargain. Newspapers the next morning proclaimed the "historic shift in power" that had ended more than a century of one-party control, and reported that senators of both parties were declaring their resolve to make the new order work.[9] But while peace was breaking out in the upper chamber, the House of Delegates leaders down the hall were contemptuous. Democratic Speaker Thomas W. Moss Jr. signaled it would be business as usual in his domain as he booted two leading Republicans, House Minority Leader S. Vance Wilkins of Amherst and conservative Delegate Kirk Cox of Colonial Heights, from key committees in retaliation for their leadership roles in the preceding fall's GOP campaigns.

A majority in either chamber still eluded Republicans as the 1997 elections for governor, lieutenant governor, attorney general, and the House of Delegates approached. And it began to seem that perhaps the long-predicted GOP legislative takeover was not imminent or even inevitable. After all, virtually the entire political establishment viewed Democrat Donald Beyer, the smart, affable and moderate two-term lieutenant governor, as the favorite in the gubernatorial contest. A year before the election, Beyer enjoyed a double-digit advantage in polls over Republican Attorney General James Gilmore despite the popularity of the Allen administration.[10] House Democrats had withstood Allen's well-funded onslaught in the 1995 midterm races, and with Beyer seemingly poised to lead a statewide Democratic rebound, it was reasonable to suppose that Democrats could fortify their House majority and preserve their perennial power base for the foreseeable future. This conventional wisdom overstated Beyer's strength. But where it really missed the mark was in underestimating the steely determination of Gilmore and his experienced political team.

Only once in the twentieth century—in the watershed Robb-Coleman race of 1981—had a lieutenant governor and attorney general squared

---

9. *Washington Post,* January 13, 1996.

10. Though both candidates were relatively little known at the time, an October 1996 survey found Beyer with an eleven-point advantage over Gilmore. *Richmond Times-Dispatch,* January 13, 1997.

off in a general-election battle for governor. But the stage was set early for the contest between Gilmore and Beyer. Beyer's nomination for governor in 1997 seemed a sure thing after he deferred to Mary Sue Terry four years earlier. Gilmore was the obvious heir-apparent on the GOP side, and the few rumblings on the Republican right—mostly from social conservatives concerned about Gilmore's middle-of-the-road stance on abortion—were quelled in March 1995 when Governor Allen announced his support for the attorney general's elevation. The Republican governor frequently showcased his ties with Gilmore, and vice versa, while Beyer was cast, somewhat uncomfortably, in the leader-of-the-opposition role. At times, it seemed the real opposition leader was Richard Cranwell; after his legislative victories over Allen in 1995, there were rumors the Vinton delegate might even challenge Beyer for the gubernatorial nod.[11] Cranwell publicly squelched the speculation, but Beyer found himself having to defend his less combative methods as the Democrats' leader. "Dick Cranwell may be a better election politician than I am because elections thrive on conflict. But as I stand here in this place and look at how things get done, my inclination is completely to look to the politics of reconciliation," Beyer said.[12] The introspective statement was little noticed at the time, but it provided a glimpse of the attributes that made Beyer so attractive as an individual and would make him so ineffectual as a gubernatorial campaign combatant.

The contending Gilmore and Beyer tickets were set after a series of maneuvers that caused even party insiders to scratch their heads. In 1996, Democrats executed what reporter Tyler Whitley called a "tactical three-cushion shot": popular Fifth District Congressman L. F. Payne Jr. announced plans to seek the lieutenant governor's post, offering a potent moderate rural complement to ticket-leader Beyer's presumed suburban appeal.[13] State Senator Virgil Goode then moved to succeed Payne in Washington—a departure that produced considerable joy in the still-smarting Senate Democratic Caucus in Richmond—while another right-leaning Democrat, Delegate W. Roscoe Reynolds of Henry County, headed for the Senate to replace Goode. Arlington lawyer William Dolan, who had run an unremarkable race for attorney general against James Gilmore in 1993, dismissed that defeat as a product of the Allen landslide and set his sights

---

11. The *Washington Post* reported on the possibility of a gubernatorial bid by Cranwell in October 1995. "Although Beyer is the party's titular head," observed reporter Peter Baker, "his sometimes tentative nature has left a void that Cranwell has sought to fill, creating a sort of dual, yen-and-yang leadership—the nice guy and the gut fighter, the philosopher and the field marshal." *Washington Post*, October 21, 1995.

12. *Washington Post*, October 21, 1995.

13. *Richmond Times-Dispatch*, February 12, 1996.

again on the third spot on the Democratic slate. Payne and Dolan quickly became strong favorites to join Beyer's ticket, creating the specter of an all-white, all-male Democratic offering for the first time since 1981. That prospect prompted former Governor Wilder to pen a letter to Beyer expressing concern over the apparent "retrogression," and former state Secretary of Education James W. Dyke Jr., a prominent African-American attorney and Wilder ally, seriously considered challenging Payne for the lieutenant governor nomination.[14] Dyke ultimately decided against the contest, and two other black leaders, Third District Congressman Robert ("Bobby") Scott and Delegate Jerrauld Jones of Norfolk, also demurred. Consistent with the decade-old pattern of uncontested Democratic statewide nominations, delegates to the party's 1997 convention then dutifully ratified the selection of the three unchallenged contenders who became the Beyer-Payne-Dolan ticket.

On the Republican side, in contrast, competition to join the Gilmore-led slate was vigorous. Former United States Attorney Richard Cullen got off to a strong early start corralling campaign contributions and grassroots support for a possible bid for attorney general, but in the summer of 1996 he opted to forgo the race.[15] Cullen's decision not to run for attorney general set off a spirited, four-way battle for the GOP nod that featured two state senators from Hampton Roads—Mark Earley of Chesapeake and Kenneth Stolle of Virginia Beach—as well as Jerry Kilgore, Governor Allen's young public safety secretary from Southwest Virginia, and Gilbert K. Davis, a Fairfax lawyer who gained national attention representing Arkansan Paula Jones in a high-profile sexual harassment suit against President Clinton. The race for the second position on the Republican slate seemed decidedly to favor T. Coleman Andrews III, a McLean businessman whose well-funded bid had generated strong support in his home region and among party conservatives statewide. But Andrews withdrew suddenly in April 1997, citing concerns about the health of one of his children, and that made his opponent, retired Richmond tobacco industry executive John H. Hager, the party's nominee for lieutenant governor by default. Republicans had opted to choose their candidates again by primary, and Earley emerged from the June voting as the GOP nominee for attorney general.[16] Less than five

14. Edds and Morris, "Virginia," p. 161.
15. Cullen became the interim attorney general a year later through gubernatorial appointment after Gilmore resigned to campaign full-time for governor.
16. Earley and Kilgore spent the least money on the race and concentrated on grassroots organization, while Stolle and Davis paid to have their messages communicated electronically. The former strategy appeared best suited for the insular GOP voting. The vote totals were: Earley—60,340 (35.8 percent); Kilgore—41,570 (24.6 percent); Stolle—35,066 (20.8 percent); Davis—31,695 (18.8 percent). The primary election

percent of registered voters turned out for the primary, a dismal showing that Republican Party executive director Christopher LaCivita sought to deflect by derisively contrasting the 169,000 GOP primary voters with the "two thousand five hundred members of the AFL-CIO and PETA who nominated the Democratic candidates."[17]

The candidates for governor did not wait for their tickets to be set before launching their active campaigns. With roughly comparable resources in their coffers, both candidates went on the air in May with television commercials touting their credentials—the earliest media-advertising start in a Virginia governor's race. Gilmore's initial missives stressed his crime-fighting successes, "partnership" with Governor Allen, and resolve to "keep Virginia moving forward." Beyer emphasized his business background and common sense. The Democrat was not just "another lawyer looking for a job in politics," his ads noted; instead, he would be "the first business leader to be governor of Virginia in forty years."[18] Neither candidate's early ads mentioned party affiliation or the defining issues that already had begun to emerge after the two men formally kicked off their bids a few weeks earlier. Their campaigns had been launched in much the same way they would end eight months later. The focused and disciplined Gilmore stressed his ties to the popular Allen and pressed a specific, poll-tested plan to reduce public school class sizes by hiring 4,000 new school teachers and phase out the local personal property tax on cars and trucks. The philosophical and meandering Beyer talked up education, hedged on taxes, and offered a hodge-podge of other ideas and opinions without a clear unifying theme.

The Democrat was first out of the box, beginning his bid in early March with the evident intention of making education his campaign's focus. In an interview published in the *Washington Post* the day before his formal announcement of candidacy, the lieutenant governor highlighted the need for billions in local school construction and talked of "building the political will" for major investments in schools, roads, and other infrastructure. Beyer's apparent plans for a tax increase to pay for such initiatives were not expressed directly, but *Post* reporters Mike Allen and Spencer Hsu thought his meaning was clear. Beyer not only had refused to rule out higher taxes,

---

results were almost directly inverse to the level of campaign spending: Davis—$1.58 million; Stolle—$1.23 million; Earley—$0.46 million; Kilgore—$0.36 million. Sabato, *Virginia Votes 1995–1998*, p. 109.

17. *Richmond Times-Dispatch*, June 11, 1997. PETA ("People for the Ethical Treatment of Animals"), an animal-rights interest group, had moved its national headquarters to Hampton Roads several years earlier.

18. *Richmond Times-Dispatch*, May 17, 1997.

they wrote, but he was poised to kick off his campaign the next day "with an ambitious but politically perilous plan to convince voters that government can be good—and that better roads and schools could be worth a tax increase."[19] The *Post* reporters contrasted Beyer's apparent forthrightness on taxes with the approach of the most recent tax-raising governor, Gerald Baliles, who had "dodged questions" about taxes (and ultimately pledged not to raise them) during his 1985 campaign, then pushed through a record tax-hike plan once in office. Beyer's candid approach, noted former Baliles speechwriter Gordon Morse, was "like putting a big 'hit me' sign on your forehead."[20] The Gilmore camp did not miss the sign; it attacked the Democrat almost instantaneously. Beyer's "liberal approach" on taxes, declared Gilmore, was a "repudiation of the fiscal conservatism we have seen exercised by Governors Allen and Wilder."[21]

Thrown off stride before he could even announce his candidacy, Beyer started back-tracking. His announcement speech on March 10 highlighted proposed increases in teacher pay and other education ideas but contained no mention of any ambitious plan to remedy the multibillion-dollar school construction backlog. Beyer then spent much of his campaign's first month trying to explain his highly nuanced stance on taxes. He finally ruled out any tax increase during a Richmond radio interview program hosted by former Governor Wilder in early April. "I'm saying very clearly that I do not intend to raise taxes, and I will not raise taxes," Beyer told Wilder and his audience.[22]

Gilmore's official campaign start came a few weeks later. Paying tribute to Governor Allen, whom he lauded as "the architect of Virginia's remarkable renaissance, my partner these four years," Gilmore made it clear that his campaign would stress solidarity with the popular incumbent but would not depend wholly on that advantage. Gilmore planned to "run George Allen's reelection campaign," his confidant and campaign strategist Boyd Marcus explained, but he would also offer his own appealing agenda. The message would be: "We've accomplished a lot; . . . let us continue and show you what [more] we can do."[23] The decision to concentrate on tax relief was inevitable, as Marcus later elaborated: "We had to pick issues based on the fact that Allen had been successful in doing a lot of things, and we had to come up with something he had not already done successfully. Cutting

---

19. *Washington Post*, March 9, 1997.
20. *Washington Post*, March 9, 1997.
21. *Daily Press*, March 11, 1997.
22. *Washington Post*, April 9, 1997.
23. *Washington Post*, January 6, 1997.

[personal] taxes was the only real failure of the Allen administration."[24] If tax relief was to be the sword, however, Marcus knew Gilmore needed a shield on the politically potent education issue. As they had done successfully in countering Allen's 1995 tax cut plan, Democrats were certain to assail the GOP tax cut proposals for forcing reductions in education funding.

The Gilmore team therefore crafted a two-prong proposal calling for new education investments—hiring 4,000 new teachers and providing merit-based college scholarships—and for phasing out the local "car tax" on most automobiles. Anticipating the Democratic counterattack, Gilmore said that the education initiatives would have funding priority and that economic growth would pay for the tax cut, as he explained in his announcement speech:

> [After] we fund our major new education investment . . . , my next priority will be to use our economic growth revenues to provide tax relief to Virginia's working families. . . . This tax relief is a dividend, paid by Virginia's growing economy to the working families of our Commonwealth, whose toil and taxes, ingenuity and investment, have made our prosperity possible. In the past, the high-tax lobby has resisted pro-growth tax cuts by scaring Virginians with lurid tales of cuts in services. That dishonest tactic will not work here. We will use growth revenues, and growth revenues alone, to phase in this tax relief."[25]

Gilmore went on to stress that the tax relief would "be delayed . . . if the [economic] growth does not occur as we hope [and] if it's not sufficient to let us sharply increase our education investment and maintain essential services." But he stressed that Allen's economic development successes and current budget forecasts provided "strong, tangible evidence" that the booming state economy would enable him to fund both his education and his tax relief plans.[26]

"If genius is discerning facts that are so obvious no one else notices them," author Garrett Epps wrote a few years later,

> then, in his career of uphill slogging, Jim Gilmore and his political brain trust had their moment of genius early in 1997. After looking at poll data and listening to focus groups, they decided to build their campaign around repealing Virginia's personal property tax on automobiles. . . . The car tax was regarded as a particularly infuriating levy. Each year, automobile owners

---

24. Marcus interview.
25. *Washington Post*, May 8, 1997.
26. *Washington Post*, May 8, 1997.

had to pay a rate set by their locality on the assessed value of their cars, no matter how long ago they bought them. While other taxes are hidden in payroll deductions or mortgage escrows, the car tax required each owner to write a check to the local revenue office.[27]

Other political figures, particularly in affluent Northern Virginia, had already noted the unpopularity of "Virginia's most hated tax."[28] State Senator Charles Colgan, a Prince William County Democrat, had received complaints about the tax from constituents for two decades, and he proposed to eliminate it entirely and raise the sales tax by a cent and a half to make up the lost revenue. But Colgan came forward with his plan only in late 1996 after Hunter Andrews had left the Senate, because the powerful Senate Finance Committee chairman had opposed the idea and refused to consider it. Among the Colgan plan's critics were Lieutenant Governor Beyer, who worried about the effect of a sales tax hike on low- and middle-income taxpayers.[29] Even with the offsetting boost in the sales tax, a January 1997 survey found that Colgan's plan was very popular with taxpaying voters around the state.[30]

Gilmore's car-tax remedy omitted Colgan's sales tax hike suggestion. Instead, the Republican called for a five-year phase-out of the tax on the first $20,000 of vehicular value—an amount sufficient to benefit most taxpayers—and for reimbursing localities from the state's growth-swollen general-fund coffers. Despite the limited and conditional nature of the Gilmore plan, Republican "No Car Tax!" signs became a familiar site in suburban neighborhoods, and GOP mailings with the same message blanketed Northern Virginia homes. In a remarkable display of campaign discipline, twenty-one of the twenty-seven television commercials produced by the Gilmore team from spring to election day mentioned the car tax cut, along with the Republican's plan to hire 4,000 new teachers.[31] By campaign's end, the "No Car Tax!" message was resonating strongly with voters, and a taxpayer revolt over a levy first imposed centuries earlier at Jamestown was being credited with producing GOP inroads among independent and Dem-

---

27. Garrett Epps, "The Outsider," *Washington Post Magazine*, August 15, 1999, p. 3.
28. *Washington Post,* December 12, 1996.
29. *Washington Post,* December 12, 1996.
30. The survey by the Mason-Dixon polling organization found that 57 percent of Virginians favored increasing the sales tax from 4.5 percent to 6 percent in exchange for repealing the personal property tax on automobiles and trucks. Only 28 percent of respondents said they opposed the idea.
31. Dick Leggitt interview, July 8, 2003.

ocratic voters. "Gilmore is the 'car-tax guy,' who with a single stroke seems to have cut across electoral demographics," reported the *Washington Post*.[32] "Originally it was a sheep tax, imposed by the old House of Burgesses on cattle in 1654 and later applied to slaves, mules, coaches, and pianos," explained reporter Mike Allen as the campaign neared its end.

> Now collected mostly on commuters, the personal-property tax has become the bane of commuters. The issue gave Gilmore, a no-nonsense, driven former prosecutor from suburban Richmond, entrée to the [Northern Virginia] turf that was to be the stronghold of Beyer, a dashing, witty Volvo and Land Rover dealer who lives in [Alexandria].[33]

"In a stroke of fortuitous coincidence for Gilmore," noted Larry Sabato, "the tax was paid in many localities just before the November election."[34]

Having stumbled in articulating his own stand on taxes when he launched his campaign in March, Beyer had even more difficulty fashioning a single, coherent position in response to Gilmore's ambitious plan to cut the unpopular car tax. The Democrat first blasted the Gilmore plan as a "declaration of war on public education" and told delegates to the state Democratic convention that the GOP tax scheme was "reckless and irresponsible."[35] But Beyer and most of his campaign advisers hailed from Northern Virginia, and the early reaction to Gilmore's plan there was intense and positive. With support for the Northern Virginia Democrat "hemorrhaging" in his indispensable home region, according to party sources, an acute sense of urgency enveloped Beyer's campaign.[36] With little notice to fellow partisans, the conflicted lieutenant governor used the candidates' first debate—a July affair before the Virginia Bar Association at the stately Greenbrier Resort in West Virginia—to offer a car-tax plan of his own. It was a less generous proposal that would give couples with a combined income of $75,000 or less a maximum income tax credit of $250 to offset their car-tax payments. Derisively dubbed "car tax lite" by reporters, the Beyer alternative proved too meager to counter the strong taxpayer appeal of Gilmore's more sweeping plan, yet it was enough of an about-face seemingly to corroborate the frequent Republican charge that the Demo-

---

32. *Washington Post*, October 30, 1997.
33. *Washington Post*, October 24, 1997.
34. Sabato, *Virginia Votes 1995–1998*, p. 133.
35. Larry O'Dell, "Gilmore Stays on Message; Capitalizes on Allen's Popularity," Associated Press, November 3, 1997; Robin Brown, "Republicans Sweep Virginia," ABC News, November 5, 1997.
36. Alan Greenblatt, "In Fall Races, Campaign Themes Sounding More Like Lullabies," *Congressional Quarterly*, October 11, 1997.

cratic candidate was guided more by opinion polls than conviction. Importantly, Beyer's concession to the GOP on taxes ceded the high ground from which moderate and liberal Democrats felt they had successfully battled Republican tax-cutters before and could again. In the wake of Beyer's shift, expected opposition to Gilmore's plan from many of the same forces that had rallied against Allen's more modest income tax relief proposal in 1995—editorial writers, business and education leaders, and even some Republican moderates—never materialized.[37]

After his November loss to Gilmore, Beyer's summer repositioning on the car-tax issue became the most frequently faulted decision of the Democratic campaign. Beyer himself candidly acknowledged the error in an interview years later:

> We understood the political power of the [car tax] issue. Many months before the election, my pollster, Geoff Garin, told me that "it wasn't the needle in the haystack; it was the haystack." We looked at it closely, but I could never find a way to [eliminate the car tax] without bankrupting the state. . . .
>
> Then, after Gilmore came out with his plan, there was a great response to it, and people kept coming to me—House of Delegates candidates and people in my running mates' campaigns and others—and saying how they were all getting killed out there by the issue and we needed to do something. There was a heated debate within my circle of advisers, and I was the last to accede to [a change of position on the issue]. But it was my mistake. I take full responsibility for it. . . .
>
> When I went to that debate and offered my plan, which everyone called "car tax lite," it did two things, and neither was good. One, it did not succeed in changing the subject. And, two, it made me look like an idiot. It made it much easier for Gilmore to make the flip-flop argument he had been trying to set up. . . . I would have been much better off sticking with my earlier position all the way through November 2. . . . [The mistake in offering my own car-tax plan] might have affected the margin; I don't think it cost me the election.[38]

The impact of Beyer's ill-fated summer repositioning on the car-tax issue was not immediately apparent, however, and the contest between the two well-funded and well-regarded statewide officials nevertheless

---

37. The projected fiscal impact of the Gilmore and Beyer car-tax proposals diverged widely. The impact of Gilmore's plan was pegged at approximately $1 billion during the five-year phase-in period and at more than $600 million annually thereafter. Beyer's plan would deprive state tax collectors of only about $200 million annually. Sabato, *Virginia Votes 1995–1998*, p. 134.

38. Beyer interview.

remained a dead heat all the way to October. In the "battle of moderates," as CNN's Gene Randall dubbed it, there seemed to be little substantive difference between the two candidates.[39] Some commentators disparaged the race as dull—"the bland leading the bland," one wag called it; a "charisma-free zone," declared another[40]—but political reporter Peter Baker found the relatively placid contest to be "a welcome relief from the dysfunctional soap-opera politics of recent times" in Virginia, the "seething hatreds" that had come to the fore in the 1994 Senate contest, and the intense negativism of other high-decibel Virginia political battles. With Beyer and Gilmore, Baker observed, voters were afforded a generally positive choice "between two competent public servants who worked their way up through state government, adhered to relatively mainstream views, and . . . waged a . . . reasonably clean campaign."[41]

Perspectives on the quality of the contest varied, but the fact that Gilmore and Beyer remained even in opinion polls during most of the race was good news mainly for the Republicans. The personable Democrat's expected edge as the more likeable candidate never came through, and it was the GOP's Gilmore who seized the initiative on key issues. Not only did Gilmore have the more popular tax plan, but, on education, both candidates backed Allen's Standards of Learning program, and Gilmore's plan to hire thousands of new teachers and reduce class sizes enjoyed stronger support from voters than did Beyer's proposal to spend a comparable amount on raising teacher salaries.[42] With a popular Republican incumbent, a booming economy, and high levels of voter satisfaction with the status quo, the burden was on Beyer to make the case for change. He never did so. Instead, the race turned primarily on a character contrast that Gilmore's savvy team set out to frame from the beginning. GOP pollster John McLaughlin, who advised Gilmore, explained:

> Like George Allen, Jim Gilmore was going to run on new ideas. But the other part of it was the character contrast. Campaigns for the Senate and

---

39. CNN website, May 8, 1997.

40. *Washington Post*, October 13, 1997.

41. *Washington Post*, November 2, 1997.

42. The candidates debated education issues over the airwaves during the first half of September. The Gilmore campaign's internal polls indicated that, although voters supported both hiring more teachers and paying teachers more, the former option was viewed as significantly more likely to improve educational quality. The Republican ads therefore offered a direct contrast between Beyer's teacher-pay proposal and Gilmore's plan to hire 4,000 new teachers, with the result that the two sides battled to a draw on the usually Democratic issue during much of the fall campaign. Marcus interview.

Congress usually turn on who is right or wrong on issues. But in a race for an executive office like president or governor or mayor, it becomes a question of character, of leadership, of who can get it done. At the beginning of the 1997 race, everyone was saying, "Oh, Beyer is this charismatic guy; he is like Clinton in getting votes; people like him," and so forth. So we did a survey and asked people what they thought of Gilmore, and what popped up in the responses was that he was *honest*—what you see is what you get. So we decided we were going to emphasize his working-class roots, his honesty, that here is a down-to-earth guy who is going to tell you the truth. Here is a leader, a lot like Allen, who keeps his promises, says what he means, and delivers. And the other guy . . . is just another flip-flopping politician who will tell you whatever you want to hear so he can get elected.[43]

As the race unfolded, the candidates seemed to go out of their way to fit the contrast outlined by McLaughlin. Beyer's shifts on taxes seemed tailor-made to lend credence to the GOP's flip-flopper charge, while Gilmore, the straight-talking ex-prosecutor, proved remarkably disciplined in staying "on message" throughout the campaign.

The candidates had spent millions, dueled over the airwaves on their credentials and major topics like taxes and education, and yet were still deadlocked as the campaign's final month neared. The problem for Gilmore, according to pollsters for the *Washington Post*, was that two-thirds of Virginia voters said they approved of the job Allen had done as governor, yet only about half of those happy with Allen were supporting Gilmore; about a third were in the Beyer column as of mid-September.[44] From the beginning of the campaign, the GOP's task—well understood by Gilmore strategists Marcus and McLaughlin—had been to persuade voters satisfied with Allen that Gilmore could be trusted to continue and build on the work begun by the popular governor. "We told Jim [Gilmore] that all of his potential votes existed within George's favorables," recalled pollster McLaughlin. "Just like Reagan passed off to Bush in 1988, Allen was going to pass off to Gilmore. Internally they may not be the closest, but publicly they were joined at the hip."[45]

Although Gilmore from his campaign's start embraced Allen's accomplishments, touted their work together as governor and attorney general, and highlighted the governor's endorsement in television ads, Beyer successfully avoided criticizing Allen so as not to prod him energetically into the fray. "I'm running against Jim Gilmore; I'm not running against Governor Allen," the Democrat pointedly declared.[46] The campaign's focus on

---

43. McLaughlin interview.
44. *Washington Post*, September 21, 1997.
45. McLaughlin interview.
46. *Washington Post*, September 3, 1997.

the candidates' competing tax relief and education initiatives seemed to serve Beyer's purpose by largely bypassing Allen. In late summer, Gilmore engendered the governor's ire by declaring that, if elected, he would not reappoint Allen's conservative secretary of natural resources, Becky Norton Dunlop, to her post—a move, among others, that was designed to distance Gilmore from the incumbent's controversial record on environmental issues. The same day, Democrat Beyer pulled an upset win in capturing the influential endorsement of the Fraternal Order of Police, which had strongly backed Allen—and Gilmore—in the 1993 statewide contests. Reporter Spencer Hsu cited the two unconnected developments as indicative that "the Allen-Gilmore relationship is more complex than the pair lets on, filled with personal and philosophical differences." The two events, wrote Hsu, "revived the fear among some Virginia GOP leaders of what they privately call the 'Reagan-Bush syndrome'—that although Gilmore may be a worthy heir, he lacks Allen's charisma and ideological verve."[47]

Fortunately for Gilmore, a series of events in late September and early October brought the set of issues most closely associated with his and Allen's tenure—public safety and the abolition of parole—dramatically to the fore at the very time when many voters were just tuning in to the gubernatorial contest. Gilmore precipitated the exchange with a hard-hitting television ad that attacked Beyer for a tie-breaking vote in 1992 to allow prison officials to release criminals three months early. The Beyer campaign responded over the air with a missive—not reviewed in advance by the Democratic candidate—that highlighted his endorsement by the Fraternal Order of Police and, almost in passing, took credit for helping Allen abolish parole. The parole claim provided Gilmore's team with an opening, and they raced to seize it. In Europe on a trade mission, Governor Allen was awakened late in the evening with word of the developments. He agreed to issue a pointed statement refuting Beyer's claim and portraying the lieutenant governor as more of an impediment than aid in the legislative fight to abolish parole. Gilmore ad-maker Dick Leggitt was hurriedly dispatched to the home of former United States Attorney General William Barr, a leader of the parole-abolition campaign, who went on camera to denounce the Democratic candidate for misleading voters.[48] Beyer, ad-libbed Barr, had as much to do with abolishing parole as "the man in the moon."[49]

---

47. *Washington Post*, September 3, 1997.
48. Leggitt interview.
49. Beyer ruefully recalled the episode later as

a disaster. . . . When I saw the ad text, there was nothing in there about parole. But when they went to film the FOP endorsement, the media people thought it would be just great if the FOP gave me credit for abolishing parole in the ad. It was a horrible mistake. . . . Allen had given me plenty of opportunities to be part of the anti-parole leadership, and I had turned them all down. But now this ad was running taking credit for it. I had no clue

The combined Allen/Barr attack on Beyer's parole claim—and ultimately on his credibility—proved highly effective. Stung by the exchange,
Beyer then used an early October debate to attack Gilmore's record as a
local prosecutor, citing plea bargains entered in child molestation cases while
he was Henrico County's commonwealth's attorney. The punch momentarily seemed to find its target, as Gilmore, fighting a severe bout with the
flu during the encounter as well as Beyer's unexpected charge, responded
quizzically. But Beyer's criticism was quickly punctured factually by the fast-
responding Gilmore camp, and, by the next day, local prosecutors in both
parties were coming to the Republican's defense, noting the distinctive evi-
dentiary problems that often prevent them from taking child sexual abuse
cases to trial. Why Beyer or his handlers thought the legendarily tough Gilmore could be convincingly attacked as soft on crime is unclear. But it was
quickly apparent that their errant attack had done double damage, prolong-
ing the campaign discourse on public safety issues owned by the Republicans and further eroding perceptions of Beyer's credibility. It was, according
to the Associated Press's Larry O'Dell, "the most serious gaffe of the campaign."[50]

In a move reminiscent of Democrat Mary Sue Terry's eleventh-hour
assault on Allen four years earlier, Beyer in early October also pummeled
his GOP opponent for "genuflecting" to Pat Robertson, the Christian
Coalition, and the Republican Party's most conservative elements on such
issues as abortion and private school vouchers.[51] One evocative Democratic
ad highlighted Robertson's six-figure contribution to the GOP cause and
charged that a beholden Gilmore would carry out Robertson's education
agenda by "tak[ing] money out of public schools and put[ting] it into private and religious schools."[52] The Republican camp had long expected the
abortion- and Robertson-related attack, and was ready with an immediate
rejoinder. "It's what we've always seen before, an effort to create fear," said
a dismissive Gilmore. "They tried it against Governor Allen; they tried it
against Senator Warner. It didn't work against them [and] it's not going to
work against me."[53] To make sure of that, the GOP team weeks earlier had

---

that it was in the ad, and when the press asked me about it, I literally had no answer. . . .
When I found out what was in there, I was embarrassed, humiliated, angry beyond belief.

Beyer interview.

50. Larry O'Dell, "Gilmore Stays on Message; Capitalizes on Allen's Popularity,"
*Associated Press*, November 3, 1997.

51. *Washington Post*, October 2, 1997.

52. *Washington Post*, October 2, 1997.

53. *Washington Post*, October 2, 1997.

taped a soothing rebuttal in which a cardigan-clad Gilmore reassured voters that he only favored "reasonable restrictions" and would not seek to outlaw abortion. The ad had been pre-positioned in the homes of Gilmore partisans in each of the state's media markets and was quickly delivered to TV stations in each area as soon as the Beyer attack aired there. Ads featuring Senator John Warner enthusiastically embracing Gilmore soon were airing heavily in the moderate, swing-voting suburban areas of Northern Virginia and Hampton Roads. The Democratic attack seemed to fall flat and, like the similar Terry fusillade four years earlier, apparently backfired. "It was like the sixth time a jack-in-the-box pops up—" Beyer observed later, "it doesn't scare you anymore."[54] "[M]oderate voters in Northern Virginia seem more concerned about [the car tax] than social issues," commented CNN's Stuart Rothenberg. "Even worse for the Democrats, Beyer's attacks on abortion and Pat Robertson have mobilized social issue conservatives, who initially seemed less than enthused about Gilmore."[55]

With Beyer's thrusts on education, crime, and abortion each parried in succession, the GOP campaign down the stretch focused its considerable resources on driving home its positive message favoring car-tax relief, hiring 4,000 new teachers, and continuing the Allen administration's popular reforms. In what Larry Sabato termed an especially "potent combination," Allen stumped for Gilmore and his running mates in the more conservative areas downstate late in the campaign while John Warner continued to make the case for the GOP team over the airwaves and on the ground in Northern Virginia and other moderate, swing-voting areas.[56] Fresh off his reelection battles of the previous year, Warner seemed to relish his newfound role as Republican cheerleader. "My name was used six times last night in the debate between Don Beyer and Jim Gilmore, and seven times in the debate

---

54. Beyer interview.

55. Stuart Rothenberg, "AllPolitics," CNN, October 9, 1997. Gilmore's abortion stance—he favored abortion restrictions only after the first two or three months of pregnancy—brought criticism from some conservative commentators, including Fred Barnes of the *Weekly Standard*. Barnes opined that the GOP nominee should have exhibited Reaganesque clarity on the controversial issue rather than attempting to define a nuanced middle ground and reassure voters that the *Roe v. Wade* decision was invulnerable as a practical matter. Fred Barnes, "Abortion and Taxes in Virginia," *Weekly Standard*, October 27, 1997. In another political year, Gilmore's position on abortion might have cost him crucial support on the Republican right, but not so in 1997. Beyer's attack solidified the social conservative base for Gilmore, who also handled the issue deftly. "Republican candidates are running smarter [and] the Christian Right is maturing," observed commentator Mark Rozell. "They're learning how to work with candidates who are not 100 percent on their issues." Linda Feldmann, "Abortion Litmus Test Eases for GOP Candidates," *Christian Science Monitor*, November 7, 1997.

56. *Daily Progress*, October 17, 1997.

before that," he told the Associated Press in mid-October. "You'll find there [are] quite a few references to the senior senator as the campaign goes along."[57] Reflecting the uncommon degree of GOP unity, the party's devoutly conservative national committeeman, Morton Blackwell, even ventured that Warner likely would enjoy the backing of the party's social conservative wing if he ran again for the Senate.[58]

While the Republican juggernaut continued its relentless, largely pre-programmed advance on the ground, the high-flitting Beyer campaign seemed to run out of things to say and came crashing down. The campaign's early October misfires on parole, plea bargains, and abortion pushed Beyer's credibility—already suspect because of his multiple, conflicting tax stands—beyond the tipping point. By the third week of October, a race that was basically tied for months had broken decisively for Gilmore; a published poll showed the Republican with a seven-point lead, and the campaign's internal polls indicated an even wider, and widening, advantage.[59] Beyer's campaign kitty was already stretched thin, and the pace of new donations slowed, while Gilmore's coffers were growing. Most important, Gilmore appeared to have won the believability debate and now seemed the more credible candidate on a range of issues, including his commitment to actually deliver on his car-tax-cut promise.

Then, on October 20, came a haymaker from Beyer's former running mate, Douglas Wilder. The former governor had deferred an endorsement until after the gubernatorial candidates squared off at an October 6th debate at Virginia Commonwealth University, in which Wilder, now teaching at the university, served as moderator. President Clinton called just before the debate to urge Wilder to endorse Beyer, but the former governor held off for another two weeks, allowing the drama to build, before announcing his decision on his weekly talk-radio program in Richmond. When it finally came, the Wilder decision was to make no endorsement at all. It was remarkably reminiscent of the dramatic 1952 radio address in which Virginia's patriarch, Harry F. Byrd Sr., pointedly declined to endorse the Democratic presidential ticket headed by Adlai Stevenson. And just as Democrat Byrd's "golden silence" was intended to, and did, aid Republican Eisenhower in that watershed race, so did Democrat Wilder's inexplicit but unmistakable nod boost Republican Gilmore in the hotly contested governor's duel nearly a half-century later.

The cagey Wilder had postured as undecided before only to come on

---

57. *Daily Progress*, October 17, 1997.
58. *Washington Post*, November 2, 1997.
59. *Washington Post*, October 23, 1997.

board belatedly and dramatically behind Democratic candidates (including even his nemesis, Charles Robb), and Beyer hoped, even assumed, it would happen again.[60] But Gilmore had spent time consulting and courting Wilder for several years, and had stressed reaching out to minority voters throughout his career. The GOP attorney general's vigorous response to an outbreak of African-American church burnings in 1996 had particularly impressed the former governor.[61] Beyer, in contrast, failed to show Wilder similar attention; prominent Democrats, including some African-American lawmakers, practically goaded the former governor, suggesting that Wilder's influence had waned and his endorsement was largely irrelevant.[62] With his dramatic non-endorsement, Wilder triggered an avalanche of criticism from aggrieved Democrats and a mini-debate over whether his views still mattered. "The former governor's political striptease had been widely portrayed as selfish showmanship," wrote Mike Allen. "But Wilder, a grandson of slaves who was the first black American to be elected governor, remains a revered figure in many parts of Virginia, with his portrait flanking that of the Rev. Martin Luther King Jr. in many a church's fellowship hall."[63] Wilder himself had no doubt about his importance. In the wake of the 1997 election, he issued virtually the same verdict he had rendered after successfully sacking fellow Democrat Owen Pickett in 1982, at the beginning of his own gubernatorial odyssey. "No longer can anyone take the African-American vote for granted," he declared.[64]

With his Democratic base in Northern Virginia and elsewhere collapsing under the weight of the "No Car Tax!" bandwagon, Wilder's defection, and the GOP's well-honed suburban appeal, Beyer acted to save fellow Democratic candidates, if not himself, by returning to his roots (and his initial position) on the pivotal car-tax issue. "My God," the frustrated candidate exclaimed at a late October rally, "we have to have a bigger vision than this of what Virginia can become."[65] The "No Car Tax!" slogan, he

---

60. *Richmond Times-Dispatch*, October 6, 1997; Beyer interview.

61. Wilder interview; James S. Gilmore III interview, November 30, 2004, and January 4, 2005.

62. Beyer interview; Wilder interview. "No one in the [Democratic] party ever showed any appreciation of my support of Robb [in 1994], and people were telling Robb he would have won anyway," Wilder later recalled. "And you had people associated with Beyer publicly saying that my support didn't matter. So, when you had people saying that, plus I didn't know what was going on in the Beyer campaign anyway, why would I endorse him? If he felt it wasn't going to do him any good, why would I do it?" Wilder interview.

63. *Washington Post*, October 22, 1997.

64. *Washington Post*, December 17, 1997.

65. *Washington Post*, October 24, 1997.

declared, "insults the intelligence of the people of Virginia. . . . 'No car tax?' No roads, no education, no hope, no future."[66] Joined in Alexandria by President Clinton, who portrayed the Republican car-tax initiative as an appeal to taxpayer selfishness, Beyer made a passionate election-eve case for protecting school funding and other vital services from Gilmore's proposed raid on the state treasury. Gone from the Beyer message, as large "Save our Schools!" banners fluttered in the background, was the alternative tax–cut proposal that earlier had confounded and demoralized his party's most ardent activists. The Alexandria speech, said liberal Congressman Robert Scott of Newport News, "outlined what the campaign should have been."[67] While Beyer's final shift on the car-tax issue came too late to stem the GOP tide, polls later showed it at least brought some Democrats back into the fold and likely prevented the surging Republicans from capturing the House of Delegates.

While Beyer and Democrats struggled to contain their losses in the contest's closing weeks, Gilmore and strategist Boyd Marcus, both dedicated GOP party-builders since their youths, turned their attention to electing other Republicans. The candidate's schedule was modified to send him into areas with hotly contested House of Delegates races, where he made a strong pitch for election of new Republican legislators who would help him eliminate the car tax and accomplish other promised goals. Gilmore also mounted an all-out effort to elect his running mates. Mark Earley had little need for assistance from the top of the ticket in his bid for attorney general; the Chesapeake Republican had amassed a broad coalition spanning from the Christian Right to normally Democratic organized-labor and education groups. But while Earley enjoyed a healthy lead in the race for attorney general, Republican John Hager remained a decided underdog in his bid for lieutenant governor against moderate, four-term congressman L. F. Payne Jr. Veteran GOP consultant and Gilmore adviser Kenneth Klinge drew upon a two-decade-old lesson in urging the campaign's high command to spare no effort to assist Hager. Had landslide-bound John Dalton made a similar effort for his running mate, Joe Canada, in 1977, Klinge reminded his colleagues, Charles Robb would not have gained the lieutenant governorship that year and launched the political career that propelled Democrats to a string of statewide victories in the 1980s.[68] Gilmore, who hardly needed convincing, agreed with the imperative of electing Hager and instructed his

66. *Washington Post*, October 24, 1997.
67. *Washington Post*, November 4, 1997.
68. J. Kenneth Klinge interview, May 27, 1980, August 30, 1984, and July 8, 2003; see *The Dynamic Dominion*, Chapter 30.

campaign to channel resources to help produce an upset.[69] A late infusion of cash from Hager's supporters in the business community and other GOP sources enabled the Republican candidate for lieutenant governor to tell his inspiring story over the airwaves—a story that included overcoming polio as a young adult to achieve success as a business executive, community leader, and, in his spare time, a wheelchair-marathon competitor.

The result was the first-ever Republican statewide sweep in Virginia—an accomplishment unparalleled by the GOP anywhere in the South and described as a "breakthrough" by Professor Merle Black of Emory University, an expert on Southern politics.[70] Gilmore's textbook campaign captured 55.8 percent of the vote; Hager, the first disabled person elected to state office in Virginia, edged Payne with 50.2 percent; and Earley, the first avowed champion of the Christian Right to win statewide, garnered 57.5 percent over his now-twice-defeated foe.[71] The Henrico Republican outpolled his gubernatorial opponent in every income group, won a majority of women (52 percent) as well as men (61 percent), and—aided by Wilder as well as his transcendent car-tax appeal—captured roughly one of every five African-American votes.[72] For the third straight gubernatorial election, Republicans fared well in both the state's rural areas and in the swing-voting suburbs.[73] Not on the ballot, but winning the approval of two-thirds of voters responding to exit polls, was incumbent Governor Allen.[74]

The widely watched race had earlier been proclaimed a national "bellwether" by the optimistic chairman of the Democratic Governors Association, Vermont Governor Howard Dean.[75] But Republicans were the ones

69. Gilmore interview; Marcus interview.

70. *Washington Post*, November 5, 1997.

71. The vote totals in the contest for governor were: Gilmore (R)—969,062 (55.8 percent); Beyer (D)—738,971 (42.6 percent); Sue DeBauche (Reform)—25,955 (1.5 percent). The vote totals in the election for lieutenant governor were: Hager (R)—839,895 (50.2 percent); Payne (D)—754,404 (45.1 percent); Bradley Evans (Reform)—75,024 (4.5 percent). The vote totals in the race for attorney general were: Earley (R)—953,455 (57.5 percent); Dolan (D)—702,523 (42.4 percent). Sabato, *Virginia Votes 1995–1998*, p. 143.

72. Sabato, *Virginia Votes 1995–1998*, pp. 144–145. African-American voters made up just 12.5 percent of the electorate in the 1997 governor's race, compared to 14 percent in 1993 and 17 percent in 1989.

73. Beyer appeared to have written off rural Southside and Southwest Virginia early in the campaign. Among other positions that proved problematic for the Democrat in rural areas, he endorsed having the Federal Drug Administration regulate tobacco as a drug. *Richmond Times-Dispatch*, April 18, 1997.

74. Sabato, *Virginia Votes 1995–1998*, p. 148.

75. *Washington Post*, September 5, 1997. Dean went on to become a national figure, leading the early jockeying for the 2004 Democratic presidential nomination—with Beyer's active support in Virginia—before losing the nod to Senator John F. Kerry of

talking up the contest's national implications in its wake. The Gilmore-led GOP had delivered a resounding message about the broad-based electoral appeal of a populist message stressing working-family tax relief and support for public education. "It has been nearly three decades in the making," wrote Eric Lipton of the *Washington Post,*

> but Virginia Republicans finally completed their Richmond revolution yesterday. By gaining all three statewide offices and a chance to control the Virginia Senate [thanks to Hager's tie-breaking vote as lieutenant governor], the party that was merely an irritant to the long-dominant Democrats for most of this century is now clearly in charge. The shift in power can be traced to Governor-elect James S. Gilmore III's simple slogan—"No Car Tax!" But even some Democrats acknowledged yesterday that the causes run deeper— that the GOP appears to have won the trust of Virginia voters by setting the agenda on such issues as education, crime, welfare, family values and economic growth.[76]

The reversal of fortunes for state Democrats in the 1990s had been as striking as the sudden Virginia Republican collapse in the 1980s.[77] Commentators not only credited Allen and Gilmore, but were sharply critical of failed Democratic standard-bearers Terry and Beyer. "Eight years, $15 million spent and not a single memorable idea," exclaimed political scientist Robert Holsworth. "[T]here have been two statewide campaigns run in which not a single idea that Virginians could remember or cared about was the centerpiece of a Democratic campaign."[78]

---

Massachusetts. Shortly after the 2004 election, Dean gained the chairmanship of the Democratic National Committee.

76. Eric Lipton, "Once Dormant GOP Conquers Richmond; Sweep of Top Virginia Offices Reflects Political Shifts That Began Decades Ago," *Washington Post,* November 5, 1997.

77. Commentators found parallels easy to draw between the two decades' mirror-image partisan outcomes. Just as Charles Robb's gubernatorial breakthrough for Democrats in 1981 was often compared with Allen's watershed win for the GOP in 1993, so was Gerald Baliles's retention of the governorship for Democrats in 1985 compared with Gilmore's claiming of a second term for Republicans in 1997. Larry Sabato wrote:

> [In 1985,] the Democrats had won back the governorship four years earlier following a twelve-year period of GOP gubernatorial rule. The incumbent governor, Chuck Robb, was quite popular at the time, and he urged voters, in essence, to give him the second term the state constitution prohibited by electing his shrewd but bland attorney general, Gerald Baliles, as his successor. Substitute "George Allen" for "Chuck Robb" and "Jim Gilmore" for "Gerald Baliles," and the previous sentence is an accurate summary of 1997. Even the winning percentages of 1985 and 1997 tracked closely: 55.2 percent for Baliles and 55.8 percent for Gilmore.

Sabato, *Virginia Votes 1995–1998,* p. 135.

78. *Washington Post,* November 5, 1997.

On election night, Gilmore celebrated his ticket's historic sweep, but partisans who swarmed to congratulate the governor-elect were struck that, even in his hour of triumph, the Republican standard-bearer kept expressing disappointment at his failure to pull in a GOP majority in the House of Delegates. He and his party had come ever so close to achieving that still-elusive goal. In the election's wake, Democrats held fifty of the one hundred seats, and following a recount they retained the fifty-first, a hotly contested Norfolk seat, by an eleven-vote margin. While GOP regulars cheered the near-parity gained in the House and applauded the election of the first black Republican in the lower chamber—young Paul Harris from George Allen's former Albemarle County district[79]—Gilmore was unsatisfied. The next day, he summoned his political aides to plot strategy. What ensued was a series of special legislative elections occasioned mainly by the governor-elect's designation of lawmakers in both parties to serve in high-level posts in his new administration. By the time the General Assembly convened in January, Gilmore had found a way to deny Democrats a functioning majority in either legislative chamber.

With the election of Earley as attorney general and the designation of Senate GOP leader Joseph Benedetti to head the state's criminal justice services agency under Gilmore, a series of special legislative elections were triggered in Chesapeake and Richmond.[80] But the moves that mattered most involved two senior Democratic legislators from Northern Virginia—Senator Charles Waddell of Loudoun County and Delegate David Brickley of Prince William County. Gilmore recruited Waddell to serve as his deputy secretary of transportation, and Brickley agreed to leave the House of Delegates to head the state agency that oversees the park system. The governor-elect trumpeted the qualifications of both men and portrayed their appointments as evidence of *bipartisan* statesmanship, but irate Democratic leaders perceived Gilmore was using state positions to *buy partisan* hegemony in the legislature. Both Waddell and Brickley hailed from GOP-leaning districts that were likely to elect Republican replacements, and indeed voters there promptly did so. Spearheaded by Gilmore's political operation and relying on the same car-tax and education messages that had fueled the GOP's state-

79. See Paul Harris, "Sharpening My Oyster Knife," in *Notes from the Sausage Factory,* eds. Day and Dale, pp. 56–58.

80. Successive special elections were held in Chesapeake to fill Earley's Senate seat and then, following Delegate Randy Forbes's election to the Senate, to fill the resulting vacancy in Forbes's House of Delegates seat. Back-to-back special elections similarly occurred in the Richmond area, where Delegate John Watkins of Chesterfield won election to succeed Benedetti, and another contest was then held to replace Watkins in the lower chamber.

wide wins, Republican candidates swept to victories in all six special elections.[81] Without funds in the bank to pay for the hasty campaign efforts, Gilmore instructed political aide Ray Allen Jr. to spend the money necessary to win the races and he would raise it later.[82] The remarkable, GOP-dominated overtime campaign ended just before the General Assembly convened for an opening day that no one present would ever forget.[83]

The governor-elect had appointive powers, campaign strategists, fund-raising capability, a road-tested message, and Republican-leaning districts all in his favor as he sought to alter the legislative landscape between the November election and January inauguration. What he lacked was time. Although Republicans won all the special elections, the political calendar did not assure the new members would all be seated in time for the opening-day organization of the General Assembly, when the partisan numbers would determine, among other things, which party owned the House of Delegates speakership and set the session's rules. Three House of Delegates elections, necessitated by the respective GOP incumbents' successes in just-completed special contests for the Senate, were not held until January 13, and that left only one day before the start of the legislative session for the State Board of Elections to certify the official results.

Though none of the special election outcomes was close and Republican appointees comprised a two-to-one majority on the election board, presiding board secretary Bruce Meadows, an Allen appointee, balked at certifying the new delegates' elections faster than was customary. The move surprised and cheered Democrats, but it enraged outgoing Governor Allen and interim Attorney General Richard Cullen, who went to court to compel faster action. Failure to do so, they argued, would effectively disfranchise voters in the three new delegates' districts. The Virginia Supreme Court found the election board's action to be within its legal discretion, however, and refused to intervene. The court decision came on the same day Republicans swept the three special elections; one newspaper headline, "GOP Loses in Court, Wins at Polls in Virginia," seemed to tell the whole story.[84] The rapid-fire events set the stage for 97 of the 100 duly elected House

---

81. Republicans also won a seventh special election that was held after the General Assembly convened. The contest was to fill the vacated House seat of GOP Delegate William Mims, who won the Senate seat formerly held by Waddell.

82. Ray Allen Jr. interview, July 8, 2003.

83. Between the 1997 election and 1998 legislative session, Gilmore's chief of staff, Boyd Marcus, and House Republican leader Vance Wilkins met separately with several Democratic delegates, most from conservative-voting rural areas, in a bid to persuade them to switch parties or caucus with the House Republicans. Having gained election as Democrats, none of those contacted felt free to accede to the GOP entreaties. Marcus interview; S. Vance Wilkins interview, March 11, 2005.

84. *Washington Post*, January 14, 1998.

members, a thin majority of them Democrats, to call the shots on opening day and reinstall House Speaker Thomas W. Moss Jr. for another two-year term.

The special elections left House Democrats with fifty seats; the Republican total rose to forty-nine; and the legislature's lone Independent, conservative thirty-six-year House veteran Lacey Putney of Bedford, was publicly mum about his plans but privately poised to caucus with the GOP, creating an even split.[85] With the Senate's successful power-sharing precedent fresh in mind, some Democratic moderates from conservative-leaning areas, including Delegates Whittington W. Clement of Danville and Thomas M. Jackson Jr. of Hillsville urged Speaker Moss and fellow partisans to take a longer view and make concessions to reflect the evident Republican parity in the chamber.[86] But no one stepped forward forcefully, in the manner of Senator Virgil Goode in 1996, to make a power-sharing demand backed by a threat to defect on the organizational voting. Asked whether any of his fellow Democratic delegates might make a Goode-like stand, veteran Roanoke lawmaker Clifton A. Woodrum answered, "Not and live."[87] The sun was evidently setting on the Democrats' century-old reign, but Moss and his allies felt aggrieved by Gilmore's post-election machinations. Having been thrown a lifeline at the last minute by a maverick GOP-controlled election board, they were not about to pass up the chance to hold on to the powerful speakership and other advantages for another two years.

In a raucous first-day session wracked by procedural controversy, desk-pounding objections from the Republican side, and all manner of bad humor, Democrats retained their last significant position in state government. The next day, reporters Jeff Schapiro and Pamela Stallsmith described the unique scene:

> Democrats yesterday rammed through the re-election of Speaker Thomas W. Moss Jr., of Norfolk, capping a day of legislative "Wrestlemania" that Republicans said wrongly denied them an equal say in the almost-evenly divided House. Contentious but dignified debate yielded to shouts of "Objection! Objection!" as some Republicans rhythmically slammed their desk tops while Democrats installed Moss as Speaker. . . . Republicans hol-

---

85. Even before the 1997 legislative elections, Putney had secretly assured House GOP leader Vance Wilkins that he would align himself with the Republican caucus and provide the decisive additional vote if the GOP contingent were to reach forty-nine or fifty members. Wilkins thereafter intervened behind the scenes to prevent Republicans in Putney's district from nominating a GOP foe for the veteran Independent in the 1997 election contests. Wilkins interview; Lacey E. Putney interview, April 26, 2005.

86. *Washington Post*, January 16, 1998.

87. *Daily Press*, January 14, 1998.

lered "Shame! Shame!" and three turned their backs as Chief Justice Harry J. Carrico swore in Moss. The dramatic opening to the 1998 General Assembly, at times evocative of the British Parliament because of its raucous outbursts, likely portends a nasty 60-day session in which legislators are expected to act on such popular issues as [the car tax.].[88]

Republicans, led by House minority leader Vance Wilkins, were ready to use their parity to bog down the body with filibusters, refuse to confirm judges, and take other obstructionist measures until, as Wilkins put it, the Democrats came to accept the "realities of political life and the idea of representative democracy."[89]

An instigator of the decidedly un-Virginia-like opening-day revolt on the House of Delegates floor, conservative Delegate Robert Marshall of Prince William County, recalled his role in the dramatic events:

> "Mr. Chairman, Mr. Chairman, Mr. Chairman . . . ," I shout more than a hundred times, adding a second word to my parliamentary vocabulary: "Objection, Objection, Objection, Objection," again probably more than a hundred times. Even moderate Republicans join in: "OBJECTION, OBJECTION, OBJECTION . . . ," another hundred times, accompanied by the crashing musical cadence of desk tops repeatedly being slammed down, hard wood on hard wood, repeated over and over and over.
>
> Tom [Brokaw of NBC Nightly News] leads the evening news with the Assembly uproar and lets America watch the melee—a combination of a frat party that had its beer cut off, a board of bankers trying to stop a run on the bank, a family of squirrels whose winter nuts had been pilfered by bats, and a school of sharks closing in on Titanic survivors. Was there ever such a spectacle in Virginia, or America?
>
> As Speaker Moss is sworn in by Chief Justice Carrico, Delegate [John ("Jack")] Reid [of Henrico] turns his back and folds his arms akimbo. Carrico has a hard time hearing Tom Moss repeat the oath of office as it is drowned out by varied Republican catcalls, yells of "Sherman's March through Georgia," and other descriptors.
>
> We are foiled but not for long.[90]

Watching the raw exercise of power by the Moss-led Democrats and the vehement GOP reaction, an angry Governor-elect Gilmore found the scene oddly reminiscent of the death pangs of despotism a few years earlier in the Soviet Union and Eastern Europe. What Democrats justified as simply applying the rules to their benefit, Gilmore saw in the larger context of

---

88. *Richmond Times-Dispatch*, January 15, 1998.
89. *Virginian-Pilot*, January 16, 1998.
90. Bob Marshall, "A Pilgrim's Diary: Hey God! Over Here! It's Me! Bob!" in *Notes from the Sausage Factory*, eds. Day and Dale, pp. 186–187.

his lifelong struggle for a two-party system against an oligarchic regime that, since the Byrd days, had perpetuated itself in power at the expense of basic democratic principles. It was, he felt, more than an entrenched machine; it was a political and social culture imbued with the arrogant belief that its ruling class was ordained to govern, particularly in the state legislature, perpetually and unaccountably. If there was any doubt that Gilmore's driving mission as governor would be achieving political reform by ending the century-plus-old single-party domination of the General Assembly, the doubt was removed on that bizarre January day when the nation's oldest continuous legislative body resembled a rowdy, banana-republic assemblage.[91]

No one felt good about what happened on that day, and no one wanted to see it repeated. Having retained the powerful speaker post, House Democrats shortly thereafter reluctantly entered into negotiations with their Republican counterparts. Delegate Lacey Putney openly declared his alignment with the GOP, making the 50–50 split in the chamber official.[92] By 9:00 p.m. on the second day of the historic session, the deal was cut, and Moss emerged from behind closed doors to announce that each party would have equal membership on committees and every panel except the Rules Committee would be led by Republican and Democratic co-chairs. Somewhat resembling the Senate deal struck two years earlier, the House power-sharing agreement would remain in effect for at least four years unless one party or the other surged to fifty-five members during that period, and it would continue thereafter until a party captured at least fifty-three seats. In the Senate, a special election triggered by Gilmore's appointive maneuvering had given the GOP its first-ever outright majority in the upper chamber (a 21–19 advantage), but the four-year compact crafted in 1996 ensured the power-sharing arrangement would continue in force through the 1999 session. Virginia thus became the first state in modern times to have power-sharing agreements simultaneously governing both houses of its legislature.[93] The House pact ended exclusive Democratic control, but some GOP members wondered aloud whether they had been wise to commit to a multi-year power-sharing deal when an outright Republican majority seemed right around the corner. Democrats, on the other hand, were uniformly

---

91. Gilmore interview.

92. Asked why he had decided to caucus with the Republicans after remaining unaligned with either party for three decades, Putney explained simply: "I felt that the Republican philosophy, generally speaking, was more conservative than the Democrats' [philosophy], especially by this time, and that it was in the best interest of the people of Virginia for me to side with what I considered the more responsible and more conservative wing in the General Assembly." Putney interview.

93. Sabato, *Virginia Votes 1995–1998*, p. 174.

despondent. Said Democratic floor leader (no longer the "majority" leader) Richard Cranwell, "I feel like a pallbearer."[94]

With the new order installed and the inauguration soon past, the General Assembly convened in joint session to hear Governor Gilmore's first legislative address. The new chief executive made clear his intention to honor his popular if costly campaign promises, but his message also emphasized bipartisan conciliation and cultural inclusiveness. It signaled an iron-fist-in-velvet-glove approach that would characterize much of Gilmore's administration as he endeavored, sometimes incongruously, to advance a conservative and partisan agenda while at the same time seeking to broaden the GOP's appeal to minority voters and centrist Democrats and independents. Gilmore's eagerness to emerge from his predecessor's shadow by striking a more amicable pose was apparent, and commentators were soon portraying Allen as the revolutionary firebrand and Gilmore as the conciliatory administrator. "Gilmore is playing Bush to Allen's Reagan, and the easy phrase is a 'kinder, gentler conservatism,' " said Mark Rozell, now at American University. "Fundamentally, they are conservatives . . . but they go about the task of leading very differently."[95] Under Governor Gilmore, wrote Spencer Hsu,

> it appears that the most rowdy aspects of Virginia's Republican Revolution, led by Governor George Allen, are a thing of the past. To allies, Gilmore's stepping back from the symbolic and rhetorical dramas of Allen's term are less a retreat than a quiet consolidation of GOP gains across state government. "I don't think the revolution is over," said Gilmore's chief of staff, M. Boyd Marcus Jr., "but if it is, it's because we won."[96]

Like the overtime legislative campaigns, the battles over Gilmore's car-tax plan and a competing Democratic initiative to aid local school construction pushed the sixty-day legislative session several days beyond its scheduled adjournment—a first for the Commonwealth. Delivering the invocation on the sixty-third day of the session, Reverend George Williams, a former deputy clerk of the House of Delegates, spoke of "trust and word-keeping difficulties . . . angry words and voices exploding," before imploring, "Please let your people go—home."[97] When lawmakers departed later that day, the GOP governor had won passage of the car-tax phase-out, and he and Democrats had reached a compromise of sorts, with details to be

94. *Virginian-Pilot,* January 16, 1998.
95. *Washington Post,* April 12, 1998.
96. *Washington Post,* April 12, 1998.
97. Associated Press, March 17, 1998.

worked out later, on increased school construction funding.[98] But clouding the session's success for Gilmore, and setting the stage for future controversies, was his administration's acknowledgment that the cost of reimbursing localities for forgoing car-tax collections would be sharply higher than advertised during the campaign. Instead of a $600 million annual drain on the state treasury when fully implemented, the program was projected to sap more than twice that amount each year. Lawmakers were well aware of the higher cost projections when they approved the car-tax legislation, and with a go-go economy producing abundant revenues, the escalating cost did not bother Gilmore. Indeed, the notion of giving taxpayers an even bigger break and restraining state spending in the process cheered the new chief executive.[99] But all that would soon change dramatically. A national economic downturn, deepened and extended by fall-out from the September 11, 2001, terrorist attacks and wartime uncertainty, would bring an abrupt end to the strong revenue growth the Old Dominion and other states had been enjoying for much of the decade.

Those deflating developments were still beyond the horizon, however, and with the Virginia economy (especially its high-tech sector) booming, Gilmore and legislators had two years of rapidly expanding revenues to allocate to a host of initiatives—education, mental health, the environment, and transportation, among others—as well as to "fund" broad-based tax relief. It was the governor's relentless push for working-family tax cuts that seemed to define his political persona and trigger interest across the country. At home, his effort to roll back two regressive levies on necessaries—the car tax and the sales tax on food and nonprescription medicines—prompted inevitable comparisons with the state's preeminent populist of an earlier era. "The late Lieutenant Governor Henry Howell was just a little ahead of his time," wrote Bob Gibson. "He ran to 'keep the big boys honest' and stumped against the food tax. . . . Governor Jim Gilmore, a populist Republican, became a Henry Howell Democrat when he shrewdly appropriated food tax repeal and just about every other major spending issue Democrats have tried to put in the cupboard."[100] The irrepressible Howell, bane of establishmentarians in both parties, had passed away during the previous year's gubernatorial campaign, two decades after his own last try for the Commonwealth's highest office. An eloquent eulogy by his early friend and follower, Larry Sabato, had illuminated how much the happy warrior from

---

98. A three-day special session of the General Assembly was required in April 1998 to balance the state budget and fix funding for the school construction and car-tax reimbursement programs.

99. Gilmore interview.

100. *Daily Progress*, November 22, 1998.

Norfolk, in defying the conventional wisdom of his day, had foreshadowed changes in state policy and politics.[101]

Though James Gilmore and Henry Howell were poles apart philosophically, the fact that they could be discussed in the same breath also highlighted how much the GOP had changed in the Reagan era and years since. Empowering working families was now the mantra, and conservative reforms vied with liberal remedies as the best prescription for accomplishing that goal. Neither party seemed particularly eager to be portrayed as a tool of business or governmental elites. Somewhat ironically, the increasing appetite among larger business interests in Virginia for increased public investments—and, if necessary, higher taxes—actually seemed to push some business groups and leaders traditionally associated with the GOP toward alignment with the state's centrist Democrats. Whether this circumstance was a Virginia anomaly or another of those trends for which the dynamic dominion would prove a harbinger was impossible to tell. What was clear, however, was that Gilmore's persona took the Virginia GOP's increasingly populist tenor to a new level. The son of a meat cutter and a secretary, the Henrico Republican culturally was far more comfortable with upwardly mobile suburbanites than with the old-money, country-club elites often associated with the GOP in the popular imagination. In a colorful profile, Garrett Epps well captured this distinctive aspect of Gilmore and his governorship:

> The story is not an unusual one in American politics, where humble origins stretch from Springfield, Ill., to Hope, Ark. But in Virginia, as the state's foremost populist, the late Henry Howell, used to say, "Everybody wants to wear velvet underwear." Family, blood and breeding, even at the verge of the twenty-first century, are serious matters in the Old Dominion. Virginia politics, in particular, have always been dynastic. Candidates were known not by who they were but by who sired them.
>
> In the departed days of the Byrd organization, the equivalent of divine anointment was supplied by "the nod," the solemn signal from Senator Harry Byrd Sr. that a chosen candidate was acceptable to him. In the years

---

101. Sabato eulogized Howell as "a Virginia original whose populism drew odd-couple support" from liberals and conservatives and "who [sought] power not for its own sake but to help others, to serve people and *not* the political class." Sabato noted that Howell's stances on issues such as poll tax abolition, population-based reapportionment, consumer protection, and removal of the sales tax on food, though denigrated by his political foes at the time, had come to receive widespread support in the years since Howell championed them. Text of remarks on file with the author. Mills Godwin, the man who emerged from retirement in 1973 to bar Howell from the governor's mansion, died in February 1999. For a description of the intertwined careers and campaigns of Howell and Godwin, see *The Dynamic Dominion*, Chapters 17, 21, 25, 29.

since the organization crumbled, Virginia, like a middle-European kingdom between the wars, has scoured the earth for pretenders with a drop of royal blood. Chuck Robb was a prince consort of the Lyndon Johnson family. John Warner was once married to Hollywood's Queen of Egypt. Oliver North proudly claimed the bar sinister of the House of Reagan. Even George Allen came from a football dynasty.

But Jim Gilmore resists the urge to don the purple. He remains identified with the working and lower middle classes that gave him birth. He drinks Miller Genuine Draft; he's been known to catch a Hootie and the Blowfish concert; his favorite restaurant is Pizza Hut. On a Saturday afternoon, he still hangs out at Price Club. He is Governor Six-Pack, *Homo suburbanus*, and, in the hallowed halls of Virginia's historic capitol, an outsider.[102]

Even Gilmore's determined focus on tax relief was traceable to his working-class roots. "Underlying [his conservative political] philosophy," wrote Epps, "is a vision of ordinary people—folks not unlike his parents—getting enough money to have real freedom."[103]

The 1999 legislative elections presented the last opportunity for Gilmore the outsider to overcome the establishment, cement his legacy, and achieve his political dream of breaking Democratic hegemony in the General Assembly. All 140 senators and delegates were again to face the voters, giving the governor a chance to be the GOP commander who led the final, successful assault on the last citadel of Democratic Party power in the Old Dominion.[104]

In this endeavor, Gilmore had an indispensable ally in House Republican leader S. Vance Wilkins. A staunch conservative, Wilkins had come to the House of Delegates in 1978, joining a twenty-five-person GOP contingent that was outnumbered three-to-one by Democrats. The indignities suffered by Republican lawmakers at the hands of the body's Democratic leaders had seemed to cow some of the minority's members, but the treatment had only served to steel Wilkins's resolve to bring about change.[105] By 1992, he had become the minority leader for an expanded, forty-one-

102. Epps, "The Outsider," p. 1.

103. Epps, "The Outsider," p. 3.

104. As the 1999 election showdown loomed, veteran political commentator Bill Wood of the University of Virginia's Sorenson Institute of Political Leadership observed that Republicans had been largely irrelevant in the state legislature for the first two-thirds of the twentieth century. But in the three decades since the election of the first Virginia GOP governor in the century, the 140-member General Assembly had undergone an "amazing turnabout," transitioning from a 109–31 Democratic majority in 1970 to a virtual tie—seventy Republicans, sixty-nine Democrats, and one Independent—when lawmakers convened in January 1999. Bill Wood, "Change Came Slowly the First 65 Years—And Then at Warp-Speed," *Richmond Times-Dispatch*, January 12, 1999.

105. Recalling the experience years later, Wilkins reeled off a litany of notorious examples. In one memorable episode, during a marathon Saturday session of the House

member House Republican caucus, and his competitive energies were focused on a single goal—winning a GOP majority. Wilkins sold his family-owned construction firm and set about the full-time business of traveling the state to recruit and train legislative candidates, raise money, plan strategy, and prod members of his caucus to do their political homework. In a conversation with College of William & Mary professor George W. Grayson, with whom he served in the House of Delegates, Wilkins recalled the long-running effort to whittle away at Democratic control:

> Like [General] Washington, who won the war after losing nearly every battle to the overwhelming strength of the British, we lost most of the legislative battles but won a war of attrition in the trenches of individual district legislative elections. This, in spite of being outspent nearly two to one in every election until 1999.[106]

Aptly labeled "Virginia's Republican Moses" by Democrat Grayson, Wilkins had spent years laying the groundwork for the final push into the Promised Land of GOP control. Before the 1999 contests were over, his political committees had donated nearly $400,000 to that election cycle's House contenders. But far more important, Wilkins had personally recruited or helped persuade dozens of prominent local citizens to offer themselves as GOP candidates for the House of Delegates.[107]

Wilkins's relentless efforts dovetailed well with the governor's sophisticated political operation. Led by consultant Ray Allen Jr., chief of staff Boyd Marcus, and Marcus's deputy Stephen A. Horton, Gilmore's team got started even before the 1999 legislative session. Districts were surveyed to determine where Democratic incumbents were vulnerable, yielding insights that later produced some surprising upsets; messages were tested; challengers

Courts of Justice Committee, he had waited in the committee room all day for a key bill he sponsored to be considered. When he finally bowed to hunger late in the day and slipped out of the committee room briefly to get something to eat, the committee quickly took up his bill and killed it, denying him an opportunity to speak on it. Wilkins interview.

106. George W. Grayson, "Virginia's Republican Moses," in *Notes from the Sausage Factory*, eds. Day and Dale, pp. 152–158. Grayson represented the Williamsburg area in the House of Delegates from 1974 to 1982 and 1984 to 2001. In his retrospective on Wilkins, the former delegate also faulted his own party's legislative hierarchy for actions that contributed to the eventual loss of majority status to the Republicans. *Notes from the Sausage Factory*, eds. Day and Dale, pp. 156–157.

107. *Richmond Times-Dispatch*, November 11, 1999. Among Wilkins's key lieutenants in the 1999 campaign effort were then-Delegate Eric Cantor of Henrico, who rendered crucial assistance with fund-raising, and Delegate Kirk Cox of Colonial Heights, who helped school candidates on campaign issues, strategy, and tactics. Wilkins interview.

were recruited; GOP incumbents were bolstered; consultants were engaged; campaign funds were raised.[108] When necessary, Gilmore did not hesitate to intervene in GOP nominating contests on behalf of candidates he deemed more electable or—as in the case of his unsuccessful bid to unseat Richmond Delegate Anne G. ("Panny") Rhodes[109]—more loyal to the Republican cause. The governor and his team also were careful to stay a step ahead on key policy matters, taking the initiative on such varied topics as food tax repeal, college tuition relief, and transportation funding partly as a means of denying rival Democrats any potent issues for the 1999 legislative campaigns.

Gilmore's political operation called the shots behind the scenes, but publicly the governor consistently rejected suggestions that the legislative elections were a referendum on his administration. The Allen-led takeover effort four years earlier had faltered, Gilmore's strategists believed, because it had relied too much on television advertising and had cast the choice as one of support or opposition to the governor and his policies. The 1999 legislative contests would be decided on local issues, the Gilmore team reasoned, and so they would pick the right districts, recruit strong candidates, tailor the campaign message to local circumstances, and use direct-mail and phone banks to deliver that message directly to targeted households.[110] The governor, in stumping, would emphasize the local message and candidate strengths, and indulge himself only occasionally in public reflection on the elections' larger implications. A Republican victory would "shatter the presumption [of Democratic hegemony] and liberate everyone in the system," he declared shortly before the voting. "My goal for decades has been to liberate people from one-party politics in this state."[111]

"Despite a highly personal quest for victory, involving more than a

---

108. Stephen A. Horton interview, July 8, 2003; Ray Allen Jr. interview.

109. Rhodes, a GOP moderate and frequent critic of Republican Governors Allen and Gilmore, faced conservative Ruble A. Hord III in a spring nomination battle. Gilmore, joined by Seventh District Congressman Thomas J. Bliley Jr., Attorney General Mark Earley, and much of the GOP establishment, backed challenger Hord against the incumbent. Rhodes, with support from Senator John Warner, emphasized her credentials as an independent-minded female and appealed strongly for independent and Democratic "crossover" support in the open primary contest. She won renomination with 56 percent of the primary vote in an outcome widely perceived as a rebuff to Gilmore. Larry J. Sabato, *Virginia Votes 1999–2003* (Charlottesville, VA: Weldon Cooper Center for Public Service, University of Virginia, forthcoming), p. 4. Rhodes's victory proved fleeting, however. After Republicans gained control of the General Assembly in 2000, their redistricting handiwork deprived Rhodes of a viable seat, and she did not seek re-election.

110. Ray Allen Jr. interview; Horton interview.

111. *Richmond Times-Dispatch,* October 31, 1999.

year of fund-raising and campaigning across the state, Gilmore insists that the election is not about him," wrote veteran reporter Robert Melton of the *Washington Post*.

> [But his] painstaking effort to capture the legislature has been pure Gilmore, involving a handpicked band of campaign-hardened loyalists, mind-numbing hours of planning and travel, record amounts of money that the governor himself raised and controlled, and a district-by-district ground war that left no Republican incumbent unprotected and lifted several GOP challengers into competitive positions.[112]

Gilmore made more than fifty campaign appearances in the sixteen months before the election and raised and spent a whopping $3.4 million on the legislative contests.[113] An additional infusion of cash came from Eleventh District congressman Thomas Davis. With his eye on the Virginia legislature's impending role in congressional reapportionment, Davis used his position as chairman of the National Republican Congressional Committee and his own political action committee to funnel nearly $600,000 to the GOP legislative campaign effort.[114] Even with those unprecedented Republican fund-raising efforts, however, the Democrats who were fighting to retain their longstanding grip on the House of Delegates still enjoyed a modest advantage in total campaign cash. The Republicans who narrowly controlled the Senate had the upper hand in fund-raising for those contests, resulting in a slight, 52 percent edge for Republicans overall in General Assembly election spending. Reflecting the partisan stakes in the watershed, pre-redistricting legislative contests, total campaign spending in the 1999 legislative races approached $28 million—a 36 percent increase over the unprecedented amount spent four years earlier.[115]

"Republicans Rule!" blared the banner headline across the front page of the *Virginian-Pilot* after the showdown on November 2 produced a six-

---

112. *Washington Post*, October 30, 1999.

113. *Washington Post*, October 30, 1999; *Washington Post*, November 3, 1999.

114. Davis interview; *Washington Post*, October 21, 1999. A GOP power for years in Northern Virginia and now in Congress, Davis's strong foray into downstate politics reinforced speculation that he might be planning a statewide bid for governor or senator. Charlie Cook, a prominent congressional analyst and political columnist, observed that Davis was "setting himself up to be the kingmaker in Republican politics in the state." "The question," Cook added, "is, 'Can he ever be king?'" *Washington Post*, October 21, 1999. In a 2005 interview, Davis acknowledged his longstanding interest in moving to the United States Senate upon John Warner's retirement. Davis interview.

115. Sabato, *Virginia Votes, 1999–2003*, pp. 13, 17–18.

seat Republican advantage in the House of Delegates and continuation of the GOP's 21–19 majority in the Senate.[116] The newspaper's readers in Hampton Roads had been at ground zero of the historic clash. Not only was Speaker Thomas Moss of Norfolk deposed by his party's loss of House control, but veteran Norfolk Democrat Stanley Walker, who had become the Senate president pro tempore under the upper chamber's power-sharing arrangement, was easily defeated in his bid for reelection. Also upended unexpectedly was longtime Democratic stalwart Glenn Croshaw of Virginia Beach, whose vulnerability in a GOP-leaning House of Delegates district had been quietly diagnosed months earlier by Gilmore's political planners.[117] "Virginia Republicans capped their decade-old drive to capture Richmond yesterday," wrote reporter Craig Timberg, "not with the hard-edged conservatism of the past but with a softer pitch to the moderate suburbs" of Northern Virginia and Hampton Roads.[118] The governor, widely credited as the architect of the long-coveted breakthrough, now was able to celebrate on election night. "Free at last, free at last, free at long last!" he exclaimed at the GOP's victory party. "Democracy has finally come to the Commonwealth!"[119]

"The time of the greatest victory is the time of greatest danger," observed Richard Evelyn Byrd, who served as Speaker of the Virginia House of Delegates at the beginning of the twentieth century, and whose party and family were largely responsible for the powerful political regime that Gilmore had labored at length to bury.[120] The elder Byrd's grandson,

---

116. *Virginian-Pilot*, November 3, 1999. Republicans won fifty-two seats and would have fifty-three votes to organize the House because the body's lone Independent, Delegate Lacey Putney, continued to caucus with the GOP. Statewide, Republican House candidates polled 55 percent of the vote, a new record for the GOP in legislative races. Democratic candidates, however, won a majority (52 percent) of the vote in two-party contested races even while their party was winning just forty-seven House seats and losing control of the chamber. Sabato, *Virginia Votes 1999–2003*, p. 9.

117. The wins over Walker and Croshaw by Republicans Nick Rerras and Terrie L. Suit, respectively, capped a stunning string of GOP victories in Hampton Roads during the 1990s that converted the area's formerly Democrat-dominated legislative delegation into a Republican stronghold. GOP consultant Tim Phillips, who advised Rerras and other candidates, noted that the party's gains in the vote-rich region not only supplied crucial seats for the new Republican legislative majorities in the General Assembly but also provided a political start for several statewide GOP candidates and helped boost Republican voting in other statewide and congressional races. Tim Phillips interview, January 14, 2006; see also Preston Bryant, "Eastern Stars," in *Notes from the Sausage Factory*, eds. Day and Dale, pp. 250–254.

118. *Washington Post*, November 3, 1999.

119. *Washington Post*, November 3, 1999.

120. James Latimer, "'Young Harry' Byrd Turning 85; Ex-Senator Reflects, Predicts and Advises," *Richmond Times-Dispatch*, December 19, 1999.

Harry F. Byrd Jr. was just ten years old when he heard Speaker Byrd's admonition, but it stuck with him. Now, with the ascendant Republicans having
captured the last bastion of Virginia's once-dominant Democrats, the retired
senator shared words of warning with the state's triumphant GOP leaders.
"Virginia apparently has now become more Republican than it has ever
been before," Byrd commented to reporter James Latimer. "But the
Republicans need to be very careful how they handle their new power. It
may not be as vast as they think."[121]

The elder statesman compared the Virginia Republicans' situation in
1999 with the GOP's congressional takeover five years earlier, when the
exultant Republicans led by new House Speaker Newt Gingrich were
widely perceived as having overplayed their legislative and rhetorical
hand.[122] And former Senator Byrd was not the only one making that comparison. Elected as the fifty-third speaker of the Virginia House of Delegates—the first Republican to hold the post since Reconstruction—Vance
Wilkins was mindful of "the Gingrich example" and was determined to
ensure that his administration of the venerated body was measured, adminis-
tratively efficient, and successful.[123] Nominated for the speakership on January 12, 2000, by the most senior GOP delegate, Fairfax's Vincent F.
Callahan Jr., the sixty-three-year-old Wilkins followed his historic installation with a brief, conciliatory message that garnered praise across party lines.
The historic scene was observed from the balcony of the House of Delegates
chamber by Governor Gilmore, who told reporter Christina Nuckols the
events provided satisfying proof that "democracy does work in the Commonwealth of Virginia."[124] For his part, Wilkins was determined to show

---

121. James Latimer, " 'Young Harry' Byrd Turning 85; Ex-Senator Reflects, Predicts
and Advises," *Richmond Times-Dispatch*, December 19, 1999.

122. Congressman Thomas Bliley, who became chairman of the House Commerce
Committee following the 1994 elections through his ties to the new speaker, concluded
retrospectively that it was a "mistake" for Gingrich to assume the role of speaker. "Newt
reminded me of [World War II General] George Patton," recalled Bliley. "He was a
great leader and battlefield commander but he just did not have the patience to work
with and massage the members." Bliley interview; see also Black and Black, *The Rise of
Southern Republicans*, p. 31 (observing that "Gingrich's harsh, argumentative, and relentlessly confrontational style gave fellow Republicans a hard lesson in how not to
govern").

123. Wilkins interview.

124. Christina Nuckols, "House Applauds New Speaker as Session Starts," *Roanoke
Times*, January 13, 2000. Wilkins's historic installation as speaker almost obscured two
other notable legislative firsts: Delegate H. Morgan Griffith of Salem became the first
Republican majority leader in the House of Delegates in more than a century, while in
the Senate, John Chichester became the first GOP president pro tempore. Among those
on hand for the momentous events was former Congressman Caldwell Butler, who was
a Republican leader in the House of Delegates in the 1960s. The installation of a Repub-

that a greater measure of democracy would work in the hemisphere's oldest continuous legislative body. He soon announced the most far-reaching set of organizational changes in the body since venerated Speaker John Warren Cooke of Mathews County modernized House operations in the early 1970s,[125] and the resulting improvements brought the new Republican speaker bipartisan accolades.

University of Richmond political scientist John Whelan, a longtime student of state legislative processes in Virginia and elsewhere, analyzed Wilkins's organizational reforms four years later, and found that the streamlined committee system and other changes made by the new speaker had markedly increased the body's efficiency. Various studies over time had highlighted a pressing need for reorganization, Whelan reported, but the change in partisan control of the House of Delegates, and especially "the determined leadership of [Wilkins]," had created the opportunity and catalyst for action.[126] "The changes made for the better in a very short time under Vance Wilkins as speaker were greater than those I had seen during my entire forty years in the General Assembly, [and people] on both sides of the aisle agree with that," commented Independent Delegate Lacey E. Putney, who owned the distinction of being the longest-serving state legislator in the country.[127]

Wilkins's determination to preside with equanimity over the House of Delegates did not diminish his intense, partisan desire to assure a sustained Republican majority in the body. He planned to use the unprecedented circumstance of simultaneous GOP control of the governorship and both legislative chambers to pass redistricting legislation that would erase the Democratic advantage from earlier line-drawing and substitute a pro-Republican configuration. Wilkins envisioned—and soon obtained—a fortified GOP majority that would preserve his party's newly gained control

---

lican speaker "was inevitable," said Butler. "The only question was whether I would live that long." Christina Nuckols, "House Applauds New Speaker as Session Starts," *Roanoke Times*, January 13, 2000; see *The Dynamic Dominion*, Chapter 15.

125. Cooke was elected to the House of Delegates in 1942, and served as speaker from 1968 until his retirement in 1980. For a description of reforms instituted pursuant to the recommendations of his Commission on the Legislative Process, see Richard Kirk Jonas, "Modernization of the Virginia General Assembly: The Commission on the Legislative Process, 1972–73," unpublished thesis, University of Richmond, 1977.

126. John T. Whelan, "Reorganization in the House: Republicans Make Their Mark," *The Virginia News Letter* (Charlottesville, VA: Weldon Cooper Center for Public Service, University of Virginia, February 2004), pp. 5–6; John T. Whelan, "A New Majority Takes Its Turn at Improving the Process in Virginia," *Journal of the American Society of Legislative Clerks and Secretaries* (Fall 2001): 13–17.

127. Putney interview.

well into the future. In the first post-redistricting balloting, Republicans claimed a sixty-four-seat majority in the hundred-member House of Delegates in the 2001 elections, a result exceeding even the highest hopes of Wilkins and his lieutenants.[128] The decisive GOP victory brought an end to power-sharing in the House of Delegates two years after it had ended in the state Senate, and it also brought to a close the colorful legislative career of Delegate Richard Cranwell. The chief architect of House Democrats' aggressive redistricting plan in the early 1990s, Cranwell ten years later was effectively redistricted out of his own Roanoke-area seat by Wilkins's line-drawing handiwork.[129]

Like Wilkins, Gilmore enjoyed heady days in the immediate aftermath of the 1999 victories. In addition to his state duties, the Virginia governor was tapped by Congress and the Clinton White House to head a panel examining the threat posed by terrorist groups' potential access to weapons of mass destruction, a role that gave him expertise in an area that soon would be thrust to the fore with the September 2001 attacks on the World Trade Center and the Pentagon.[130] Politically, Gilmore bestowed an influential early endorsement on the presidential candidacy of fellow Governor George W. Bush of Texas in spring 1999, and then helped Bush to a pivotal victory in Virginia Republicans' first-ever binding presidential primary on February 29, 2000.[131] The front-running Bush's campaign had stumbled with an early loss in New Hampshire to Senator John McCain of Arizona, and the Texan's win in the Old Dominion put him back on track to gain the nomination handily. Bush rewarded Gilmore for his support—and rec-

---

128. The once-dominant Democrats claimed only thirty-four seats. Delegate Watkins Abbitt Jr., of Appomattax, son of the late Fourth District congressman and Byrd Democratic kingpin, joined Delegate Lacey Putney in seeking reelection as an Independent, though Abbitt, unlike Putney, did not caucus with the majority Republicans. Reflecting the effects of GOP-controlled redistricting, Republican candidates captured sixty-four of the hundred House seats despite winning only 55.5 percent of the total statewide legislative vote and only 52.9 percent of the vote in party-contested races. Sabato, *Virginia Votes, 1999–2003*, p. 154.

129. After a brief respite from politics, Cranwell became chairman of the state Democratic Party in 2005.

130. Gilmore was appointed as chairman of the Congressional Advisory Panel to Assess Domestic Response Capabilities for Terrorism Involving Weapons of Mass Destruction in 1999. Recommendations by the panel (generally known as the "Gilmore Commission") later were influential in shaping development of the federal Department of Homeland Security.

131. In the only other GOP presidential primary of the twentieth century in Virginia, state Republicans held a non-binding ("beauty contest") primary vote in spring 1988 and then selected their presidential convention delegates in state and congressional district conventions.

ognized his notable party-building labors and successes—by tapping the Virginia governor to serve as chairman of the Republican National Committee (RNC).

It was not long, however, before both Gilmore and Wilkins were suffering setbacks, affirming the truth of Speaker Byrd's timeless admonition. Pulled in three directions by his gubernatorial, terrorism panel, and RNC roles, the preoccupied Gilmore quickly found that working with a legislature controlled by the chief executive's own party—even when that control has been achieved with the governor's help—can be more difficult than building coalitions across party lines. The national and state economies began to slow in late 2000 and early 2001, triggering a bitter fight between Gilmore and the GOP-controlled Senate, led by Senate Finance Committee chairman John Chichester, over the sufficiency of growth revenues to fund the next phase of previously legislated car tax relief. The dispute resulted in an unprecedented legislative impasse in 2001 that blocked the usual mid-biennium adjustments to the budget and gave Democrat Mark Warner a managerial competence issue on which to center his campaign for the governorship that same year. Republicans had just captured legislative majorities promising change, yet the most notable change was a new peak in legislative-executive acrimony and an embarrassing failure to compromise sufficiently to pass a budget bill. "It took the Republicans a hundred years to take control of the General Assembly," quipped Democratic Delegate Clifton A. ("Chip") Woodrum, "but it took them only one year to show why it had taken them a hundred years."[132]

As governor, Gilmore bore the brunt of the political fallout from the legislative meltdown. After reclaiming that post for Democrats, Governor Mark Warner heaped scorn on his predecessor for bequeathing mounting budget shortfalls—an effective political device even though Virginia's budget problems paralleled those in states across the country and were chiefly the result of the national economic downturn, September 11th terrorist attacks, six-month closure of Reagan National Airport, and troop deployments from Hampton Roads.[133] Adding to his woes, Gilmore and his lieu-

---

132. Remarks during 2004 Virginia General Assembly Project Conference, University of Virginia Center for Politics, Richmond, VA, July 23, 2004.

133. Although Warner as governor frequently cast blame on his Republican predecessor for errant state revenue estimates and resulting budget shortfalls, revenue forecasts in Virginia invariably were developed by career state employees who served in multiple administrations. After accurate revenue forecasting later proved at least as elusive for Warner as his predecessors, triggering sharp criticism from GOP legislators, the Democratic governor's finance secretary, John Bennett, reminded lawmakers that essentially the same staff had been generating the revenue forecasts for administrations of both parties continuously since the mid-1980s. *Richmond Times-Dispatch*, June 21, 2005.

tenants fell out of favor with the political operatives in the Bush White House, and Gilmore exited the national party chairmanship after a year in the post.

In contrast to the serial political setbacks suffered by Gilmore late in his gubernatorial tenure, Wilkins's problems were impelled by personal controversy and were far more devastating. At the pinnacle of legislative power, only two years in the speaker's perch that had long been his goal, the Amherst Republican resigned in 2002 after disclosure that he earlier had paid a six-figure sum to settle a former employee's sexual harassment claim. Wilkins and his top legislative aide also were snared in yet another Virginia political eavesdropping scandal, this one involving an employee of the state Republican Party who illicitly gained access to conference calls in which Governor Warner, Democratic lawmakers, and others discussed pending litigation over redistricting.[134] The details of the sexual harassment matter were never disclosed, and Wilkins's involvement in the eavesdropping matter seemed peripheral, but the speaker faced public and private pressure to resign from the state's top elected GOP state official (Jerry W. Kilgore, who had been elected attorney general in 2001) and from fellow Republican lawmakers. Other elected officials—notable among them President Clinton and Senator Robb—had weathered sexual misconduct scandals that seemed at least as serious as Wilkins's, but GOP politicians and activists who preached family values had little stomach for defending the embattled Republican leader. For his part, Wilkins was disappointed that more of his fellow lawmakers did not stand by him, but he also understood the stakes. Having devoted decades to winning a Republican majority in the legislature, the first GOP speaker in Virginia in more than a century resolved to step aside quietly rather than place the political fortunes of his caucus further

---

134. In March 2002, Republican Party executive director Edmund A. Matricardi III joined the conference call using an access code illicitly provided by a disgruntled former Democratic Party staffer. Three days later, Matricardi and Wilkins aide Claudia Tucker listened in on another similar call. Matricardi, Tucker, and Joseph Willis Lee III (the Democratic operative who supplied the access code) pled guilty to federal criminal charges and paid fines. State GOP chairman Gary Thomson, who after learning of the first instance of misconduct failed to prevent the second, resigned the party chairmanship in August 2003 and also paid a fine pursuant to a federal plea arrangement. A subsequent civil suit brought against the state Republican Party and various individual defendants, including Wilkins, by thirty-three Democrats who participated in the conference calls resulted in a $750,000 out-of-court settlement. See George Whitehurst, "Democrats sue over eavesdropping," *Danville Register & Bee*, March 20, 2004. The scandal, like the episode a decade earlier involving various members of the Robb Senate staff, appeared to catch the offending operatives unaware that their ethically suspect actions were also illegal under federal eavesdropping prohibitions. See chapter 4.

at risk with a probably futile effort to overcome perceptions of his personal misconduct.[135]

Those travails, however, were in the future and out of sight as the curtain rang down on the twentieth century, with Gilmore and Wilkins widely heralded as uniquely successful partisan leaders. Many had played a part, but the final GOP legislative breakthrough—the signal event marking consummation of the decades-long political realignment of the Commonwealth—had come on their watch, and almost assuredly would not have come then without their determined efforts. The triumphant pair could claim a full measure of credit for pulling off the political feat that was each's longstanding goal. In America's oldest legislature—indeed, in Virginia politics—there was now a new world.

---

135. Interviewed three years later, Wilkins expressed no second thoughts about the wisdom of his decision to relinquish the speakership amid the controversy. "I had some philosophical goals I still wanted to achieve, but I had pretty much achieved my political goals," he said, adding, "I got the [Republican majority in the] House to where they can't lose it for at least ten years unless they really try to." Reiterating that the sexual harassment claim that led to his political demise was without merit, Wilkins averred that his "big mistake" was in secretly paying the claimant to avoid disclosure of the sexual harassment allegations during the heat of a pivotal legislative campaign. When the payment was later disclosed, many members of the GOP caucus and others took it as proof that the underlying charges were true, he noted. Wilkins interview.

*Part III*

MARK WARNER AND THE
"SENSIBLE CENTER,"
2000–2006

# 9

# TAXING TIMES AND THE TACTIC
# OF BIPARTISANSHIP

> We've shown that here in Virginia, Democrats and Republicans can
> come together, put politics aside, and make tough decisions when
> times demand it. . . . With the budget that we passed last year, we
> . . . made the tax code fairer for Virginia's families. We provided the
> funding necessary to meet our core commitments in education,
> health services and public safety. And we restored Virginia's fiscal
> integrity.[1]
>
> —Governor Mark R. Warner, 2005

A s the dawn of the new millennium approached, the overarching concern was that the newly ubiquitous computers that impacted virtually
every aspect of human activity would fall victim to the dreaded Y2K bug
when the big moment arrived, causing the global citizenry to spend January
1, 2000, in Stone Age–like darkness beset by multifarious miseries that could
scarcely be imagined. As disasters go, the Y2K bug was a bust—though it
would never be quite clear whether the threatened crisis had been skillfully
averted or grossly exaggerated.

As it turned out, however, the sighs of relief on the first day of the new
millennium were premature. While the Y2K disaster never materialized, the
first years of the new century would be witness to unprecedented trials of
other kinds. Even after living through it, a list of the troubles reads more
like a second-rate Hollywood script than a plausible chronicle of the times:
a terrorist attack felling the World Trade Center towers and damaging the
Pentagon; a global war against a technologically sophisticated organization
of murderous Islamic radicals; devastating hurricanes and other natural disasters; mortal threats, man-made and natural, from lethal biological agents and

---

1. Text of 2005 State of the Commonwealth Message, Governor's Press Office, January 12, 2005.

261

killer viruses; a string of sniper attacks that terrorized the nation's capital and surrounding portions of Virginia and Maryland; and sundry other major events that in less extreme circumstances would easily merit mention. To those crises could be added a list of unusually daunting public policy challenges: conflicting international ambitions and a wave of anti-Americanism in the post–Cold War world; a battered global economy and national recession; ballooning of the federal deficit and national debt; a cascade of vexing policy issues precipitated by rapid technological advances; increased economic competition from abroad; a wave of illegal immigration; acute polarization of the American electorate on cultural issues; and mounting cynicism about the trustworthiness of public officials.[2] Of course, each of the crises and challenges had a positive flip-side, presenting opportunities to provide leadership, supply vision, advance human achievement, and foster a culture of community and ethic of service. Whether the troubled times were a sign of greater hardship to come or a crucible in which a stronger American character would be refined, or both, was too early to tell. It was clear, however, that the times were extraordinarily challenging for those engaged in government and politics. And with its four-century mark approaching, Virginia, the birthplace of representative government in America, was right in the thick of it.

The first two statewide elections of the new century cemented the positions of George Allen and Mark Warner as leaders of their respective parties in Virginia, and placed them in the wings, soon to emerge on the national political stage as highly influential players. George Allen's capture in 2000 of the Senate seat occupied by Charles Robb completed the GOP's conquest of the center-left Democrats who had dominated the state's politics a decade earlier, and it attested to the durable appeal of Allen's Reaganesque brand of reform-minded populism. Mark Warner's election in 2001 and popular tenure as governor signaled that a Democrat could not only win but prosper in the Republican-leaning Commonwealth by eschewing partisan politics-as-usual and clinging to what Warner branded the "sensible center."[3] The emergence of two major political figures in Virginia whose respective successes spoke persuasively to their fellow partisans

---

2. Viewing the imposing scene in 2005, Virginia's foremost elder statesman, former Senator Harry F. Byrd Jr., observed to a correspondent, "Excepting Lincoln and FDR, George W. Bush has on his plate simultaneously more problems of great magnitude than any of the other 40 [Presidents]." Letter from Harry F. Byrd Jr. to the author, September 28, 2005.

3. Mark Warner interview; see also Warren Fiske, "Warner Eyes Final Year in Office," *Virginian-Pilot*, January 12, 2005; Mark R. Warner, "The Sensible Center," in *Notes from the Sausage Factory*, eds. Day and Dale, pp. 288–289.

around the country was, in itself, palpable evidence of Virginia's return to the vanguard of American politics.

Allen accomplished an unusual feat—dislodging an incumbent United States senator—in a relatively close contest that focused on the two contenders' gubernatorial records, their competing views on education, and Robb's Senate tenure, including his close alignment with outgoing President Clinton.[4] Though the incumbent senator had avoided controversy since his 1994 reelection, Robb's public persona never recaptured the luster lost with the scandalous disclosures of the early 1990s. To many observers, it seemed as if the senator's heart was not in his 2000 reelection bid—an impression Robb later largely confirmed, conceding that he lacked "fire in the belly" during the contest.[5] Having gained a second term in 1994 primarily through the support of his party's most loyal—and liberal—adherents, Robb appeared to move leftward as a range of social issues came to the fore during his 1995-2000 tenure, and he rung up a rate of support for President Clinton—80 percent—that surpassed most of his Democratic colleagues in the Senate. With Clinton viewed unfavorably by three out of five Virginia voters, Allen's tack in 2000 was inevitable.[6] He never raised the various Robb personal controversies, but he implicitly indicted both the senator's leftward lean and past indiscretions by repeatedly charging that Robb embodied "Clinton values" while he (Allen) represented "Virginia values." The double entendre worked for Allen in part because Vice President Albert Gore Jr., the Democratic presidential nominee, was evidently dis-

---

4. The vote totals were: Allen (R)—1,420,460 (52.3 percent); Robb (D)—1,296,093 (47.7 percent). Although the Republican challenger led in opinion surveys throughout the race and outspent Robb by $10.9 million to $6.6 million, the advantages of Senate incumbency and the competitiveness of the state's politics were apparent in the closeness of the final tally. Allen's winning percentage was nearly identical to George W. Bush's 52.5 percent share of the vote in the simultaneous presidential balloting in Virginia. Sabato, *Virginia Votes 1999–2003*, pp. 44, 58.

5. Robb interview. Recalling the contest nearly five years later, Robb cited "ideology, age and enthusiasm" as deciding factors in Allen's win. Robb also observed that popular former governors in Virginia generally have an edge in running against incumbent senators, and he pointed to the difficulty of running as a Democrat during a presidential contest in GOP-leaning Virginia. "In the end, however, I didn't lose because of the presidential election," Robb said. "52 percent of the voters preferred George Allen while only 48 percent preferred Chuck Robb. And both of us are content with the result." Robb interview. Robb's post-Senate contentment stemmed in part from his status as a respected elder statesman. Among other activities, he was tapped by President George W. Bush for a high-profile assignment as leader of a bipartisan presidential commission charged with investigating United States intelligence failures in connection with the 2003 invasion of Iraq.

6. Sabato, *Virginia Votes 1999–2003*, pp. 44, 49; see also John B. Judis, "From Hell," *The New Republic*, December 19, 1994.

tancing himself from Clinton and the sexual controversies that had plagued the president and had prompted his impeachment in 1998.

Mostly, though, Allen secured the Senate seat by battling Robb to a draw, and even better than a draw, on the pivotal issue of education. For weeks after the traditional Labor Day start of the campaign, the two heavy-weight contenders sparred over the airwaves on the question of who possessed the most genuine commitment to public education. Robb's electronic missives assailed education spending "cuts" that Allen had rec-ommended when he advanced an ill-fated tax cut plan as governor in 1995, while the Republican countered with a surprising charge that Robb, too, had proposed education funding reductions as governor. Both sides had a kernel of truth on their side—but only a kernel. Each governor, inheriting a weak economy and budget gap, had at some point recommended modest reductions in the anticipated rate of education spending increase. But far more relevant was the fact that each, over the full course of his gubernatorial tenure, had recommended funding increases for elementary and secondary education that, by the standards of the day, were unusually large. Each man thus could plausibly claim the "education governor" mantle, and did. But the long-running battle eventually broke Allen's way, partly on the strength of his claim that higher student test scores showed the wisdom of the Republican's insistence on combining the increased dollars with significant reforms through the "Standards of Learning" accountability program. Allen's cause also was helped by his popular plan to give parents a $1,000 per child tax credit for education-related purchases, such as computers, the services of tutors, and other learning aids. The proposal combined tax relief with support for education in a way that resonated positively with moderate suburban voters as well as the Republican's conservative base. By election day, voters, by a margin of 47 percent to 34 percent, said they viewed Allen as the candidate more likely to improve education.[7] That was an unusual result: Republican candidates typically had enjoyed an edge among voters on economic and criminal justice issues, while Democrats usually had held the advantage in voter confidence on educational matters. Allen had joined the education battle with Robb and defeated the Democrat on his own ground.

As a first-term senator, Allen seemed to exert unusual influence. When controversy enveloped Senate Majority Leader Trent Lott in 2002—the Mississippian was accused of racial insensitivity when, at a century-mark birthday celebration for Senator Strom Thurmond of South Carolina, he made laudatory remarks about the former Dixiecrat's early career—Allen

---

7. McLaughlin interview.

and fellow Virginian John Warner took the decisive first steps to nudge Lott out as Senate leader and replace him with Tennessean William ("Bill") Frist.[8] Allen joined the Senate leadership team in 2003, succeeding Frist as chairman of the National Republican Senatorial Committee. In that role during the pivotal 2004 elections, the junior senator from Virginia saw his political stock rise sharply after his electoral efforts helped produce a 55-seat GOP majority in the 100-member Senate and contributed to the surprising ouster of the body's combative Democratic leader, Thomas A. Daschle of South Dakota. With his Senate term set to expire in 2006, Allen girded for a possible reelection battle against popular Democratic Governor Warner. But Warner signaled in 2005 that he had set his sights instead on the presidency, averting, at least for a time, a showdown between the two political powerhouses.

The White House, meanwhile, was occupied by George W. Bush, eldest son of the 41st president, and the nation was preoccupied with a war against the Al Qaeda terrorist organization and its shadowy allies. Bush's victory in the February 2000 Virginia primary helped him secure the GOP nomination despite Arizonan John McCain's vigorous challenge.[9] The Texas governor and his seasoned running mate, former defense secretary Richard B. Cheney, then went on to a razor-thin, "overtime" win in the hard-fought general election contest against the Democratic ticket of Vice President Gore and Senator Joseph Lieberman of Connecticut.[10] For the ninth consecutive time, Virginia dutifully gave its electoral votes—in 2000, they were all precious—to the national Republican slate.[11] Less than a year

---

8. According to the *Washington Post*, Allen was the first senator to call Lott directly and urge him to resign as the negative publicity from the Mississippian's statements mounted. Allen and Warner both played key early roles in recruiting Frist as a candidate for the majority leader post and were among several Southern Republicans who worked behind the scenes to arrange Lott's ouster and Frist's elevation, outflanking other potential contenders for the position. *Washington Post*, December 22, 2002; John Warner interview.

9. The vote totals in the Virginia primary were: Bush—350,588 (52.8 percent); McCain—291,488 (43.9 percent); Alan L. Keyes—20,356 (3.1 percent). Sabato, *Virginia Votes 1999–2003*, p. 22.

10. The Democratic ticket garnered more popular votes nationwide, but Bush and Cheney gained an Electoral College edge by narrowly carrying Florida, a result that was confirmed only after an extended period of recounts and state and federal litigation. Among the many accounts of the historically close and controversial 2000 presidential election, see Larry J. Sabato, *Overtime! The Election 2000 Thriller* (New York: Longman, 2002).

11. The Virginia vote totals were: Bush (R)—1,437,490 (52.5 percent); Gore (D)—1,217,290 (44.4 percent); Ralph Nader (Green)—59,398 (2.2 percent). Sabato, *Virginia Votes 1999–2003*, p. 41. Ironically, Gore would have been elected president if Virginia's electoral votes had been apportioned on the basis of the popular vote results in the state

in office, Bush and his presidency were transformed by the terrorist attacks on the World Trade Center in New York and the related tragedies at the Pentagon and in Pennsylvania. After deploying American forces successively to oust the Taliban regime and Al Qaeda leadership from Afghanistan and to topple the Baathist government of Saddam Hussein in Iraq, Bush pressed for democratic reforms in the Middle East and elsewhere in a bid simultaneously to advance American democratic ideals and remedy conditions contributing to terrorism. But the controversial decision to extend the war effort to Iraq bedeviled the Bush administration after a key rationale for the conflict—fears that the malevolent regime possessed weapons of mass destruction—proved unfounded and terrorists waged an extended and bloody campaign to thwart the introduction of democratic institutions in the country. Virginia's Senator John Warner served as chairman of the Senate Armed Services Committee during much of the Bush presidency and persistently supported the president's defense and foreign policy initiatives.[12]

Republicans regained a majority in the congressional delegation from Virginia in 2000 and quickly fortified it through redistricting, incumbency, and a party switch. In addition to Allen's capture of the Senate seat, GOP candidates for the House of Representatives in 2000 swept the open-seat races to succeed retiring congressmen Herbert H. Bateman, Owen B. Pickett, and Thomas J. Bliley Jr.[13] Fifth District Representative Virgil Goode, who broke with fellow Democrats in voting to impeach President Clinton

---

or, as in Maine and Nebraska, according to congressional district victories. Legislation to provide for the latter method of apportionment was introduced in Virginia in the early 1990s, when Democrats still possessed majorities in both legislative houses and Democrat Douglas Wilder was governor. The measure passed easily in the House of Delegates but died in the state Senate. See Grayson, "Virginia Senator Hunter B. Andrews's Impact on the Nation," pp. 333–334.

12. John Warner was not the only Virginian to play a notable role during the younger Bush's presidential administration. Richmonder John Snow, chief executive of railroad giant CSX Corporation, became secretary of the treasury in February 2003 and was reappointed to the post after Bush won a second term in 2004. Governor James Gilmore served a yearlong stint as chairman of the Republican National Committee; former lieutenant governor John Hager was appointed to an education department post; and numerous other senior officials from the Allen and Gilmore state administrations were tapped for Bush administration positions.

13. Republicans Bliley and Bateman (who died in 2000 after announcing his retirement) were succeeded by Delegates Eric Cantor of Henrico and Jo Ann Davis of Yorktown, respectively. Congressman Pickett, a Democrat, was succeeded by GOP state senator Edward Schrock of Virginia Beach, who overcame Democratic attorney Jody M. Wagner, also of Virginia Beach, in a spirited contest. Wagner went on to become state treasurer under Governor Mark Warner and secretary of finance under Warner's successor, Timothy Kaine. Schrock served in Congress until 2004, when he was succeeded by Delegate Thelma Drake, a Norfolk Republican.

in 1998, sought reelection as an Independent in 2000, caucused with House Republicans for two years, and then formally joined the GOP in 2002.[14] And former Republican state chairman J. Randy Forbes won a special election to succeed long-serving Fourth District Democrat Norman Sisisky, who died in 2001. The result was an eight-seat GOP majority in the eleven-member delegation, an advantage that was cemented with the Republican-controlled reapportionment process in 2001–2002. Longevity, political acumen, and good fortune then combined to make the Virginia delegation one of the most influential in Congress. In addition to the prominent legislative and political roles played by Senators Warner and Allen, Representative Frank Wolf served as a powerful Appropriations subcommittee chairman; Congressman Robert W. Goodlatte chaired the important Agriculture Committee; the Seventh District's Eric Cantor joined the House leadership as chief deputy majority whip;[15] and Representative Thomas M. Davis, III, led the National Republican Congressional Committee before becoming chairman of the Committee on Government Reform. These and other key positions held by members of Congress from Virginia gave the Commonwealth its most powerful congressional delegation at least since the days of Harry F. Byrd Sr.[16]

All of this contributed to a perception that the Republican Party was dominant in Virginia, and indeed the GOP had registered major gains as the decades-old partisan realignment in the state reached fruition. But the seeming dominance was mostly an illusion. Since the state's rapid realignment of the late 1960s and early 1970s, the occasional swings of party fortune and resulting perception of dominance—whether by the Republicans in the 1970s and 1990s or by the Democrats in the 1980s—had been more apparent than real. Elections in realigned Virginia continued to be decided by the independent swing voters who held the political balance. And it was there that Mark Warner went looking for votes in a bid to overcome his party label and capture the governorship in 2001.

With a keen political instinct, appealing personality, and moderate

---

14. Though many played a part over time in his recruitment to the GOP, Goode credited Eleventh District Congressman Thomas M. Davis III and Fifth District Republican chairman Tucker Watkins with the pivotal roles in his conversion. Watkins' Fifth District Democratic counterpart, Carl Eggleston Jr., also provided impetus for the switch by leading the criticism of Goode in the wake of his vote to impeach President Clinton. Goode interview.

15. See Susan J. Crabtree, "The Chosen Republican: Richmond's Eric Cantor Joins the House GOP Leadership," *Weekly Standard,* January 27, 2003. Cantor became chief deputy majority whip, the fourth-ranking leadership post, in 2002.

16. For a description of the congressional elections in Virginia after 2000, see Sabato, *Virginia Votes 1999–2003*, pp. 27–31, 56–59, 167–176.

manner, unfettered by a nettlesome voting record (since he had never held public office), and aided by a bank account as deep as his long arms were ready and able to reach, the lanky and frenetic Mark Warner brought huge assets to the race for governor. His preparations were extensive and were not limited to amassing personal wealth through the timely capture of cellular telephone franchises and other high-tech ventures. Politically, he had earned his spurs as campaign captain for Douglas Wilder in 1989, as Democratic state party chairman in the early 1990s, and in a variety of other roles. He had run a hard-hitting Senate campaign against John Warner in 1996 that gave few clues he later would present himself convincingly to moderate-conservative Virginians as a new kind of Democrat. But Mark Warner's strong showing against the Republican incumbent in 1996 impressed his fellow partisans and political observers alike. That performance, along with the financial lifeline he was able to throw his sinking party, assured his nomination for governor in 2001.

Warner knew, however, that getting nominated was the easy part and that winning a statewide general election as a Democrat in GOP-leaning Virginia would be infinitely more difficult. He had been paying close attention as Republicans captured suburban support in the 1990s with promises and results on educational accountability, crime-fighting, welfare reform, tax relief, and other popular measures. He had paid attention, too, as his own party's hapless nominees had tried unsuccessfully to pry away those same suburban voters with social issue appeals—notably on gun control and abortion—and strident attacks on the GOP's ties to religious conservatives. By the time he readied his own gubernatorial bid, it was apparent to Mark Warner that the main effect of those attacks had not been to bring the suburbs into the Democratic column but to drive culturally conservative voters en masse to the GOP candidates. The result had been such lopsided Republican margins in conservative rural areas that a Democrat had to win by nearly a landslide in suburbia—an exceedingly difficult task in the competitive Commonwealth—to have a chance of assembling a statewide majority.

Warner's response was a canny strategy that punctured the social liberal stereotype of non-rural Democratic politicians and emphasized his efforts over time to bring the promise of the knowledge-based economy to rural communities. As chairman of a healthcare foundation and in his own business ventures, he had made a concerted effort to build relationships in the rural Southside and in Southwest Virginia.[17] Now those efforts bore fruit, as Warner the candidate went aggressively after rural support, combining a down-home pitch with a centrist stance on values-laden social issues that, if

---

17. Mark Warner interview.

not calculated to endear, at least would not antagonize.[18] Once nominated, he used his Democratic running mates effectively as foils, publicly distancing himself from their more liberal stands on the death penalty, gun control, and same-sex civil unions.[19] Meanwhile, in the swing-voting suburbs, he presented himself as the urbane apostle of the new economy and a proven businessman able to restore steady stewardship to the state's increasingly shaky fiscal affairs.

There were few galvanizing issues in the 2001 campaign because Warner endeavored to minimize the perceived differences with Republicans, except on the timely question of which candidate could provide the more sound fiscal management to the state. On each and every popular issue that the GOP had ridden to success in the 1990s—chief among them, parole abolition, education standards, welfare reform, and car tax relief—Warner pledged his fidelity. If there was a weakness in this centrist Democratic campaign plan, it was the absence of any big idea or distinctly appealing innovation that would provide a strong affirmative case for what a Warner governorship would accomplish for the people of Virginia. The Democrat's huge financial advantage might have been enough to save his bid from this otherwise problematic omission.[20] But that would never be known, because self-inflicted wounds on the Republican side kept the contest from being close.

The GOP's problems were manifold, but three missteps loomed especially large in retrospect, as indeed they appeared to many knowledgeable observers at the time. First, the two beneficiaries of the Gilmore-led sweep in 1997—Lieutenant Governor John Hager and Attorney General Mark Earley—waged a nonstop, four-year struggle for the gubernatorial nomination that sapped the energy, attention, and resources of both and precluded either from being effectively positioned as the GOP heir-apparent. As such intraparty battles go, the Earley-Hager contest was not unduly acrimonious. But it did continue long after the outcome (Earley's nomination) was inevitable, and it siphoned off campaign dollars that were indispensable against the well-heeled Warner. Despite repeated urgings from Governor Gilmore

---

18. Democratic rural strategist David ("Mudcat") Saunders and Warner campaign manager Steve Jarding received much of the credit for the innovative rural strategy and later championed the courting of rural "NASCAR dads" in advising various Democratic candidates across the country. See William Schneider, "How to Woo NASCAR Fans," *National Journal*, December 13, 2003.

19. *Roanoke Times*, June 22, 2001; Sabato, *Virginia Votes 1999–2003*, pp. 117–118.

20. Warner outspent Earley by roughly a two-to-one margin. When spending by the candidates' various campaign committees was aggregated, Warner's committees spent $22.5 million compared to $11.5 million invested in the Earley effort. Sabato, *Virginia Votes 1999–2003*, p. 114.

and other GOP leaders, both contenders missed multiple opportunities to join forces on the Republican ticket and thereby unify the party's discordant factions. An apparent consequence of the Earley-led GOP's failure to find room on its ticket for Hager was the defection to Warner in the fall by numerous wealthy Richmond-area business leaders who were close to Hager. Never enthusiastic about Earley's social conservatism, the Republican-leaning business leaders' contributions fueled the campaign efforts of a "Virginians for Warner" group—a throwback to the similarly named independent support groups that had been common in Virginia politics two decades earlier.[21] A key political figure from that earlier era, former GOP national committeewoman Judy Peachee Ford, organized the Virginians for Warner campaign effort, which provided a patina of bipartisan support that Warner would continue to cultivate assiduously as governor.

A second factor aiding the Democrats in 2001 was the ugly GOP civil war on the budget. The bitter election-year battle that pitted Senator Chichester and his moderate followers against Governor Gilmore, House Speaker Wilkins, and their conservative allies provided essential campaign fodder for Warner. He hardly needed a big idea or bold initiative when his case for a leadership change could rest soundly upon his business credentials and his pledge to end the political squabbling and produce a budget. Faced with this problem not of his making, Republican Earley seemed perpetually unsure how to handle it. He could have embraced the strong tax cut position of incumbent Gilmore, whose popularity among voters remained reasonably high,[22] and defined the budget controversy in polarizing pro-tax versus anti-tax terms. Or he could have distanced himself from Gilmore and embraced the stance of his former colleagues in the Senate, whose resistance to additional car tax relief increasingly seemed justified as the downturn in the economy deepened during the election year. But Earley needed the governor's financial help—funding from the Gilmore-chaired Republican National Committee was indispensable—even as he heard continually from normally Republican business leaders who viewed the incumbent's fiscal policies with mounting disdain. As a result, the GOP standard-bearer

---

21. For a description of "Virginians for . . ." organizations in state campaigns during the 1970s and 1980s, see chapter 2; see also *The Dynamic Dominion*, Chapters 23, 25, 27, 30, and 33.

22. A survey conducted for the *Richmond Times-Dispatch* just before the November election gave Gilmore a 61 percent approval rating at a time when Warner enjoyed a double-digit lead over Earley in the gubernatorial race. *Richmond Times-Dispatch*, November 4, 2001. A Republican-sponsored post-election poll suggested that a race between Warner and Gilmore would have ended in a statistical dead heat, with Warner holding a 47-to-45 percent advantage. Sabato, *Virginia Votes 1999–2003*, p. 133.

wavered somewhere between the two polar positions in his party and failed to offer any consistent response to his Democratic foe's central message: that Republicans had brought disorder to the Commonwealth's fiscal house and only businessman Warner could set it right.

Finally, although Warner failed to offer a compelling vision of reform or improvement as the rationale for his candidacy, that shortcoming was at least matched by the GOP campaign. After nearly a decade of popular innovating, the Republican reform cupboard fell bare in 2001. In the contest of the two "Marks," Earley had the superior advocacy skills, and his personal story—a journey that took him to the Phillipines as a young missionary—rivaled Warner's rags-to-riches tale for inspirational quality. But at no point in the contest did the versatile Chesapeake Republican offer voters any concrete idea of what he hoped to achieve as their governor. The failure was the more remarkable because of Earley's unconventional political appeal in past contests. Four years earlier, Mark J. Rozell, a political scientist and frequent commentator on the religious conservative movement, had noted the unusual range of his support. "Earley could be the model candidate for the future success of the Christian right," wrote Rozell. "He's an elected official with serious public credentials and with crossover appeal to African Americans and labor unionists, as well as to white evangelical social conservatives."[23] Ironically, in addition to failing to project an issue-oriented appeal to swing voters in the state's pivotal suburbs, the Earley campaign had persistent difficulty rallying its social conservative base, in part because of Democrat Warner's centrist stance and de-emphasis of hot-button social issues.

After a brief suspension of the gubernatorial campaign as shell-shocked Virginians came to grips with the events of September 11, Warner seemingly glided to victory—though the final margin showed the contest had been closer than most observers believed and than most preelection surveys indicated.[24] The state's Republican lean was generally cited by analysts as the reason for the unexpected closeness, but post-September 11th anxiety at the prospect of a chief executive without past governmental experience also played a part. The biggest reason for the strong close by the GOP, how-

---

23. *Washington Post*, October 21, 1997.

24. The vote totals were: Warner (D)—984,177 (52.2 percent); Earley (R)—887,234 (47.0 percent). Sabato, *Virginia Votes 1999–2003*, p. 126. One consequence of the September 11th terrorist attacks was that President Bush, suddenly cast in the role of wartime leader, decided it would be unseemly to campaign in the 2001 elections. His refusal to come to Virginia, which may also have been influenced by opinion polls suggesting Earley was headed for likely defeat, had a major negative impact on the Republican campaign effort. Sabato, *Virginia Votes 1999–2003*, pp. 120–121.

ever, was the tax issue. After Warner offered a transportation plan premised on millions in new tax revenue (subject to voter approval by referendum), Republicans in the campaign's closing weeks mounted a familiar-sounding electronic assault on the Democrat's alleged tax-raising designs. Warner responded firmly—"You've heard a lot of false charges from my opponent in this year's governor's race. Let me set the record straight: I will not raise taxes."[25]—and then used his huge financial advantage to bury Earley in an avalanche of television ads in which the reassuring Democrat repeated his emphatic denial.[26]

The Democrat's gubernatorial victory a year after George W. Bush reclaimed the White House for Republicans continued a pattern—the party that loses the White House wins the Virginia governorship the next year—that had been repeated without interruption since the mid-1970s. Pundits and politicians debated whether the phenomenon reflected some profound underlying truth about the split-ticket tendencies of Virginia voters, or was a matter of happenstance, or perhaps contained elements of both. Some students of Virginia politics, such as Congressman Thomas M. Davis III, suggested that Virginia's gubernatorial elections in the state's competitive era had been behaving like midterm congressional elections, when the party in the White House traditionally loses seats in Congress.[27] But even that plausible theory had its limits when applied to the 2001 Virginia contest, since Republicans gained seats under Bush in the next year's midterm congressional elections. The best explanation for Warner's win in 2001 seemed to be, not some invisible hand of national politics, but the Democratic candi-

---

25. See Tyler Whitley and Jeff E. Schapiro, "Warner: 'I Will Not Raise Taxes'; Final Debate Slated Tonight in Roanoke," *Richmond Times-Dispatch*, October 10, 2001; R.H. Melton, "Virginia Tax Referendum Tops Issues on Eve of Final Candidate Debate," *Washington Post*, October 10, 2001; Bob Lewis, "Candidates Resume Jousting over Taxes," *Associated Press*, October 10, 2001.

26. Also important to Warner's win was an expansive get-out-the-vote effort made possible in part by the Democratic National Committee's million-dollar-plus financial support. See Paul Bradley, "Winning Campaign a Mixture of High-Tech, Knocking on Doors," *Richmond Times-Dispatch*, November 7, 2001. Mike Henry, who directed the Democrats' voter turnout program in 2001, went on to serve as director of Timothy Kaine's successful campaign to succeed Warner as governor four years later.

27. Four years later, on the verge of a second consecutive gubernatorial victory by Virginia Democrats during the George W. Bush administration, Davis told political commentator Fred Barnes that "Virginia governor's races are in a sense a mid-term election. People give their verdict on the president." Fred Barnes, "Virginia Governor's Race is a Test of the President's Popularity," *The Weekly Standard*, October 24, 2005. Political analysts Larry Sabato and Charlie Cook offered similar interpretations. See Robert Barnes, "On Virginia's Gubernatorial Race, National Politics Gains a Role," *Washington Post*, October 19, 2005; Charlie Cook, "Virginia Likes to Send the President a Message," *Cook Report*, October 8, 2005.

date's own effective positioning and lavish campaign spending, aided by voter annoyance at the squabbling Virginia Republicans.

Elected with Warner was his running mate for lieutenant governor, Richmond Mayor Timothy M. Kaine. The son-in-law of Linwood Holton, the state's first GOP governor since Reconstruction, Kaine was the latest in a line of Virginia candidates with intergenerational political connections, joining the ranks of such prominent Virginia political families as the Byrds, Battles, Daltons, and Millers.[28] But Kaine came to statewide politics somewhat serendipitously, gaining the nod for lieutenant governor in a three-way Democratic primary after the expected nominee, popular state Senator Emily W. Couric of Charlottesville, became gravely ill with cancer in 2000 and had to forgo the race.[29] In the general election contest, Kaine faced conservative Delegate Jay Katzen, a little-known legislator from Fauquier County who also had gained his party's nod after withdrawal of the favored candidate. Former GOP chief J. Randy Forbes had been the strong front-runner for the Republican nomination for lieutenant governor but withdrew from the race to seek the Fourth District congressional seat upon the death of Congressman Norman Sisisky in March 2001. As the only other candidate in the field, Katzen inherited the GOP nomination by default and then lost narrowly to Kaine in November.[30]

---

28. United States Senator Harry F. Byrd Jr. was the son of governor and United States Senator Harry F. Byrd, from whom the state's Democratic "Byrd" organization drew its unofficial name. Former Ambassador William C. Battle, the 1969 Democratic nominee for governor, was the son of Governor John S. Battle. Governor John N. Dalton was the son of state Senator and former two-time Republican gubernatorial nominee Ted Dalton; the younger Dalton's widow, state senator Edwina ("Eddy") Dalton, was the GOP nominee for lieutenant governor in 1989. Two-term state Attorney General Andrew P. Miller, a Democrat who sought the governorship in 1977 and a seat in the United States Senate a year later, was the son of gubernatorial candidate and Byrd organization foe Francis Pickens Miller. See *The Dynamic Dominion*, Chapters 1, 4, 7, 15–17, 20, 30. Although Virginia's dynastic tendencies appear to have subsided in more recent decades, the most notable example of offspring (or in-laws) of famous politicians making it big in state politics remains Governor and United States senator Charles Robb, son-in-law of President Lyndon B. Johnson. See chapter 1.

29. In retrospect, it appears likely that the intervention of Couric's illness prevented her from becoming Virginia's first female governor. A gifted politician who enjoyed a measure of star quality—her sister, Katie, was the well-known cohost of the popular *Today* morning show for the NBC television network—Couric evidently would have been even better positioned to succeed popular outgoing Governor Mark Warner in 2006 than his actual successor, Timothy Kaine. For a reflection on Couric's potential by a senior legislative colleague, Senate minority leader Richard Saslaw of Fairfax County, see Dick Saslaw, "Memory of a Dear Friend, Emily Couric," in *Notes from the Sausage Factory*, eds. Day and Dale, pp. 132–134.

30. The vote totals in the general election for lieutenant governor were: Kaine (D)—925,974 (50.3 percent); Katzen (R)—883,886 (48.1 percent). Sabato, *Virginia Votes 1999-2003*, p. 126.

In the contest for attorney general, Jerry W. Kilgore, the former Allen public safety secretary from Scott County in far Southwest Virginia, defied history by becoming the first Virginia Republican ever to win a down-ballot contest while a Democrat was capturing the governorship. Kilgore's winning margin—more than 20 percentage points over trial attorney Donald A. McEachin, an African-American delegate from the Richmond area—was the most decisive of any of the statewide winners.[31] With Kilgore's lopsided victory (he received 122,000 more votes than gubernatorial winner Mark Warner) and the startlingly strong showing by GOP candidates for the House of Delegates, who captured 64 of the chamber's 100 seats, it was tempting to dismiss the Republican-sounding Warner's stand-out win as an aberration. But the reality was that Virginia remained a two-party competitive state, and Warner had recharted the path to power for a Democratic Party that had lost its way in the 1990s. Exiting the governorship in 2006 with Democrat Kaine as his successor, Warner could credibly claim to have found a formula for Democratic competitiveness even in states that routinely had given their electoral votes to GOP presidential contenders.

The Couric tragedy delayed for an undetermined time the next test of Virginians' readiness to elect a female candidate to statewide office.[32] And the weak showing by a third African-American statewide nominee—McEachin's bid for attorney general had been preceded by Republican Maurice Dawkins's long-shot Senate candidacy in 1988 and Democrat Douglas Wilder's gubernatorial breakthrough in 1989—caused some to suggest anew that race remained a formidable barrier in Virginia politics. But another indication of the state's eagerness to sweep away such barriers came in February 2003, when the associate justices of the Supreme Court of Virginia elected Leroy Hassell of Norfolk as the first African American to serve as the state's chief justice.[33] One of the youngest to serve in that post,

---

31. The vote totals in the general election for attorney general were: Kilgore (R)—1,107,068 (60.0 percent); McEachin (D)—736,431 (39.9 percent). Sabato, *Virginia Votes 1999-2003,* p. 126. McEachin had gained his party's nomination after Southside Delegate Whittington W. Clement and Roanoke state Senator John S. Edwards split the moderate vote in the Democratic primary. After Warner's election, Clement joined his cabinet as state transportation secretary.

32. Virginia Republicans also lost one of their foremost female leaders to tragedy when the party's new national committeewoman, Jennifer Curtis Byler, and her young daughter Sarah died in a 2001 boating accident in the Chesapeake Bay. In Byler's memory, new GOP chairman Kate Obenshain Griffin in 2004 established the Jennifer Byler Institute, a training program for female Republican leaders, activists, and candidates. Griffin's father, Richard D. Obenshain, had preceded her in the state GOP chairmanship by two decades. See *The Dynamic Dominion,* Chapter 23.

33. Hassell, only the second African American to serve on the state's Supreme Court, had been appointed to that post by Governor Gerald Baliles in 1989, and had been elected to another term by the Republican-controlled General Assembly in 2001.

the Harvard-educated Hassell succeeded Harry Carrico, an indefatigable and widely revered jurist from Fairfax who served in the state's top judicial position longer than any of his predecessors.

Meanwhile, the intrepid former Governor Wilder, who years earlier had declared the end of his elective career, came roaring back. The seventy-one-year-old Richmonder turned his sights on the capital's problem-plagued and scandal-ridden city government, teaming with former Richmond mayor and congressman Thomas J. Bliley Jr., to press for significant structural changes. The bipartisan duo mounted a successful grassroots campaign in 2002–2003 to change the city charter so that, among other reforms, the mayor would be chosen by direct citywide election.[34] When others he deemed suitable did not seek the post, Wilder then became a mayoral candidate himself, and he proceeded to poll 80 percent of the vote in ousting incumbent Mayor Rudolph C. McCollum Jr. in the November 2004 contest.[35] In the fourth decade of a history-making career, Wilder found himself making common cause with Republicans almost as often as Democrats in his new role.[36] It was apparent he had no intention of going quietly into the history books anytime soon.

Except for the Indian summer of the Wilder career, the elections of 2002–2004 produced few surprises in Virginia. The president's party actually gained seats in both houses of Congress in the 2002 midterm contests, and Congressman Virgil Goode's long-anticipated formal conversion to the GOP that year added a symbolic exclamation point to rural Virginia's partisan realignment.[37] Reelected to a fifth term without Democratic opposition, seventy-five-year-old Senator John Warner saw his chairmanship of the Armed Services Committee re-secured and his place assured as the second longest-serving United States senator from Virginia.[38] With the sudden

---

34. Bliley, Wilder interviews; *Richmond Times-Dispatch*, July 26, 2002. Wilder's longtime aide, Paul Goldman, spearheaded the effort to gather the petition signatures necessary to put the charter change measure on the ballot in Richmond.

35. *Richmond Times-Dispatch*, November 4, 2004.

36. Addressing an assemblage of conservative House of Delegates Republicans in June 2004 after vocally opposing a statewide sales tax increase, Wilder was greeted with an enthusiastic ovation and jocular chants of "Four more years!" *Daily Press*, August 15, 2004.

37. See *Midterm Madness: The Elections of 2002*, ed. Larry J. Sabato (Lanham, MD: Rowman & Littlefield Publishers, Inc., 2003).

38. Warner became chairman of the Senate Armed Services Committee in January 1999, but he surrendered the post in May 2001 after Vermont's liberal Republican senator, James Jeffords, became an Independent and caucused with Senate Democrats, giving them control of the Senate. Warner returned to the committee chairmanship after Republicans regained the Senate majority in the 2002 elections. The longevity milestone for the state's senior senator came in April 2005, when he passed United States Senator Carter Glass of Lynchburg in length of Senate service (Glass was senator from 1920 to

departure of Vance Wilkins from the House of Delegates in 2002, the affable and conciliatory William J. Howell, a fifteen-year delegate from Stafford County, became the consensus choice of his colleagues to assume the speaker's post.[39] The sweeping Republican legislative gains of 2001 receded slightly during the ensuing years, leaving Howell and his fellow partisans with a still-comfortable, 57-seat GOP majority in the House of Delegates, while Republicans in the state Senate enjoyed a 23-to-17 advantage.

With Howell's elevation to the House speakership and John Chichester's continuing tenure as president pro tempore of the state Senate, both legislative houses were led by members of the same party from the same county. Despite that unusual circumstance, the two Stafford County Republicans seemed to represent distinct faces of the Virginia Republican Party as it entered a new century. Chichester, a Byrd Democrat turned Republican, embodied the moderate-conservative Godwin-Dalton-Warner GOP tradition long aligned with the state's largest business interests. Howell, a lifelong suburban Republican, reflected the grassroots economic and social conservatism of the Reagan era, championed in Virginia by GOP leaders Obenshain, Allen, and Gilmore. The two also had divergent priorities and found different allies among Democrats. Howell, who stressed tax restraint and greater governmental *reform,* found himself most often in accord with former governor Wilder, an ardent tax foe. Chichester, who stressed debt restraint and greater public *investment,* frequently aligned himself with Governor Warner and his pre-Wilder Democratic predecessors. Howell's viewpoint was shared by a greater number of majority-party lawmakers, but the relative seniority of Chichester's allies and the frequent support for his position among Democratic legislators leveled the playing field. Despite their sometimes-differing outlooks, the two Republican leaders found common ground on some issues, and their personal relationship helped to temper the strife that continually threatened to engulf the contending GOP factions in the legislature.[40]

1946). Among Virginians, only Senator Harry F. Byrd Sr., who served from 1933 to 1965, held the office longer than Warner.

39. Howell followed Independent Delegate Lacey Putney, the 40-year legislative veteran, who succeeded to the speakership of the House of Delegates upon Wilkins's resignation and held the post until the House of Delegates next convened and elected Howell in January 2003. Putney, who continued to caucus with the majority Republicans after first doing so in 1998, could have completed Wilkins's two-year term as speaker. Instead, he stepped aside in deference to the wishes of GOP delegates who deemed it important to have a lawmaker elected as a Republican in the leadership post. Putney interview.

40. William J. Howell interview, April 26, 2005; Chichester interview; Jo Becker and Chris L. Jenkins, "Split on Taxes Begins at Top of Virginia GOP: Stafford Legislators Guide Rival Camps," *Washington Post,* February 9, 2004.

If the dawn of the new millennium brought times of trial nationally and internationally, the economic shocks at the national level ensured Virginia would experience taxing times as well. Indeed, the issue of taxes—whether and how much to cut them in times of robust state economic and revenue growth, and whether and how much to raise them during economic downturns and revenue shortfalls—became the dominant topic in state politics, dividing the GOP majority in the legislature and roiling the state's political elite.

For all its fury, tax-related controversy actually had arrived comparatively late in the Old Dominion. Many state capitals were scenes of raging tax debates beginning in the early 1990s, when state levies were raised across the country to cope with the effects of a national recession. Led by Democratic Governor Wilder, Virginia defied that tax hike trend and instead balanced the recession-battered state budget in the early 1990s primarily through a combination of spending cuts and college tuition increases. Within a few years, economic growth in Virginia was again eclipsing the nation's, prompting state spending levels to increase sharply in absolute terms and to rebound strongly in comparison to other states. After Republican Governor Gilmore was elected in 1997 largely on the strength of his promise to cut the unpopular local car tax and use the state's growing coffers to reimburse localities for the lost revenue, power-sharing lawmakers in both parties and both houses dutifully agreed on a billion-dollar-plus plan to phase out the tax as state revenues grew. The measure served to pay a dividend to taxpaying citizens and to restrain the level of government spending growth as the economy boomed.

In 2000–2001, however, the economy began to slow nationally and in Virginia. In the state Senate, senior members of both parties doubted the sustainability of revenue growth and balked at Gilmore's effort to implement the next scheduled phase of previously enacted car tax relief. But the governor, supported by the new GOP majority in the House of Delegates, feared the phase-out would never be completed if allowed to stall. Gilmore and his House backers prevailed in the sense that the tax cut program preceded to the next phase and taxpayers gained increased relief. But the clash also produced an unprecedented legislative impasse that prevented passage of annual budget legislation in 2001. Democrat Mark Warner then reaped the harvest of popular dissatisfaction with the bickering Republicans and gained the governorship.

Warner's winning campaign stressed his credentials as a businessman and his commitment to taming the budget strife without raising taxes. He applauded former Governor Wilder's no-tax-hike stewardship during the recession of the early 1990s and made a number of specific promises. He would not, Warner repeatedly insisted, propose any increase in taxes. He would not allow any tax hikes except those first approved by voters in a referendum. He would complete the phase-out of the unpopular car tax. And he would prevent any repeat of the unseemly state budget deadlock that occurred early in the 2001 election year. "I will not raise taxes," Warner declared in response to his GOP critics. "As a fiscal conservative . . , I've simply said let's trust the people. . . . Not all the wisdom resides with the politicians in Richmond."[41]

When the September 11, 2001, terrorist attacks and ensuing wartime uncertainties produced a longer and deeper recession than anyone had envisioned, Warner and the GOP-controlled legislature were forced to confront an eventual $6 billion biennial budget shortfall. In Washington, President Bush persuaded Congress to enact successive tax-cutting plans, financed in part through federal deficits, in an effort to stimulate an economic turnaround. But in Virginia, where a balanced budget was legally required, Warner and lawmakers first enacted a series of deep spending cuts to close the gap. Then, in 2004, the Democratic governor joined with GOP Senator Chichester and a bipartisan Senate majority to pass a $1.4 billion tax increase package. The measure ultimately was adopted—nearly two months after the legislature's scheduled adjournment—when 17 Republicans in the House of Delegates broke with their party's anti-tax leadership and joined Democrats in approving the measure.[42]

Neither the governor nor most legislators in either party had acknowledged any tax hike plans during the 2003 legislative election contests, and the measures adopted by the General Assembly and signed by the governor

---

41. R. H. Melton, "Virginia Tax Referendum Tops Issues on Eve of Final Candidate Debate," *Washington Post*, October 10, 2001 (quoting Warner statement in television ad). During his first year in office, Warner campaigned in support of sales tax increases for transportation in regional referenda held in Northern Virginia and Hampton Roads. Though voters in both regions decisively rejected the tax hike proposals, statewide voters overwhelmingly endorsed Warner-backed bond issues for state colleges and parks in the November 2002 balloting. See Quentin Kidd, "The Failed Transportation Tax: A Simple Message from Voters?" *The Virginia News Letter* (Charlottesville: Weldon Cooper Center for Public Service, University of Virginia), January 2003; Sabato, *Virginia Votes 1999–2003*, pp. 176–179, 181–184.

42. Two Republican moderates, Senator Thomas K. Norment Jr. of James City County and Delegate L. Preston Bryant of Lynchburg, played instrumental roles in forging the final budget compromise, which raised taxes less than the Senate GOP leadership preferred but more than was acceptable to the Republican leaders in the House of Delegates. In the aftermath of the controversy, House of Delegates Speaker William J. Howell declined to reappoint Bryant to the influential House Appropriations Committee; a year later, Bryant left the House of Delegates to accept appointment as secretary of natural resources in the administration of Democratic Governor Timothy Kaine.

in the spring of 2004 contradicted each of the four campaign pledges Warner had made in gaining the office three years earlier. Warner did not refrain from proposing higher taxes as promised; to the contrary, he recommended one of the largest increases ever in the state's history. He did not hew to his "trust the people" mantra by putting his tax hike proposals to a referendum; instead, when Senator George Allen and former Governor Douglas Wilder came to the State Capitol during the 2004 legislative session to decry the broken promises on taxes and urge a popular vote before imposition of new levies, Warner derisively threatened a veto if a referendum requirement were added to the measure. Although he proposed completion of the car tax phase-out as part of his tax package, Warner did not insist on it; rather, he backed Senate-sponsored legislation in 2004 permanently capping car tax relief, and he persisted in supporting that cap even after state revenues rebounded sharply later in the year.[43] And, as for his often-repeated pledge to avoid another unseemly budget deadlock like the one that propelled him to the state's top office, the governor not only did not avoid one; he virtually assured one, by weaving the new tax dollars throughout his biennial budget blueprint and promising to veto the entire appropriations act if his proposed revenue increases were not included in the measure ultimately enacted by the legislature.

For a governor who had been faulted for a lack of executive leadership during his first two years in office, the tax initiative was strikingly bold. The full political effects of the governor's strong action on the budget would not be fully apparent until his own next bid for public office, but there was no indication in the aftermath of the 2004 legislative battle that the chief executive's strong standing with Virginia voters had been diminished at all by the fight. To the contrary, even after it became apparent that Warner and his financial advisers had significantly underestimated the size and swiftness of the state's economic rebound—a billion-dollar-plus surplus materialized less than a year after the tax hikes were enacted and the unanticipated revenues continued to mushroom thereafter[44]—the governor continued to

---

43. Warner's original tax proposal included completion of the car tax phase-out. With proposed increases in the sales and income tax levies, the effect of the Warner-introduced tax package was a net tax increase of approximately $1 billion in the state's biennial budget.

44. News of the emerging surplus surfaced almost as soon as lawmakers concluded their prolonged work on the budget and tax legislation in late spring 2004. When the General Assembly reconvened in mid-June for the constitutionally mandated follow-up session to consider gubernatorial vetoes and amendments, a surplus of several hundred million dollars had already appeared. "I hate to be the one who said [I] told you so," said GOP Delegate David B. Albo of Fairfax, a tax hike foe. "But, I told you so. . . . If we had stayed a few extra days, we would have found that there was $300 million out there that we just didn't know about." Tax hike proponents countered that the new

enjoy sky-high public approval ratings in published polls.[45] Virginians seemed to understand that Warner had inherited a sick economy and state budget, and they applauded him for braving political perils to deal with it, even if the remedy—budget cuts and tax hikes—was bitter medicine. The governor celebrated the anniversary of his tax initiative in a well-received "State of the Commonwealth" address in January 2005 that complimented legislators of both parties and lavished particular praise on those who had stood with him in the long-running budget battle:

> We've shown that here in Virginia, Democrats and Republicans can come together, put politics aside, and make tough decisions when times demand it. We began where the need was greatest, with the budget. Together, we made the tough choices necessary to balance the budget. We cut spending. We cut the size of the state workforce. We consolidated agencies. . . .
>
> Tax reform was an essential component of our work to fix Virginia's finances and to build the foundation for a stronger economy. . . . With the budget that we passed last year, we . . . made the tax code fairer for Virginia's families. We provided the funding necessary to meet our core commitments in education, health services and public safety. And we restored Virginia's fiscal integrity.[46]

Just a year earlier, reporters noting the dearth of executive accomplishments had suggested the governor was in over his head, implying that it had been a mistake for the young leader to start his public service in the state's top post.[47] But with a single session, the likeable Warner had deftly turned the tables on his critics. Having demonstrated during two years of difficult budget cuts that he was not some spendthrift "national" Democrat, Warner couched his tax-raising initiative in the benign language of "tax reform" and as a fiscally conservative measure necessary to right the state's battered finances and preserve its prized—and apparently endangered—triple-A credit rating. In this effort, Warner was aided immeasurably by his Republican allies in the state legislature, especially in the Senate, and by worthies in

---

levies were necessitated not only by immediate funding needs but also by projected growth in education costs, Medicaid, and other programs. *Washington Post*, June 17, 2004.

45. In a late October 2004 survey, 61 percent of Virginians rated Warner's gubernatorial performance as good or excellent, and 56 percent said the tax increase package was necessary. *Richmond Times-Dispatch*, November 1, 2004. By summer 2005, Warner's approval rating among Virginians had climbed to 74 percent. *Richmond Times-Dispatch*, July 26, 2005.

46. Text of 2005 State of the Commonwealth Message, Governor's Press Office, January 12, 2005.

47. See Michael D. Shear, "After a Rocky First Half, Warner to Set Agenda," *Washington Post*, January 14, 2004.

the GOP-leaning business community. Their support for his tax increase initiative—indeed, many of them suggested even steeper tax hikes[48]—made Warner appear not only moderate, but as that most appealing of political figures: a statesman able to transcend partisan divisions and take political risk to act in the best long-term interest of the state.[49]

Politically, Warner the Democrat had cut a new path to popularity with the broad, independent middle of the Virginia electorate. The two other leading Virginia political figures, John Warner and George Allen, had accomplished largely the same thing by different means. In the 1990s, John Warner had proven to independents that he was not a typical partisan politician when he defied his party and, at evident risk to himself, repudiated fellow GOP candidates that he regarded as outside the political mainstream. George Allen had proven to independents that he was not a typical partisan politician when he made sweeping promises of state policy reform and then, acting as the antithesis of the stereotypical politician, he actually pushed them through a Democratic-controlled legislature. Mark Warner proved to independents that he was not a typical partisan politician by resolutely refraining from combat with the state's GOP legislative majority and by demonstrating an ability to work in a businesslike manner across party lines, first for painful budget cuts and then for a tax hike that seemed impelled by fiscal circumstances.[50]

Shortly after passage of the major tax legislation in Virginia, Warner began his year-long tenure as chairman of the National Governors Association, and he took to the hustings nationally to tout his Virginia legislative successes and back the Kerry-Edwards national ticket.[51] State Democrats

48. Senator Chichester, the influential Finance Committee chairman, led Republican moderates in backing Warner's tax-raising initiative and even recommended a significantly larger increase than that proposed by the governor. Chichester cited the rumored threat to the state's credit rating as his paramount concern. Echoing sentiments expressed by Warner, the Senate leader said he was "absolutely determined that we were not going to lose that triple-A rating on my watch." Chichester interview.

49. Warner's selection of three prominent Republicans for his gubernatorial cabinet—former Lieutenant Governor John Hager, former state Senator Jane Woods, and former Delegate Robert Bloxom—also bolstered his bipartisan credentials.

50. For a discussion of Virginia's experience with divided government in the context of the 2004 budget controversy and otherwise, see Thomas R. Morris, "Divided Government Is Not a Disaster," in *Notes from the Sausage Factory*, eds. Day and Dale, pp. 49–52. A Republican moderate, Morris left the presidency of Emory & Henry College in 2006 to join the cabinet of Governor Timothy Kaine as secretary of education.

51. The Democratic national ticket in 2004 featured two sitting United States senators, the first time that had occurred since the Kennedy-Johnson entry in 1960. Senator Kerry was nominated for president after the front-running campaign of Vermont Governor Howard Dean faltered in the early caucus and primary voting. Kerry then chose the

had early hopes of capturing Virginia's 13 electoral votes for the first time in forty years, but President Bush ultimately amassed a solid 54 percent majority in the state and became the first president since Reagan to capture an actual majority of the popular vote nationally.[52] Throughout the 2004 presidential campaign, leading Democrats, pundits, and journalists had seemed convinced that Kerry would succeed in ousting Bush, who was beset by doubts about his military policy in Iraq and by an economic recovery that failed to gain traction at home. When the votes were in and the president had been reelected, many surprised Democrats began to point fingers at the cultural liberalism of the Kerry candidacy as the culprit.[53] It was not long before Warner's successes in GOP-leaning Virginia were being touted as a model for Democratic renewal nationally. Virginia had been in that position before—Charles Robb had pointed to his Virginia party's centrist successes when Democrats were looking for a way to stem the tide of Reaganism in the 1980s—but the talk about Warner seemed especially serious. "The Democratic Party needs to do now what we did during the period between 1989 and 1992," commented Al From of the centrist Democratic Leadership Council. "It needs to redefine itself by challenging a lot of the old orthodoxies. Mark Warner's biggest contribution to our party can be redefining our brand and what it stands for."[54]

Warner's moderate stance on values-laden social issues, his emphasis on fiscal discipline, and his conciliatory, bipartisan tenor had made him successful and popular in the Old Dominion, and the fact that his stock was high in conservative Virginia in turn made him a rare political property—and rising star—in a struggling national Democratic Party that had lost back-to-

---

leading Southern contender, North Carolina's first-term senator, John Edwards, to be his running mate.

52. The presidential election vote totals in Virginia were: Bush (R)—1,716,959 (53.7%); Kerry—1,454,742 (45.5%). Virginia State Board of Elections website (www.sbe.state.va.us). Nationally, Bush received 50.7 percent of the popular vote and 286 of 538 electoral votes. See *Divided States of America: The Slash and Burn Politics of the 2004 Presidential Election,* ed. Larry J. Sabato (New York: Pearson Education, Inc., 2006).

53. Another key factor was the Kerry campaign's failure to respond to summertime attacks on the candidate's military record. Virginian Christopher LaCivita, a Gulf War veteran who had served as Virginia GOP executive director, spearheaded the influential efforts of "Swift Boat Veterans for Truth," a group that publicly assailed Kerry's actions during and after the Vietnam conflict. The organization's broadsides played a key role in impugning Kerry's credentials as a wartime leader and were widely credited with helping to turn the tide in favor of Bush's reelection. See John J. Miller, "What the Swifties Wrought," *National Review,* November 29, 2004; David S. Broder, "Hits and Misses in '04," *Washington Post,* December 30, 2004.

54. *Washington Post,* November 14, 2004.

back presidential contests.[55] "More than three years before the 2008 presidential election," wrote Michael Shear of the *Washington Post*, "Warner has become one of the Democratic Party's most often-mentioned hopes for taking back the White House. Warner is a tax-increasing, one-term governor with no foreign policy experience. But he's also a moderate Democratic governor in a conservative Southern state."[56] The Virginia governor had a national platform with his National Governors Association chairmanship, but it was his tax and budget legislation that earned him accolades from the political establishment. *Governing* magazine, for example, named him "Public Official of the Year" in 2004 in addition to giving the state top marks on management.[57] The tax legislation did more for Warner than demonstrate his ability to build bipartisan coalitions. It converted a governorship that initially could claim little accomplishment other than sure-handed budget triage into a nationally noteworthy tenure that merged fiscal discipline with a progressive policy of targeted investment.[58]

It was Lieutenant Governor Timothy Kaine's victory in the 2005 race for governor, however, that provided the biggest boost to Warner's impending presidential campaign against the seemingly formidable frontrunner, New York Senator and former First Lady Hillary Rodham Clinton. Virginia's off-year elections are often scrutinized for signs of national trends, and the 2005 balloting was widely viewed as a harbinger of big trouble ahead for the GOP in the 2006 midterm elections. Beset by a series of setbacks ranging from continuing violence in Iraq and investigations of top GOP officeholders to a failed Supreme Court nomination,[59] much-maligned

---

55. See Gerald Seib, "Party Irregular: Can Warner Show Democrats a Path?" *Wall Street Journal*, November 17, 2004; George F. Will, "Virginia's Democratic Contender," *Washington Post*, December 19, 2004.

56. *Washington Post*, March 3, 2005.

57. The magazine's eight award recipients included two Virginians, Warner and Senator John Chichester, and the magazine featured the bipartisan pair on the cover of its "Public Officials of the Year 2004" issue in November 2004. While stressing passage of the tax hike legislation, the magazine also lauded Warner for reducing state expenditures by $6 billion, eliminating 3,000 state employee positions, abolishing 50 state boards, and cutting spending in every agency except K–12 education in response to the sharp revenue downturn that commenced in 2001. Alan Greenblatt, "Solidarity on Solvency," *Governing: The Magazine of States and Localities*, November 2004, pp. 24–25.

58. Mark Warner interview.

59. After years of anticipation over impending vacancies on the Supreme Court, Bush successfully tapped conservative Circuit Judge John G. Roberts Jr. to succeed deceased Chief Justice William H. Rehnquist in mid-2005. But his attempt to replace retiring Associate Justice Sandra Day O'Connor, the first female member of the Court, with White House counsel Harriett Miers failed after GOP conservatives and other critics pilloried her for lacking jurisprudential knowledge and interest. After weeks of

response to Gulf Coast hurricane devastation, and soaring gasoline prices, President Bush's popularity in fall 2005 plummeted to 37 percent nationally and 42 percent in Virginia, a state he had carried handily less than a year earlier.[60] The widespread voter discontent with partisan polarization and the problem-plagued state of affairs in Washington contrasted with the largely positive perception of Mark Warner's bipartisan approach and seemingly steady hand at the Virginia helm.[61]

Kaine had been routinely identified as a committed liberal by reporters and commentators four years earlier,[62] but in 2005 he presented himself as Warner's centrist apostle. He touted his support for Warner's "tax reform" initiative and chided his Republican foe, former Attorney General Jerry Kilgore,[63] for opposing the "bipartisan solutions" of the "Warner-Kaine administration" that had earned Virginia accolades as "the best managed state in America." With the state's economy humming again and the bitter budget battles quickly receding from memory, satisfied voters gave the governor the lion's share of the credit. A poll published by the *Washington Post* days before the November election put Warner's approval rating at an astonishing 80 percent and found that 70 percent of Virginians considered the state to be on the right track.[64] "Virginia is the last state with a one-term limit, and we have a tradition in Virginia of a popular governor being able to designate a successor and get him elected," explained Larry Sabato. "That's the reason Tim Kaine won."[65] Warner's popularity with the crucial

mounting opposition, the embattled nominee withdrew shortly before the November 2005 election and Bush nominated Circuit Judge Samuel Alito for the post. The conservative Alito won Senate approval in early 2006 after a contentious confirmation process.

60. See Michael Sluss, "Decline in Job Approval Mirrors National Trend," *Roanoke Times,* September 17, 2005.

61. In contrast to 2001, when President Bush declined to campaign for GOP gubernatorial nominee Mark Earley in the immediate aftermath of the September 11th attacks, the president made a strong personal pitch for Kilgore at a well-attended Richmond rally on the eve of the 2005 election. Believing the race to be close, Kilgore strategists hoped the presidential glitz would boost the candidate's support in the dispirited GOP base and increase Republican turnout. For their part, Governor Warner and Democrats welcomed the opportunity to contrast the state of affairs in Washington, D.C., with their performance in Virginia.

62. See Sabato, *Virginia Votes 1999–2003,* pp. 85, 117.

63. Adhering to an odd Virginia tradition, Kilgore resigned as attorney general in February 2005 to devote full-time attention to his gubernatorial campaign. Judith Williams Jagdmann, a Kilgore deputy, was elected by the General Assembly to complete the GOP standard-bearer's term.

64. *Washington Post,* October 30, 2005.

65. *Hannity & Colmes,* Fox News Channel, November 8, 2005. In the modern competitive era in Virginia politics, voters typically have not tired of the incumbent governor and his party after just four years, and have worked around the one-term limit on gubernatorial service by giving the constitutionally precluded second term to a perceived

swing-voting independents in the state's burgeoning suburbs was especially important to the Democratic campaign. Lacking the moderate governor's rural appeal, Kaine focused his media advertising, personal campaigning, and sophisticated grassroots organizational activities on the vote-rich suburbs, and his strong showing even in some historically GOP-leaning areas of Northern Virginia and Hampton Roads eclipsed Warner's own tally four years earlier.[66]

Although Governor Warner and President Bush loomed over the 2005 gubernatorial campaign as dominant images, Kilgore and Kaine were no mere bystanders. Seeking to re-create some of the reformist luster that had propelled his mentor, George Allen, to the governorship a dozen years earlier, the front-running Kilgore spent much of the spring outlining detailed policy proposals, a positive agenda he branded as "Honest Reform." In the fall, however, Kilgore and his advisers accentuated the negative, having become convinced that the only way to win in a political environment decidedly favorable to continuity and adverse to Republicans was to separate Kaine from Warner. The GOP campaign tried to do so by calling attention to the lieutenant governor's support for additional tax hikes, his past liberal stances on hot-button issues such as the death penalty, and his record as Richmond mayor. In the end, the relentless—and expensive—Republican effort to define Kaine over the airwaves largely precluded the Kilgore campaign from conveying their own candidate's personal narrative and policy ideas to Virginians. "In the 1990s," recalled commentator Robert Holsworth, "the Republicans were the party that brought forth the [Standards of Learning], welfare reform, the elimination of parole, the partial elimination of the car tax, and juvenile justice reform." But unlike in the Allen and Gilmore gubernatorial bids, "[t]he Republican campaign [in 2005] failed to establish any forward-looking issue that Kilgore 'owned.'"[67]

proxy. Warner's hand-off to Kaine represented the fourth time in three decades that popular governors who themselves had gained office through a change of parties were succeeded by their partisan allies. The other instances were the Allen-Gilmore (1998), Robb-Baliles (1986), and Holton-Godwin (1974) successions.

66. Mike Henry interview, January 11, 2006. The vote totals in the election for governor were: Kaine (D)—1,025,942 (51.7 percent); Kilgore (R)—912,327 (45.9 percent). Virginia State Board of Elections website (www.sbe.state.va.us). A third candidate, state Senator H. Russell ("Russ") Potts Jr., of Winchester, polled less than 50,000 votes (2.2 percent) in his self-styled "Independent Republican" bid. Though reporters, pundits, and editorialists lavished attention on Potts earlier in the year when he announced his breakaway effort, the vocal sports promoter's campaign calling for higher transportation levies attracted little support and proved inconsequential in November.

67. Robert Holsworth, "Many Things Combined to Cripple Kilgore's Gubernatorial Hopes," *Richmond Times-Dispatch*, November 13, 2005.

Except for an expensive plan to educate more of the state's four-year-olds, Kaine's campaign devoted even less time to promoting new policy initiatives than did Kilgore's. But the Democrats enjoyed the advantage of incumbency; it was the Republicans' burden to make the case for change.

The steady barrage of GOP attacks on Kaine kept the contest deadlocked until its final days, but the negativism eventually took its toll as undecided voters in the vote-laden suburban areas broke strongly toward the Democrat on election day. Several factors appeared to explain why disenchantment with Kilgore in the end trumped doubts about Kaine. First, in attempting to engage Kaine on the GOP's tried and true issue of taxes, Kilgore was compromised throughout by the seeming inconsistency between his 2004 opposition to the $1.4 billion tax hike package and his refusal to call for its repeal a year later despite the existence of large state budget surpluses. Kilgore's dilemma had been apparent from the moment Republican moderates in the General Assembly provided the crucial votes to pass the Warner tax plan. Hoping to avoid reopening the deep GOP wounds from that tax fight and to avert a direct clash with the popular Warner over his signature initiative, Kilgore in 2005 declined to urge repeal of the new levies. Instead, he recommended several other tax relief measures and a constitutional requirement that future tax hikes be submitted to the voters by referendum. The nuanced position never made its way into Kilgore's television advertisements, and to the extent voters were aware, the stance appeared to satisfy neither the moderate suburbanites who were pleased with Warner's stewardship nor the already disaffected anti-tax base of the GOP. With the tax issue clouded and Kaine stoutly disavowing tax hike intentions, Kilgore made little headway with his frequent charge that the Democrat would add a higher gasoline levy to the already soaring prices at the pump.[68]

---

68. Kilgore's charges were prescient if unavailing. Kaine had been in the governorship only days when he contradicted his campaign pronouncements on taxes. While his predecessor's about-face on new levies had come amid budget shortfalls and after two years of deep budget reductions, Kaine moved swiftly—in the face of a large state budget surplus—to propose his own billion-dollar annual tax increase, this time to pay for a backlog of major transportation projects. The Kaine tax hike plan triggered a reprise of the 2004 budget struggle, generating bipartisan support in the moderate Senate, strong opposition from the conservative GOP majority in the House of Delegates, and another unseemly budget impasse. Whether Kaine's reversal on taxes ultimately would meet with success (as with the 1986 Baliles and 2004 Warner gambits) or failure (as with Governor Thomas Stanley's much earlier 1954 fiasco) was unclear as this book went to press. "Looking back on it, I am the only Democrat who said he wouldn't raise taxes and kept his word," observed former Governor Douglas Wilder in a 2005 interview, recalling similarities between the no-tax-hike pronouncements and contrary actions of Governors Baliles and Warner. Wilder interview. While some commentators applauded Kaine's courage in tackling the perennial transportation conundrum, others echoed Wilder's

Second, while Warner never criticized Kilgore over the airwaves, the trusted incumbent's much-advertised endorsement of Kaine gave the Democratic nominee a decided edge in the candidates' underlying battle for believability. The Warner imprimatur, together with the nimble Kaine's superior candidate skills and adroit repositioning on the issues, largely shielded the Democrat from the long-expected GOP fusillade on his record. In the 2001 campaign, Warner had publicly repudiated his running mate Kaine's opposition to the death penalty and support for gun control and same-sex civil unions. By 2005, Kaine was flatly denying any heresy on guns and gays, but on the death penalty he was unapologetic. Instead, he repeatedly invoked his long-held religious beliefs—he had taken a year off from Harvard Law School to serve as a missionary in Honduras—as the principled ground for his opposition to capital punishment and his personal antipathy toward abortion. "My faith teaches life is sacred, that's why I personally oppose the death penalty," Kaine said in one much-run television ad, before issuing the reassuring disclaimer, "As governor, I'll carry out death sentences handed down by Virginia juries because that's the law."[69]

Kaine's tactic recalled President John F. Kennedy's response to critics who feared a Catholic president's unquestioning fealty to the pope, and it appeared similarly effective.[70] As the Democrat's focus groups had shown, voters who saw Kaine earnestly attesting to his religious conviction were reluctant to believe GOP charges that he was a liberal.[71] Whether born of tactical ingenuity or simple necessity, the former missionary's faith shield withstood the heat from the Republican attacks and helped cement his new centrist image in voters' minds. Just a year after John Kerry's awkward presidential campaign had highlighted the estrangement of the national Democratic Party's liberal elite from much of religious America, Kaine seemingly

lament about the dearth of candor. "The Commonwealth has come a long way from the first President—Virginia-born George Washington, who could not tell a lie—to its recent Governors, who cannot seem to tell the truth," quipped editorialist Barton Hinkle. See A. Barton Hinkle, "Did Leighty (Accidentally, Of Course) Tell the Truth?" *Richmond Times-Dispatch*, March 7, 2006.

69. *Washington Times*, November 6, 2005.

70. In his 1960 campaign, Kennedy worked to allay fears that he would take his marching orders from the Vatican as president. While reiterating his Catholic faith, he stressed that he would owe his allegiance to his presidential oath rather than the papal throne.

71. A senior Kaine aide revealed the focus group research to columnist E. J. Dionne Jr. after the election. See E. J. Dionne Jr., "A Party Finds the Right Words," *Washington Post*, November 10, 2005. The research apparently helped spur a change in Kaine's 2005 election strategy. In his statewide bid four years earlier, the Democrat did not highlight his religiosity.

had reconnected with the faith community in Virginia. Democratic strategists across the nation took notice.[72]

Locked in a persistently close race according to most opinion surveys, Kaine and Kilgore also enjoyed unprecedented fund-raising success, breaking all records for raising and spending campaign cash in a Virginia contest for governor.[73] A significant share of the Democratic funds went to pay for a blizzard of television ads in which Governor Warner, speaking directly to the camera, vouched for Kaine's character and solidarity with the Warner agenda and bipartisan approach. Had the influential governor supplied the Democratic nominees for lieutenant governor and attorney general with the same direct, power-packed electronic endorsement, Kaine's running mates might also have prevailed in the distinctly hospitable environment Democrats enjoyed in fall 2005. But former Congresswoman Leslie Byrne, the pugnacious Northern Virginia liberal running for lieutenant governor on the Kaine ticket, had sparred with Warner for the 1996 Senate nomination and had no hope of such an embrace. On election day, she fared far better than anyone had predicted when the race began but still succumbed to conservative Republican state Senator William T. Bolling of Hanover County by 22,000 votes.[74] In the race for attorney general, GOP Delegate Robert F. McDonnell of Virginia Beach came out 360 votes ahead following a recount in the closest statewide election in modern Virginia history.[75] McDonnell's Democratic opponent, state Senator R. Creigh Deeds of Bath County, waged a Warner-like campaign rooted in rural Virginia but could not overcome the advantage McDonnell enjoyed because of his political

72. See Howard Fineman, "A Faith-Based Initiative: What the Democrats Can Learn from Kaine's Virginia Victory," *Newsweek*, November 21, 2005. Kaine's success seemed to confirm the wisdom of advice that other Democratic centrists, such as Senator Evan Bayh of Indiana, had been giving their fellow partisans for some time. A potential rival to Mark Warner for the moderate mantle in the 2008 presidential campaign, Bayh had admonished Democrats in 2003 that "the Democratic Party can't afford to be perceived as cultural elitists. If we appear to be hostile to people of faith . . . , they will believe 'the Democrats don't understand people like us.'" Gil Klein, "Strategists Warn Democrats," *Richmond Times-Dispatch*, October 24, 2003.

73. The three candidates for governor raised more than $46 million. Kilgore set the record with nearly $25 million; Kaine spent $20 million; and Potts raised roughly $1.3 million. See Virginia Public Access Project website (www.vpap.org).

74. The vote totals in the election for lieutenant governor were: Bolling (R)—979,265 (50.5 percent), Byrne (D)—956,906 (49.3 percent). Virginia State Board of Elections website (www.sbe.state.va.us).

75. The vote totals in the election for attorney general, as adjusted following the statewide recount, were: McDonnell (R)—970,886 (49.96 percent), Deeds (D)—970,563 (49.95 percent). *Washington Post*, December 22, 2005.

base in populous Hampton Roads.[76] Despite the most favorable climate for Democrats in decades—a "perfect storm for a Democratic candidate," Sabato called it[77]—Warner's party failed to capture two of three statewide offices and registered only a one-seat net gain in the House of Delegates.[78] But the big prize was the governorship; the governor and his party had focused their resources there, and they had a solid win to show for it.

In the wake of the 2005 election, a triumphant Warner touted his success in the moderate-conservative Old Dominion as a remedy for the Democrats' national ills and a way back to the White House. The morning-after reaction of ABC's George Stephanopoulos to the off-year election results reflected a media consensus that, while a setback for President Bush, the "big winner out of last night is Virginia Governor Mark Warner. He wants to run for president in 2008 [and he] was a big factor behind Tim Kaine's win in Virginia. He's heading up to New Hampshire next week."[79] Appearing on CBS's *Face the Nation,* Warner stressed that his centrist approach could put Republican-leaning "red states" in play in 2008 and appeal to voters' desire for a chief executive able to get results by working across party lines:

> If Democrats continue to put forward candidates that can only be competitive in 16 or 17 states, I think we do [the Democratic Party and] the country a disservice. . . . A Democratic candidate that only competes for 16 states and then tries to hit a triple bank shot to get that 17th state—even if you win under that scenario, can you govern? What this country desperately needs is someone who not only can win but can govern.[80]

---

76. Another key factor was the stance taken by Richmond Mayor Douglas Wilder. In a move reminiscent of his refusal to endorse Democrat Donald Beyer in the 1997 race for governor, Wilder declined to endorse fellow Democrat Deeds, citing the Democrat's opposition to the Wilder gubernatorial administration's signature initiative limiting handgun purchases to one per month. *Richmond Times-Dispatch,* November 1, 2005.

77. *Daily Press,* November 9, 2005.

78. Democratic gains in legislative districts in Northern Virginia were largely offset by the GOP's downstate pick-ups. Democrats increased their House of Delegates representation from 38 to 39 members; Republicans lost an additional seat to an Independent, lowering their total from 60 to 58 delegates. The GOP strength in the House continued to be bolstered by the usual support of conservative Independents Lacey Putney and Watkins Abbitt; the Independent newcomer, Katherine Waddell, steered a more centrist course. In early 2006, a series of special legislative elections occasioned by Bolling's elevation and the tapping of lawmakers for appointive posts by Kaine and McDonnell left Republicans with a 23-seat majority in the 40-member state Senate and 57 seats in the 100-member House of Delegates.

79. *Good Morning America,* ABC News, November 9, 2005.

80. *Face the Nation,* CBS News, November 13, 2005.

Distinguishing Kaine's faith-based appeal from his own emphasis on "mak[-ing] sure rural communities and small-town America [don't] get left behind," Warner said, "[W]e Democrats need to put forward . . . people who are comfortable talking about their faith, talking about values, comfortable in parts of America where, let's face it, . . . Democrats perhaps haven't been welcome as much recently."[81] Warner's themes not only represented a departure from Democratic orthodoxy; his emphasis on reaching across party lines and moving "Forward Together"[82] posed a direct challenge to the polarizing stratagems employed by the political masterminds atop both national parties. "As attention properly focuses on Warner as a potential presidential candidate in 2008, the lesson of his tenure is clear for national Democrats," wrote *Boston Globe* columnist Thomas Oliphant. "Success at the polls still leaves a stark reality that demands bipartisan governance if huge budget messes are to be cleaned up and other major challenges are to be confronted."[83] "The last two Democrats to reach the White House were charming southern governors," observed *The Economist* in reporting the American off-year election verdict. "Mr. Warner's stealth campaign to slow down the coronation of Hillary Clinton has hitherto seemed somewhat quixotic; after this week's results, he seems a realistic alternative."[84]

Warner concluded his governorship in January 2006 on a high. Though he could boast of few groundbreaking policy changes, his bipartisan imagery and businesslike approach to governmental management had won him the respect of a broad cross-section of Virginia voters, as a wave of positive commentaries at the close of his tenure attested.[85] Even Republican foes, such as House of Delegates GOP caucus chief R. Steven Landes, acknowledged that Warner possessed a certain "star quality" that had served him well as governor and might create opportunities for political success

---

81. *Face the Nation*, CBS News, November 13, 2005.

82. Warner's political action committee was dubbed "Forward Together," a familiar slogan that had figured prominently in campaigns and speeches by, among others, President Richard Nixon and British Prime Minister Winston Churchill.

83. Thomas Oliphant, "As Virginia Goes," *Boston Globe*, November 10, 2005.

84. "At Last, Something for the Democrats to Cheer About; the Off-Year Elections," *The Economist*, November 12, 2005; see also David S. Broder, "Warner's Rising Star," *Washington Post*, November 24, 2005.

85. See, e.g., Michael D. Shear, "Warner's Triumphant Legacy No Easy Feat," *Washington Post*, January 10, 2006. Warner's chief of staff summarized the managerial achievements of the "Businessman Governor" in an end-of-term retrospective that highlighted bipartisanship, diversity, accountability, openness, and innovation as administration hallmarks. See Bill Leighty, "Governor Warner Leaves Successor Solid Foundation," *Richmond Times-Dispatch,* January 8, 2006. A career state employee who served governors of both parties, Leighty himself was credited with executing many of the managerial measures and was tapped to continue in the chief of staff role by Governor Kaine.

beyond the state's borders.[86] "His years were tumultuous, at times dictated by circumstances beyond his control," wrote reporters Michael Hardy and Jeff E. Schapiro, citing vicissitudes ranging from budget shortfalls and job losses to sniper attacks and a succession of natural disasters.

> Among them was an economy that went bust to boom, a cycle reflecting Warner's political fortunes. Once derided as weak because of early setbacks, Warner leaves office angling for another: the presidency in 2008. To some, this might seem bewildering, given that the centerpiece of Warner's legacy is a broken promise that actually drove up his approval rating, which now surpasses 70 percent.[87]

Recalling that his first two years in office were "crummy" and that "holding it together" was a daunting job, Warner opined that the fiscal adversity and his businesslike response had set the stage for his later success: "All the bad news helped create the opportunity that something had to be done."[88] It was clear that Virginians' verdict on his tenure was broadly positive. Whether his centrist record and conciliatory message would also resonate with the ideological faithful who typically turn out for Democratic presidential primary balloting was the major unanswered question as Virginia's multimillionaire ex-governor began his quest for the White House.

Unlike Governor Warner, Senator George Allen did not see his presidential prospects improve with the outcome of Virginia's odd-year gubernatorial election. To the contrary, Democrats emboldened by Kaine's win seemed eager to recruit a credible, well-funded candidate to contest Allen's November 2006 reelection to the Senate.[89] But like Warner, Allen had left the governorship as one of the five most popular state executives in the nation after getting his way in a legislature controlled by the other party, and the hard-charging Republican had remained highly visible after capturing the state's junior Senate seat in 2000. With Vice President Richard Cheney publicly declaring his resolve not to seek the top post in 2008, the GOP presidential field lacked a clear conservative favorite, and throughout 2005 the buzz grew in national Republican circles that Allen could well be the new conservative hope. Though he barely registered in early public

---

86. Chris Graham, "Will a Homegrown Candidate Go All the Way?" *The Hook*, January 5–11, 2006.

87. Michael Hardy and Jeff E. Schapiro, "His Specialty: Seizing Chances from Setbacks," *Richmond Times-Dispatch*, January 7, 2006.

88. Hardy and Schapiro, "His Specialty: Seizing Chances from Setbacks."

89. Two contenders stepped forward to seek the Democratic nod to take on Allen: former Fairfax County Democratic Party chair Harris Miller, a high-tech lobbyist, and James Webb, who served as secretary of the Navy during the Reagan administration.

opinion polls on the presidential race, the nonpartisan *National Journal* in April published a survey of several hundred GOP "insiders" in the nation's capital who rated the Virginia senator as the person most likely to become the Republican presidential nominee in 2008—a finding that was echoed at the end of 2005 by a repeat survey.[90] Other influential voices—ranging from veteran columnist George Will to conservative icon Rush Limbaugh and anti-tax guru Grover Norquist to pundits Stuart Rothenberg, Chuck Todd, and others on the Capitol Hill beat—weighed in with positive observations about Allen's record, style, ideas, and prospects.[91] Declaring the Virginia Republican to be "quite possibly the next President of the United States," the conservative *National Review* featured Allen's beaming visage on its cover in November 2005. Editor Richard Lowry elaborated:

> It is not hard to do a calculation that says at this early stage in the '08 race George Allen has a better chance of winning the nomination than any other Republican. He combines the people skills of Bill Clinton, with the convictions of a Ronald Reagan, with the non-threatening persona of George W. Bush circa 2000, before he became a hate-figure for the Left. Profile writers often invoke Reagan and Bush in describing Allen, but the senator is emphatically his own man, with a personal history that has forged a rare and particular political talent, blending amiability with competitive ruthlessness in a way that makes him, at age 53, one of the nation's top politicians.[92]

Though the Virginian lacked the high profile of Arizona Senator John McCain, the most well known of the prospective Republican contestants, Allen seemed both in tune with the GOP's conservative base and capable of transcending that base in the general election with a Reaganesque appeal. "[He is] in the sweet spot of Republican politics . . . on good terms with every piece of the coalition," observed Grover Norquist, a frequent barometer of opinion on the Republican right.[93] Accompanying Allen on a trip to New Hampshire, George Will observed that the Virginian possessed

---

90. See "2008 Republican Insiders Poll," and "2008 Democratic Insiders Poll," *National Journal,* December 17, 2005.

91. See George F. Will, "Warming Up to Hit Hard," *Washington Post,* July 7, 2005; Interview with Rush Limbaugh, *Hannity & Colmes,* Fox News Channel, October 19, 2005; Grover Norquist, "The Best and the Brightest," *The American Spectator,* December 2005–January 2006; Stuart Rothenberg, "Are Republicans Ready for Another George?" *Roll Call,* March 28, 2005; Chuck Todd, "Return of the Gipper?" *Washingtonian,* August 2005; David Nather, "George Allen's Sporting Chance for 2008," *Congressional Quarterly,* October 24, 2005.

92. Richard Lowry, "Buckling His Chin Strap: Senator George Allen—Likable, Conservative and Tough—Prepares to Run for President," *National Review,* November 7, 2005.

93. Lowry, "Buckling His Chin Strap."

"Reagan's knack for expressing strong views in an unthreatening manner."[94] Stuart Rothenberg cited an unnamed observer's convincing view that the senator had been "blessed with the talent to connect with people" and the "ability to take complex issues and break them down to the average person."[95] Further attesting to Allen's communication skills and policy depth was his unusually successful, reform-oriented governorship, which garnered renewed attention and provided his chief credential as an executive leader.

Once in the Senate, Allen had enjoyed opportunities to bolster his visibility and mastery of key national issues through key appointments to the Foreign Relations, Commerce, and Energy and Natural Resources committees. His duties took him, among other places, to the two areas of the world that seemed certain to command American foreign policy attention for the foreseeable future—postwar Iraq and up-and-coming China. Among his favorite policy initiatives in the Senate were educational measures to promote American competitiveness in math, science, engineering, and related fields, legislation to provide technology grants to historically black colleges and other minority-serving schools,[96] and opposition to taxation of the Internet. A frequent guest on nationally televised interview programs, the easygoing Virginian appeared comfortable making his way through the minefield of hot topics issues that increasingly bedeviled the ruling Republicans in the nation's capital. But as he pondered a White House bid, the major question for Allen—aside from his own reelection to the Senate in 2006—was whether the conservative populist and self-described "insurgent" could fashion a message blending continuity and change that would sell on the heels of the two-term Bush presidency.

Ranked by Washington insiders among the top two presidential prospects in each party, Virginia's two ascendant political figures and the com-

---

94. *Washington Post*, July 7, 2005.

95. *Roll Call*, March 28, 2005

96. Allen's racial progressiveness had been questioned by Democratic foes as they sought to galvanize African-American voters in his 1993 and 2000 campaigns. Critics pointed to Allen's younger days when he had included a Confederate banner in a home flag display and a hangman's noose among western artifacts in his law office. Allen adamantly rejected any suggestion of racial insensitivity, and his electoral track record—he garnered better-than-average African-American support for a Republican—tended to belie such criticism. In addition to his proposal for technology grants for minority-serving institutions, Allen as senator led a high-profile tour of civil rights sites and successfully sponsored legislation apologizing for the Senate's failure to ban lynching in the South. In so doing, he called on his colleagues to "learn from history, never again sit quietly, and never again turn one's head away when the ugly specter of racism, anti-Semitism, hate and intolerance rises again." Nather, *Congressional Quarterly*, October 24, 2005.

petitive system that produced them became subjects of interest in the national news media.[97] In a late 2005 article entitled "The Virginians," *Newsweek*'s Howard Fineman wrote:

> As a new election cycle begins, Virginia—and the double-helix career of [Warner and Allen]—is moving to center stage. Differing in background, tone and philosophy, they offer competing models of how to succeed in the South, where Democrats must be competitive if they hope to win the White House again. . . .
>
> Virginia itself is part of their story—and a test bed for political change in the country as a whole. As the 400th anniversary of the founding of Jamestown approaches—soon to be a major motion picture—Virginia remains suffused with the Jeffersonian aura and the gentle green landscape of an agrarian democracy. But today Virginia is far less about cigarette tobacco than digital technology, and its devotion to segregation has long since been rendered moot by the election of the nation's first African-American governor (Doug Wilder, in 1989) and by a global influx of immigrants, drawn by the economic buzz of several of the nation's largest semiconductor [fabrication plants] and the vast headquarter campuses of companies such as AOL and Nextel. President Lyndon B. Johnson won the state in 1964. No Democrat has since. But the changing economics and demographics could put it in play in 2008.[98]

While reporters focused on their differing personalities, methods, and messages, the two presidential prospects from Virginia were not without similarities. Each had been transplanted in the "new dominion"—Allen was a California native; Warner was born in Indiana—and each had waged just two statewide campaigns (one each for governor and senator). While they could easily have been rivals, especially for the United States Senate in 2006, they appeared aware that a premature battle between them for primacy in Virginia would be costly, damaging, and potentially career-limiting for both. As a result, the two seemed to steer clear and, if anything, spent more time complimenting than criticizing each other.[99] Meanwhile, each took

---

97. "2008 Republican Insiders Poll" and "2008 Democratic Insiders Poll," *National Journal,* December 17, 2005.

98. Howard Fineman, "The Virginians," *Newsweek,* December 26, 2005–January 2, 2006.

99. The generally genial relations between the two Virginia political titans was not new. As they prepared for their respective statewide campaigns in 2000 and 2001, Republican Allen and Democrat Warner had teamed up as co-chairs of a "Communities in Schools" initiative designed to promote private-sector involvement in underperforming school divisions. See David Lerman, "State Could Produce Two Presidential Hopefuls," *Daily Press,* March 13, 2005; Michael D. Shear, "A Matchup to Imagine; Could Virginia's Boys Square Off in 2008?" *Washington Post,* August 7, 2005. In January

concrete steps to prepare for a presidential bid, hiring top campaign aides with high-profile national experience,[100] raising campaign cash, trudging through early primary states, and taking advantage of largely favorable national news coverage. The fascination with the pair in the national media left in-state reporters, who tended to view both politicians more critically, bemused. "Intoxicated by an initial wave of uncritical coverage by the national press, Warner and Allen are giddily . . . attempting to reinvent themselves for an out-of-state audience," observed an often-skeptical Virginia reporter, who suggested the pair should bear in mind "one of the cardinal rules of politics: Don't believe your own clips."[101]

Whatever the future held for George Allen and Mark Warner, this much was clear: Virginia had been transformed dramatically in several decades' time from a staid, one-party Democratic bastion characteristic of the Old South to a highly competitive, two-party political system on the cutting-edge of national politics and governmental affairs. In this competitive Virginia environment, party fortunes had ebbed and flowed, producing stand-out Democratic and Republican leaders who now commanded the attention of and bid for support from fellow partisans around the country, monitored closely by the nation's political elite. Opinions of their prospects varied and were sure to rise and fall like shifts in barometric pressure as 2008 approached. But no one doubted that Virginia—the 400-year-old birthplace of the nation and early "Mother of Presidents"—had returned to the vanguard of American politics.

---

2006, Allen and Warner again touted the benefits of business-education collaboration, convening a Richmond news conference to endorse new state investments in university-based research and development.

100. Allen tapped Dick Wadhams, a highly sought political operative who helped engineer the ouster of Senate Majority Leader Thomas Daschle in 2004, to serve as his senatorial chief of staff. Warner hired Monica Dixon, a former top aide to former Vice President Albert Gore Jr., to spearhead his federal political action committee.

101. Jeff E. Schapiro, "Warner and Allen Bask in Media's Glow," *Richmond Times-Dispatch*, December 25, 2005.

# EPILOGUE:
# A CONCLUDING REFLECTION ON
# VIRGINIA'S LEGACY OF FREEDOM

[T]he destiny of the republican model of government [is] justly considered as deeply, perhaps as finally, staked on the experiment
entrusted to the hands of the American people.[1]

—President George Washington, First Inaugural Address, 1789

As this book went to press, the 400th anniversary of Jamestown—and
thus of Virginia and America—loomed just ahead in 2007. Virginians
were preparing to lead the nation and the world in a timely reflection on
the remarkable advance of freedom and democracy in the four centuries
since starry-eyed English settlers braved an oceanic crossing and—aided by
the native peoples and, later, by slaves from Africa—planted a new nation
and representative government on the banks of the James. A wide array of
commemorative activities, star-studded celebrations, VIP visits, cultural fes-
tivals, community initiatives, educational programs, and university-based
conferences on the future of democracy were being planned for the anniversary year. Jefferson's Virginia Capitol was undergoing a major renovation
in time to welcome anniversary-year visitors. And a major public-private
and federal-state partnership was transforming the complementary museums
and interpretive facilities at Jamestown into a tourist destination without
peer. New discoveries were being made, too, as excited archaeologists
probed the recently found headquarters of the two cultures that encountered each other in early Virginia: the English settlers' original James Fort

---

1. W. W. Abbot, *The Papers of George Washington, Presidential Series*, vol. 2, April–
June 1789. (Charlottesville: University Press of Virginia, 1987), pp. 152–158.

on the James River and Chief Powhatan's "capital" at Werewocomoco on the banks of the York.[2]

Though vitally important instruments of history, the Jamestown settlers actually were late arrivals on the scene. So, too, for that matter, were the Virginia Indians who greeted them. Long before, in fact some 35 million years before, the three small ships made their way across the Atlantic, another traveler—a celestial body, variously described as a meteorite, comet, asteroid, ice ball, or bolide—made its way to Virginia from an unknown point of origin in the universe. The three-mile wide object, traveling at 75 times the speed of sound, crashed into the shallow ocean at the site of present-day Cape Charles, Virginia, producing a tsunami so large it lapped the Virginia mountains and leaving a crater in the ocean floor twice the size of the state of Rhode Island and nearly as deep as the Grand Canyon. This celestial event, discovered only in recent years by scientists with the U.S. Geological Survey at Woods Hole, Massachusetts, featured the biggest object ever to impact the Western Hemisphere, the most massive anywhere since the cataclysmic death of the dinosaurs, and one of the six largest ever to hit the planet.[3] For our purposes, the event's relevance lies in its direct causal relation to Virginia's role as the cradle of democracy in the modern world.

As the waters of the ocean receded over time, the crater became a vital agent in forming the Chesapeake Bay and the rich estuary system adjoining

---

2. In a great historical irony, both sites were discovered independently in the years just preceding the Jamestown 400th anniversary milestone. Long thought to have been lost to the river, the James Fort discovery was announced by archaeologist William Kelso, joined by Governor George Allen and other state dignitaries, on September 12, 1996. Dr. Kelso's "Jamestown Rediscovery Project," sponsored by the Association for the Preservation of Virginia Antiquities (APVA), had commenced in 1994. See Andrew Petkofsky, "Finder of Fort Impatient," *Richmond Times-Dispatch*, September 12, 1996. In 2003 and 2004, archaeologists E. Randolph Turner III, of the state Department of Historic Resources, and Martin Gallivan, of the College of William & Mary, reported finding convincing evidence that Werewocomoco, the expansive Indian village that had been a center of native civilization for many centuries, was located on the present-day farm of Robert and Lynn Ripley on Purtan Bay in Gloucester County. See Andrew Petkofsky, "Has Legend Found a Home? Archaeologists Believe Goucester Site Is Pocahontas' Village," *Richmond Times-Dispatch*, May 7, 2003; Andrew Petkofsy, "Ditches at Indian Site Date to 1400s; System at the Home of Chief Powhatan May Match Map from 1608," *Richmond Times-Dispatch*, August 5, 2004. Archaeological digs were ongoing at both sides at this writing, and were expected to continue for many years.

3. The crater discovery is described in C. Wylie Poag, *Chesapeake Invader: Discovering America's Giant Meteorite Crater* (Princeton, NJ: Princeton University Press, 1999), pp. 3–66; see also J. Hunter Barbour, "The Freshest Advices: The Bolide, the Horse Path, and History," *Colonial Williamsburg*, Winter 2002–2003, pp. 13–15.

it. Nature and man then interacted in ways that changed the course of human history.

The nurturing Chesapeake estuary became home to the Powhatan Confederacy, a hierarchical Indian society that was already highly developed when Englishmen, also attracted to the natural protections and abundance of the Chesapeake region, came to found a settlement in 1607. Without the assistance of the Powhatans in the nourishing bosom of the bay, the Jamestown settlement would not have survived. But survive it did, and in nearby Williamsburg a century and a half later its heirs—the giants of the founding generation—worked out their revolutionary ideas and mustered the mettle to assert independence from colonial rule.

The ensuing war ended—history being rich with irony—just down the road at Yorktown, where the Chesapeake combined with the self-serving aims of a foreign power to lay a fatal trap for the vaunted British army of General Cornwallis. Because George Washington, the victor, chose to return to his serene home on the banks of the Potomac rather than be king—an event destined to rank forever among the most consequential acts of self-denial in human history—a republic took root, and a nation at length was forged. The question of nationhood was not resolved, however, until a rebellious Richmond finally fell to the forces of Union in 1865 after four years of carnage, much of it in the blood-soaked soil of the Chesapeake watershed.

Two hours north, another city in the Chesapeake estuary, the capital that appropriately bears Washington's name, has for two centuries been the locus of decisions that provided hope for people around the world seeking freedom. Among those decisions were the orders that dispatched great aircraft carriers and other vessels from Hampton Roads, near Cape Henry where the English settlers first landed, to the climactic engagements of the twentieth century that turned back the tide of totalitarianism and saved liberty.

If we see these and other remarkable events of the past 400 years and longer as random occurrences, owing only to the vagaries of nature, time, place, and circumstance, then they should occupy our thoughts little now. But if we see the remarkable progress of mankind toward democracy as a Providential gift that confers both opportunity and obligation, then our presence here in Virginia—the cradle of American democracy and *ground zero* for an explosion of freedom that has transformed the world—should be at once inspiring and sobering. We should see the ongoing business of politics and governance not only as a collection of ordinary, mind-numbing tasks (which it often is) but also as part of an extraordinary enterprise at a pivotal moment—a tide of freedom, if you will, to be taken at the flood lest the venture be lost.

Importantly, the issues that were present at the founding of the American Republic—indeed, were present in the settlement at Jamestown and long before—still resonate in our politics today: *How much should a person contribute from his labors to support the common purposes of the society in which he lives? And how should that be decided?*

Although far more has been written about Captain John Smith's swashbuckling exploits than his education and religious upbringing, the indispensable leader of the early Virginia colony undoubtedly was familiar with the practical instruction the apostle Paul sent to one of the early Christian communities: "If a man will not work he shall not eat."[4] Recognizing the realistic imperative behind Paul's seemingly uncharitable admonition, Smith shocked the toil-averse gentlemen among the settlers at Jamestown into reluctant effort with the same edict. Since that rather hard beginning, the axiom that there is "no such thing as a free lunch" has been often repeated in America. Economist Milton Friedman invoked it to highlight the reality that governmental beneficence comes at a cost to individual liberty and societal prosperity.[5] More recently, the saying has been invoked for the proposition that if one wants government to provide a host of services—from the advancement of American interests and ideals abroad to the provision of a wide array of services at home—then one must be willing to pay for them with his taxes. Both truths are inescapable, whether one turns for insight to a sectarian saint like Paul, a secular icon like Smith, or a contemporary Democrat or Republican.

Because ours is a republican form of government, the understanding that government's benefits must be purchased necessarily focuses the matter on the question of who is to decide, and how. The very cause of American independence, encapsulated famously in Patrick Henry's "liberty or death" exhortation, was rooted in objection to taxation by a remote and powerful government in which the colonial citizens had no effective voice. This concern about centralized power, its power to tax, and thus its power to destroy, lurked behind virtually every debate the American founders and framers had and every decision they made. It produced most of the grand difficulties in the Grand Experiment. Indeed, despite the potent "Spirit of '76," wariness of centralized power in general and taxation in particular nearly cost the colonials their Continental Army and hence their independence.

---

4. II Thessalonians 3:10.

5. See Milton Friedman, *There's No Such Thing as a Free Lunch* (LaSalle, IL: Open Court Publishing Company, 1975).

Though the debate over the proper way to array, exercise, and restrain government power has continued in various forms from the earliest to the present day, the framers of the Constitution embraced the then-radical idea that the authority to govern—and thus the crucial power to, as Jefferson later put it, "take from the mouth of labor the bread it has earned"[6]— proceeded from The People, was legitimized through their consent, and would remain accountable to their will. *But accountable how?* Are political candidates to share their intentions with voters in advance and hew to those assurances once in office? Are they to withhold their intentions at election time, act as they see fit in office, and be held to account only if and when they face voters thereafter? Is there a bond of trust between those who govern and the governed; if not, should there be; and if so, what should be its terms?

These points of context—the extraordinary train of cause and effect that has brought us to this moment of great democratic promise in the world and the recurring presence in our political labors of issues that go to the very character of democracy—are indispensable subjects as Virginians assess their times and shape their future with an eye toward an exciting new century. And if these points provide essential context for the discussion among Virginians, then they also are the nub of the American debate about the national mission, and ought to occupy the deliberations of democrats and republicans around the world.

People of goodwill can disagree and debate at length on the appropriate level of taxation and its implications for government, the economy, public needs, and private interests. Indeed, *debate taxes* is what Virginians have done in earnest since 1997. The point for reflection is not the merit of any particular tax measure, or the proper level and mix of taxes, or any other specific policy choice. The debate over taxes is central to the American experience because it goes to the heart of the question, how much government is the right amount? From the perspective of the taxpayer, the question is, how much should my family and I be required to pay? From the perspective of the recipient of government benefits, the question is, how much should government do to help me? From the perspective of the policymaker, the question is, how much and what form of taxation will produce the greatest good for the greatest number? The question, however it is framed, always reduces to a decision about the proper balance to strike between private right and public initiative. This debate is, as noted earlier, as old as the American Republic, as old as Virginia, as old as Christendom— indeed, older than all of them.

---

6. Thomas Jefferson, First Inaugural Address, March 4, 1801.

What is largely new—at least since the Enlightenment and the revolutionary American system of representative government it yielded—is our focus on the *process* of deciding, on the relationship between "taxation and representation." And the thing that ought to concern all people interested in the health of democracy is the apparently growing disconnect between what politicians say at election time and what they do in office, not only on taxation but other matters. Democracy, as noted at the beginning of this volume, occupies an exceedingly small space in the vast expanse of human history. And it requires no great insight for one to recognize that democracy's future depends on the creation and persistence of a bond of trust between those who govern and those who choose them to exercise that power. Why would citizens long remain loyal and active participants in a republic if they lacked confidence that the decisions they made at the ballot box were reliably informed choices with corresponding consequences?

To pose this question is not to suggest that elected representatives ought to parrot or pander to "the public" and blow with the winds of popular whim or passion. Burke's familiar formulation—*a representative owes you his conscience*—still resonates as right. But what does not work in a free society is the reality or even the perception of unaccountability, and thus futility, that derives from deceit by political leaders. It is fine for a politician to refuse to make a pledge he doubts he can keep and instead to say in effect, "Trust me to do the right thing by the lights of my conscience." It is also quite acceptable for a politician to make a responsible promise with honest intention but later confess error and reverse direction in response to genuinely unanticipated circumstances or newly acquired information. What a politician cannot do—at least, not without diminution of the trust that is the marrow of democracy—is to make a pledge such as, "I won't raise your taxes," when he does not really mean it. Nor can comparable harm be avoided when a politician says, "I won't raise your taxes," yet at the same time denies the reality (if it be so) that the price of restraining taxes either will be a lesser level of publicly financed services or an increased debt burden on succeeding generations. There have been plenty of both kinds of dissembling in the years since the Reagan "revolution" and its supply-side nostrums reached the state capitals and came into contact (and often conflict) with state-level balanced-budget imperatives. A lack of candor in the communication from those who seek office to those who grant it is not the province of liberals or conservatives, Democrats or Republicans, pro-taxers or anti-taxers. It is an equal-opportunity offender.

One may reasonably ask why there is this digression—of all places, in a book about politics—into such seeming moralizing about truthfulness. After all, does not the republican form of government contain its own policing mechanism—the wrath of voters at election, or reelection, time? The answer, of course, is "yes" and "but." Yes, the people ultimately have their say, and in the Madisonian formulation they are further aided in restraining rogue politicians by the systemic collision of contending interests and factions. But there are two sides to Madison's visionary equation, just as human nature is heir to both virtue and vice. "[W]hat is government itself, but the greatest of all reflections on human nature?" Madison asked.

> If men were angels, no government would be necessary. If angels were to govern men, no external nor internal controls on government would be necessary. In framing a government which is to be administered by men over men, the great difficulty lies in this: you must first enable the government to control the governed; and in the next place oblige it to control itself.[7]

The familiar aspect of this proposition involves deploying human nature, especially the *vice* of self-interested ambition, to *restrain* government. But the other, too often overlooked side of the Madisonian equation is the necessity of *virtue* in effectuating positive governmental *initiative*. To put it simply, most people will only follow leaders they trust, and most leaders can earn trust only by exhibiting virtue, and the transcendent virtue that most people demand of their leaders is honesty. So if we want merely to restrain government, we can perhaps rely on negative impulses to block wrong action. But if we want government to be an instrument for good—if we envision it as an agent of *reform* in the public interest—then it must be pulled along by a positive vision honestly espoused by trusted leaders. The cynicism that is bred by discovery that trusted officials, once imagined to possess such vision and values, are in reality deceptive, self-seeking politicians is highly destructive of democracy. And it is an illusion to suggest that this cynicism is mitigated meaningfully by the electorate's opportunity to wreak vengeance on the offender in the next election. The whole enterprise of representative government depends deeply on a bond of trust between the representative and the governed; without it, the business becomes an exercise in futility that ultimately will disillusion and disengage the electorate. An emphasis on honesty thus does belong in a book about politics—this one and every one—because even if one does not regard honesty in the political sphere as a moral imperative, it is a practical one.

Virginians need to reflect upon this fundamental proposition as they consider the future of their democracy in 2007 and beyond. But they need to go even a step further and ask themselves why democracy is so important anyway. Autocratic governments, after all, have often proven far more "efficient" in achieving certain aims. And one need only look a little past the American Revolution to the French one to see that majoritarian oppres-

---

7. James Madison, The Federalist No. 51.

sion can be as lethal as the monarchical or dictatorial variety. The importance of democracy—at least, the American scheme of ordered liberty—lies not in the oft-repeated mantra that the "majority rules," but in its creation of conditions in which *individuals rule* and *majorities act* in common pursuit. The most consequential aspect of freedom—religious, political, commercial, and otherwise—is the opportunity it enables for individual choice on matters ranging in importance from the faith that decides one's place in eternity to the relationships that determine one's place in the world down to the comparatively inconsequential preferences that direct what one eats for breakfast, drives to work, or watches on television. Yet, the individual's freedom to choose is not the only thing that matters in fashioning a governmental arrangement, because we know that individuals generally achieve by working together. And, even if men fancied themselves as islands and had no interest in common effort and achievement, some surrender of individual autonomy to society would be essential because there are not enough islands for each person to have one. In the close proximity in which we find ourselves on this shrinking planet, it is seldom long before one person's exercise of freedom through action becomes an imposition upon, and thus a loss of freedom for, another. To paraphrase Churchill, neither democracy nor its more refined cousin, republicanism, provides a perfect solution to this dilemma. It just seems to be the fairest one so far conceived.

It is human nature to take for granted the state of affairs one finds around him, and to consider little how it came about or how fragile it may yet be. But, even at this seemingly late hour, we take the health of our democracy for granted at our peril. In his first inaugural address, George Washington declared, "[T]he destiny of the republican model of government [is] justly considered as deeply, perhaps as finally, staked on the experiment entrusted to the hands of the American people."[8] In the same situation a dozen years later, Thomas Jefferson said,

> Sometimes it is said that man cannot be trusted with the government of himself. Can he, then, be trusted with the government of others? Or have we found angels in the form of kings to govern him? Let history answer this question.[9]

Washington did not presume to know the importance the American democratic experiment ultimately would attain in history any more than Jefferson was really willing, in the manner of a detached observer, to "let history decide" the matter. These two remarkable Virginians and Americans, so dif-

---

8. George Washington, First Inaugural Address, April 30, 1789.
9. Thomas Jefferson, First Inaugural Address, March 4, 1801.

ferent in so many fundamental ways, shared a ferocious commitment to the republican cause. They recognized that the age-old question would be answered only in the fullness of time, yet they also knew theirs was a moment that mattered. And when history's verdict at last was rendered, neither wanted his labors to be found wanting.

In much the same way, the gift of democracy entrusted to generations since their time provides a unique opportunity and imposes a singular obligation, regardless of political persuasion. "Once to every man and nation," wrote James R. Lowell in the words to an inspiring anthem,

> Comes the moment to decide,
> In the strife of truth with falsehood, For the good or evil side;
> Some great cause, some great decision, Off'ring each the bloom or blight,
> And the choice goes by forever 'Twixt that darkness and that light.[10]

The opportunity in our time to make democracy work is indeed a fleeting one, presenting a cascade of choices and chances that will not pass by again. "Politics is a good thing," as Professor Sabato reminds us, because it is the vehicle through which ordinary citizens can seize these opportunities and translate democracy's abstract promise into concrete governance. If, as I suggested at the start of *The Dynamic Dominion,* the measure of that governance is its proximity to the intersection of men's maximum freedom and highest ideals, then the people and their politicians have a vital choice to make. They can glide down freedom's road on a self-centered joy ride, or they can make their way toward that intersection with purpose, adhering to a moral standard and applying their talents to help others.

For those Virginians—voters and policymakers—who choose the latter course, there is a lot of work to do. It is fine to dwell at length, as politicians and voters recently have, on the subject of taxes. But it is finer still to dwell on the subject of improvement. And it is essential to dwell on how public and private institutions can best be mobilized and arrayed, together and separately, to help people improve their lives and the life of their communities. A policy, generally ascribed to contemporary liberalism, that says "government must always do it" not only denies the superior efficacy of many private institutions but it ultimately will sap their vitality. Free people, being possessed of will and spirit, simply do not respond to confiscation with the same enthusiasm and energy they give to opportunities for voluntary initiative. At the same time, a constant drumbeat of opposition to government— the "just say no" refrain frequently heard from some conservative

---

10. James R. Lowell, "Once to Every Man and Nation," in *Sing Joyfully,* ed. Jack Schrader (Carol Stream, IL: Tabernacle Publishing Company, 1989) p. 609.

quarters—denies the necessity of people to arrange themselves in a society in which both rights and responsibilities are accepted and a perceived common good can be energetically pursued. The reason so many people in this mature democracy are turned off by politics is that it seems to attract and prosper those political beings for whom unvarnished personal ambition, rank partisanship, abstract ideology, or some combination of the three is the polestar. The notion that the whole enterprise is about using one's precious time on the planet to improve people's lives routinely gets lost in the political shuffle.

Virginia politicians in both parties can identify the reforms calculated to produce such improvement, though partisanship, ideology, ambition, alliances, finances, or any of a host of other factors may prevent them from admitting or acting upon it. Contemporary policy arguments are typically couched in strident, almost cataclysmic terms for political effect. Yet, if thoughtful political figures on either side of the partisan divide could be temporarily relieved of the appetite for self-advancement and encouraged to make considered lists of effectual reforms, it is likely the lists would be similar in many respects.

They would recognize protecting the safety, security, and liberty of citizens as government's first responsibility and demand a relentless campaign to free citizens from violence and intimidation in strife-ridden central cities and drug-plagued rural communities no less than in prosperous suburbs.

They would call for a rational and sustainable policy of infrastructure investment—schools, water and wastewater facilities, roads and transit systems, and the like—to support the essential purposes of people in a progressive and productive society.

They would acknowledge the need to reassess Virginia's aging governmental structures and, among other reforms, promote greater efficiency and more dynamic democracy by empowering citizens and officials to act through sensible regional arrangements.

They would concede that, even in one of the nation's best-managed states, long-term planning and fiscal discipline are sorely needed to prevent the best-laid plans from falling victim to unpredictable turns in the business cycle.

They would stress the need for performance incentives and accountability in all aspects of government, especially in the realm of education, on which, more than any other single factor, individual and societal hopes rest.

They would affirm the efficacy of free markets and honest competition in producing excellence; and, having so affirmed, they would restrain governmental interference in the marketplace and open every aspect of public and private endeavor to competition's healthy impact, including education.

They would look beyond government bureaucracy to the innovative private sector—both to for-profit companies and not-for-profit organizations—for assistance in achieving a broad range of public purposes.

They would demand a reasoned interpretation of the religious freedom guarantee so that faith-based institutions—no less than any other entities and, because of their demonstrated efficacy, more than most—could help meet pressing human needs.

They would circumscribe the policymaking prerogatives of the courts, recognizing that the accretion of such power by unelected and largely unaccountable jurists, especially at the federal level where they enjoy life tenure, threatens the very foundation of republicanism.

They would insist on the protection and wise use of natural resources, preserve open space, bring coherence to land-use planning, and commit the Commonwealth to sustained efforts to revitalize the Chesapeake Bay and its tributaries, the richest estuary in the world.

And they would recognize that a range of deeply felt convictions are held on the fundamental and sometimes competing values of life, liberty, and equality, necessitating a more civil discourse as society, no less than the individuals who comprise it, struggles in search of ultimate truth.

More, of course, could be added to this hypothetical list. But above and ahead of all these things, Democrats, and Republicans and independents alike would acknowledge that the power public officials wield and the resources they allocate are not the province or property of the government. They comprise, rather, a trust created by citizens who have surrendered a measure of their natural liberty and the fruits of their labors to the pursuit of common purposes. As fiduciaries, public officials not only must wield that power and allocate those resources with prudence; they must also deal *honestly* with the ultimate owners.

It is this sense among Virginia leaders that has kept the Commonwealth remarkably free from the financial corruption that has frequently plagued state and local governments elsewhere. Whether that same ethic is strong enough to prevent political corruption—specifically, the failure of honest discourse between the governors and the governed—is a more uncertain matter. It is a more important one, too, because without politically faithful trustees, democracy at length cannot survive.

Through more than half a century of dramatic change in the Old Dominion, much has remained the same. From the New Deal to the Reagan "revolution," from the Byrd organization to the Allen "renaissance," from Ted Dalton and Richard Obenshain to Charles Robb and Mark Warner, and from Governor Tuck to Governor Wilder, the Commonwealth's sudden, often surprising, political twists and turns have masked a more gradual and logical political, social, and economic evolution. A substantial partisan realignment has occurred, an era of vigorous two-party competition has arrived, and, through it all, many of the tenets that guide political behavior in Virginia have emerged intact. The Mother of States and Statesmen[11] appears poised to contribute in new and significant ways to the great American experiment in democracy.

Such grand reflections are undoubtedly appropriate, but Virginia politics also requires a sense of humor. Truth can indeed be stranger than fiction, and politics late in the Commonwealth's fourth century has followed a bizarre script seemingly calculated to temper Virginians' legendary sense of self-importance and keep everyone shaking their heads. Not just any Tom, Dick, or Harry has run for office in the once-staid Old Dominion. Virginia's Senate candidates have included Elizabeth Taylor's umpteenth husband, the recipient of a nude massage from a beauty queen, and a swashbuckling patriot who sold missiles to mullahs and lied to Congress. Its gubernatorial candidates have been less ostentatious but still curious characters: a counterespionage agent turned master-politician; a Navy skipper who happened upon JFK and his PT 109 survivors in the Pacific; missionaries to the Philippines and Honduras; the tobacco-chewing son of a Hall of Fame football coach; a telecommunications tycoon vaguely reminiscent of Industrial Age robber-barons; and a grandson of slaves who never learned the meaning of the word "can't." Contemporary Virginians, in short, seem to have mastered the art of the improbable. And that seems oddly appropriate, since nothing could have been more improbable than three tiny ships of fortune-seekers, adventurers, and misfits landing on a mosquito-infested island in the middle of nowhere and changing the course of history.

For Virginians mindful of their past, there remains an abiding conviction that their Commonwealth possesses something unique and well worth preserving. As the fresh breeze of freedom whistles across the dunes on distant shores, there is a sense that what began when pioneers first set foot on Virginia's Atlantic sands is profoundly good, but far from perfect—and still unfinished. In his Second Inaugural Address, Governor Mills Godwin placed responsibility for the future where it inevitably must lie. During a time of promise yet cynicism not unlike today, he said, "Let us abandon the hunt for someone or something we can blame for whatever offends or

---

11. An official salute to the Virginia state flag adopted by the General Assembly a half-century ago includes reference to two state nicknames—the "Old Dominion" and the "Mother of States and Statesmen."

aggrieves us. Where the people govern, no citizen can hold himself completely blameless if government be found wanting."[12]

Freedom is God's gift to mankind, Virginia's legacy to America, and America's mission in the world. As a new generation of Virginians ushers in a fifth century, striving to preserve the Commonwealth's distinctive heritage while adapting to the brisk winds of change, the challenges no doubt will be formidable. Political conflict, partisan and otherwise, will be sharp. But in this process the venerated tenets of individual freedom and responsibility, limited government, religious liberty, free enterprise, equal opportunity, public integrity, and private charity will find new expression. And, Virginians will affirm again the timeless wisdom of their state Constitution: "That no free government, nor the blessings of liberty, can be preserved to any people, but . . . by frequent recurrence to fundamental principles."[13]

---

12. *Leadership in Crisis: Selected Statements and Speech Excerpts of The Honorable Mills E. Godwin, Jr., Governor of Virginia, 1974–1978* (Richmond: Commonwealth of Virginia), p. vii.

13. Constitution of Virginia, Art. I, §15.

# BIBLIOGRAPHY

## BOOKS, ARTICLES,
## AND BROADCASTS

II *Thessalonians* 3:10.

"2004 Report," *Pollina Corporate Top-10 Pro-Business States*, February 22, 2004.

Abbot, W. W. *The Papers of George Washington, Presidential Series,* vol. 2, April–June 1789. Charlottesville: University Press of Virginia, 1987.

"At Last, Something for the Democrats to Cheer About; the Off-Year Elections," *The Economist*, November 12, 2005.

Atkinson, Frank B. *The Dynamic Dominion*, second ed. Lanham, MD: Rowman & Littlefield Publishers, 2006.

———. "Dalton Taught State GOP How to Win," *The Richmond News Leader*, September 19, 1986.

———. "George Allen's 1,000 Days Have Changed Virginia," *University of Virginia News Letter*. Charlottesville: Weldon Cooper Center for Public Service, University of Virginia, September 1996.

———. "The Reapportionment Dilemma: Lessons from the Virginia Experience," *Virginia Law Review* 68 (March 1982): 541–570.

Baker, Donald P. *Wilder: Hold Fast to Dreams*. Cabin John, MD: Seven Locks Press, 1989.

Barbour, J. Hunter. "The Freshest Advices: The Bolide, The Horse Path, and History," *Colonial Williamsburg*, Winter 2002–2003.

Barnes, Fred. "Abortion and Taxes in Virginia," *The Weekly Standard*, October 27, 1997.

———. "Virginia Governor's Race Is a Test of the President's Popularity," *The Weekly Standard*, October 24, 2005.

Barnes, James A., and Peter Bell. "2008 Democratic Insiders Poll," *The National Journal*, December 17, 2005.

———. "2008 Republican Insiders Poll," *The National Journal*, December 17, 2005.

———. "Insiders Poll," *The National Journal*, April 30 2005.

Barnes, Robert. "On Virginia's Gubernatorial Race, National Politics Gains a Role," *Washington Post*, October 19, 2005.

Barone, Michael, and Richard E. Cohen. *The Almanac of American Politics 2006.* Washington, DC: National Journal Group, 2005.

Becker, Jo, and Chris L. Jenkins. "Split on Taxes Begins at Top of Virginia GOP: Stafford Legislators Guide Rival Camps," *Washington Post*, February 9, 2004.

Billings, Warren M. *A Little Parliament.* Richmond, VA: The Library of Virginia, 2004.

Black, Earl, and Merle Black. *Politics and Society in the South.* Cambridge, MA: Harvard University Press, 1987.

———. *The Rise of Southern Republicans.* Cambridge, MA: The Belknap Press of Harvard University Press, 2002.

Bowman, Gary M. *Highway Politics in Virginia.* Fairfax, VA: George Mason University Press, 1993.

Bradley, Paul. "Winning Campaign a Mixture of High-Tech, Knocking on Doors," *Richmond Times-Dispatch*, November 7, 2001.

Broder, David S. "Hits and Misses in '04," *Washington Post*, December 30, 2004.

———. "Warner's Rising Star," *Washington Post*, November 24, 2005.

Brown, Robin. "Republicans Sweep Virginia," ABC News, November 5, 1997.

Byrd, Bill. "Coleman Blasts Racial 'Double Standard,'" *Virginian-Pilot*, November 3, 1989.

Byrd, William, II. *History of the Dividing Line Betwixt Virginia and North Carolina.* 1733 (electronic edition available through Early America Digital Archive, Maryland Institute for Technology in the Humanities, University of Maryland, College Park, MD.)

Cannon, Lou. *Governor Reagan: His Rise to Power.* New York: Public Affairs, 2003.

Carlson, Peter. "State's Rites," *Washington Post*, February 25, 1996.

Christie, Mark. "Virginia's Education Reform Works," *The Virginia News Letter.* Charlottesville: Weldon Cooper Center for Public Service, University of Virginia, August, 2001.

———. "Virginia's Education Reform Works—II," *The Virginia News Letter.* Charlottesville: Weldon Cooper Center for Public Service, University of Virginia, January 2004.

Coleman, Marshall. *Agenda for the '90s: Fulfilling Virginia's Promise*, Coleman for Governor Campaign, November 1988.

Cook, Charlie. "Virginia Likes to Send the President a Message," *The Cook Report*, October 8, 2005.

Crabtree, Susan J. "The Chosen Republican: Richmond's Eric Cantor Joins the House GOP Leadership," *Weekly Standard*, January 27, 2003.

Crain, Mark W. *Volatile States.* Ann Arbor: University of Michigan Press, 2003.

Cutler, R. J., and David Van Taylor. *A Perfect Candidate.* New York: First Run Features, 1996.

Daniels, Josephus. *The Life of Woodrow Wilson.* Will H. Johnson, 1924.

Davis, Donald E., and Eugene V. Trani. *The First Cold War.* Columbia: University of Missouri Press, 2002.

Day, Barnie. "Remembering A. L. Philpott," *Notes from the Sausage Factory*, ed. Barnie Day and Becky Dale. Lawrenceville, VA: Brunswick Publishing, 2005.

Dillin, John. "Jackson, Wilder Vie for Turf as Top Black Leader," *Christian Science Monitor*, April 13, 1990.

Dionne, E. J., Jr. "A Party Finds the Right Words," *Washington Post*, November 10, 2005.

*Divided States of America: The Slash and Burn Politics of the 2004 Presidential Election*, ed. Larry J. Sabato. New York: Pearson Education, Inc., 2006.

Edds, Margaret. *Claiming the Dream: The Victorious Campaign of Douglas Wilder of Virginia*. Chapel Hill, NC: Algonquin Books, 1990.

Edds, Margaret, and Thomas R. Morris. "Virginia: Republicans Surge in the Competitive Dominion," *Southern Politics in the 1990s*, ed. Alexander P. Lamis. Baton Rouge: Louisiana State University Press, 1999.

Eisenberg, Ralph. "The Emergence of Two-Party Politics," *The Changing Politics of the South*. Baton Rouge: Louisiana State University Press, 1972.

Ellis, Joseph J. *Founding Brothers*. New York: Alfred A. Knopf, 2001.

Emblidge, Mark. "SOLs Prove Their Value with Higher Scores," *Richmond Times-Dispatch*, February 13, 2005.

Epps, Garrett. "As Virginia Goes . . ." *Washington Post Magazine*, January 25, 1981.

———. "The Outsider," *Washington Post Magazine*, August 15, 1999.

Evans, Harold. *American Century*. New York: Knopf Publishing, 1998.

*Face the Nation*, CBS News, November 13, 2005. (Mark R. Warner interview).

Feldmann, Linda. "Abortion Litmus Test Eases for GOP Candidates," *Christian Science Monitor*, November 7, 1997.

Fineman, Howard. "A Faith-Based Initiative: What the Democrats Can Learn from Kaine's Virginia Victory," *Newsweek*, November 21, 2005.

———. "The Virginians," *Newsweek,* December, 26, 2005–January 2, 2006.

Fisher, Margie. "Abortion Debate Fizzles," *Roanoke Times & World-News*, October 1, 1989.

Fiske, Warren. "A Legacy of Reform; Allen Rekindled GOP by Picking, Winning His Fights," *Virginian-Pilot & Ledger-Star,* January 11, 1998.

———. "Warner Eyes Final Year in Office," *Virginian-Pilot*, January 12, 2005.

———. "Wilder Looks Unscathed as Smoke Clears," *Virginian-Pilot & Ledger-Star*, November 5, 1989.

Franklin, Billy, and Judy Tull. *Tough Enough: The Cocaine Investigation of United States Senator Chuck Robb*. Virginia Beach, VA: Broad Bay Publishing Co, Inc., 1991.

Friedman, Milton. *There's No Such Thing as a Free Lunch*. LaSalle, IL: Open Court Publishing Company, 1975.

Garreax, Joel. "Virginia Is for . . . Losers?" *Washington Post*, March 28, 1994.

Germond, Jack W., and Jules Witcover. *Mad as Hell: Revolt at the Ballot Box*. New York: Warner Books, Inc., 1993.

Gibson, Bob. "One Full Term," *The Daily Progress*, January 11, 1998.

Goldman, Paul. "Ms. Terry Must Accept Responsibility for Loss," *Richmond Times-Dispatch*, November 5, 1993.

———. Why Warner and Others Didn't Back Wilder," *Notes from the Sausage Factory*, ed. Barnie Day and Becky Dale. Lawrenceville, VA: Brunswick Publishing, 2005.

Goldman, Peter, Thomas M. DeFrank, Mark Miller, Andrew Murr, and Tom Mathews. *Quest for the Presidency*. College Station: Texas A&M University Press, 1994.

*Good Morning America*, ABC News, November 9, 2005. George Stephanopolous discussing 2005 Virginia gubernatorial race.

Goolrick, John C. *A Life in the 'Burg*. Victoria, BC: Trafford Publishing, 2003.

Grayson, George W. "Virginia Senator Hunter B. Andrew's Impact on the Nation," *Notes from the Sausage Factory*, ed. Barnie Day and Becky Dale. Lawrenceville, VA: Brunswick Publishing, 2005.

———. "Virginia's Republican Moses," *Notes from the Sausage Factory*, ed. Barnie Day and Becky Dale. Lawrenceville, VA: Brunswick Publishing, 2005.

Greenblatt, Alan. "In Fall Races, Campaign Themes Sounding More Like Lullabies," *Congressional Quarterly*, October 11, 1997.

———. "Solidarity on Solvency," *Governing: The Magazine of States and Localities*, November 2004.

Grier, Peter. "Robb's Moderate Image Wins Out," *Christian Science Monitor*, November 10, 1994.

*Hannity & Colmes*, Fox News Channel, November 8, 2005. Interview with Larry J. Sabato.

Hardin, Peter. "Reclaiming History: The Struggle of Virginia's Indians," *Richmond Times-Dispatch*, March 5–6, 2000.

Hardy, Michael, and Jeff E. Schapiro. "Allen Fulfilled Most Promises," *Richmond Times-Dispatch*, January 11, 1998.

———. "Allen Successful in His Last Session," *Richmond Times-Dispatch*, February 23, 1997.

———. "His Specialty: Seizing Chances from Setbacks," *Richmond Times-Dispatch*, January 7, 2006.

Harris, John, *Th Survivor: Bill Clinton in the White House*. New York: Random House, 2005.

Harris, Paul, "Sharpening My Oyster Knife," *Notes from the Sausage Factory*, ed. Barnie Day and Becky Dale. Lawrenceville, VA: Brunswick Publishing, 2005.

Harwood, Richard. "Tilt! Tilt!" *Washington Post*, November 19, 1989.

Hayes, Jack Irby Jr. *Dan Daniel and the Persistence of Conservatism in Virginia*. Macon, GA: Mercer University Press, 1997.

Holsworth, Robert. "Many Things Combined to Cripple Kilgore's Gubernatorial Hopes," *Richmond Times-Dispatch*, November 13, 2005.

Holton, Linwood. "An End to the Southern Strategy?" *New York Times*, December 23, 2002.

Hsu, Spencer S. "The Transformation of Governor Allen—And Virginia," *Washington Post*, January 9, 1998.

Hunter, Jack R. "Linwood Holton's Long Quest for the Governorship of Virginia and Its Impact on the Growth of the Republican Party." Unpublished thesis, University of Richmond, 1972.

Jackson, Thomas. "Students and the SOLs Ended Year Successfully," *Richmond Times-Dispatch*, July 9, 2004.

Jenkins, Kent Jr. "Baliles Contradicts No-Tax Pledge," *Virginian-Pilot & Ledger-Star*, September 14, 1986.

Johnson, Paul. *A History of the American People*. New York: Harper Perennial, 1999.

Johnson, Steven Daniel. "Charles S. Robb and the Reserved Governorship." Unpublished dissertation, University of Virginia, 1990.

Jonas, Richard Kirk. "Modernization of the Virginia General Assembly: The Commission on the Legislative Process, 1972-73." Unpublished thesis, University of Richmond, 1977.

Judis, John B. "From Hell," *The New Republic*, December 19, 1994.

Key, V.O., Jr. *Southern Politics in State and Nation*. New York: Alfred A. Knopf, Inc., 1949.

Kidd, Quentin. "The Failed Transportation Tax: A Simple Message from Voters?" *The Virginia News Letter*. Charlottesville: Weldon Cooper Center for Public Service, University of Virginia, January 2003.

Kirn, Walter. "When Sex Is Not Having Sex," *Time*, February 2, 1998.

Klein, Gil. "Strategists Warn Democrats," *Richmond Times-Dispatch*, October 24, 2003.

Latimer, James. "A Different Dominion: The Republican Renaissance," WCVE-TV 1986 (videotape).

———. " 'Young Harry' Byrd Turning 85; Ex-Senator Reflects, Predicts and Advises," *Richmond Times-Dispatch*, December 19, 1999.

Leighty, Bill. "Governor Warner Leaves Successor Solid Foundation," *Richmond Times-Dispatch*, January 8, 2006.

Lerman, David. "State Could Produce Two Presidential Hopefuls," *Daily Press*, March 13, 2005.

Lewis, Bob. "Candidates Resume Jousting over Taxes," Associated Press, October 10, 2001.

———. "State Earns A Grade in Management Survey," Associated Press, January 31, 2005.

Lipton, Eric. "Once Dormant GOP Conquers Richmond; Sweep of Top Virginia Offices Reflects Political Shifts That Began Decades Ago," *Washington Post*, November 5, 1997.

"Live Free or Move," *Forbes*, May 24, 2004.

Lloyd, T. Preston, Jr. "Endangered Guardians: Campaign Finance Reform and the Embattled Two-Party System." Unpublished undergraduate thesis, University of Virginia, April 20, 2004.

Lowell, James R. "Once to Every Man and Nation," *Sing Joyfully*, ed. Jack Schrader. Carol Stream, IL: Tabernacle Publishing Company, 1989.

Lowry, Richard. "Buckling His Chin Strap: Senator George Allen—Likable, Conservative and Tough—Prepares to Run for President," *National Review*, November 7, 2005.

Lublin, David, *The Republican South: Democratization and Partisan Change*. Princeton, NJ: Princeton University Press, 2004.

Madison, James. *The Federalist No. 51*, Springfield, VA: Global Affairs Publishing Company, 1987.

Marshall, Bob. "A Pilgrim's Diary: Hey God! Over Here! It's Me! Bob!" *Notes from the Sausage Factory*, ed. Barnie Day and Becky Dale. Lawrenceville, VA: Brunswick Publishing, 2005.

Matalin, Mary, and James Carville. *All's Fair*. New York: Random House, Inc., 1994.

McGrory, Mary. "Wilder's Way of Winning," *Washington Post*, April 12, 1990.

Melton, R. H. "Virginia Tax Referendum Tops Issues on Eve of Final Candidate Debate," *Washington Post*, October 10, 2001.

*Midterm Madness: The Elections of 2002*, ed. Larry J. Sabato. Lanham, MD: Rowman & Littlefield Publishers, 2003.

Miller, John J. "What the Swifties Wrought," *National Review*, November 29, 2004.

Morris, Thomas R. "Divided Government Is Not a Disaster," *Notes from the Sausage Factory*, ed. Barnie Day and Becky Dale. Lawrenceville, VA: Brunswick Publishing, 2005.

———. "Virginia: L. Douglas Wilder, Governing and Campaigning," *Governors and Hard Times*, ed. Thad L. Beyle. Washington, DC: CQ Press, 1992.

Morrison, Jeffrey H. *John Witherspoon and the Funding of the American Republic*. Notre Dame, IN: University of Notre Dame Press, 2005.

Nather, David. "George Allen's Sporting Chance for 2008," *Congressional Quarterly*, October 24, 2005.

Nockols, Christina. "House Applauds New Speaker as Session Starts," *Roanoke Times*, January 13, 2000.

Norquist, Grover. "The Best and the Brightest," *The American Spectator*, December 2005–January 2006.

North, Oliver L. *Under Fire: An American Story*. New York: HarperCollins Publishers, 1991.

O'Dell, Larry. "Gilmore Stays on Message; Capitalizes on Allen's Popularity," Associated Press, November 3, 1997.

Oliphant, Thomas. "As Virginia Goes," *Boston Globe*, November 10, 2005.

Paolantonio, S. A. "Iowa Crowns Democrats' Newest Star," *Philadelphia Inquirer*, June 25, 1990.

Petkofsky, Andrew. "Ditches at Indian Site Date to 1400s; System at the Home of Chief Powhatan May Match Map from 1608," *Richmond Times-Dispatch*, August 5, 2004.

———. "Finder of Fort Impatient," *Richmond Times-Dispatch*, September 12, 1996.

———. "Has Legend Found a Home? Archaeologists Believe Goucester Site Is Pocahontas' Village," *Richmond Times-Dispatch*, May 7, 2003.

Poag, Wylie C. *Chesapeake Invader: Discovering America's Giant Meteorite Crater*. Princeton, NJ: Princeton University Press, 1999.

Reed, Ralph. Active Faith: *How Christians are Changing the Soul of American Politics*. New York: The Free Press, 1996.

Rich, Richard. "News from Virginia," *Virginia Reader: A Treasury of Writings from the First Voyages to the Present*. New York: E. P. Dutton and Company, 1948.

Rothenberg, Stuart. *AllPolitics*, CNN, October 9, 1997. Interview with Stuart Rothenberg discussing the Virginia gubernatorial race.

———. "Are Republicans Ready for Another George?" *Roll Call*, March 28, 2005.

Rozell, Mark J. "Virginia: The New Politics of the Old Dominion," *The New Politics of the Old South*. Lanham, MD: Rowman & Littlefield Publishers, 2003.

Rozell, Mark J., and Clyde Wilcox. *Second Coming: The New Christian Right in Virginia Politics*. Baltimore and London: The Johns Hopkins University Press, 1996.

Sabato, Larry J. *Feeding Frenzy*. New York: The Free Press, second edition, 1993.

———. *Overtime! The Election 2000 Thriller*. New York: Longman, 2002.

Sabato, Larry J. *PAC Power: Inside the World of Political Action Committees*. New York: W. W. Norton & Co., 1984.

———. *Virginia Votes 1979–1982*. Charlottesville: Institute of Government, University of Virginia, 1983.

———. *Virginia Votes 1983–1986*. Charlottesville: Institute of Government, University of Virginia, 1987.

————. *Virginia Votes 1987–1990.* Charlottesville: Center for Public Service, University of Virginia, 1991.

————. *Virginia Votes 1991–1994.* Charlottesville: Weldon Cooper Center for Public Service, University of Virginia, 1996.

————. *Virginia Votes 1995–1998.* Charlottesville: Weldon Cooper Center for Public Service, University of Virginia, 1999.

————. *Virginia Votes 1999 to 2003.* Charlottesville: Weldon Cooper Center for Public Service, University of Virginia, forthcoming.

Saslaw, Dick. "Memory of a Dear Friend, Emily Couric," *Notes from the Sausage Factory*, ed. Barnie Day and Becky Dale. Lawrenceville, VA: Brunswick Publishing, 2005.

Schapiro, Jeff E. "Hunter Andrews's Spirit Lives On, Loud and Clear," *Notes from the Sausage Factory*, ed. Barnie Day and Becky Dale. Lawrenceville, VA: Brunswick Publishing, 2005.

————. "Story Details Historic Contest for Governor," *Richmond Times-Dispatch*, June 10, 1990.

————. "Warner and Allen Bask in Media's Glow," *Richmond Times-Dispatch*, December 25, 2005.

Schneider, William. "How to Woo NASCAR Fans," *The National Journal*, December 13, 2003.

Seib, Gerald. "Party Irregular: Can Warner Show Democrats a Path?" *Wall Street Journal*, November 17, 2004.

Shakespeare, William. *Julius Caesar*, Act I, Sc. II.

Shear, Michael D. "A Matchup to Imagine: Could Virginia's Boys Square Off in 2008?" *Washington Post*, August 7, 2005.

————. "After A Rocky First Half, Warner to Set Agenda," *Washington Post*, January 14, 2004.

————. "Warner's Triumphant Legacy No Easy Feat," *Washington Post*, January 10, 2006.

Shogan, Robert. "Wilder's Political Travels Stir Talk of '92 Ambitions," *Los Angeles Times*, June 25, 1990.

Short, Marc. "How the North Campaign Went South." Unpublished paper, University of Virginia, December 17, 2003.

Shroder, Kirk T. "Standards, Accountability and Education Reform . . . from the President of a State Board of Education," *Southern Regional Education Board*, September 2003.

Sluss, Michael. "Decline in Job Approval Mirrors National Trend," *Roanoke Times*, September 17, 2005.

Todd, Chuck. "Return of the Gipper?" *Washingtonian*, August 2005.

Warner, Mark R. "The Sensible Center," *Notes from the Sausage Factory*, ed. Barnie Day and Becky Dale. Lawrenceville, VA: Brunswick Publishing, 2005.

Whelan, John T. "A New Majority Takes Its Turn at Improving the Process in Virginia," *Journal of the American Society of Legislative Clerks and Secretaries*, Fall 2001.

Whelan, John T. "Reorganization in the House: Republicans Make Their Mark," *The Virginia News Letter*. Charlottesville: Weldon Cooper Center for Public Service, University of Virginia, February 2004.

Whitehurst, George. "Democrats sue over eavesdropping," *Danville Register & Bee*, March 20, 2004.

Whitley, Tyler and Jeff E. Schapiro. "Warner: 'I Will Not Raise Taxes'; Final Debate Slated Tonight in Roanoke," *Richmond Times-Dispatch*, October 10, 2001.

Wilder, L. Douglas. "When the Dream Became Reality," *The Virginia News Letter*. Charlottesville: Weldon Cooper Center for Public Service, University of Virginia, August, 2003.

Wilhelm, Daniel F. and Turner, Nicholas R. "Is the Budget Crisis Changing the Way We Look at Sentencing and Incarceration?" *Issues in Brief*, New York: Vera Institute of Justice, June 2002.

Will, George F. "Virginia's Democratic Contender," *Washington Post*, December 19, 2004.

———. "Warming Up to Hit Hard," *Washington Post*, July 7, 2005.

Williams, Juan. "One-Man Show," *Washington Post Magazine*, June 9, 1991.

Wood, Bill. "Change Came Slowly the First 65 Years—And Then at Warp-Speed," *Richmond Times-Dispatch*, January 12, 1999.

Yancey, Dwayne. *When Hell Froze Over*. Roanoke, VA: Taylor Publishing Company, 1988.

## GOVERNMENT PUBLICATIONS

Commission Draft, "Review of State Spending: December 2004 Update," Joint Legislative Audit and Review Commission, Commonwealth of Virginia, December 13, 2004.

Constitution of Virginia, Art. I, section 15.

Interim Report, "Review of State Spending," Joint Legislative Audit and Review Commission, Commonwealth of Virginia, January 2002.

Leadership in Crisis: Selected Statements and Speech Excerpts of The Honorable Mills E. Godwin, Jr., Governor of Virginia, 1974-1978. Richmond: Commonwealth of Virginia.

Report, "Review of State Spending: June 2002 Update," Joint Legislative Audit and Review Commission, Commonwealth of Virginia, January 2002.

United States Chamber of Commerce's State Liability Systems Ranking, study no. 14966, January 11, 2002.

Virginia Criminal Sentencing Commission. *A Decade of Truth-In-Sentencing in Virginia*. Richmond: Commonwealth of Virginia, 2005.

## JUDICIAL DECISIONS

*Blakely v. Washington*, 125 S.Ct. 21 (2004).

*Davis v. Michigan*, 489 U.S. 803 (1989).

*Harper v. Virginia Department of the Treasury*, 509 U.S. 86 (1993).

*Roe v. Wade*, 410 U.S. 113 (1973).

*Webster v. Reproductive Health Services*, 492 U.S. 490 (1989).

# NEWSPAPERS

*Boston Globe*
*Chesterfield Gazette*
*Daily Progress*
*Danville Register & Bee*
*Los Angeles Times*
*New York Times*
*Philadelphia Inquirer*
*Richmond News Leader*
*Richmond Times-Dispatch*
*Roanoke Times & World News*
*Virginian-Pilot & Ledger-Star*
*Wall Street Journal*
*Washington Post*
*Washington Times*


# WEBSITES

Virginia Pubic Access Project website (www.vpap.org).
Virginia State Board of Elections website (www.sbe.state.va.us).


# SPEECHES AND TRANSCRIPTS

Jefferson to the Virginia Assembly, 1826.
Remarks during the 2004 Virginia General Assembly Project Conference, University of Virginia Center for Politics, Richmond, VA, July 23, 2004.
Remarks of President George W. Bush at Whitehall Palace, London, England, White House Press Office, Washington DC, November 19, 2003.
Remarks of President George W. Bush, Second Inaugural Address, White House Press Office, Washington DC, January 20, 2005.
Remarks of President George W. Bush upon the 20th Anniversary of the National Endowment for Democracy, White House Press Office, Washington DC, November 6, 2003.
Remarks of President George Washington, Farewell Address to the People of the United States, delivered September 17, 1796, U.S. Government Printing Office, 1991.
Remarks of President George Washington, First Inaugural Address, April 30, 1789.
Remarks of President Thomas Jefferson, First Inaugural Address, March 4, 1801.
Remarks of Governor Mark R. Warner, 2005 State of the Commonwealth Message, Governor's Press Office, January 12, 2005.
Transcript of Proceedings, "Virginia Governor's Project—The Honorable Charles S. Robb, Governor of Virginia, 1982–1986,' Center for Politics and the Weldon Cooper Center for Public Service, University of Virginia, July 18–19, 2001.

Transcript of Proceedings, "Virginia Governor's Project—The Honorable Gerald L. Baliles, Governor of Virginia, 1986–1990," Center for Politics and the Weldon Cooper Center for Public Service, University of Virginia, July18–19, 2002.

## AUTHOR INTERVIEWS

Alderson, John E., September 24, 1984, and March 11, 2005.
Allen, George, April 5, 2005.
Allen, Ray, Jr., July 8, 2003.
Baliles, Gerald L., November 30, 2004, and January 5, 2005.
Beyer, Donald S., Jr., March 18, 2005.
Bliley, Thomas J., Jr., March 15, 2005.
Broyhill, Joel T., April 11, 1984.
Chichester, John H., February 9, 2005.
Cullen, Richard, December 15, 2004.
Dalton, John, July 1, 1980, and September 10, 1984.
Davis (Beamer), Betsy, July 16, 2003.
Davis, Thomas M., III, March 17 2005.
Dendy, H. Benson, III, February 7, 2005.
Farris, Michael, March 15, 2005.
Franklin, Anson, June 4, 1980, and September 17, 1984.
Gastanaga, Guthrie, March 16, 2005.
Gilmore, James S., III, November 30, 2004, and January 4, 2005.
Godwin, Mills E., September 9, 1979, September 18, 1984, and May 8, 1990.
Goode, Virgil, March 14, 2005.
Henry, Mike, January 11, 2006.
Holton, Linwood, May 28, 1980, and September 17, 1984.
Horton, Stephen A., July 8, 2003.
Howell, William J., April 26, 2005.
Kern, Richard P., Ph. D., April 21, 2006.
Klinge, J. Kenneth, May 27, 1980, August 30, 1984, and July 8, 2003.
LaCivita, Christopher, July 16, 2003.
Leggitt, Dick, July 8, 2003.
Lihn, Charles, September 28, 1984.
Marcus, M. Boyd, Jr., July 8, 2003.
McLaughlin, John, July 8, 2003, and July 16, 2003.
Meese, Edwin, III, November 16, 2004.
North, Oliver, April 5, 2005.
Parris, Stanford E., September 26, 1984.
Peachee, Judy F., September 14, 1979, August 30, 1984, and September 20, 1984.
Putney, Lacey E, April 26, 2005.
Robb, Charles S., October 5, 1984 and April 16, 2005.
Smith, W. Roy, July 21, 1980, and October 8, 1984.
Stottlemyer, Todd A., December 15, 2004.
Terry, Mary Sue, March 22, 2005.

Thomas, Michael E., July 16, 2003.
Timmons, Jay W., July 16, 2003.
Trible, Paul S., March 18, 2005.
Wampler, William C., February 22, 1984.
Warner, John W., June 27, 1980, May 17, 1990, and December 8, 2004.
Warner, Mark R., March 21, 2005.
Wilder, L. Douglas, March 22, 2005.
Wilkins, S. Vance, March 11, 2005.

# INDEX

Abbitt, Watkins, 38
abortion issue, 12–13; 1985 gubernatorial campaign, 57–58; 1989 gubernatorial campaign, 87–89, 97–99, 105; 1993 gubernatorial campaign, 143–44, 171–72, 174; 1997 gubernatorial campaign, 232–33
Adams, John, 179
African-American candidates, 274–75. *See also* Dawkins, Maurice A.; Jackson, Jesse L.; Wilder, L. Douglas
African-American voters, 10, 19; 1977 attorney general campaign, 40; 1981 gubernatorial campaign and, 40–42; 1985 lieutenant governor campaign and, 49–50, 54–56, 60–62; 1989 gubernatorial campaign and, 102; 1994 Senate elections and, 200; Allen and, 175; middle class, 61, 84; Republican candidates and, 20–21
Agee, G. Steven, 164
Alanis, Ray Jr., 248
Alcorn, Daniel, 191
Alderson, John, 28–29, 31, 33–34, 57, 59n35
Allen, George F., xvii, xxiii, 77; 2004 legislative session and, 279; abortion proposals, 143–44, 171–72, 174;

advertising campaign, 169–70; battles with Democrats, 203–4; campaign issues and, 142–43, 161–62; congressional committees, 293; criminal justice proposals, 162; economic development and, 142–43; educational reform agenda, 129–31, 139–42, 161–62; election to Congress, 113, 154; financing issues, 158–59; Gilmore, support for, 233; as governor, 203–4; grassroots emphasis, 158–59; honest change theme, 130, 169, 175, 178, 204; inauguration speech, 132–33; independents and, 281; Mark Warner and, 203, 210; nomination of, 163–64; North campaign and, 189, 198, 208; personal characteristics, 125–26, 128, 160–61, 172–73; populism of, xxi, 126–28; presidential aspirations, xxii, 291–95; reform agenda, 132–45; Republican lack of support for, 159–60; State of the Commonwealth address, 142, 218; tax proposals, 134–38, 144; United States Senate campaign, 178, 262–64; as U.S. senator, 132, 264–65; welfare reform bill, 137–38; worldview, 128–29. *See also* gubernatorial campaign, 1993

Allen, Mike, 223–24, 227, 235; on 1994 Senate campaign, 203, 209; on North, 197; on Terry, 170, 171–72

Allen, Ray Jr., 157, 240

Almond, Lindsay, 153

Andrews, Hunter B., 46, 107, 136, 138–39, 226

Andrews, T. Coleman III, 222

aristocracy of ability, 68

asteroid, 298

attorney general, 26

attorney general campaign: 1977, 17, 19, 22–25, 40; 1993, 175; 1997, 222–23; 2005, 288–89

Ayres, Drummond, 116

Bagley, Richard M., 54

Baker, Donald, 73, 113–14, 115

Baker, Peter, 196, 208, 229

Baliles, Gerald L., 5, 15, 43, 52, 87, 224; as 1985 gubernatorial candidate, 54, 56, 63, 65; Allen and, 136; as governor, 70–75; leaks about Durrette and, 59; race issues and, 60–61; support for Wilder, 80, 94

Barger, Hazel, 53

Barr, William, 134, 162, 231

Bateman, Herbert H., 30–31, 32, 51n12, 52, 266; former Democrats' interest in, 35–37

BDM International, 155

Benedetti, Joseph B., 103, 239

Bentsen, Lloyd, 77

Beyer, Donald S., 103, 130; 1993 gubernatorial campaign and, 157, 163, 169; 1994 Senate campaign and, 189; 1996 legislative session and, 218; 1996 Senate campaign and, 214; Allen and, 136, 139–40; announcement speech, 224; car tax and, 227–28; Clinton's support for, 234, 236; criticism of negative ad campaign, 177; on John Warner, 157; nomination, 1993, 163; personal characteristics, 221; reelection campaign, 176–77; Wilder's lack of support for, 234–35. See also gubernatorial campaign, 1997

Black, Earl, 11, 87, 88

Black, Merle, 11, 87, 88, 237

Blackwell, Morton, 234

Bland, James, 64

Bliley, Thomas J. Jr., 77, 92, 154–55, 187, 266; 1993 gubernatorial campaign and, 155, 156; 1994 Senate campaign and, 188–89

Bolling, William T., 288

Boothe, Armistead, 6

Bork, Robert, 76, 98, 182–83, 207

Bosher, William, 141n42

Boucher, Frederick C., 52

Brady Bill, 168

Brickley, David, 239

Bridge, Christine, 115

Broyhill, Joel, 33–34, 207

Buckley, William F. Jr., 128

Bush, George H. W., 77, 108–9, 114, 117–18, 156, 205

Bush, George W., xiv, 127, 141, 265–66, 272, 278, 284; as candidate, 254–55

business, profession and occupation licensing (BPOL) tax, 135

business leaders, 20, 23–24, 31, 34–35, 57, 270

Butler, Caldwell, 31, 52, 57, 192

Byrd, Bill, 107

Byrd, Harry Flood Jr., 7–8, 11, 25, 29, 251–52; as Independent candidate, 202; independent stance of, 180, 202; retirement, 48

Byrd, Harry Flood Sr., xvi, xvii, 51n11, 106, 130, 246; 1952 radio address, 234; golden silence, 180; as Independent candidate, 180

Byrd, Richard Evelyn, 251

Byrd, Thomas, 27, 29–30

Byrd, William II, xv(n.5)

Byrd organization, 6–7, 21; 1957 elections and, 153; decline of, 40, 85; New Republicans, 160

Byrne, Leslie L., 118, 201, 210, 288

cabinet secretary of technology, 146

Callahan, Vincent F., Jr., 252

campaign financing, 6, 13–14, 18, 24, 102–3

Campaign for Honest Change, 178

Canada, Joe, 32–33, 76, 79, 236

Cantor, Eric, xxiii, 267

Cape Charles, 298

capital punishment issue, 97

Carico, Melville ("Buster"), 31

Carlson, Peter, 219

Carrico, Harry J., 242

Carrico, Henry, 275

"Carry Me Back to Ol' Virginy" (Bland), 64–65

car tax, 146–47, 223, 225–28, 244, 277–78; as 1997 issue, 235–36

Carter, Jimmy, 38, 52

Center for Politics (University of Virginia), xxi, 68

charter schools, 144, 146

Cheney, Richard B., 265, 292

Chesapeake Bay, 144, 298–99, 307

Chichester, John, 57, 63–64, 74, 142, 218, 255, 270, 276–77

Christian Coalition, 89n10, 207, 232

Christian Right, 7, 13, 34, 200, 237, 270; 1993 gubernatorial campaign and, 164, 171

civil rights, xvi

Civil War, xvi, 180, 299

Clement, Whittington W., 241

Clinton, Hillary, 283

Clinton, William ("Bill"), 114, 125, 149, 201, 204, 263; 1996 election results, 214; 1996 Senate campaign and, 211–12; Beyer, support for, 234, 236; endorsement of Robb, 191; impeachment, 266–67; North on, 196; unpopularity of, 167, 169–70, 194; welfare reform, 138

Coalition, 7–8, 18, 34, 85; Coleman and, 22–27, 37–38; race issues and, 60, 63; two aspects of, 23–24

Coker, Brad, 109

Cold War, 4

Coleman, J. Marshall, 6–8, 64, 155; 1977 attorney general campaign, 17, 19, 25,

40; 1981 Republican convention and, 31–32; 1985 gubernatorial campaign and, 57; 1989 gubernatorial campaign and, 91–93, 167; 1994 Senate campaign and, 184, 187, 195–96, 200; abortion issue and, 97; aggressive style, 21, 22–24; as attorney general, 17, 22–24; Coalition and, 22–27, 37–38; conservatism questioned, 21–22, 39; desegregation issue and, 22–23; as Independent candidate, 192; lottery referendum and, 77; negative campaigning and, 96–97; race issues and, 88, 100–101; strategies used, 19–20; supporters, 20, 22, 24, 26, 40–43. *See also* gubernatorial campaign, 1981

Colgan, Charles, 136, 226

Colin, Richard, 162

Committee on Government Reform, 267

communities, xx

competitive political system, xvii, xx, 5, 16, 274, 295

Confederacy, xvi

Congress, xvi, 4, 124–25. *See also* House of Representatives

congressional elections, 272–73

consent of the governed, 128

constituency groups, 19

Contract with America, 204

Cooke, John Warren, 253

Cornwallis, General, 299

Couric, Emily W., 273, 274

Cox, Kirk, 220

Cramer, Alfred, 27, 48

Cranwell, C. Richard, 12, 72, 97, 218, 221, 254; Allen's governorship and, 131, 134–36, 146; as floor leader, 244

creative conservatism, 178

criminal justice, 98, 148; 1993 issues, 162, 167–69; 1997 issues, 231–33; bifurcated trials law, 133; capital punishment, 97; criminal record check, 168; handgun bills, 115, 168–69; juvenile justice reform, 144; parole abolition initiative, 133, 134, 168, 175, 231–32; three strikes law, 133; truth-in-sentencing system, 148n58, 162

Croshaw, Glenn, 251
Crusade for Voters (Newport News), 62, 65, 71
Cullen, Richard, 134, 222, 240
Curry, Jerry R., 79

Dalton, Edwina P. ("Eddy"), 76, 103, 273n28
Dalton, John, 4, 8, 14–15, 57, 236; on 1981 convention, 34; as Coleman's mentor, 20–21, 24, 26, 41; on tax issue, 70; Trible and, 48
Dalton, Ted, xvii, 14
Daniel, Robert, 52
Daniel, W. C. ("Dan"), 8, 52, 79
Darden, Colgate, 37
Daschle, Thomas A., 265
Davis, Betsy, 157–58, 174
Davis, Charles, 4
Davis, Gilbert K., 222
Davis, Richard J. ("Dick"), 5, 9, 11, 43, 48–49, 54
Davis, Thomas M. III, xxiii, 155, 201, 250, 267, 271
Dawkins, Maurice A., 57, 78–79, 274
Dean, Howard, 237
DeBolt, Edward, 59, 156
Deeds, R. Creigh, 289
DeMary, Jo Lynne, 141–42n42
democracy, xiii–xv, 128, 301–2
Democratic Black Caucus of Virginia, 10
Democratic Leadership Council (DLC), xxii, 10–11, 16, 70, 110, 282
Democratic Party, xvii, xix, 3–4; campaign financing, 13–14; centrist strategy, xxi, 5–9, 19, 40, 124–25, 268–69; coalitions, 4–6, 50–51; conventions, 37, 60, 222; defections from, 21; domination of General Assembly, 217–18; factionalism, 9, 18, 50; former Democrats, 35–37, 53–54; governors, 126; legislative party, 45; legislative resistance to Allen, 135; national response to post-Reagan realities, 124–25; New Dominion ticket, 60, 66; New South generation, 87; primaries, 93, 190–91;

Robb Democrats, 6–7, 86; strategy, 1989, 93–95; suburban strategy, 12–13; successes in 1980s, 11–16; unity, 8–9. *See also* Byrd organization
Dendy, H. Benson III, 45
Denton, Robert, 139
devolution, 125
Dillard, Laura, 101
Dolan, William D. III, 163, 171, 175, 221–22
Dole, Robert, 204–5, 207, 211, 214
Dukakis, Michael, 77
Dunlop, Becky Norton, 231
Durrette, Wyatt B. Jr., 15, 17, 21–22, 67, 155; 1977 campaign, 25; 1981 Republican convention and, 31–32; 1985 gubernatorial campaign and, 57–62; as candidate for attorney general, 27, 43; race issues and, 60–62, 88
Dyke, James W. Jr., 191, 222

Earley, Mark, 76–77, 143, 216, 222, 236–37, 239, 269–71
economy, national, xvii–xix, 48, 51–52, 255, 277–78
economy, Virginia, xvii–xix, 52–53, 75, 109, 142–43, 245, 277–80; 1980s, 83–86; 1990s, 106–7; 2000–2001, 147, 255–56
Edds, Margaret, 80, 92, 93, 94, 100, 159
education, xix–xx, 44, 67, 264; 1997 proposals, 225, 229; accountability standards, 141, 146, 147n54; Allen's agenda, 129–31, 139–42, 161–62; charter schools, 144, 146; college tuition restrictions, 133; desegregation issues, 22–23; funding for black colleges, 146; lottery profits for, 137, 146; school construction funding, 244–45; Standards of Accreditation, 146; Standards of Learning, 141, 147n54, 229, 264
Eisenhower, Dwight, 150
Eisman, Dale, 170–71
entrepreneurial individualism, 88
Epps, Garrett, 20, 225, 246–47

Falwell, Jerry, 27, 30, 34, 40, 89; 1993 gubernatorial campaign ads and, 171–72, 176; endorsement of Coleman, 42–43

Farley, Guy O. Jr., 27–34, 40–41, 53; concession speech, 32–33

Farris, Michael P., 164, 170–71, 176–77, 183; 1996 Senate campaign and, 205; John Warner's lack of support for, 187, 202; on North, 199–200

Ferebee, Smith, 28, 58

Ferrarro, Geraldine, 53

Fineman, Howard, xxi, 294

Fisher, Margie, 15

Fiske, Warren, 107, 128

Fitzpatrick, Joseph T., 9

Forbes, J. Randy, 178, 209, 267, 273

Ford, Judy Peachee, 216, 270. *See also* Peachee, Judy

former Democrats, 35–37, 53–54

France, 303–4

Franklin, Anson, 19–20, 21–22

Fraternal Order of Police (FOP), 169, 231

Friddell, Guy, 113

Friedman, Milton, 300

Frist, William ("Bill"), 265

From, Al, 282–83


Gamage, Stewart, 9

Garin, Geoff, 228

Garland, Ray, 39, 80, 182

Gartlan, Joseph V. Jr., 219

Gastanaga, Claire Guthrie, 174n77

General Assembly. *See* Virginia General Assembly

George Mason University, xxi

Gibson, Bob, 202, 245

Giesen, A. R. ("Pete"), 57

Gigot, Paul, 109

Gilley, Wade, 23

Gilmore, James S. ("Jim") III, 77, 92, 150, 216; 1993 gubernatorial campaign and, 171; 1999 legislative elections and, 247–52; Allen's initiatives and, 131–32, 145–46, 254–55, 277; Allen's support for, 233; appointments, 239–40; as attorney general, 144, 175; Bush, support for, 254–55; car tax proposal, 146–47, 223, 225–28, 244, 277–78; as chairman of Republican National Committee, 254–55, 256; compared with Howell, 245–46; family background, 246–47; as governor, 240–56; legislative address, 244; power-sharing agreement and, 241, 243–44, 254; as prosecutor, 232. *See also* gubernatorial campaign, 1997

Gingrich, Newt, 204–5, 210, 252

globalization, xiv–xv

Godwin, Mills, 5–7, 20, 130, 159; 1981 gubernatorial campaign and, 24, 32, 37, 39–40; 1985 gubernatorial campaign and, 57, 64–65; 1989 gubernatorial campaign and, 51; on 1996 Senate campaign, 202; Allen, opposition to, 137; break with tradition, 85; Coleman and, 22, 24, 32, 41–42; desegregation issue and, 22–23; education and, 139; Miller, support for, 207; race issues and, 60, 64–65, 99; Second Inaugural Address, 308–9

Goldman, Paul, 11, 55, 62, 108, 173–74; 1985 gubernatorial campaign and, 69–70

Goode, Virgil Jr., 60, 215, 221; 1994 Senate campaign and, 191; 1996 legislative session and, 218–19; conversion to GOP, 275; Republicans, support for, 139–40, 266–67

Goodlatte, Robert W., 267

Gore, Albert Jr., 78, 263–64, 265

governance, xviii–xix, 300–305

*Governing* magazine, 283

government, debates over, 300–303

governors, xxii; Democratic, 126; term limits, xx

Gray, Elmon, 25–26, 29, 139

Grayson, George W., 248

Great White Fleet, xiv

Grier, Peter, 198–99

gubernatorial campaign, 1965, 6

gubernatorial campaign, 1981, 4–8, 15,

17–46, 147; Coleman's liabilities, 21–22; election day results, 43; incumbency and, 17–18; issues, 39–42; legislative election outcomes, 43; lieutenant governor campaign, 26–34, 43; patronage and, 23–24; race issues in, 40–42; Reagan campaign and, 28–29; Republican mistakes, 17–18; Republican search for alternate to Coleman, 24–26; Virginians for Robb, 38–39, 41. *See also* Republican conventions, 1981; Robb, Charles

gubernatorial campaign, 1985, 5, 15, 47–81; 1982 elections and, 51–52; abortion issue, 57–58; African-American vote and, 49–50; background developments, 47–49; Democratic candidates, 54–55; election day results, 67–68; lieutenant governor campaign, 5, 54–81; past-versus-future imagery, 66–67; race issues in, 54–56, 64–67; Republican strategy, 60–62, 66; tax issues, 70–72. *See also* Wilder, L. Douglas

gubernatorial campaign, 1989, 5–6, 16, 83–119, 167; abortion issue, 87–89, 97–99, 105; campaign financing, 102–3; capital punishment issue, 97; debates, 92; Democratic strategy, 93–95; election day results, 101–2, 174; "Let's Make History" theme, 94, 95; media and, 95, 99–100, 103–4, 109; negative campaigning, 96–99; past-versus-future imagery, 94, 99; race issues in, 94–95, 100–101; Republican primary, 89–92

gubernatorial campaign, 1993, 127–28, 151, 153–78; abortion issue, 143–44, 171–72, 174; advertising campaigns, 164–66, 169–72, 176–77; criminal justice issues, 162, 167–69; election day results, 174–75; issues, 161–74; John Warner and, 150, 156–57; nominations, 163–64; poll results, 166–67, 170–71; redistricting, 154–55; Republican gains, 175–76

gubernatorial campaign, 1997, 177, 184, 220–40; abortion issue, 232–33; advertising campaigns, 230–33; car tax proposal, 146–47, 223, 225–28, 244, 277–78; character contrast, 229–30; criminal justice issues, 231–33; election day returns, 237–38; issues, 223–31; special legislative elections, 239–43

gubernatorial campaign, 2001, 146–47, 267–73; issues, 268–69

gubernatorial campaign, 2005, 283–88; advertising campaigns, 285–86

Hager, John H., 222, 236–37, 238, 269–70

Hampton Roads, 6, 13

handgun bills, 115, 168–69

Haner, Steve, 72

Hardin, Peter, 209

Hardy, Michael, 130, 291

Harris, Herbert, 52

Harris, Joel W., 58–59

Harris, John, 115, 158, 211

Harris, Paul, 239

Harrison, Edythe C., 53

Harwood, Richard, 103, 105

Hasell, Leroy, 275

Hazel, John T. ("Til"), 136–37, 158

Health, Education and Welfare Department (HEW), 22–23

Henry, Patrick, 300

Hill, Oliver, xvi, 195

Holsworth, Robert, 75, 109, 115, 132; on 2005 gubernatorial campaign, 286; on Democratic campaigns, 238; on John Warner, 188; on Terry, 161

Holton, Linwood, 6, 18–19, 150, 160, 273; 1985 gubernatorial campaign and, 59–60, 65; Allen and, 136; support of Miller, 36

Hord, Ruble A. III, 249n110

Horton, Stephen A., 248

Houck, Edd, 208

House Appropriations Committee, xxiii

House of Delegates, Virginia, 5, 51n13, 134, 139, 218; 1981 elections, 44;

1993 elections, 175–76; 1997 election results, 239; speakership, 150, 240–42, 252–53
House of Delegates Finance Committee, 136
House of Delegates Rules Committee, 243
House of Representatives, xxiii, 215, 266–67
Howell, Henry, 8, 9, 18, 21, 245–46; 1981 gubernatorial campaign and, 25, 26; as Independent candidate, 180, 202; Robb as successor to, 38; tax issues and, 245
Howell, Janet, 190–91
Howell, William J., 276
Howell-Miller schism of 1970s, 50
Hsu, Spencer, 223–24, 231, 244
Huffman, Donald W., 54, 86, 199
Hussein, Saddam, 196

ideology, 11, 41, 88–89, 305–6; New Right, 28, 30
income, per capita, xvii–xviii
incumbency, 11, 17–18
Independent candidates, 6, 19, 191, 216
individualism, 88
infrastructure, xix–xx
initiative, 303
innovation, xix–xx, xxi
Internet, xviii
Iran-Contra controversy, 76, 92, 184–86, 193–94, 196, 199–200
Iraq war, 265–66, 282

Jackson, Jesse L., 10, 74, 78, 110
Jackson, Thomas M. Jr., 241
James Fort, 297–98
Jamestown, xiii, xv, xvii, xx, 217, 297–99
Jamestown Exposition, xiv
Jefferson, Thomas, xv, xvi, 68, 128, 179, 301, 304
Jenkins, Kent Jr., 185, 192
Johnson, David, 187
Johnson, Lyndon B., xxii, 5, 38, 43
Johnson, Steven D., 108

Jones, James P., 141
Jones, Jerrauld, 144, 222
Jones, Robley S., 140
juvenile justice reform, 144

Kaine, Timothy M., 149, 273, 283–90
Katzen, Jay, 273
Keeter, Scott, 172
Kemp, Jack, 214
Kennedy, John F., 287
Kerry, John, 282, 288
Kilberg, Bobbie, 164
Kilgore, Jerry W., 222, 256, 274, 284–88
Kincaid, Anne B., 143
King, Tom, 167
King holiday proposal, 41, 49
Klinge, Kenneth, 155–56, 236

LaCivita, Christopher, 166, 223
Landes, R. Steven, 291
Lane, Edward, 21–22
Latimer, James, 14, 25–26, 252
Lauterberg, Robert, 140
Laxalt, Paul, 192
leadership, xx–xxiii
Leggitt, Dick, 231
legislative elections: 1981, 43; 1987, 76–77; 1991, 112–13, 154; 1994 midterm, 194; 1995 midterm, 203–4, 220; 1997, 239–43; 1999, 247–52; 2001, 254
legislative sessions: 1995, 136–38; 1996, 139–43, 218–20; 2004, 279
Leno, Jay, 192
Lewis, Lawrence Jr., 24, 156, 160, 165
libertarian conservatism, 89
liberty, xxiii–xiv
Lieberman, Joseph, 265
lieutenant governor campaigns: 1977, xvi, 8; 1981, 26–34, 43; 1985, 5, 54–81; 1989, 103; 1997, 221–22, 236–37; 2001, 273; 2005, 288. *See also* Wilder, L. Douglas
Limbaugh, Rush, 292
Lipton, Eric, 238
Locke, John, 128

Lott, Trent, 264–65
lottery, 77, 137, 146
Lowell, James R., 304
Lowry, Richard, 292
Lucas, Louise, 218–19

Mackenzie, Ross, 193
Madison, James, xv, 303
Marcus, Boyd, 92, 156, 224–25, 230, 236, 244, 248
Marsh, John O. Jr., 25
Marshall, Robert, 242
Mason, George, xv
Massive Resistance, 13, 21, 65, 88
McCain, John, 254, 265, 292
McCollum, Rudolph C. Jr., 275
McDonnell, Robert F., 288–89
McEachin, Donald, 274
McGrory, Mary, 109, 110
McLaughlin, John, 166–67, 168, 229–30
McMath, George, 86
McSweeney, Patrick, 177–78, 187, 206
Meadows, Bruce, 240
media, 14; 1985 gubernatorial campaign and, 65, 69–70; 1989 gubernatorial campaign and, 95, 99–100, 103–4, 109; Allen and, 158; North and, 193–94
Medicare, 210
Meese, Edwin, 127, 192
Mercatus Center (George Mason University), xxi
Merritt, Mark, 187–88
middle class, African-American, 61, 84, 88
Miller, Andrew P., 5, 8, 9, 48, 273n28
Miller, Clinton, 155
Miller, James C., 186–87, 202, 206–7
Miller, Kevin G., 52
Miller, Nathan, 27–28, 29, 31–34, 36, 57
Milton, Robert, 250
Mitchell, George J., 111
Mondale, Walter, 53
Moral Majority, 13, 27, 28, 30, 34, 40, 42, 88
Moran, James P. Jr., 164, 191
Morris, Thomas R., 107, 151, 189–90, 211–12

Morse, Gordon C., 176, 224
Moss, Thomas W. Jr., 134–35, 220, 241–42, 251
Mulligan, Hugh, 28

Nakashima, Ellen, 211
National Governors Association, xxiii, 282, 283
*National Journal*, 292
national political trends, xxi, 11, 283–84
National Republican Congressional Committee, xxiii, 250, 267
National Republican Senatorial Committee, xxiii, 265
*National Review*, 292
National Rifle Association, 168–69
National Right to Work Committee, 99–100
Native Americans, xx
negative campaigning, 96–99, 177
New Right, 7, 28, 29–30, 57, 60, 89
*Newsweek*, 294
No Child Left Behind Act, 141
Norquist, Grover, 292, 293
North, Betsy, 197
North, Oliver, 76, 183–85, 192–202, 208, 213; 1996 Senate campaign and, 202, 205; on advertising, 197–98n67; Iran-Contra controversy and, 184–87, 193–94, 196, 199–200; media and, 193–94; misstatements by, 196–97; Reagan and, 186–87, 195, 197–98; Warner's opposition to, 184–89, 195, 198
Northern Virginia, xx, 6, 13, 104–5
Nuckols, Christina, 252

Obenshain, Helen, 33, 53
Obenshain, Richard, xvii, xxii, 8, 20, 54, 84, 128; death of, 7, 15, 181
O'Brien, W. R. ("Buster"), 57
O'Dell, Larry, 232
Old Dominion, as term, xvi(n10)
Olin, James R., 52
Oliphant, Thomas, 290

Parker, William T., 77
Parkerson, William F. Jr., 76

Parris, Stanford, 26, 48, 57–59, 92, 98
party loyalties, 18–19
patronage, 23–24
Payne, L. F. Jr., 79, 215, 221–22, 236, 237
Peachee, Judy, 23–24, 27–29, 34–35, 57, 59; on decline of Coalition, 85; gubernatorial campaign of 1989 and, 91. *See also* Ford, Judy Peachee
Perot, Ross, 118
Persian Gulf War, 108, 194
*Philadelphia Inquirer*, 109–10
Philpott, A. L., 173
Pickett, Owen B., 49–50, 63, 79, 235, 266
political action committees, 28, 178
political parties, early controversy over, 179–80
*Politics and Society in the South* (Black and Black), 11
population growth, 13
populism, 124, 127, 147–48, 238
Powell, Lewis F., 106
power-sharing agreement, 218–21, 241, 243–44, 254
Powhatan, Chief, 298
Powhatan Confederacy, 299
presidential aspirations, xxii–xxiii; Allen, xxii, 291–95; Mark Warner, 265, 282–85, 289–90, 294–95; Robb, 11, 108–12, 117; Wilder, 11, 108–11, 113–17
presidential campaigns: 1988, 77–78; 1992, 117–18; 1996, 204–5; 2004, 282; Republican winning streaks, 117, 124
presidents, xxi–xxii
primaries: Democratic, 93, 190–91; presidential, 254, 265; Republican, 89–92, 163, 208–9; Super Tuesday proposal, 78
prison construction, 134
protest candidacies, 181
public-private partnerships, 144
Putney, Lacey E., 241, 243, 253, 275n39

Quayle, Dan, 78, 207

race issues, 12–13; 1981 gubernatorial campaign, 40–42; 1985 gubernatorial campaign, 54–56, 64–67; 1989 gubernatorial campaign, 94–95, 100–101; Coalition and, 60, 63; education, 22–23; Holton and, 59–60; Wilder and, 41, 54–56, 62–63, 66, 113–14
Randall, Gene, 229
Reagan Democrats, xxi, 16, 123
Reagan, Nancy, 195, 197, 198
Reagan Republicans, 6, 12–13
Reagan, Ronald, 3, 59n36, 97, 123, 198; 1980 presidential campaign, 42, 52; 1981 gubernatorial campaign and, 28–29; economic recession and, 48, 51; Iran-Contra controversy and, 76, 92, 186; North and, 186–87, 195, 197–98; populism of, 124, 127; portrayal of, 172; reelection, 53
Reagan-Bush syndrome, 231
Reaganism, 11
Reaganomics, 84, 123–24
Reagan-style populism, 124, 127
realignment of politics: in America, 180–81; in Virginia, 18–19, 123, 126, 132, 149, 180, 267, 308
redistricting, 51n13, 52, 112, 154–55, 253–54
referenda, 147
reform, 303
Reform Party, 118
Reiley, Mary ("Mame"), 164
representative government, xv, 128, 301–2
Republican conventions: 1977, 27, 58–59, 92; 1978, 27–28; 1981, 31–37, 40–41, 52–53, 92; 1984, 53; 1985, 92; 1993, 163–64; 1994, 188
Republican National Committee (RNC), xxiii, 255
Republican Party, xvii, xix; 1980–81 elections, 3–4; 1985 strategy, 60–62; 1990s successes, 147–48; campaign financing, 18, 24; conservative coalitions, xxi, 7–8, 18–21, 27, 89; factionalism, 7–8, 27, 29, 34–35, 53, 56–57,

89; failure to capitalize on gains, 18, 85–86; former Democrats in, 35–37; lack of party loyalty, 18–19; legislative elections, 1981, 43; legislative elections, 1991, 112–13, 154; moderate-conservative coalition, 19–20, 27, 35; mountain-valley faction, 27, 57, 59; Obenshain faction, 19, 21–22, 27, 28; post–1964 winning streak, 117; presidential winning streaks, 117, 124; primaries, 89–92, 163, 208–9; Reagan's redefinition of, 123; representation, 1979–1989, 5; Richmond Main Street business leaders, 23–24, 31, 34–35, 57, 270; scandals, 1980s, 76; search for alternate to Coleman, 24–26

Republican Policy Committee, 86

Republicans for Baliles, 59

Reynolds, W. Roscoe, 221

Rhodes, Anne G. ("Panny"), 249

Richmond-based establishment, 6, 23–24, 31, 34–35, 57

*Richmond Times-Dispatch*, 100

Right to Work Law, 99–100

Robb, Charles, xxii, 4–5, 48, 147, 236, 282; 1977 lieutenant governor campaign, xvi, 8; 1985 gubernatorial campaign and, 48, 69–70; 1988 Senate campaign and, 78–79; 1994 Senate campaign and, 189–201; 2000 Senate campaign and, 262–63; centrist strategy, 5, 8–9, 40; Clinton's endorsement of, 191; feud with Wilder, 10–11, 50, 55, 72–73, 108, 111–12, 115–17, 163, 190; as governor, 44–46; letters about Wilder, 96, 116–17; presidential aspirations, 11, 108–12, 117; scandals, 111–12, 117, 184, 190, 263; supporters, 38–40; on tax issue, 1985, 71; unpopularity of, 116, 154, 169; voter base and, 19. *See also* gubernatorial campaign, 1981

Robb, Lynda Johnson, xxii

Robb-Wilder coalition, 10, 12

Robertson, M. G. ("Pat"), 67, 77, 89, 232, 233; 1993 gubernatorial campaign ads and, 171, 172, 176

Robinson, J. Kenneth, 25, 53

Robinson, Spottswood, xvi

*Roe v. Wade,* 97

Roosevelt, Theodore, xiv

Rothenberg, Stewart, 233, 292, 293

Rozell, Mark J., 130–31, 173, 244, 271

rural Virginia, 19, 131

Sabato, Larry, 3, 86, 111, 194, 206, 305; on 1981 gubernatorial campaign, 41, 43; on 1985 gubernatorial campaign, 55–56, 61, 74; on 1989 gubernatorial campaign, 97; on 1993 gubernatorial campaign, 163, 166, 169–70; on 1994 Senate campaign, 199; on 1996 Senate campaign, 212; on 1997 gubernatorial campaign, 227, 238n78; on 2005 attorney general campaign, 289; on Allen, 159; eulogy for Howell, 245–46; on Mark Warner, 285; on media bias, 95, 100, 103–4

Saslaw, Richard, 219

Satterfeld, David, 8

Saunders, N. Leslie Jr., 72

Schapiro, Jeff E., 50, 109, 110, 199, 241–42

Scott, Robert ("Bobby"), 191, 195, 222, 236

Scott, William, 150

Senate Democratic Caucus, 221

Senate Finance Committee, Virginia, 142, 220, 226, 255

Senate Health and Education Committee (Virginia), 143

Senate, Virginia, 5, 138–39, 218. Senate Armed Services Committee, xxiii, 156, 182, 215–16, 266

September 11, 2001, terrorist attacks, xviii, 245, 254, 255, 261, 265–66, 271, 278

Shafran, George, 27

Shapiro, Jeff E., 291

Shear, Mike, 283

Shropshire, J. T. ("Jay"), 64, 99

Sisisky, Norman, 52, 267, 273

Slaughter, D. French Jr., 53–54, 113, 154

Slaughter, Kay, 154
slavery, xxiii
Smith, Alson, 172–73
Smith, John, 300
Smith, Roy W., 7, 53, 57; 1981 guberna-
    torial campaign and, 38–39; Coleman
    and, 22, 23; support for Robb, 38–39;
    tax issue, view of, 70–71
social issues, 124–25
South, 6, 11, 180
Southside Virginia, xx
Spong, William, 9
Stallsmith, Pamela, 241–42
Stanhagen, William, 28, 33, 57
state politics, 11–12, 20
state song, 64–65, 99
Stephanopoulos, George, 289
Stevens, Greg, 173
Stevenson, Adlai, 234
Stolle, Kenneth, 222
Stottlemyer, Todd, 156
"Strike Force" (citizen group), 140
suburban sprawl, 83–84
suburban voters, 10, 23; 1981 gubernato-
    rial campaign and, 30, 43; 1985 guber-
    natorial campaign and, 67; 1989
    gubernatorial campaign and, 104–5;
    1993 gubernatorial campaign and, 131,
    164, 168, 174–75, 177; 1999 legisla-
    tive elections, 251; abortion issue and,
    12–13, 87–88; issues and, 39, 84–85,
    104–5, 118–19; John Warner and,
    183–84; race issues and, 60, 61
Super Tuesday primary, 78
Supreme Court, *Webster* decision, 88–89,
    97, 98
swing states, 16

tax issues, 133, 264, 300, 301; 1994, 134–
    38, 144; 1994 proposals, 135; 1997,
    223–28, 235–36; 2004, 286; car tax,
    146–47, 223, 225–28, 235–36, 244,
    277–78; controversies, 1990s, 148–49;
    sales tax, 226; Wilder's stand on, 70–
    72, 106–7, 109–10, 277–78
technology initiatives, xviii, 146

term limits, xx
Terry, Mary Sue, 153–54, 211; advertising
    campaign, 171–72, 232; as attorney
    general, 4, 16, 56, 67, 80, 103, 115;
    campaign issues and, 161–62; endorse-
    ment of Goode, 191; failure to capital-
    ize on assets, 164–66; personal
    characteristics, 160–61, 166; Wilder
    and, 162–63. *See also* gubernatorial
    campaign, 1993
Thomas, John Charles, 45
Thomas, Michael, 156, 157, 159, 166, 174
Thurmond, Strom, 264
Tidewater, 13
Timberg, Craig, 251
Timmeck, Paul, 135
Timmons, Jay, 160
Todd, Chuck, 292
totalitarianism, xiv
transportation issues, 71, 74, 87, 144
Traywick, Flo, 187
Trible, Paul S. Jr., 11, 48, 76, 205; abor-
    tion issue and, 98; credibility problem,
    90–91; gubernatorial campaign of
    1989 and, 90–91, 96; retirement, 78
truthfulness, 302–3
Tuck, Bill, 6
two-party system, 179–80, 202, 242–43

United States Senate campaign, 1978, 5,
    48
United States Senate campaign, 1982, 48–
    49, 51–52
United States Senate campaign, 1994:
    advertising campaigns, 197–98; Cole-
    man and, 184, 187, 195–96, 200; elec-
    tion day results, 200–201; Warner's
    opposition to North, 184–89, 195,
    198; Wilder and, 184, 190–91, 194–
    95, 201–2
United States Senate campaign, 1996, 183;
    advertising campaigns, 206–8, 210–13;
    election results, 213–14; false photo
    incident, 212–13
University of Virginia, xxi, 68

values, Virginia, xix, xx, 69
Viguerie, Richard, 57

Virginia: balanced budget required, 278; competitive political system, xvii, xx, 5, 16, 274, 295; constitution, 309; importance of, xiv, 45; international interests, 75; as Mother of Presidents, xv, xxi–xxii; Northern Virginia, xx, 6, 13, 104–5; as one-party state, xvi–xvii; population trends, 1980s, 83–84; post–Civil War, xvi–xvii; realignment of politics, 123, 126, 132, 149, 180, 267; rural, 19, 131; state motto, 47; state song, 64–65, 99; triple-A credit rating, 281; two-party system, 179–80, 202, 242–43. *See also* economy, Virginia
Virginia Economic Development Partnership, 143
Virginia Education Association, 140
Virginia General Assembly, 5; Democratic domination of, 217–18; Republicans in, 1980s, 86–87. *See also* House of Delegates, Virginia; Senate, Virginia
Virginia Military Institute, 163
Virginia Retirement System, 133–34, 163
Virginia Supreme Court, 45, 240
*Virginian-Pilot*, 100
"Virginians for" groups, 180
Virginians for Robb, 38–39, 41
Virginians for Trible, 51
Virginians for Warner, 270
Voter News Service, 213–14
voter registration issue, 41, 42
voters: independent, 6, 180–81, 200, 202, 267, 281; liberal, 10, 19–21; women, 174n77, 200. *See also* African American voters; suburban voters

Waddell, Charles, 218, 239
Wahlquist, Andrew, 78
Walker, Stanley, 142, 251
Wampler, William C., 36, 52
Wampler, William C. Jr., 77
Warner, John W., xxiii, 5, 27, 53, 76; 1978 Senate campaign and, 48; 1993 gubernatorial campaign and, 177; 1996 Senate campaign and, 183, 202–5; Bork issue and, 182–83; career of,

181–82; Coleman, support of, 192; considers gubernatorial bid, 150, 156–57; elected to fifth term, 275–76; endorsement of candidates, 183–84; false photo incident and, 212–13; independent stance of, 178, 181, 182–83, 281; Lott incident and, 265; military service, 185, 206–7; North, opposition to, 184–89, 195, 198; returns to GOP, 149–50; on Senate Armed Services Committee, 156, 182, 206, 215–16, 266, 275
Warner, Mark R., xxi, xxii, 77, 108, 146–49, 162, 183, 255, 262, 278; 1996 Senate campaign and, 207, 209–14; on Allen, 164, 172–73, 203; approval rating, 2005, 284–85; as governor, 132, 279–81, 290–91; independent voters and, 267–68, 281; presidential aspirations, 265, 282–85, 289–90, 294–95; Robb and, 191; support for Kaine, 288; taxes and, 279
Washington, George, 179, 299, 304
*Washington Post*, 99–100, 103, 105, 113, 115
*Webster* decision, 88–89, 97, 98
welfare, xix, 137–38
Wheat, James C., III, 173n72
Wheeler, Garth, 169
Whelan, John, 253
*When Hell Froze Over* (Yancey), 54–55
Whitehurst, G. William, 79
Whitley, Tyler, 206, 212, 221
Wilder, L. Douglas, xxii–xxiv, 4, 7, 9–11, 15–16, 84; 1985 lieutenant governor campaign and, 5, 54–81; 1994 Senate campaign and, 184, 190–91, 194–95, 201–2; 1996 Senate campaign and, 213; 2004 legislative session and, 279; African American leaders and, 194–95; African American votes and, 49–50, 54–56; Beyer, lack of support for, 234–35; campaign trail, 68–69; character issues, 98–100, 107, 109; criminal justice record, 98; distancing from Robb and Baliles, 72–74; early strate-

gies for governorship, 72–74; economic policies, 106–7; feud with Robb, 10–11, 50, 55, 72–73, 108, 111–12, 115–17, 163, 190; Gilmore and, 216; as governor, 106–9; as Independent candidate, 191, 194, 201–2; independent stance of, 69, 70, 73; legislative record, 95–96; New Mainstream theme, 11, 110, 113; Northern Virginia voters and, 104–5; personality, 105–6; Pickett and, 79; political appointments, 108; presidential aspirations, 108–11, 113–17; race issues and, 41, 54–56, 62–63, 66, 113–14; Richmond mayoral campaign, 275; Robb and 1985 campaign, 48, 69–70; Sabato on, 55–56; strategy, 1989, 93–94; taxes and, 70–72, 106–7, 109–10, 277–78; Terry and, 162–63; unpopularity of, 108, 116, 154, 169; Virginia Senate terms, 47–48. *See also* gubernatorial campaign, 1989

Wilkins, S. Vance, 150, 220, 242, 247–48, 276; scandals, 256–57; as Speaker, 252–54
Will, George, 293
Willey, Edward E., 21
Williams, Earle C., 155–60, 163
Williams, George, 244
Wilson, Woodrow, xxii, 4n4, 129
Wolf, Frank, case., 267
women voters, 174n77, 200
Wood, Bill, 248n105
Woodrum, Clifton A. ("Chip"), 241, 255
World War II, 6
Wrenn, Sue, 208

Y2K bug, 261
Yancey, Dwayne, 49, 54–55, 73–74, 104
Young, Leonidas, 59n34

# ABOUT THE AUTHOR

**Frank B. Atkinson** is the chairman of McGuireWoods Consulting LLC and a partner in McGuireWoods LLP in Richmond, Virginia. He has participated in and written about Virginia politics for three decades, and is a frequent lecturer on political history at Virginia colleges and universities. From 1994 to 1996, he served in the cabinet of Governor George Allen as counselor and director of policy. During the Reagan administration, he served as special counsel and deputy chief of staff to the U.S. Attorney General.